MULTINATIONAL COMPANIES IN UNITED STATES INTERNATIONAL TRADE

MULTINATIONAL COMPANIES IN UNITED STATES INTERNATIONAL TRADE

A Statistical and Analytical Sourcebook

F. Steb Hipple

QUORUM BOOKS
Westport, Connecticut • London

Library of Congress Cataloging-in-Publication Data

Hipple, F. Steb.
     Multinational companies in United States international trade : a
statistical and analytical sourcebook / F. Steb Hipple.
       p.   cm.
    Includes bibliographical references and index.
    ISBN 0–89930–820–1 (alk. paper)
    1. International business enterprises—United States. 2. United
States—Foreign economic relations. 3. Investments, Foreign—United
States. I. Title.
HD2785.H57 1995
338.8′8873—dc20   94–46200

British Library Cataloguing in Publication Data is available.

Library of Congress Catalog Card Number: 94–46200
ISBN: 0–89930–820–1

First published in 1995

Quorum Books, 88 Post Road West, Westport, CT 06881
An imprint of Greenwood Publishing Group, Inc.

Printed in the United States of America

The paper used in this book complies with the
Permanent Paper Standard issued by the National
Information Standards Organization (Z39.48–1984).

10 9 8 7 6 5 4 3 2

CONTENTS

TABLES

PREFACE

The basic conception of this book is very simple -- to put an unnoticed but definitive data set into the hands of researchers and analysts. The book contains detailed information on the role of multinational companies in the international trade of the United States. This material provides the basis for empirical analysis in the fields of international business, international trade, and international finance.

THE NEED FOR THIS BOOK

For the past twenty years, the U.S. Government has collected statistical information on the domestic and international operations of multinational companies (MNCs). The principal vehicle in this effort has been a series of six benchmark surveys of foreign direct investment (FDI) conducted by the Bureau of Economic Analysis.

The FDI surveys represent the most complete and definitive sources of data available on the operations of multinational companies in the U.S. economy. Sadly, these benchmarks have been largely ignored by researchers and analysts. The reason is simple -- the data are presented in a format and in a time frame which make accurate and consistent analysis almost impossible.

The fundamental problem is that the operations of USA-based MNCs and foreign-based MNCs have always been surveyed separately. The two disparate groups of multinational companies have never been the subject of a unified benchmark survey. Consequently, the categories of data collected have varied between the outward investment surveys and the reverse investment surveys. In addition, the surveys have never been conducted on a regular basis.

This book presents the international trade data from the six benchmark surveys in a form which can be used for empirical analysis. To accomplish this end, a common format was created for the trade data from the different benchmark sources, and the trade data were converted to a common time period.

As a result, this book can present data on the trading activities of multinational companies as though complete and consistent benchmark surveys had been conducted in 1975, 1982, and 1989. The coverage of the subject is exhaustive -- affiliate related trade, intrafirm related trade, bilateral trade with major trading partners, trade by ultimate beneficial owners, commodity (SITC) trade, and affiliate industry group trade.

TWENTY YEARS OF RESEARCH

In a sense, this book and the benchmark surveys have evolved together. The research had its beginnings in the Department of Commerce in 1974 with the original FDI benchmark survey. The author was one of the analysts who contributed to that seminal data collection effort. Then in 1982, the author produced a government study which combined the results of the 1974 reverse investment benchmark and the 1977 outward investment benchmark study. That paper first identified the affiliate trade overlap problem.

After returning to academe in 1982, several further papers were written, including a comparison study which added the 1980 and 1982 benchmarks. It was very clear that the time period covered by the four available surveys was too brief to provide accurate insights into the operations of multinational companies. The added perspective of another set of benchmark surveys was needed. The last two benchmark surveys covered 1987 and 1989, with the final results released in early 1993.

It took the federal government twenty years to collect the data on MNC operations. It then took the author fifteen months to develop the 63 standardized trade tables which form the core of the book. The writing phase occupied the summer and early fall of 1994.

ACKNOWLEDGEMENTS

A preface always concludes with acknowledgements. During my years with the International Trade Administration, U.S. Department of Commerce, I had the privilege of working with the foremost international economics research staff in Washington. The early analytical work was supported by two research directors, Franklin J. Vargo and then Allen J. Lenz. The research benefitted from the comments of colleagues Lester A. Davis, Georg Mehl, and Victor Bailey. The trade data expertise of Victor Bailey was especially valuable.

After returning to academe in 1982, I was very fortunate to receive the support and encouragement of Professor H. Peter Gray of Rutgers University.

This led, in part, to a series of presentations at the Eastern Economics Association meetings. One of those papers, on the definition of MNC-related trade, was published in *The American Economic Review* in 1990.

At East Tennessee State University, the book has benefitted from the comments and criticisms of colleagues Dr. Jon Smith and Dr. Frederick W. Mackara. I am also very indebted to Dr. George Poole and Dr. Larry Neal of the Mathematics Department who provided invaluable assistance in refining the stochastic techniques used in the data conversion process. My secretary Ms. Sandra Wilson has provided continuing help in all phases of the project. My graduate assistant Mr. Jeff Burleson has been especially untiring in double checking data and identifying incorrect words which were correctly spelled. Finally, my family has been very patient and enduring as holidays and weekends were devoted to "the book."

In the end, the author still remains responsible for all errors of commission and omission. The topical coverage of the book is very extensive, however, so nearly all the errors will be those of commission.

PART I

INTRODUCTION TO MULTINATIONAL COMPANIES

CHAPTER 1

THE RISE OF THE MULTINATIONAL COMPANY

Multinational companies have come to characterize global business, and to dominate industries and national economies. As a result, these enterprises are the focus of continuing public concern and policy debate. Sadly, these important discussions are often forestalled by a lack of quantitative information on the operations of multinational companies. The purpose of this book is to provide a detailed source of data and analysis on the role of multinational firms in U.S. international trade.

MULTINATIONAL COMPANIES IN THE GLOBAL ECONOMY

Foreign direct investment (FDI) is an aggregate measure of the growth of multinational companies (MNCs). The multinational enterprise is created when a business firm in one nation makes an equity investment in a firm in a second nation. That equity investment is counted as part of the outward direct investment from the source country, and as part of the reverse direct investment in the host country.

In 1967, total outward direct investment in the world economy was $112.3 billion. The United States was the key source of investment funds. In that year, U.S. direct investment abroad was $56.6 billion, for a 50.4% share of the world total. In contrast, foreign investment in the United States was only $9.9 billion or 9.4% of the recorded worldwide reverse investment of $105.5 billion.

By 1980, world outward investment had increased 12.4% per year to reach $518.3 billion. American direct investment abroad had grown 11.0% per year to reach $220.2 billion. Accordingly, the United States was down to a 42.5% world share. In contrast, foreign investment in the United States had increased by 17.8% per year to reach $83.0 billion, or a 16.3% share of worldwide reverse investment.

These trends continued during the 1980s. In 1987, total outward investment in the world had doubled to $1,023.4 billion, increasing 10.2% each year. The United States was fading as a source of new foreign direct investment capital -- U.S. outward investment had increased only 5.6% per year. In 1987, American direct investment abroad was $322.2 billion and had fallen to a 31.5% share of the world total. In contrast, foreign direct investment in the United States grew 18.5% each year to a level of $271.8 billion in 1987. The United States was now host to a 25.2% share of global reverse investment.

In 1967, the United States was the source of one-half of the worldwide outward direct investment, but host to less than 10% of the reverse investment. In comparison, Europe and Canada had 30% and 20% shares of worldwide reverse investment.

By 1987, two decades later, the United States held only 30% of global outward investment, falling behind Europe, which had moved up to be the source of one-half of the outward investment in the world. In contrast, the nation had become a magnet for foreign direct investment. In 1987, some one-fourth of worldwide reverse investment was in the United States [Rutter 7].

THE CREATION OF A MULTINATIONAL COMPANY

Multinational companies evolve from domestic firms that go beyond simple exporting and importing activities to acquire foreign affiliates. The affiliate trade linkages can be as buyer and/or supplier. In an "upstream" investment, the affiliate is a supplier; in a "downstream" investment, the affiliate is a buyer.

The change from a domestic company into a multinational company usually involves several stages. At first, the firm becomes very involved in importing and/or exporting. The growth and prosperity of the company become entwined with business linkages to foreign firms. In a downstream linkage, the foreign buyer takes a larger share of sales. In a upstream linkage, the foreign supplier provides a larger proportion of material inputs.

At some point, the linkages become too important to be left to informal "arms-length" relationships, and the domestic firm will seek a formal connection with the foreign partner. This change often does not involve any financial investment, but rather will take the form of a franchise or licensing agreement. For example, the first steps in creating a foreign distribution network involve the establishment of licensed agencies and franchisees.

As the business linkages deepen between the two firms, the need for broad coordination and cooperation emerges. The next step involves taking an investment position in the foreign partner. The investment is usually in terms of debt capital -- the domestic firm makes a loan by purchasing debt obligations issued by the foreign firm. This creates even stronger links between the two business firms, and gives the domestic company a strong stake in the financial success of its overseas partner.

The final step in the process involves equity investments in the foreign company. At first, the equity investment is meant to be a permanent capital injection which, unlike a loan, does not have to be repaid. At some point, a decision is made to acquire a management voice in the foreign firm through additional equity investments.

The U.S. Government considers a 10% or more equity position as a significant ownership interest with an effective voice in management. The two linked firms are viewed as a multinational company, where the domestic firm is the "parent firm" and the foreign firm is the "foreign affiliate." This definition is applied to U.S.-based firms that have acquired affiliates in other countries (outward investment) and to foreign-based firms that have acquired affiliates in the United States (reverse investment). If the equity position rises above the 50% level, the affiliate is described as a majority owned foreign affiliate (MOFA) and consolidated reporting of financial statements is permitted [Mataloni 44].

The final step in the development of the multinational company is true global integration of all business activities. Manufacturing, distribution, and research and development operations will be situated without regard to national boundaries. The automobile industry is probably the most advanced in this regard. The major firms are world players with assembly and related operations scattered over the globe.

Why do domestic firms become transformed into multinational companies? Several different reasons have been suggested including: (1) to reduce the cost of international transactions previously done on an arms-length basis, (2) to achieve economies of scale through growth beyond the confines of the home market, (3) to acquire geographic production and sourcing flexibility, (4) to gain knowledge advantages through cultural diversity in research, design, manufacturing, and marketing, and (5) to acquire market power over purely domestic competitors.

INFORMATION PROBLEMS

In the 1950s and 1960s, American-based firms, taking advantage of favorable currency and political conditions, began investing abroad. This created popular concern about "runaway factories" and job losses. By the 1970s, foreign firms were investing heavily in the United States. Policy concerns now focused on the "selling of America" and the growth of foreign influence in domestic markets and political processes.

Unfortunately, these policy debates were being conducted in a vacuum -- no solid data existed on the operations of multinational companies in the United States economy. At the order of the U.S. Congress, the Department of

Commerce began to assemble information on the operations of MNCs. The Bureau of the Census collected the raw data and the Bureau of Economic Analysis (BEA) performed the analysis and issued the reports and studies.

The first benchmark survey was conducted in 1974 and covered foreign direct investment in the United States (reverse investment). The second benchmark was conducted in 1977 and covered U.S. direct investment abroad (outward investment). Additional benchmarks were performed in 1980, 1982, 1987, and 1989. To supplement the census benchmark surveys, the Bureau of Economic Analysis has also issued a series of smaller annual surveys.

However, these reports and studies still do not provide a coherent source of quantitative information on the impact and role of multinational companies in the American economy. The benchmark surveys are the primary sources of information on MNC operations, yet the different census surveys on reverse investment and outward investment have never been conducted during the same year. The operations of the two large groups of multinational companies -- U.S.-based MNCs and foreign-based MNCs -- have never been the subject of a unified benchmark survey.

In addition, the reverse investment and outward investment surveys do not have a matching data content (especially regarding trade data). And finally, the timing intervals between and among the benchmark surveys have been irregular. Due to these factors, it is impossible to accurately analyze the trends and structural changes in MNC operations.

The annual surveys suffer from different problems. They are smaller and thus do not provide a high level of detailed data. The annual surveys are also based on the previous benchmark survey, and are never revised after a new benchmark has been conducted.

THE PURPOSE AND PLAN OF THE BOOK

The subject of this book is the international operations of multinational companies in the United States. The purpose of this book is to provide a coherent source of quantitative information on the role of MNCs in U.S. international trade.

The activities of multinational firms may be generally divided into "domestic" operations and "international" operations. Domestic operations would concern such topics as investments, assets, sales, employment, and employee compensation. The international operations would cover the international trade activities.

The book consists of twenty-six chapters organized into four separate parts. Parts I and II contain six chapters and form the introduction to the book. Parts III and IV are the core of the work and contain twenty chapters based on various categories of geographic and product trade.

Part I on "Introduction to Multinational Companies" outlines the significance of MNCs and details the data sources for the empirical study of multinational companies. Part II on "The Trade Role of Multinational Companies" presents the model and analytical concepts that are used in the book to examine the trade role of MNCs. Chapter 6 on "Total Merchandise Trade" provides a first perspective on the trade role of MNCs.

Part III on "Geographic Patterns of MNC-Related Trade" contains five chapters. Four of the chapters examine trade with Canada, Europe, Japan, and Other Areas. Chapter 7 on "Total Geographic Trade" is an aggregate of merchandise trade with the four geographic areas.

Part IV on "Product Patterns of MNC-Related Trade" contains fifteen chapters. Twelve of the chapters examine trade in specific product categories -- such as Food, Petroleum, Chemicals, and Road Vehicles. Chapter 12 on "Total Product Trade," Chapter 13 on "Non-Manufactured Goods Trade," and Chapter 20 on "Manufactured Goods Trade" are aggregates of product trade.

The book provides three different perspectives on the role of multinational companies in total U.S. trade. The first perspective is overall merchandise trade. Chapter 6 on "Total Merchandise Trade" directly analyzes the affiliate related and intrafirm related trade activities of MNCs. The second perspective is geographic trade. Chapter 7 on "Total Geographic Trade" is an aggregate of the MNC-related trade with four geographic areas. The third perspective is product trade. Chapter 12 on "Total Product Trade" is an aggregate of the MNC-related trade in twelve product categories.

Each perspective of MNC-related trade is self contained, to the point of some repetition. Each part of the book includes (1) a full analysis of affiliate related and intrafirm related trade and (2) a full discussion of data derivation from the original U.S. Government sources.

CHAPTER 2

SOURCES OF DATA ON
MNC OPERATIONS

The Bureau of Economic Analysis is the official provider of data and analysis on the operations of multinational companies in the United States. There are two sources: (1) the infrequent benchmark surveys of foreign direct investment and (2) a series of annual surveys. The census benchmark surveys contain the most detailed information available on MNC activities.

THE DEFINITION OF THE MULTINATIONAL COMPANY

Following World War II, the American economy dominated world production and world trade. In the 1950s and 1960s, taking advantage of these favorable currency and political conditions, American firms began to invest abroad. This created the first popular concern over multinational companies and "runaway factories." The firms were accused of exporting jobs, and strategists worried about the eroding industrial base.

By the late 1960s and the early 1970s, the situation had reversed itself. Foreign firms, led by the Japanese, were investing heavily in the United States. Policy concerns now focused on the "selling of America" and the loss of technological leadership. Strategists lamented the growth of foreign influences in domestic markets and foreign business involvement in American political processes.

The policy debates at the time were being conducted in a vacuum -- no solid data existed on the operations of multinational companies in the U.S. economy. There was no organized program in the federal government to collect and analyze information on the operations of multinational companies in the United States.

In 1974, the Congress instructed the Department of Commerce through its two statistical agencies -- the Bureau of the Census and the Bureau of Economic Analysis (BEA) -- to assemble information on the operations of foreign companies doing business in the United States. The Bureau of the Census collected the data and the Bureau of Economic Analysis, under the supervision of the Office of the Secretary, performed the study. The 1974 benchmark survey of foreign direct investment in the United States was issued in 1976.

The first benchmark survey was followed by a 1977 survey on outward direct investment. Pairs of reverse and outward investment benchmark surveys followed in 1980 and 1982, and in 1987 and 1989. (A set of surveys for 1992 and 1994 is in process). To supplement the benchmark surveys, the BEA began a series of smaller annual surveys in the late 1970s. The reverse investment series began in 1977 and the outward investment series in 1983.

The following key terms are used by the Bureau of Economic Analysis to describe the members of U.S.-based multinational companies [Mataloni 44]:

> *U.S. multinational company (MNC):* The U.S. parent and all of its foreign affiliates.

> *U.S. parent:* A person, resident in the United States, who owns or controls 10 percent or more of the voting securities, or the equivalent, of a foreign business enterprise. "Person" is broadly defined to include any individual, branch, partnership, associated group, association, estate, trust, corporation or other organization (whether or not organized under the laws of any State), or any government entity. If incorporated, the U.S. parent is the fully consolidated U.S.A. enterprise consisting of (1) the U.S. corporation whose voting securities are not owned more than 50 percent by another U.S. corporation, and (2) proceeding down each ownership chain from that U.S. corporation, any U.S. corporation (including Foreign Sales Corporations located within the United States) whose voting securities are more than 50 percent owned by the U.S. corporation above it. A U.S. parent comprises the domestic (U.S.) operations of a MNC.

> *Foreign affiliate:* A foreign business enterprise in which there is U.S. direct investment, that is, in which a U.S. person owns or controls 10 percent or more of the voting securities or the equivalent. Affiliates comprise the foreign operations of an MNC.

> *Majority-owned foreign affiliate (MOFA):* A foreign affiliate in which the combined ownership of all U.S. parents exceeds 50 percent.

> *Nonbank:* An entity (MNC, parent, or affiliate) whose primary activity is not banking. Only nonbanks are covered by this article.

The members of foreign-based multinational firms are described by similar language, with appropriate word substitutions.

Two points need emphasizing. First, the BEA has used the 10% equity rule since the first 1974 benchmark to define the parent-affiliate linkage. This level of ownership interest is considered sufficient to give the "parent" firm management influence in the operations of the "affiliate" firm. Second, the foreign direct investment benchmark and annual surveys have always excluded financial firms. When these firms ("banks") are surveyed, they are reported on a separate basis and are not combined with the nonbank firms.

INFORMATION COVERAGE OF THE BEA SURVEYS

The MNC operations that are of policy concern and interest are revealed by the types of business data collected and published in the BEA surveys. Fortunately for analysts, the types of financial and operating data collected have remained largely unchanged since the 1970s.

Reverse Investment Surveys

The 1974 benchmark survey of foreign direct investment in the United States contained 132 tables. There were nine categories of key interest as shown in the summary table: the number of affiliates, the value of foreign direct investments, the value of total assets, the value of plant and equipment, sales, employee compensation, employment, exports, and imports [BM74 Table 1].

The last benchmark on reverse investment covered 1987, and contained 164 tables. According to the summary table, the major data categories were ten in number: the value of total assets, the value of plant and equipment, expenditures for plant and equipment, sales, net income, employee compensation, employment, land owned, exports, and imports [BM87 Table 6]. The number of categories had increased by one since 1974, but the focus had changed more to operating measurements rather than foreign direct investments.

In comparison, the annual surveys contained around 70 tables and have less detailed information. The twelve main areas of data coverage are the number of affiliates, the number of companies consolidated, the value of total assets, the value of plant and equipment, expenditures for plant and equipment, sales, net income, employee compensation, employment, land owned, exports, and imports.

Outward Investment Surveys

The 1977 benchmark survey of United States direct investment abroad contained 399 tables, more than triple the data content of the 1974 reverse investment benchmark. As shown in the summary table of selected items, there were eight data categories of key interest: the number of affiliates, the value of total assets, total income, net income, employment, employee compensation, the value of U.S. direct investments, and direct investment income [BM77 Table B]. The merchandise trade categories were not included!

The last benchmark on outward investment covered 1989, and contained 291 tables (nearly twice the number as the 1987 reverse benchmark). According to the summary table, the major data categories still numbered eight, but were now the number of affiliates, the value of total assets, total sales, net income, employment, employee compensation, the value of U.S. direct investments, and direct investment income [BM89 Table 7]. The merchandise trade categories were still excluded.

In comparison, the annual surveys contained around 70 tables (the same as the reverse investment surveys) and have less detailed information. The six main areas of data coverage are the number of affiliates, the value of total assets, sales, net income, employee compensation, and employment. Even here, trade data was banished to the detail tables.

Deficiencies in the BEA Surveys

The BEA surveys of foreign direct investment provide very large data sets covering the operations of multinational companies. The benchmark surveys possess staggering levels of detail while the annual surveys present time series information for important aggregate series. However, these benchmark and annual surveys do not provide a coherent source of quantitative information on the operations of multinational companies in the American economy.

The problems with the BEA surveys are both large and small. For example, the survey respondents always report their financial and operating data on a fiscal year basis. Yet the survey results are routinely compared to calendar year data, such as in the calculation of trade shares.

Most significantly, the benchmark surveys on reverse investment and outward investment have never been conducted during the same year. The operations of the two disparate groups of multinational companies -- U.S.-based MNCs and foreign-based MNCs -- have never been the subject of a unified benchmark survey.

This creates fundamental difficulties in conducting any analysis since the census benchmarks are the primary sources of information on MNC operations. The greatest problem is the time gap between the reverse and outward surveys. And since the surveys are conducted at different times, there is no pressure to collect similar data, as noted above.

The timing intervals between the benchmark surveys have been very irregular. The 1974 and 1977 benchmark set was separated by three years; all the subsequent benchmark sets are separated by two years. The gap between the 1974/1977 set and the 1980/1982 set was six and five years; the gap between the 1980/1982 set and the 1987/1989 set was seven years.

The annual surveys possess different problems. They are samples whereas the benchmarks are a census. As a result, the annual surveys cannot provide (1) as high a level of detailed data and (2) as high a level of statistical reliability. The annual surveys are also based on the previous benchmark survey, and are not revised after a new benchmark has been conducted. Thus the "time series" drawn from the annual series suffer from significant discontinuities.

Due to these factors, it is still difficult to accurately analyze the trends and structural changes in MNC operations. The BEA reports and studies on foreign direct investment provide a mountain of data covering the operations of multinational companies. Unfortunately, it is the common situation in the computer era of having too many numbers and not enough information.

CHAPTER 3

THE BENCHMARK SURVEYS OF
FOREIGN DIRECT INVESTMENT

Since 1974, the Bureau of Economic Analysis has completed six benchmark surveys on reverse and outward direct investment. The census benchmarks form three sets profiling the operations of multinational companies in the mid-1970s, the early 1980s, and the late 1980s.

THE BENCHMARK SURVEYS

The benchmark surveys of foreign direct investment are conducted by the U.S. Department of Commerce to fulfill a mandate from the Congress to collect information on the operations of multinational companies in the American economy. Responsibility for the surveys has been assigned to the Bureau of Economic Analysis.

To date, six benchmark surveys have been completed covering the period 1974 to 1989. The list follows and the shorthand reference is shown in brackets:

U.S. Department of Commerce, Office of the Secretary. *Foreign Direct Investment in the United States: Volume 2: Benchmark Survey, 1974.* Washington, DC: USGPO (April 1976). [BM74].

U.S. Bureau of Economic Analysis. *U.S. Direct Investment Abroad, 1977.* Washington, DC: USGPO (April 1981). [BM77].

___. *Foreign Direct Investment in the United States, 1980.* Washington, DC: USGPO (October 1983). [BM80].

___. *U.S. Direct Investment Abroad: 1982 Benchmark Survey Data.* Washington, DC: USGPO (December 1985). [BM82].

___. *Foreign Direct Investment in the United States: 1987 Benchmark Survey, Final Results.* Washington, DC: USGPO (August 1990). [BM87].

___. *U.S. Direct Investment Abroad: 1989 Benchmark Survey, Final Results.* Washington, DC: USGPO (October 1992). [BM89].

The benchmarks for 1974, 1980, and 1987 cover the operations of foreign-based MNCs in the United States or "reverse investment." The 1977, 1982, and 1989 benchmarks cover the operations of U.S.-based multinational firms or "outward investment." The benchmarks form three sets for 1974/1977, 1980/1982, and 1987/1989 which cover the operations of the two groups of multinational companies. Two more benchmarks are in process covering 1992 and 1994. Preliminary results from the reverse FDI 1992 benchmark were released in late 1994 [Zeile]. Data from the complete set should not be available until 1997.

Before 1974, a few scattered surveys had been conducted on the operations of multinational companies. During World War II, a survey of foreign direct investment in the United States was done to identify enemy property for seizure. In 1966, a survey was conducted on U.S. direct investment abroad. The first "modern" survey was the 1974 benchmark census. This was conducted under congressional mandate, and was directly supervised by the Office of the Secretary of Commerce. The information content of the 1974 benchmark has provided the basis for all subsequent surveys.

INFORMATION CONTENT OF THE BENCHMARK SURVEYS

The three benchmarks on reverse investment provide consistent financial and operating data in the following areas: (1) the number of affiliates, (2) the value of foreign direct investments, (3) the value of total assets, (4) the value of plant and equipment, (5) sales, (6) employee compensation, (7) employment, (8) direct investment income, and (9) merchandise trade.

The three benchmarks on outward investment provide consistent financial and operating data in the following areas: (1) the number of affiliates, (2) the value of U.S. direct investments, (3) the value of total assets, (4) sales, (5) net income, (6) employee compensation, (7) employment, (8) direct investment income, and (9) merchandise trade.

The first seven items on each list are considered to be "domestic" operations while the last two items -- direct investment income and merchandise trade -- are considered to be "international" operations which affect the balance of payments. The impact of multinational companies could be analyzed from the perspective of any of these types of operations. This book focuses on the impact of merchandise trade.

TRADE DATA COVERAGE IN THE BENCHMARK SURVEYS

This book considers the merchandise trade impact of multinational companies from the perspective of geographic trade and product trade. In each case, a different set of benchmark source tables was used.

Geographic Trade Source Tables

The benchmark tables used as sources for geographic trade data are listed below. For each benchmark, export and import source tables are shown for affiliate related trade and intrafirm related trade. Intrafirm trade is the trade between the affiliate firm and the parent firm in the MNC. Affiliate trade is the total trade conducted by the affiliate and includes intrafirm trade.

The data format in the source tables was affiliate industry rows with geographic columns. The industry rows were collapsed into Petroleum, Manufacturing, Wholesale, and Other Industry categories. This structure was dictated by the set of affiliate industry data available in the 1974 benchmark. The geographic columns were collapsed into Canada, Europe, Japan and Other Areas. This structure was dictated by analytical interest and the availability of data.

BM74: Foreign Direct Investment in the United States
    Affiliate Related Trade
        Exports: Tables E-2, E-6, E-7, E-8
        Imports: Tables E-2, E-6, E-7, E-8
    Intrafirm Related Trade
        Exports: Tables E-2, E-6, E-7, E-8
        Imports: Tables E-2, E-6, E-7, E-8

BM77: U.S. Direct Investment Abroad
    Affiliate Related Trade
        Exports: Table II.I.4
        Imports: Table II.I.20
    Intrafirm Related Trade
        Exports: Table II.I.7
        Imports: Table II.I.23

BM80: Foreign Direct Investment in the United States
    Affiliate Related Trade
        Exports: Table G-18
        Imports: Table G-32
    Intrafirm Related Trade
        Exports: Table G-20
        Imports: Table G-34

BM82: U.S. Direct Investment Abroad
  Affiliate Related Trade
      Exports: Table II.G.3
      Imports: Table II.G.20
  Intrafirm Related Trade
      Exports: Table II.G.7
      Imports: Table II.G.24

BM87: Foreign Direct Investment in the United States
  Affiliate Related Trade
      Exports: Table G-23
      Imports: Table G-29
  Intrafirm Related Trade
      Exports: Table G-25
      Imports: Table G-31

BM89: U.S. Direct Investment Abroad
  Affiliate Related Trade
      Exports: Table II.H.5
      Imports: Table II.H.22
  Intrafirm Related Trade
      Exports: Table II.H.9
      Imports: Table II.H.26

There are a total of twenty-four tables listed. The BM74 trade data are organized by the four affiliate industry groups, so four source tables are cited in each of the four cases listed under that benchmark heading.

The Ultimate Beneficial Owner, or UBO, is the location of the parent firm. In outward investment, the UBO is always the United States, thus the identity of the UBO is pertinent only to reverse investment. These data were derived from the following source tables in the reverse investment benchmarks:

BM74: Foreign Direct Investment in the United States
  Affiliate Related Trade
      Exports: Tables E-2, E-15, E-16, E-17, E-19
      Imports: Tables E-2, E-15, E-16, E-17, E-19
  Intrafirm Related Trade
      Exports: Tables E-2, E-15, E-16, E-17, E-19
      Imports: Tables E-2, E-15, E-16, E-17, E-19

BM80: Foreign Direct Investment in the United States
  Affiliate Related Trade
      Exports: Table G-19
      Imports: Table G-33

Intrafirm Related Trade
Exports: Table G-21
Imports: Table G-35

BM87: Foreign Direct Investment in the United States
Affiliate Related Trade
Exports: Table G-24
Imports: Table G-30
Intrafirm Related Trade
Exports: Table G-26
Imports: Table G-32

The data format used in the source tables was UBO rows with geographic columns. The UBO rows were collapsed into Canada, Europe, Japan and Other Areas UBOs. The geographic columns were collapsed into the same four categories.

Product Trade Source Tables

The benchmark tables used as sources for product trade data are listed below. For each benchmark, export and import source tables are shown for affiliate related trade and intrafirm related trade. Intrafirm trade is the trade between the affiliate firm and the parent firm in the MNC. Affiliate trade is the total trade conducted by the affiliate and includes intrafirm trade.

The data format in the source tables was affiliate industry rows with product columns. The industry rows were collapsed into Petroleum, Manufacturing, Wholesale, and Other Industry categories. This structure was dictated by the set of affiliate industry data available in the 1974 benchmark. All twelve product columns were retained: Food, Beverages and Tobacco, Crude Materials, Petroleum and Products, Coal, Other Products, Chemicals, Machinery, Road Vehicles and Parts, Other Transport Equipment, Metal Manufactures, and Other Manufactures.

BM74: Foreign Direct Investment in the United States
Affiliate Related Trade
Exports: Tables E-1, E-3, E-4, E-5
Imports: Tables E-1, E-3, E-4, E-5
Intrafirm Related Trade
Exports: Tables E-1, E-3, E-4, E-5
Imports: Tables E-1, E-3, E-4, E-5

BM77: U.S. Direct Investment Abroad
Affiliate Related Trade
Exports: Table III.I.2

Imports: Table III.I.18
Intrafirm Related Trade
Exports: Table III.I.6
Imports: Table III.I.22

BM80: Foreign Direct Investment in the United States
Affiliate Related Trade
Exports: Table G-12
Imports: Table G-24
Intrafirm Related Trade
Exports: Table G-14
Imports: Table G-26

BM82: U.S. Direct Investment Abroad
Affiliate Related Trade
Exports: Table III.G.2
Imports: Table III.G.19
Intrafirm Related Trade
Exports: Table III.G.6
Imports: Table III.G.23

BM87: Foreign Direct Investment in the United States
Affiliate Related Trade
Exports: Table G-10
Imports: Table G-16
Intrafirm Related Trade
Exports: Table G-12
Imports: Table G-18

BM89: U.S. Direct Investment Abroad
Affiliate Related Trade
Exports: Table III.H.4
Imports: Table III.H.21
Intrafirm Related Trade
Exports: Table III.H.8
Imports: Table III.H.25

There are a total of twenty-four source tables for product trade. The BM74 trade data are organized by the four affiliate industry groups, so four source tables are cited in each of the four cases listed under that benchmark heading.

PART II

THE TRADE ROLE OF MULTINATIONAL COMPANIES

CHAPTER 4

CONCEPTS OF MNC-RELATED TRADE

This chapter uses the trade matrix model to define four concepts of MNC-related trade. Two definitions -- affiliate related trade and intrafirm related trade -- provide the best context for analyzing the trade role of multinational companies.

THE TRADE MATRIX MODEL

The trade matrix model was developed by the author for a U.S. Government report on the trade role of multinational companies in 1977 [Hipple 1982]. It consists of a trade matrix placed within a flow of funds format to analyze the behavior of different groups of trade transactors. The model has been used in several studies of the trade role of multinational companies, notably two articles that appeared in *The American Economic Review* and *The International Trade Journal* in 1990.

The trade flows between the United States and other countries may be disaggregated in different ways. The procedure used here is to define trade relationships in terms of the identity of trade transactors. Following the practice of the Bureau of Economic Analysis, first divide the world into the United States (USA) and the rest of the world (ROW).

The international trade in the world is conducted by two types of business firms -- multinational companies and domestic companies. The multinational companies consist of parent firms and affiliate firms. U.S.-based MNCs have their parent firms in the United States and their affiliates in the ROW. Foreign-based MNCs have their parent firms in the ROW and their affiliates in the United States. As defined by the BEA, the parent firm has a 10% or more ownership (equity) interest in the foreign affiliate. The other trade transactors are purely domestic companies who engage in international trade on an "arms-length" basis only.

The trade transactors in the world may be classified as parent companies p, affiliate companies a, and other companies o. Exports X and imports M will be defined from the perspective of the United States. That is, X is imports for the ROW, and M is exports for the ROW.

Three sets of trade transactors are located in the United States: the parent firms of U.S.-based MNCs; the foreign affiliate firms of ROW-based MNCs; and U.S. domestic companies. Three sets of trade transactors are located in the rest of the world: the parent firms of ROW-based MNCs; the foreign affiliate firms of U.S.-based MNCs; and ROW domestic companies.

Total U.S. exports may be shown as:

$$X = Xp + Xa + Xo \qquad (1)$$

Let the terms Xp, Xa, and Xo represent exports by U.S. parent firms, the U.S. affiliates of foreign multinational companies, and other U.S. companies respectively.

The destination of U.S. exports can be shown as:

$$Xp = Xpp + Xpa + Xpo \qquad (2a)$$

$$Xa = Xap + Xaa + Xao \qquad (2b)$$

$$Xo = Xop + Xoa + Xoo \qquad (2c)$$

The first lower case letter represents the domestic U.S. seller, and the second lower case letter represents the ROW buyer. For example, the term Xpo is the value of U.S. exports originated by U.S. parent companies and sold to the "other" group of foreign companies.

Similarly, the buyers and sellers of U.S. imports can be shown as the following:

$$M = Mp + Ma + Mo \qquad (3)$$

$$Mp = Mpp + Mpa + Mpo \qquad (4a)$$

$$Ma = Map + Maa + Mao \qquad (4b)$$

$$Mo = Mop + Moa + Moo \qquad (4c)$$

The first lower case letter represents the domestic U.S. buyer, and the second lower case letter represents the ROW seller. For example, the term Mpo is the value of U.S. imports purchased by U.S. parent companies from the "other" group of foreign companies.

The matrix equation system in (2) and (4) shows nine categories of paired buyers and sellers. For example, the *po* category would include *Xpo* and *Mpo*. The categories involving multinational companies are shown by the letters *p* and/or *a*. The various concepts of the trade role of multinational companies can be illustrated by different sets of the nine categories of paired buyers and sellers. Each set forms a "definition" of MNC-related trade.

FOUR DEFINITIONS OF MNC-RELATED TRADE

Each definition is based on an alternative view of the types of trade transactions that can be properly linked with the activities of multinational companies. The four definitions focus on trade related to parents and affiliates combined, parents alone, affiliates alone, and intrafirm shipments between parents and affiliates. These definitions were used as the basis of the 1990 articles in *The American Economic Review* and *The International Trade Journal*.

1. Parent and Affiliate Related Trade

Under this concept, the trade role of MNCs includes all the trade transactions where the parent firm or the affiliate firm participates as a buyer and/or seller. In terms of the matrix equations, it would include all the categories with *p* and/or *a*. Under this nearly all-inclusive definition, only the *oo* category of trade transactions is excluded. In the export and import equations below, the included transaction categories are shown in bold type.

$$Xp = Xpp + Xpa + Xpo \qquad (5a)$$

$$Xa = Xap + Xaa + Xao \qquad (5b)$$

$$Xo = Xop + Xoa + Xoo \qquad (5c)$$

$$Mp = Mpp + Mpa + Mpo \qquad (6a)$$

$$Ma = Map + Maa + Mao \qquad (6b)$$

$$Mo = Mop + Moa + Moo \qquad (6c)$$

This concept of the MNC trade role is used by the BEA to calculate the level of merchandise trade "associated" with U.S.-based multinational companies for the annual articles which appear in the *Survey of Current Business* [Mataloni 51]. Since this concept includes the trade activities of parent firms, trade data are available only for U.S.-based multinationals.

2. Parent Related Trade

This concept of MNC-related trade focuses on the activities of the parent firm. All trade transactions in which the parent firm participates as a buyer or seller are included. In terms of the trade matrix equations, it would include all categories with p.

$$Xp = Xpp + Xpa + Xpo \qquad (7a)$$

$$Xa = Xap + Xaa + Xao \qquad (7b)$$

$$Xo = Xop + Xoa + Xoo \qquad (7c)$$

$$Mp = Mpp + Mpa + Mpo \qquad (8a)$$

$$Ma = Map + Maa + Mao \qquad (8b)$$

$$Mo = Mop + Moa + Moo \qquad (8c)$$

This concept of MNC-related trade has not been extensively used. The data have been published for U.S. multinational companies in the recent benchmark surveys of U.S. direct investment abroad. Since this concept involves the trade activities of parent firms, trade data are available for U.S.-based MNCs only.

3. Affiliate Related Trade

This concept focuses on the trading activities of the affiliate firms. The MNC trade role includes all the trade transactions in which the affiliate company participates as a buyer or seller. In terms of the matrix equations, it would include all categories with a.

$$Xp = Xpp + Xpa + Xpo \qquad (9a)$$

$$Xa = Xap + Xaa + Xao \qquad (9b)$$

$$Xo = Xop + Xoa + Xoo \qquad (9c)$$

$$Mp = Mpp + Mpa + Mpo \qquad (10a)$$

$$Ma = Map + Maa + Mao \qquad (10b)$$

$$Mo = Mop + Moa + Moo \qquad (10c)$$

This concept of the MNC trade role has been the focus of BEA analysis and data collection efforts. Both the annual reports and the benchmark surveys include information on affiliate operations. Extensive trade data are available for U.S.-based and ROW-based multinational companies.

4. Intrafirm Related Trade

This concept of the MNC trade role is limited to transactions where units of the multinational firm are at both ends of the trade. In terms of the matrix equations, it would include the two categories with *pa* and *ap*. It should be noted that intrafirm shipments are included in all of the preceding concepts of MNC-related trade.

$$Xp = Xpp + Xpa + Xpo \qquad (11a)$$

$$Xa = Xap + Xaa + Xao \qquad (11b)$$

$$Xo = Xop + Xoa + Xoo \qquad (11c)$$

$$Mp = Mpp + Mpa + Mpo \qquad (12a)$$

$$Ma = Map + Maa + Mao \qquad (12b)$$

$$Mo = Mop + Moa + Moo \qquad (12c)$$

This is the most narrow perception of the MNC trade role. It focuses on the distinction between "arms-length" and "intrafirm" transactions. The transactions between a parent and affiliate are not set by market forces or valued at market prices, but represent the production and distribution operations of the vertically-integrated, multinational company. The value of the transactions are transfer prices, needed for customs declarations, and set for internal MNC accounting purposes [Hipple 1990 JIBS]. The BEA annual reports and benchmark surveys provide trade data for both U.S.-based and ROW-based MNCs. The intrafirm data, however, are not as plentiful as the data on affiliate operations.

SOME ESTIMATES OF MNC-RELATED TRADE

The trade matrix model and the four definitions of MNC-related trade served as the basis for two articles published in 1990. The *American Economic Review* article measured the value of MNC-related trade in 1982 under all four definitions [Hipple 1990 AER]. The *International Trade Journal* article used the affiliate related trade and intrafirm related trade definitions to analyze MNC-related trade for 1977, 1982, and 1987, especially regarding the growing U.S. trade deficit [Hipple 1990 ITJ].

The *American Economic Review* article required a "heroic" assumption -- the trade behavior of ROW parent firms is the same as the behavior of U.S. parent firms. As noted above, the Bureau of Economic Analysis has collected partial data on the business operations of the parent firms of U.S.-based MNCs. No data have been collected on the parent firms of foreign-based MNCs, yet these data were needed to specify all the values in the trade matrix model. Under the assumption of identical behavior, it was possible to create a complete trade data set.

Under the first definition -- parent and affiliate related trade -- the article showed that U.S.-based MNCs and ROW-based MNCs together accounted for a 99.4% share of all merchandise trade in 1982. The definition was so broad that it included nearly all trade transactors. Under definition two -- parent related trade -- the trade share for all MNCs fell slightly to 82.9%. Both of these definitions were too broad to be of any analytical value.

In contrast, definitions three and four provided a useful perspective on the role of MNC-related trade in total merchandise trade. Affiliate related trade accounted for a 50.7% share of total trade in 1982. And intrafirm related trade, the critical dividing line between arms-length transactions and internal MNC transfer payments, had a 34.2% share of merchandise trade.

The *International Trade Journal* article used the affiliate trade and intrafirm trade concepts of MNC-related trade to analyze the role of MNC-related trade over time, especially in regards to the growing American trade deficit. Based on data availability, the years 1977, 1982, and 1987 were selected for comparison purposes.

Beginning in 1977, in affiliate related trade, combined U.S. MNCs and ROW MNCs held a 54.2% share of total merchandise trade in 1977. More significantly, the MNCs recorded a $20,514 million deficit compared to a total merchandise deficit of $27,796 million. In intrafirm related trade, multinational companies had a 40.2% share of total trade and a $24,134 deficit. Based on trade shares, MNCs should have run deficits on the order of 40% to 50% of the total deficit. Under either definition, it was clear that multinational firms could be associated with most of the total trade deficit. The remainder of the overall deficit was linked to a small deficit in non-MNC trade.

By 1982, the merchandise trade deficit was little changed at $27,507 million (up $289 million). In affiliate related trade, MNCs had a 53.8% share (down 0.4 share points) and a deficit of $18,514 million (down $2,000 million). In intrafirm trade, MNCs had a 35.5% share (down 4.7 share points) and a deficit of $19,053 million (down $5,081 million). Multinational companies, as a group of trade transactors, remained linked to most of the deficit.

Finally in 1987, the merchandise trade deficit had exploded to a level of

$152,119 million, an increase of $124,612 million in five years. In affiliate related trade, MNCs had a 51.2% share (down 2.6 share points) and a deficit of $89,491 million (up $70,977 million). In intrafirm trade, combined MNCs had a 38.2% share (up 2.7 share points) and a deficit of $61,788 million (up $61,788 million). Multinational companies, as a group of trade transactors, still remained linked to an excessive share of the deficit. Notably, non-MNC trade had also jumped to a very large deficit position.

From this analysis, it appeared that multinational companies were a significant factor in the deterioration of U.S. trade performance -- under either the affiliate or intrafirm definition. These two concepts of MNC-related trade are used as the basis for the analysis in this book.

CHAPTER 5

AFFILIATE TRADE AND INTRAFIRM TRADE

This chapter presents and discusses the standardized trade table format which has been used in the book. The table format is based upon the affiliate and intrafirm definitions of MNC-related trade. Affiliate related trade also involves a trade overlap problem.

THE STANDARDIZED TRADE TABLES

A standardized table format has been used throughout the book to present the data on MNC-related trade. The table includes sections for affiliate related trade and intrafirm related trade. Within each section, detail data are shown for different categories of MNC-related trade. The trade data include measures of both the dollar value of trade and trade shares.

As an example, Table 6.1 from the next chapter is shown on page 33. The title of the table is "Table 6.1: Multinational Companies and U.S. Total Merchandise Trade in 1975." Three comparison years are used in this book -- 1975, 1982, and 1989. Every chapter contains three tables for these three years. The "Table 6.1" part of the title means that the table is from Chapter 6 and is the first of the three trade tables and represents 1975.

The top section of the table is labeled "Affiliate Related Trade" and the bottom section is labeled "Intrafirm Related Trade," representing the two definitions of MNC-related trade. An identical format is used in both table sections.

The table has nine data columns. The first three data columns show exports, imports, and the trade balance in millions of U.S. dollars. The remaining six data columns show two measures of trade shares in percent.

The middle set of three data columns is based upon the share of "Total" trade (the first data row in the top and bottom sections of the table). The three columns show export, import, and average trade shares. The export and import trade shares are the ratio of the export and import dollar values to the value of trade shown in the "Total" row. The average trade shares are a trade-weighted average of the export and import shares. The shares in the "Total" row are shown as "100.0" as a reference.

The last set of three data columns is based upon the share of "All MNCs" trade (the third data row in the top and bottom sections of the table). The three columns show export, import, and average trade shares. The export and import trade shares are the ratio of the export and import dollar values to the value of trade shown in the "All MNCs" row. The average trade shares are a trade-weighted average of the export and import shares. The shares in the "All MNCs" row are shown as "100.0" as a reference.

The row labels are identical in both sections of the table. The first row label is "Total" which represents the total trade being shown in the table. In Table 6.1, it is the total merchandise trade of the United States for 1975. For example, Total merchandise exports were $109,254 in 1975. This figure is shown in the "Total" data line of both sections of the table.

In other tables, "Total" could refer to total trade with a geographic area such as U.S.-Japanese trade in 1982 (see Table 10.2), or to total trade in a product category such as U.S. trade in Chemicals in 1989 (see Table 21.3). The title of the table will specify the exact nature of "Total" trade. Note that the value for "Total" will be the same for both the affiliate related and intrafirm related trade sections of the table.

The second and third row labels are "Non-MNCs" and "All MNCs." The "All MNCs" values are the sum of the four affiliate industry rows. It represents the total trade related to both U.S.-based and ROW-based MNCs combined under that definition of MNC-related trade.

In Table 6.1, under affiliate related trade, the "All MNCs" value for exports is $58,893 million. In contrast, under intrafirm related trade, the "All MNCs" value for exports is $41,566 million. The intrafirm related definition of MNC trade covers a smaller range of transactions than the affiliate related definition. Both "All MNCs" values are the sum of the related figures in the four affiliate industry groups.

The values for "Non-MNCs" on row two are the difference between the "Total" trade on row one and the "All MNCs" related trade on row three. Under affiliate related trade, "Non MNCs" exports are $50,361 million (or $109,254 million less $58,893 million).

In terms of the shares of "Total Trade," Total exports have a 100.0% share, Non-MNCs exports have a 46.1% share, and All MNCs exports account for a 53.9% share. All MNCs imports have a 55.5% share of Total imports, slightly more than the export share. The average for All MNCs is a 54.7% share. That is, multinational companies accounted for over half of U.S. merchandise trade in 1975 (under the affiliate related trade definition).

[Standardized Trade Table Format Example]
Table 6.1: Multinational Companies and
U.S. Total Merchandise Trade in 1975

	MERCHANDISE TRADE (Millions of Dollars)			TOTAL TRADE (Percent Share)			ALL MNCs TRADE (Percent Share)		
	EXPORTS	IMPORTS	BALANCE	EXP	IMP	AVG	EXP	IMP	AVG
Affiliate Related Trade									
Total	109254	96570	12684	100.0	100.0	100.0	NA	NA	NA
Non-MNCs	50361	42956	7406	46.1	44.5	45.3	NA	NA	NA
All MNCs	58893	53615	5279	53.9	55.5	54.7	100.0	100.0	100.0
USA MNCs	36181	27153	9028	33.1	28.1	30.8	61.4	50.6	56.3
ROW MNCs	26433	29367	-2934	24.2	30.4	27.1	44.9	54.8	49.6
Petro MNCs	3980	15215	-11235	3.6	15.8	9.3	6.8	28.4	17.1
USA MNCs	1805	11660	-9855	1.7	12.1	6.5	3.1	21.7	12.0
ROW MNCs	2321	4417	-2096	2.1	4.6	3.3	3.9	8.2	6.0
Manu MNCs	26007	15102	10905	23.8	15.6	20.0	44.2	28.2	36.5
USA MNCs	24984	12823	12161	22.9	13.3	18.4	42.4	23.9	33.6
ROW MNCs	2217	2947	-730	2.0	3.1	2.5	3.8	5.5	4.6
Whole MNCs	26616	21418	5198	24.4	22.2	23.3	45.2	39.9	42.7
USA MNCs	7808	1166	6642	7.1	1.2	4.4	13.3	2.2	8.0
ROW MNCs	20978	21514	-536	19.2	22.3	20.6	35.6	40.1	37.8
Other MNCs	2290	1879	410	2.1	1.9	2.0	3.9	3.5	3.7
USA MNCs	1584	1504	80	1.4	1.6	1.5	2.7	2.8	2.7
ROW MNCs	917	489	428	0.8	0.5	0.7	1.6	0.9	1.2
Intrafirm Related Trade									
Total	109254	96570	12684	100.0	100.0	100.0	NA	NA	NA
Non-MNCs	67688	54565	13123	62.0	56.5	59.4	NA	NA	NA
All MNCs	41566	42005	-439	38.0	43.5	40.6	100.0	100.0	100.0
USA MNCs	28739	21342	7397	26.3	22.1	24.3	69.1	50.8	59.9
ROW MNCs	12827	20663	-7836	11.7	21.4	16.3	30.9	49.2	40.1
Petro MNCs	3299	11770	-8471	3.0	12.2	7.3	7.9	28.0	18.0
USA MNCs	1473	9020	-7547	1.3	9.3	5.1	3.5	21.5	12.6
ROW MNCs	1826	2750	-924	1.7	2.8	2.2	4.4	6.5	5.5
Manu MNCs	20448	12433	8015	18.7	12.9	16.0	49.2	29.6	39.3
USA MNCs	19647	10247	9400	18.0	10.6	14.5	47.3	24.4	35.8
ROW MNCs	801	2186	-1385	0.7	2.3	1.5	1.9	5.2	3.6
Whole MNCs	16513	16377	136	15.1	17.0	16.0	39.7	39.0	39.4
USA MNCs	6669	896	5773	6.1	0.9	3.7	16.0	2.1	9.1
ROW MNCs	9844	15481	-5637	9.0	16.0	12.3	23.7	36.9	30.3
Other MNCs	1306	1425	-119	1.2	1.5	1.3	3.1	3.4	3.3
USA MNCs	950	1179	-229	0.9	1.2	1.0	2.3	2.8	2.5
ROW MNCs	356	246	110	0.3	0.3	0.3	0.9	0.6	0.7

Under the "All MNCs" row are two rows labeled "USA MNCs" and "ROW MNCs" which show the total trade associated with U.S.-based MNCs and ROW-based MNCs, respectively. These rows are the sum of the related figures in the four affiliate industry groups.

In Table 6.1, under affiliate related trade, U.S. MNCs exports are $36,181 million and account for a 33.1% share of Total trade and a 61.4% share of All MNCs trade. The equivalent data for ROW MNCs exports are $26,433 million, a 24.2% share of Total trade, and a 44.9% share of All MNCs trade. Note that the sum of U.S. MNCs and ROW MNCs exports is $62,614 million compared to the All MNCs figure of $58,893 million. Under Total trade, the export share sum is 57.3% compared to the All MNCs figure of 53.9%. Under All MNCs trade, the export share sum is 106.1% compared to the All MNCs figure of 100.0%. The All MNCs figures have been adjusted for the "affiliate trade overlap."

Part of the affiliate trade by U.S. MNCs and ROW MNCs is with each other. This overlap must be removed from the All MNCs figures to avoid double counting and exaggerating the level of MNC-related trade. In the example, the level of the affiliate trade overlap is estimated to be $3,721 million, 3.4% of Total trade, and 6.1% of All MNCs trade. The affiliate trade overlap at the All MNCs level represents trade between the two groups of affiliates.

In Table 6.1, under intrafirm related trade, U.S. MNCs exports are $28,739 million and account for a 26.3% share of Total trade and a 69.1% share of All MNCs trade. The equivalent data for ROW MNCs exports are $12,827 million, a 11.7% share of Total trade, and a 30.9% share of All MNCs trade. Note that the sum of U.S. MNCs and ROW MNCs exports is $41,566 million and is identical to the All MNCs figure of $41,566 million. The trade shares for U.S. MNCs and ROW MNCs also sum to the All MNCs figures. By definition, there can be no overlap in intrafirm trade.

The remaining twelve rows of data in the affiliate and intrafirm related trade sections of the table cover the four affiliate industry groups. As discussed in Chapter 3, the tables in the benchmark surveys are organized according to the industry of the affiliate firms. It has been possible to collect consistent data from all six benchmark surveys for four industry groups -- Petroleum Affiliates (Petro), Manufacturing Affiliates (Manu), Wholesale Trade Affiliates (Whole), and Other Industry Affiliates (Other).

The data for each affiliate industry group are presented in the same format as the "All MNCs," "USA MNCs," and "ROW MNCs" group discussed above. Under affiliate related trade, there is a trade overlap between the U.S. MNCs and the ROW MNCs which must be eliminated from the industry level trade. For example in Table 6.1 under Manufacturing Affiliates, the exports of "Manu MNCs" are less than the sum of the exports of U.S. MNCs and ROW MNCs. The affiliate trade overlap within Manufacturing Affiliates represents trade between (1) the two groups of manufacturing affiliates and (2) trade with affiliates in the other industry groups. Under intrafirm related trade, there is no trade overlap at the affiliate industry level.

In all the trade tables, the All MNCs data row is the sum of the four industry rows -- Petro MNCs, Manu MNCs, Whole MNCs, and Other MNCs.

The U.S. MNCs and ROW MNCs data rows under All MNCs are the sum of the related data rows in the four affiliate industry groups.

THE AFFILIATE TRADE OVERLAP PROBLEM

Intrafirm related trade is "closed trade" in the sense that the transactors on both sides are fully known, and there is no overlapping trade between the U.S.-based firms and the ROW-based firms. The export and import figures for U.S. MNCs and ROW MNCs can be directly aggregated to find totals.

Affiliate related trade is "open" in the sense that the transactors beyond intrafirm trade are not known. Affiliates do trade with each other, and this overlap must be removed to avoid overstating the significance of affiliate related trade.

The trade overlap problem can be presented in terms of the notation from the trade matrix model in Chapter 4. Let Xat and Mat represent the total exports and imports by the U.S.-located affiliates of ROW-based MNCs. Let Xta and Mta represent the total exports and imports by the ROW-located affiliates of U.S.-based MNCs.

In the following equations, the known values are shown in bold type.

$$Xat = Xap + Xaa + Xao \qquad (13a)$$

$$Xta = Xpa + Xaa + Xoa \qquad (13b)$$

$$Mat = Map + Maa + Mao \qquad (14a)$$

$$Mta = Mpa + Maa + Moa \qquad (14b)$$

The terms with the lowercase t are the total affiliate trade, while the terms with ap or pa represent intrafirm trade. The difference is the arms-length trade conducted by the affiliates with (1) the other group of affiliates shown by aa and (2) domestic firms shown by ao or oa.

The total export trade by affiliates is the sum of Xat and Xta minus the trade overlap term Xaa. Similarly, total import trade by affiliates is the sum of Mat and Mta but minus the trade overlap term Maa. The task is to provide an estimate of the overlap term that is consistent with both the U.S. MNC and ROW MNC data.

The process is to calculate the arms-length trade for both sets of MNC affiliates. The smaller amount is selected since it is a constraint on the value that can be taken by the overlapping trade in Xaa or Maa. This amount must then be allocated into trade with the other group of affiliates and trade with domestic firms. In the absence of any market share information, the allocation rule is an even split.

In previous studies, a different allocation rule was employed based on a rather complex market share formula. (See Hipple [1990 AER] for example.) The formula included unrelated trade flows in the market share denominator and, as a result, understated the size of the affiliate trade overlap.

Furthermore, the affiliate trade overlap must be calculated at the "All MNCs" level of trade. The trade overlap cannot be estimated within a subset of MNC-related trade (such as manufacturing affiliates) since there is affiliate overlap trade outside of the subset (manufacturing affiliates will trade with wholesale trade affiliates, for example). The proper procedure is to calculate the overlap at the "All MNCs" level of trade, and then allocate the overlap to subsets at the industry level.

In Chapter 6 on "Total Merchandise Trade," the affiliate trade overlap is calculated at the "All MNCs" level and is allocated to the four affiliate industry groups. In Part III on "Geographic Patterns of MNC-Related Trade," the trade overlap is calculated at the "All MNCs" level in the four geographic trade chapters and is then allocated to the affiliate industry groups. The trade data in Chapter 7 on "Total Geographic Trade" are the sum of the trade data in the detail chapters. Thus the trade overlap data in Chapter 7 are the sum of the overlap data in the four geographic trade chapters.

In Part IV on "Product Patterns of MNC-Related Trade," the trade overlap is calculated at the "All MNCs" level in the twelve product trade chapters and is then allocated to the affiliate industry groups. The trade data in Chapter 12 on "Total Product Trade," Chapter 13 on "Non-Manufactured Goods Trade," and Chapter 20 on "Manufactured Goods Trade" are the sum of the trade data in the detail chapters. Thus the trade overlap data in these aggregate chapters are the sum of the overlap data in the related product trade chapters.

CHAPTER 6

TOTAL MERCHANDISE TRADE

Total Merchandise trade provides the initial overview of the trade role of multinational companies. On this basis, MNC affiliate trade accounts for a 53% share of total trade, and MNC intrafirm trade has a 39% share. Wholesale affiliates are the dominant industry group, followed by manufacturing affiliates.

DEFINITION OF TOTAL MERCHANDISE TRADE

Total Merchandise trade, along with Total Geographic trade and Total Product trade, provide three different perspectives on the MNC role in total trade. Total Merchandise trade is the simplest perspective and consists of the direct analysis of total merchandise exports and imports.

Merchandise exports are defined as "Exports of Merchandise (Including Reexports)" and consist of goods produced in the United States and sold to foreign consumers ("Domestic Merchandise") and goods imported into the United States and reexported ("Foreign Merchandise"). The export value is the value at the U.S. point of export, or FAS value (free alongside ship).

Merchandise imports are defined as "General Imports of Merchandise" and consist of goods produced elsewhere and purchased by U.S. consumers. The import value is the value at the foreign point of export, or FAS value (free alongside ship) [BS6391 164-165].

TRENDS IN TOTAL MERCHANDISE TRADE

In 1975, Total Merchandise trade was $205,824 million. Exports were $109,254 million and imports were $96,570 million yielding a surplus of $12,684 million. Between 1975 and 1982, total trade increased 124% or

$254,570 million to reach $460,394 million. Both exports and imports enjoyed strong growth, but with imports growing one-third faster. This growth imbalance converted the modest 1975 trade surplus into a 1982 deficit of $27,510 million. The total swing in the trade balance was 317% or a decline of $40,194 million.

Between 1982 and 1989, the growth rates slowed in Total Merchandise trade. Total trade grew 82% or $376,629 million to reach $837,023 million. Imports still continued to grow one-third faster than exports. This resulted in another 298% deterioration in the trade balance of $81,889 million, pushing the deficit to $109,399 million by 1989.

THE TRADE ROLE OF MULTINATIONAL COMPANIES

This section is based on the trade data shown in Tables 6.1, 6.2, and 6.3 for 1975, 1982, and 1989, respectively. The overall trade role of multinational companies ("All MNCs" in the tables) is discussed for both affiliate related trade and intrafirm related trade.

The affiliate related data for Total Merchandise trade are different from Total Geographic and Total Product trade data due to differing estimates of the affiliate trade overlap. The intrafirm trade data are identical in all three instances.

Affiliate Related Trade

Total Merchandise trade totaled $205,824 million in 1975. Adjusted for the trade overlap, affiliate related trade was $112,508 million for a 54.7% share; Non-MNC trade was $93,317 million for a 45.3% share. The MNC-related trade position reflected a 53.9% share of export trade and a 55.5% share of import trade. The dominant MNC group was U.S.-based firms with a 30.8% share of total trade; ROW-based firms held a 27.1% share. U.S. multinational companies had a larger share of exports; ROW MNCs held the larger share of imports.

The Total Merchandise trade balance in 1975 was a surplus of $12,684 million. This reflected a $5,279 million surplus in MNC-related trade and a $7,406 million surplus in Non-MNC trade. Thus the overall trade surplus position in Total Merchandise was due to both components. In turn, the MNC-related surplus was based on a surplus position of U.S.-based multinationals which offset a small deficit position of ROW-based firms.

Between 1975 and 1982, Total Merchandise trade grew 124% or $254,570 million to reach $460,394 million. In comparison, affiliate related trade increased $130,159 million or 116% to a level of $242,667 million (adjusted for the trade overlap). Accordingly, the overall affiliate position decreased slightly from a 54.7% to a 52.7% share and Non-MNC trade rose to a 47.3% share.

Table 6.1: Multinational Companies and U.S. Total Merchandise Trade in 1975

	MERCHANDISE TRADE (Millions of Dollars)			TOTAL TRADE (Percent Share)			ALL MNCs TRADE (Percent Share)		
	EXPORTS	IMPORTS	BALANCE	EXP	IMP	AVG	EXP	IMP	AVG
Affiliate Related Trade									
Total	109254	96570	12684	100.0	100.0	100.0	NA	NA	NA
Non-MNCs	50361	42956	7406	46.1	44.5	45.3	NA	NA	NA
All MNCs	58893	53615	5279	53.9	55.5	54.7	100.0	100.0	100.0
USA MNCs	36181	27153	9028	33.1	28.1	30.8	61.4	50.6	56.3
ROW MNCs	26433	29367	-2934	24.2	30.4	27.1	44.9	54.8	49.6
Petro MNCs	3980	15215	-11235	3.6	15.8	9.3	6.8	28.4	17.1
USA MNCs	1805	11660	-9855	1.7	12.1	6.5	3.1	21.7	12.0
ROW MNCs	2321	4417	-2096	2.1	4.6	3.3	3.9	8.2	6.0
Manu MNCs	26007	15102	10905	23.8	15.6	20.0	44.2	28.2	36.5
USA MNCs	24984	12823	12161	22.9	13.3	18.4	42.4	23.9	33.6
ROW MNCs	2217	2947	-730	2.0	3.1	2.5	3.8	5.5	4.6
Whole MNCs	26616	21418	5198	24.4	22.2	23.3	45.2	39.9	42.7
USA MNCs	7808	1166	6642	7.1	1.2	4.4	13.3	2.2	8.0
ROW MNCs	20978	21514	-536	19.2	22.3	20.6	35.6	40.1	37.8
Other MNCs	2290	1879	410	2.1	1.9	2.0	3.9	3.5	3.7
USA MNCs	1584	1504	80	1.4	1.6	1.5	2.7	2.8	2.7
ROW MNCs	917	489	428	0.8	0.5	0.7	1.6	0.9	1.2
Intrafirm Related Trade									
Total	109254	96570	12684	100.0	100.0	100.0	NA	NA	NA
Non-MNCs	67688	54565	13123	62.0	56.5	59.4	NA	NA	NA
All MNCs	41566	42005	-439	38.0	43.5	40.6	100.0	100.0	100.0
USA MNCs	28739	21342	7397	26.3	22.1	24.3	69.1	50.8	59.9
ROW MNCs	12827	20663	-7836	11.7	21.4	16.3	30.9	49.2	40.1
Petro MNCs	3299	11770	-8471	3.0	12.2	7.3	7.9	28.0	18.0
USA MNCs	1473	9020	-7547	1.3	9.3	5.1	3.5	21.5	12.6
ROW MNCs	1826	2750	-924	1.7	2.8	2.2	4.4	6.5	5.5
Manu MNCs	20448	12433	8015	18.7	12.9	16.0	49.2	29.6	39.3
USA MNCs	19647	10247	9400	18.0	10.6	14.5	47.3	24.4	35.8
ROW MNCs	801	2186	-1385	0.7	2.3	1.5	1.9	5.2	3.6
Whole MNCs	16513	16377	136	15.1	17.0	16.0	39.7	39.0	39.4
USA MNCs	6669	896	5773	6.1	0.9	3.7	16.0	2.1	9.1
ROW MNCs	9844	15481	-5637	9.0	16.0	12.3	23.7	36.9	30.3
Other MNCs	1306	1425	-119	1.2	1.5	1.3	3.1	3.4	3.3
USA MNCs	950	1179	-229	0.9	1.2	1.0	2.3	2.8	2.5
ROW MNCs	356	246	110	0.3	0.3	0.3	0.9	0.6	0.7

Within the affiliate trade structure, the export share fell to 51.7% and the import share to 53.6%. These changes reflected a decline in the U.S. MNC shares which offset a rise in ROW MNC shares.

The Total Merchandise trade balance in 1982 had changed to a deficit of $27,510 million, a $40,194 deterioration from 1975. The affiliate related trade position had changed into a deficit of $18,918 million, a swing of $24,196 million. The Non-MNC trade balance had also become a deficit of $8,593 million, a swing of $15,998 million. Thus the deterioration in the Total Merchandise trade balance was due to unfavorable trends in both components. The conversion of MNC-related trade into a deficit was caused by the growing deficit position of ROW multinationals, linked to a decline in the size of the U.S. MNC surplus.

In the 1982 to 1989 period, Total Merchandise trade grew 82% or $376,629 million to $837,023 million. In comparison, affiliate related trade rose $198,896 million or 82% to a level of $441,562 million (adjusted for the trade overlap). As a result, the overall affiliate position remained little changed, increasing from a 52.7% to a 52.8% share and Non-MNC trade had a 47.2% share. Within the affiliate trade structure the export share decreased to 50.1% and the import share increased to 54.8%. The export change reflected a decline in the trade share of ROW MNCs which offset an increased share of U.S. MNCs. The import change was due to a higher trade share of ROW MNCs which offset a lower U.S. MNC share. Compared to 1975, the U.S. MNC share of total trade had fallen from 30.8% to 23.9%; the ROW MNC share had risen from 27.1% to 30.8%. ROW-based firms had supplanted U.S.-based firms as the dominant MNC group in Total Merchandise trade.

The Total Merchandise trade deficit in 1989 was $109,399 million, a rise of $81,889 million over 1982. The affiliate related trade deficit was $76,833 million, an increase of $57,916 million; the Non-MNC trade deficit was $32,566 million, an increase of $23,974 million. Thus the deterioration in the Total Merchandise trade balance reflected trends in both components. The MNC-related deficit was based on the growing trade deficit of ROW MNCs which had reached $85,531 million.

Intrafirm Related Trade

Total Merchandise trade totaled $205,824 million in 1975. Intrafirm related trade was $83,571 million for a 40.6% share (compared to a 54.7% share for affiliate related trade). Arms-length or Non-MNC trade was $122,253 million for a 59.4% share. The MNC-related trade position reflected a 38.0% share of export trade and a 43.5% share of import trade. The dominant MNC group was U.S.-based firms with a 24.3% share of total trade; ROW-based firms held a 16.3% share. U.S. multinationals had the much larger share of exports and imports, especially in exports.

The Total Merchandise trade balance in 1975 was a surplus of $12,684 million. This reflected a $439 million deficit in MNC-related trade and a $13,123 million surplus in Non-MNC trade. Thus the trade surplus was due to Non-MNC trade. The MNC-related deficit was linked to a deficit in ROW MNC trade which offset a surplus in U.S. MNC trade.

Between 1975 and 1982, Total Merchandise trade grew $254,570 million or 124% to reach $460,394 million. In comparison, the intrafirm related trade

Table 6.2: Multinational Companies and
U.S. Total Merchandise Trade in 1982

	MERCHANDISE TRADE (Millions of Dollars)			TOTAL TRADE (Percent Share)			ALL MNCs TRADE (Percent Share)		
	EXPORTS	IMPORTS	BALANCE	EXP	IMP	AVG	EXP	IMP	AVG
Affiliate Related Trade									
Total	216442	243952	-27510	100.0	100.0	100.0	NA	NA	NA
Non-MNCs	104568	113160	-8593	48.3	46.4	47.3	NA	NA	NA
All MNCs	111875	130792	-18918	51.7	53.6	52.7	100.0	100.0	100.0
USA MNCs	56718	51406	5312	26.2	21.1	23.5	50.7	39.3	44.6
ROW MNCs	60236	84290	-24054	27.8	34.6	31.4	53.8	64.4	59.6
Petro MNCs	4583	23209	-18626	2.1	9.5	6.0	4.1	17.7	11.5
USA MNCs	3304	15771	-12467	1.5	6.5	4.1	3.0	12.1	7.9
ROW MNCs	1531	8486	-6955	0.7	3.5	2.2	1.4	6.5	4.1
Manu MNCs	48204	42288	5916	22.3	17.3	19.7	43.1	32.3	37.3
USA MNCs	37180	31107	6073	17.2	12.8	14.8	33.2	23.8	28.1
ROW MNCs	12883	12386	497	6.0	5.1	5.5	11.5	9.5	10.4
Whole MNCs	55467	61941	-6474	25.6	25.4	25.5	49.6	47.4	48.4
USA MNCs	14866	2706	12160	6.9	1.1	3.8	13.3	2.1	7.2
ROW MNCs	43336	61679	-18343	20.0	25.3	22.8	38.7	47.2	43.3
Other MNCs	3620	3354	266	1.7	1.4	1.5	3.2	2.6	2.9
USA MNCs	1368	1822	-454	0.6	0.7	0.7	1.2	1.4	1.3
ROW MNCs	2486	1739	747	1.1	0.7	0.9	2.2	1.3	1.7
Intrafirm Related Trade									
Total	216442	243952	-27510	100.0	100.0	100.0	NA	NA	NA
Non-MNCs	144859	150439	-5580	66.9	61.7	64.1	NA	NA	NA
All MNCs	71583	93513	-21930	33.1	38.3	35.9	100.0	100.0	100.0
USA MNCs	46559	41598	4961	21.5	17.1	19.1	65.0	44.5	53.4
ROW MNCs	25024	51915	-26891	11.6	21.3	16.7	35.0	55.5	46.6
Petro MNCs	2585	15243	-12658	1.2	6.2	3.9	3.6	16.3	10.8
USA MNCs	1915	12646	-10731	0.9	5.2	3.2	2.7	13.5	8.8
ROW MNCs	670	2597	-1927	0.3	1.1	0.7	0.9	2.8	2.0
Manu MNCs	33462	33128	334	15.5	13.6	14.5	46.7	35.4	40.3
USA MNCs	30350	25448	4902	14.0	10.4	12.1	42.4	27.2	33.8
ROW MNCs	3112	7680	-4568	1.4	3.1	2.3	4.3	8.2	6.5
Whole MNCs	33774	43365	-9591	15.6	17.8	16.8	47.2	46.4	46.7
USA MNCs	13433	2282	11151	6.2	0.9	3.4	18.8	2.4	9.5
ROW MNCs	20341	41083	-20742	9.4	16.8	13.3	28.4	43.9	37.2
Other MNCs	1762	1777	-15	0.8	0.7	0.8	2.5	1.9	2.1
USA MNCs	861	1222	-361	0.4	0.5	0.5	1.2	1.3	1.3
ROW MNCs	901	555	346	0.4	0.2	0.3	1.3	0.6	0.9

increased $81,525 million or 98% to a level of $165,096 million. Accordingly, the overall intrafirm position decreased from a 40.6% to a 35.9% share (compared to a 54.7% to 52.7% share change for affiliate related trade). Non-MNC trade rose to a 64.1% share. Within the intrafirm trade structure, the export share dropped to 33.1% and the import share to 38.3%. These changes reflected a decline in the shares of U.S.-based MNCs; the shares of ROW-based

MNCs were largely unchanged.

The Total Merchandise trade balance in 1982 had changed to a deficit of $27,510 million, a deterioration of $40,194 million from 1975. The intrafirm related trade deficit had increased $21,491 to a level of $21,930 million. The Non-MNC trade surplus had become a deficit of $5,580 million, a decline of $18,703 million. Thus the decline in the Total Merchandise trade balance resulted from unfavorable trends in both components. The MNC-related deficit emerged due to a growing deficit in ROW MNC trade and a shrinking surplus in U.S. MNC trade.

In the 1982 to 1989 period, Total Merchandise trade grew $376,629 million or 82% to $837,023 million. In comparison, intrafirm related trade increased $165,952 million or 101% to a level of $331,048 million. As a result, the overall intrafirm position increased from a 35.9% to a 39.6% share (compared to a 52.7% to 52.8% share change for affiliate related trade). Non-MNC trade fell to a 60.4% share. Within the intrafirm trade structure, the export share rose slightly to 34.0% and the import share pushed up to 43.8%. The export change reflected an increase in the trade share of U.S. MNCs which offset a decline in the ROW MNC share. The import change was due to a jump in the trade share of ROW MNCs. Compared to 1975, the U.S. MNC share of total trade had fallen from 24.3% to 19.9%; the ROW MNC share had risen from 16.3% to 19.6%. U.S.-based firms remained the dominant MNC group by a mere 0.3% share.

The Total Merchandise trade deficit in 1989 had increased to $109,399 million, a deterioration of $81,889 million from 1982. The intrafirm related trade deficit was $83,418 million, an increase of $61,488 million; the Non-MNC trade deficit had risen $20,041 million to reach $25,981 million. Thus the growth in the Total Merchandise trade deficit was due to unfavorable trends in both components, especially in MNC-related trade. The MNC-related deficit was based on the ballooning ROW MNC deficit which had reached $95,650 million.

INDUSTRY TRADE ROLES

This section is based on the trade data shown in Tables 6.1, 6.2, and 6.3 for 1975, 1982, and 1989, respectively. The trade role of each affiliate industry group is discussed on the basis of affiliate related trade.

Petroleum Affiliates

Affiliate related trade was $19,195 million in 1975, adjusted for the affiliate trade overlap. This figure represented a 9.3% share of total trade and a 17.1% share of MNC-related trade. Overall, the industry category ranked third and was dominated by U.S.-based firms. The industry trade balance was a deficit

Table 6.3: Multinational Companies and
U.S. Total Merchandise Trade in 1989

	MERCHANDISE TRADE (Millions of Dollars)			TOTAL TRADE (Percent Share)			ALL MNCs TRADE (Percent Share)		
	EXPORTS	IMPORTS	BALANCE	EXP	IMP	AVG	EXP	IMP	AVG
Affiliate Related Trade									
Total	363812	473211	-109399	100.0	100.0	100.0	NA	NA	NA
Non-MNCs	181448	214014	-32566	49.9	45.2	47.2	NA	NA	NA
All MNCs	182365	259198	-76833	50.1	54.8	52.8	100.0	100.0	100.0
USA MNCs	102558	97394	5164	28.2	20.6	23.9	56.2	37.6	45.3
ROW MNCs	86316	171847	-85531	23.7	36.3	30.8	47.3	66.3	58.5
Petro MNCs	4340	22772	-18432	1.2	4.8	3.2	2.4	8.8	6.1
USA MNCs	2512	10079	-7567	0.7	2.1	1.5	1.4	3.9	2.9
ROW MNCs	2014	14145	-12131	0.6	3.0	1.9	1.1	5.5	3.7
Manu MNCs	98651	113727	-15076	27.1	24.0	25.4	54.1	43.9	48.1
USA MNCs	70187	77372	-7185	19.3	16.4	17.6	38.5	29.9	33.4
ROW MNCs	31873	40871	-8998	8.8	8.6	8.7	17.5	15.8	16.5
Whole MNCs	74389	118105	-43717	20.4	25.0	23.0	40.8	45.6	43.6
USA MNCs	27886	7675	20211	7.7	1.6	4.2	15.3	3.0	8.1
ROW MNCs	49096	114049	-64953	13.5	24.1	19.5	26.9	44.0	36.9
Other MNCs	4985	4593	392	1.4	1.0	1.1	2.7	1.8	2.2
USA MNCs	1973	2268	-295	0.5	0.5	0.5	1.1	0.9	1.0
ROW MNCs	3333	2782	551	0.9	0.6	0.7	1.8	1.1	1.4
Intrafirm Related Trade									
Total	363812	473211	-109399	100.0	100.0	100.0	NA	NA	NA
Non-MNCs	239997	265978	-25981	66.0	56.2	60.4	NA	NA	NA
All MNCs	123815	207233	-83418	34.0	43.8	39.6	100.0	100.0	100.0
USA MNCs	89539	77307	12232	24.6	16.3	19.9	72.3	37.3	50.4
ROW MNCs	34276	129926	-95650	9.4	27.5	19.6	27.7	62.7	49.6
Petro MNCs	2665	15260	-12595	0.7	3.2	2.1	2.2	7.4	5.4
USA MNCs	1914	7332	-5418	0.5	1.5	1.1	1.5	3.5	2.8
ROW MNCs	751	7928	-7177	0.2	1.7	1.0	0.6	3.8	2.6
Manu MNCs	67988	90362	-22374	18.7	19.1	18.9	54.9	43.6	47.8
USA MNCs	60062	62775	-2713	16.5	13.3	14.7	48.5	30.3	37.1
ROW MNCs	7926	27587	-19661	2.2	5.8	4.2	6.4	13.3	10.7
Whole MNCs	51065	99383	-48318	14.0	21.0	18.0	41.2	48.0	45.4
USA MNCs	26283	6140	20143	7.2	1.3	3.9	21.2	3.0	9.8
ROW MNCs	24782	93243	-68461	6.8	19.7	14.1	20.0	45.0	35.7
Other MNCs	2097	2228	-131	0.6	0.5	0.5	1.7	1.1	1.3
USA MNCs	1280	1060	220	0.4	0.2	0.3	1.0	0.5	0.7
ROW MNCs	817	1168	-351	0.2	0.2	0.2	0.7	0.6	0.6

of $11,235 million, compared to a total merchandise surplus of $12,684 million.

By 1982, industry trade had increased 45% to $27,792 million. This figure represented a 6.0% share of total trade (down 3.3 share points), and a 11.5% share of MNC-related trade (down 5.6 share points). The industry category ranked third, behind wholesale and manufacturing affiliates. The trade balance was a deficit of $18,626 million (up $7,391 million), compared to a total merchandise deficit of $27,510 million (a swing of $40,194 million).

Industry related trade decreased by 2.0% to $27,112 million in 1989. This figure represented a 3.2% share of total trade (down 2.8 share points), and a 6.1% share of MNC-related trade (down 5.3 share points). The industry category still ranked third, and continued to be dominated by U.S.-based firms. The trade balance was a deficit of $18,432 million (down $194 million), compared to a total merchandise deficit of $109,399 million (up $81,889 million).

Manufacturing Affiliates

Affiliate related trade was $41,109 million in 1975, adjusted for the affiliate trade overlap. This figure represented a 20.0% share of total trade and a 36.5% share of MNC-related trade. The industry category ranked second and was dominated by U.S.-based firms. The industry trade balance was a surplus of $10,905 million, compared to a total merchandise surplus of $12,684 million.

By 1982, industry trade had increased 120% to $90,492 million. This figure represented a 19.7% share of total trade (down 0.3 share points), and a 37.3% share of MNC-related trade (up 0.8 share points). The industry category ranked second, behind wholesale affiliates. The trade balance was a surplus of $5,916 million (down $4,989 million), compared to a total merchandise deficit of $27,510 million (a swing of $40,194 million).

Industry related trade increased by 135% to $212,378 million in 1989. This figure represented a 25.4% share of total trade (up 5.7 share points), and a 48.1% share of MNC-related trade (up 10.8 share points). The industry category now ranked first, and continued to be dominated by U.S.-based firms. The trade balance was a deficit of $15,076 million (a swing of $20,993 million), compared to a total merchandise deficit of $109,399 million (up $81,889 million).

Wholesale Trade Affiliates

Affiliate related trade was $48,035 million in 1975, adjusted for the affiliate trade overlap. This figure represented a 23.3% share of total trade and a 42.7% share of MNC-related trade. The industry category ranked first and was dominated by ROW-based firms. The industry trade balance was a surplus of $5,198 million, compared to a total merchandise surplus of $12,684 million.

By 1982, industry trade had increased 144% to $117,408 million. This figure represented a 25.5% share of total trade (up 2.2 share points), and a 48.4% share of MNC-related trade (up 5.7 share points). The industry category continued to rank first. The trade balance was a deficit of $6,474 million (a swing of $11,672 million), compared to a total merchandise deficit of $27,510 million (a swing of $40,194 million).

Industry related trade increased by 64% to $192,494 million in 1989, adjusted for the affiliate trade overlap. This figure represented a 23.0% share of total trade (down 2.5 share points), and a 43.6% share of MNC-related trade (down 4.8 share points). The industry category now ranked second, behind manufacturing, and continued to be dominated by ROW-based firms. The trade balance was a deficit of $43,717 million (up $37,242 million), compared to a total merchandise balance which was in deficit of $109,399 million (up $81,889 million).

Other Industry Affiliates

Affiliate related trade was $4,169 million in 1975, adjusted for the affiliate trade overlap. This figure represented a 2.0% share of total trade and a 3.7% share of MNC-related trade. The industry category ranked last and was dominated by U.S.-based firms. The industry trade balance was a surplus of $410 million, compared to a total merchandise surplus of $12,684 million.

By 1982, industry trade had increased 67% to $6,973 million. This figure represented a 1.5% share of total trade (down 0.5 share points), and a 2.9% share of MNC-related trade (down 0.8 share points). The industry category continued to rank last. The trade balance was a surplus of $266 million (down $144 million), compared to a total merchandise deficit of $27,510 million (a swing of $40,194 million).

Industry related trade increased by 37% to $9,578 million in 1989, adjusted for the affiliate trade overlap. This figure represented a 1.1% share of total trade (down 0.4 share points), and a 2.2% share of MNC-related trade (down 0.7 share points). The industry category still ranked last, and continued to be dominated by U.S.-based firms. The trade balance was a surplus of $392 million (up $126 million), compared to a total merchandise deficit of $109,399 million (up $81,889 million).

DERIVATION OF THE DATA

Total Merchandise trade, Total Geographic trade, and Total Product trade provide three different perspectives on the MNC role in total trade. Total Merchandise trade is the simplest perspective and is based on the data for total merchandise exports and imports. Total Merchandise data is generally identical to the trade data for Total Geographic trade and Total Product trade. The exception is affiliate related trade where different procedures are used to estimate the trade overlap.

Three steps are needed to derive the Total Merchandise trade data on MNC-related trade. First, the benchmark source tables which show the affiliate and intrafirm trade data must be identified. Second, all of the MNC-related trade data must be time shifted to common time periods for comparison. And third, estimates must be derived for the trade overlap in affiliate related trade.

The Benchmark Source Tables

The basic data for merchandise trade come from the six foreign direct investment surveys conducted by the U.S. Government over the past two decades. The benchmark years are 1974, 1977, 1980, 1982, 1987, and 1989, and are referred to as BM74, BM77, etc. (Full citations are shown in the Selected Bibliography.) The 1974, 1980, and 1987 benchmarks cover foreign direct investment in the United States ("reverse investment"). The 1977, 1982, and 1989 benchmarks cover U.S. direct investment abroad ("outward investment").

The benchmark tables used as sources for merchandise trade data are listed below. For each benchmark, export and import source tables are shown for affiliate related trade and intrafirm related trade. There are a total of twenty-four source tables. (The BM74 trade data are organized by the four affiliate industry groups, so four source tables are cited in each of the four cases listed under that benchmark heading.)

BM74: Foreign Direct Investment in the United States
    Affiliate Related Trade
        Exports: Tables E-1, E-3, E-4, E-5
        Imports: Tables E-1, E-3, E-4, E-5
    Intrafirm Related Trade
        Exports: Tables E-1, E-3, E-4, E-5
        Imports: Tables E-1, E-3, E-4, E-5

BM77: U.S. Direct Investment Abroad
    Affiliate Related Trade
        Exports: Table II.I.4
        Imports: Table II.I.20
    Intrafirm Related Trade
        Exports: Table II.I.7
        Imports: Table II.I.23

BM80: Foreign Direct Investment in the United States
    Affiliate Related Trade
        Exports: Table G-12
        Imports: Table G-24
    Intrafirm Related Trade
        Exports: Table G-14
        Imports: Table G-26

BM82: U.S. Direct Investment Abroad
    Affiliate Related Trade
        Exports: Table II.G.4

Imports: Table II.G.21
Intrafirm Related Trade
Exports: Table II.G.7
Imports: Table II.G.24

BM87: Foreign Direct Investment in the United States
Affiliate Related Trade
Exports: Table G-10
Imports: Table G-16
Intrafirm Related Trade
Exports: Table G-12
Imports: Table G-18

BM89: U.S. Direct Investment Abroad
Affiliate Related Trade
Exports: Table II.H.2
Imports: Table II.H.2
Intrafirm Related Trade
Exports: Table II.H.2
Imports: Table II.H.2

Conversion to Comparison Years

The common time periods for the trade data comparisons are 1975, 1982, and 1989. The time shifting of the benchmark data to these comparison years is accomplished by using information from two sources. The first source is the series of annual reports on foreign direct investment activities begun by the Bureau of Economic Analysis in the late 1970s. The second source is U.S. annual trade data.

The BEA annual reports on multinational companies are linked to the previous benchmark surveys. Thus the annual reports on reverse investment for 1988 and 1989 are based on the 1987 benchmark. The reports on outward investment for 1987 and 1988, however, are still based on the 1982 benchmark. The comparison year of 1989 can draw upon the 1989 benchmark for outward investment and the 1989 annual report on reverse investment. The same situation holds for the 1980 to 1982 period.

There are no BEA annual FDI reports for the 1974 to 1977 period, so any year in that interval could be selected as the comparison year. Since the time period between 1982 and 1989 is seven years, it is convenient to select 1975 for the initial comparison year.

The time shifting process also uses U.S. annual trade data. The source is *Business Statistics 1963-91* which provides time series data for total merchandise trade (as well as geographic and product detail trade data) for the entire period under study. The conversion to comparison years involves the following time shifts and sources.

BM74: Foreign Direct Investment in the United States
    One-year time shift forward to 1975
        Exports: BS6391, 76-78
        Imports: BS6391, 79-81

BM77: U.S. Direct Investment Abroad
    Two-year time shift backward to 1975
        Exports: BS6391, 76-78
        Imports: BS6391, 79-81

BM80: Foreign Direct Investment in the United States
    Two-year time shift forward to 1980
        Exports: FDIUS82, G-3; BS6391, 76-78
        Imports: FDIUS82, G-3; BS6391, 79-81

BM82: U.S. Direct Investment Abroad
    No time shift

BM87: Foreign Direct Investment in the United States
    Two-year time shift forward to 1989
        Exports: FDIUS89, G-1; BS6391, 76-78
        Imports: FDIUS89, G-1; BS6391, 79-81

BM89: U.S. Direct Investment Abroad
    No time shift

As noted above, industry and affiliate trade totals are available for 1982 and 1989 from the annual BEA reverse investment reports. For 1975, however, these data must be generated by multiplying the BM74 and BM77 industry and affiliate trade levels by the change in total merchandise exports or imports.

The Overlap in Affiliate Related Trade

Two sets of comparable MNC-related trade data now exist -- affiliate related trade and intrafirm related trade. Intrafirm trade can be directly aggregated, but affiliate related trade must be adjusted for a trade overlap.

Intrafirm related trade is "closed trade" in the sense that the transactors on both sides are fully known, and there is no overlapping trade between the U.S.-based firms and the ROW-based firms. The export and import figures for U.S. MNCs and ROW MNCs can be directly aggregated to find totals. For example, in Table 6.1, under the "All MNCs" heading, U.S. MNC exports were $28,739 million while ROW MNC exports were $12,827 million. These figures are added to find the All MNC export figure of $41,566 million.

Affiliate related trade is "open" in the sense that the transactors beyond intrafirm trade are not known. Affiliates do trade with each other, and this overlap must be removed to avoid overstating the significance of affiliate related trade. Returning to "All MNCs" related exports in Table 6.1, the trade level of U.S.-based MNCs is $36,181 million and ROW-based MNCs is $26,433 million. The level of All MNCs trade is not the sum of these figures or $62,614 million. Using the procedure described in Chapter 5, the trade overlap between the two groups of affiliates is estimated to be $3,721 million. This gives an All MNCs export figure of $58,893 million.

As discussed in Chapter 5, the value of the trade overlap must be calculated within a closed system. Accordingly, the dollar value of the affiliate trade overlap is calculated at the All MNCs level for exports and imports. This overlap is then allocated to total exports and imports for the four industry level subsets.

PART III

GEOGRAPHIC PATTERNS OF MNC-RELATED TRADE

CHAPTER 7

TOTAL GEOGRAPHIC TRADE

Total Geographic trade provides the second overview of the trade role of multinational companies. From this perspective, MNC affiliate trade accounts for a 54% share of total trade, and MNC intrafirm trade has a 38% share. Wholesale affiliates are the dominant industry group, followed by manufacturing affiliates.

DEFINITION OF TOTAL GEOGRAPHIC TRADE

Total Geographic trade, along with Total Merchandise trade and Total Product trade, provide three different perspectives on the MNC role in total trade. Total Geographic trade is an aggregate of merchandise trade with four geographic areas -- Canada, Europe, Japan, and Other Areas.

The four areas serve as the basis for the geographic trade chapters in Part III of the book "Geographic Patterns of MNC-Related Trade." These chapters provide the core of the analysis of MNC-related trade from the perspective of trade by geographic areas. Each chapter shows the affiliate and intrafirm related trade for the three comparison years of 1975, 1982, and 1989.

This chapter on "Total Geographic Trade" summarizes the MNC-related trade which is covered in the individual area chapters. The trade data shown in the following tables represents the aggregate dollar value of all area trade combined.

TRENDS IN TOTAL GEOGRAPHIC TRADE

In 1975, Total Geographic trade was $205,824 million. Exports were $109,254 million and imports were $96,570 million yielding a surplus of

$12,684 million. Between 1975 and 1982, total trade increased 124% or $254,570 million to reach $460,394 million. Both exports and imports enjoyed strong growth, but with imports growing one-third faster. This growth imbalance converted the modest 1975 trade surplus into a 1982 deficit of $27,510 million. The total swing in the trade balance was 317% or a decline of $40,194 million.

Between 1982 and 1989, the growth rates slowed in Total Geographic trade. Total trade grew 82% or $376,629 million to reach $837,023 million. Imports still continued to grow one-third faster than exports. This resulted in another 298% deterioration in the trade balance of $81,889 million, pushing the deficit to $109,399 million by 1989.

THE TRADE ROLE OF MULTINATIONAL COMPANIES

This section is based on the trade data shown in Tables 7.1, 7.2, and 7.3 for 1975, 1982, and 1989, respectively. The overall trade role of multinational companies ("All MNCs" in the tables) is discussed for both affiliate related trade and intrafirm related trade.

The affiliate related data for Total Geographic trade are different from Total Merchandise and Total Product trade data due to differing estimates of the affiliate trade overlap. The intrafirm trade data are identical in all three instances.

Affiliate Related Trade

Total Geographic trade totaled $205,824 million in 1975. Adjusted for the trade overlap, affiliate related trade was $115,470 million for a 56.1% share; Non-MNC trade was $90,354 million for a 43.9% share. The MNC-related trade position reflected a 55.5% share of export trade and a 56.8% share of import trade. The dominant MNC group was U.S.-based firms with a 30.8% share of total trade; ROW-based firms held a 27.1% share. U.S. multinational companies had a larger share of exports; ROW MNCs held the larger share of imports.

The Total Geographic trade balance in 1975 was a surplus of $12,684 million. This reflected a $5,737 million surplus in MNC-related trade and a $6,947 million surplus in Non-MNC trade. Thus the overall trade surplus position in Total Geographic was due to both components. In turn, the MNC-related surplus was based on a surplus position of U.S.-based multinationals which offset a small deficit position of ROW-based firms.

Between 1975 and 1982, Total Geographic trade grew 124% or $254,570 million to reach $460,394 million. In comparison, affiliate related trade increased $129,082 million or 112% to a level of $244,552 million (adjusted for the trade overlap). Accordingly, the overall affiliate position decreased slightly

Table 7.1: Multinational Companies and
U.S. Total Geographic Trade in 1975

	MERCHANDISE TRADE (Millions of Dollars)			TOTAL TRADE (Percent Share)			ALL MNCs TRADE (Percent Share)		
	EXPORTS	IMPORTS	BALANCE	EXP	IMP	AVG	EXP	IMP	AVG
Affiliate Related Trade									
Total	109254	96570	12684	100.0	100.0	100.0	NA	NA	NA
Non-MNCs	48651	41704	6947	44.5	43.2	43.9	NA	NA	NA
All MNCs	60604	54867	5737	55.5	56.8	56.1	100.0	100.0	100.0
USA MNCs	36181	27153	9028	33.1	28.1	30.8	59.7	49.5	54.8
ROW MNCs	26433	29367	-2934	24.2	30.4	27.1	43.6	53.5	48.3
Petro MNCs	4043	15546	-11502	3.7	16.1	9.5	6.7	28.3	17.0
USA MNCs	1805	11660	-9855	1.7	12.1	6.5	3.0	21.3	11.7
ROW MNCs	2321	4417	-2096	2.1	4.6	3.3	3.8	8.1	5.8
Manu MNCs	26656	15418	11237	24.4	16.0	20.4	44.0	28.1	36.4
USA MNCs	24984	12823	12161	22.9	13.3	18.4	41.2	23.4	32.7
ROW MNCs	2217	2947	-730	2.0	3.1	2.5	3.7	5.4	4.5
Whole MNCs	27522	21974	5549	25.2	22.8	24.0	45.4	40.0	42.9
USA MNCs	7808	1166	6642	7.1	1.2	4.4	12.9	2.1	7.8
ROW MNCs	20978	21514	-536	19.2	22.3	20.6	34.6	39.2	36.8
Other MNCs	2382	1929	453	2.2	2.0	2.1	3.9	3.5	3.7
USA MNCs	1584	1504	80	1.4	1.6	1.5	2.6	2.7	2.7
ROW MNCs	917	489	428	0.8	0.5	0.7	1.5	0.9	1.2
Intrafirm Related Trade									
Total	109254	96570	12684	100.0	100.0	100.0	NA	NA	NA
Non-MNCs	67688	54565	13123	62.0	56.5	59.4	NA	NA	NA
All MNCs	41566	42005	-439	38.0	43.5	40.6	100.0	100.0	100.0
USA MNCs	28739	21342	7397	26.3	22.1	24.3	69.1	50.8	59.9
ROW MNCs	12827	20663	-7836	11.7	21.4	16.3	30.9	49.2	40.1
Petro MNCs	3299	11770	-8471	3.0	12.2	7.3	7.9	28.0	18.0
USA MNCs	1473	9020	-7547	1.3	9.3	5.1	3.5	21.5	12.6
ROW MNCs	1826	2750	-924	1.7	2.8	2.2	4.4	6.5	5.5
Manu MNCs	20448	12433	8015	18.7	12.9	16.0	49.2	29.6	39.3
USA MNCs	19647	10247	9400	18.0	10.6	14.5	47.3	24.4	35.8
ROW MNCs	801	2186	-1385	0.7	2.3	1.5	1.9	5.2	3.6
Whole MNCs	16513	16377	136	15.1	17.0	16.0	39.7	39.0	39.4
USA MNCs	6669	896	5773	6.1	0.9	3.7	16.0	2.1	9.1
ROW MNCs	9844	15481	-5637	9.0	16.0	12.3	23.7	36.9	30.3
Other MNCs	1306	1425	-119	1.2	1.5	1.3	3.1	3.4	3.3
USA MNCs	950	1179	-229	0.9	1.2	1.0	2.3	2.8	2.5
ROW MNCs	356	246	110	0.3	0.3	0.3	0.9	0.6	0.7

from a 56.1% to a 53.1% share and Non-MNC trade rose to a 46.9% share. Within the affiliate trade structure, the export share fell to 52.1% and the import share to 54.0%. These changes reflected a decline in the U.S. MNC shares which offset a rise in ROW MNC shares.

The Total Geographic trade balance in 1982 had changed to a deficit of $27,510 million, a $40,194 deterioration from 1975. The affiliate related trade position had changed into a deficit of $18,949 million, a swing of $24,686 million; the Non-MNC trade balance had also become a deficit of $8,561 million, a change of $15,508 million. Thus the deterioration in the Total Geographic trade balance was due to unfavorable trends in both components. The conversion of MNC-related trade into a deficit was caused by the growing deficit position of ROW multinationals, linked to a decline in the size of the U.S. MNC surplus.

In the 1982 to 1989 period, Total Geographic trade grew 82% or $376,629 million to $837,023 million. In comparison, affiliate related trade rose $199,909 million or 82% to a level of $444,461 million (adjusted for the trade overlap). As a result, the overall affiliate position remained unchanged at a 53.1% share; Non-MNC trade had a 46.9% share. Within the affiliate trade structure the export share decreased to 50.3% and the import share increased to 55.3%. The export change reflected a decline in the trade share of ROW MNCs which offset an increased share of U.S. MNCs. The import change was due to a higher trade share of ROW MNCs which offset a lower U.S. MNC share. Compared to 1975, the U.S. MNC share of total trade had fallen from 30.8% to 23.9%; the ROW MNC share had risen from 27.1% to 30.8%. ROW-based firms had supplanted U.S.-based firms as the dominant MNC group in Total Geographic trade.

The Total Geographic trade deficit in 1989 was $109,399 million, a rise of $81,889 million over 1982. The affiliate related trade deficit was $78,686 million, an increase of $59,737 million; the Non-MNC trade deficit was $30,714 million, an increase of $22,153 million. Thus the deterioration in the Total Geographic trade balance reflected trends in both components. The MNC-related deficit was based on the growing trade deficit of ROW MNCs which had reached $85,531 million.

Intrafirm Related Trade

Total Geographic trade totaled $205,824 million in 1975. Intrafirm related trade was $83,571 million for a 40.6% share (compared to a 54.7% share for affiliate related trade). Arms-length or Non-MNC trade was $122,253 million for a 59.4% share. The MNC-related trade position reflected a 38.0% share of export trade and a 43.5% share of import trade. The dominant MNC group was U.S.-based firms with a 24.3% share of total trade; ROW-based firms held a 16.3% share. U.S. multinationals had the much larger share of exports and imports, especially in exports.

The Total Geographic trade balance in 1975 was a surplus of $12,684 million. This reflected a $439 million deficit in MNC-related trade and a $13,123 million surplus in Non-MNC trade. Thus the trade surplus was due to Non-MNC trade. The MNC-related deficit was linked to a deficit in ROW MNC trade which offset a surplus in U.S. MNC trade.

Between 1975 and 1982, Total Geographic trade grew $254,570 million or

Table 7.2: Multinational Companies and U.S. Total Geographic Trade in 1982

	MERCHANDISE TRADE (Millions of Dollars)			TOTAL TRADE (Percent Share)			ALL MNCs TRADE (Percent Share)		
	EXPORTS	IMPORTS	BALANCE	EXP	IMP	AVG	EXP	IMP	AVG
Affiliate Related Trade									
Total	216442	243952	-27510	100.0	100.0	100.0	NA	NA	NA
Non-MNCs	103641	112202	-8561	47.9	46.0	46.9	NA	NA	NA
All MNCs	112802	131751	-18949	52.1	54.0	53.1	100.0	100.0	100.0
USA MNCs	56718	51406	5312	26.2	21.1	23.5	50.3	39.0	44.2
ROW MNCs	60236	84290	-24054	27.8	34.6	31.4	53.4	64.0	59.1
Petro MNCs	4628	23477	-18849	2.1	9.6	6.1	4.1	17.8	11.5
USA MNCs	3304	15771	-12467	1.5	6.5	4.1	2.9	12.0	7.8
ROW MNCs	1531	8486	-6955	0.7	3.5	2.2	1.4	6.4	4.1
Manu MNCs	48196	42242	5954	22.3	17.3	19.6	42.7	32.1	37.0
USA MNCs	37180	31107	6073	17.2	12.8	14.8	33.0	23.6	27.9
ROW MNCs	12883	12386	497	6.0	5.1	5.5	11.4	9.4	10.3
Whole MNCs	56312	62648	-6336	26.0	25.7	25.8	49.9	47.6	48.6
USA MNCs	14866	2706	12160	6.9	1.1	3.8	13.2	2.1	7.2
ROW MNCs	43336	61679	-18343	20.0	25.3	22.8	38.4	46.8	42.9
Other MNCs	3665	3384	282	1.7	1.4	1.5	3.2	2.6	2.9
USA MNCs	1368	1822	-454	0.6	0.7	0.7	1.2	1.4	1.3
ROW MNCs	2486	1739	747	1.1	0.7	0.9	2.2	1.3	1.7
Intrafirm Related Trade									
Total	216442	243952	-27510	100.0	100.0	100.0	NA	NA	NA
Non-MNCs	144859	150439	-5580	66.9	61.7	64.1	NA	NA	NA
All MNCs	71583	93513	-21930	33.1	38.3	35.9	100.0	100.0	100.0
USA MNCs	46559	41598	4961	21.5	17.1	19.1	65.0	44.5	53.4
ROW MNCs	25024	51915	-26891	11.6	21.3	16.7	35.0	55.5	46.6
Petro MNCs	2585	15243	-12658	1.2	6.2	3.9	3.6	16.3	10.8
USA MNCs	1915	12646	-10731	0.9	5.2	3.2	2.7	13.5	8.8
ROW MNCs	670	2597	-1927	0.3	1.1	0.7	0.9	2.8	2.0
Manu MNCs	33462	33128	334	15.5	13.6	14.5	46.7	35.4	40.3
USA MNCs	30350	25448	4902	14.0	10.4	12.1	42.4	27.2	33.8
ROW MNCs	3112	7680	-4568	1.4	3.1	2.3	4.3	8.2	6.5
Whole MNCs	33774	43365	-9591	15.6	17.8	16.8	47.2	46.4	46.7
USA MNCs	13433	2282	11151	6.2	0.9	3.4	18.8	2.4	9.5
ROW MNCs	20341	41083	-20742	9.4	16.8	13.3	28.4	43.9	37.2
Other MNCs	1762	1777	-15	0.8	0.7	0.8	2.5	1.9	2.1
USA MNCs	861	1222	-361	0.4	0.5	0.5	1.2	1.3	1.3
ROW MNCs	901	555	346	0.4	0.2	0.3	1.3	0.6	0.9

124% to reach $460,394 million. In comparison, intrafirm related trade increased $81,525 million or 98% to a level of $165,096 million. Accordingly, the overall intrafirm position decreased from a 40.6% to a 35.9% share (compared to a 54.7% to 52.7% share change for affiliate related trade). Non-MNC trade rose to a 64.1% share. Within the intrafirm trade structure, the export share dropped to 33.1% and the import share to 38.3%. These changes reflected a decline in the shares of U.S.-based MNCs; the shares of ROW-based MNCs were largely unchanged.

The Total Geographic trade balance in 1982 had changed to a deficit of $27,510 million, a deterioration of $40,194 million from 1975. The intrafirm related trade deficit had increased $21,491 to a level of $21,930 million. The Non-MNC trade surplus had become a deficit of $5,580 million, a decline of $18,703 million. Thus the decline in the Total Geographic trade balance resulted from unfavorable trends in both components. The MNC-related deficit emerged due to a growing deficit in ROW MNC trade and a shrinking surplus in U.S. MNC trade.

In the 1982 to 1989 period, Total Geographic trade grew $376,629 million or 82% to $837,023 million. In comparison, intrafirm related trade increased $165,952 million or 101% to a level of $331,048 million. As a result, the overall intrafirm position increased from a 35.9% to a 39.6% share (compared to a 52.7% to 52.8% share change for affiliate related trade). Non-MNC trade fell to a 60.4% share. Within the intrafirm trade structure, the export share rose slightly to 34.0% and the import share pushed up to 43.8%. The export change reflected an increase in the trade share of U.S. MNCs which offset a decline in the ROW MNC share. The import change was due to a jump in the trade share of ROW MNCs. Compared to 1975, the U.S. MNC share of total trade had fallen from 24.3% to 19.9%; the ROW MNC share had risen from 16.3% to 19.6%. U.S.-based firms remained the dominant MNC group by a mere 0.3% share.

The Total Geographic trade deficit in 1989 had increased to $109,399 million, a deterioration of $81,889 million from 1982. The intrafirm related trade deficit was $83,418 million, an increase of $61,488 million; the Non-MNC trade deficit had risen $20,041 million to reach $25,981 million. Thus the growth in the Total Geographic trade deficit was due to unfavorable trends in both components, especially in MNC-related trade. The MNC-related deficit was based on the ballooning ROW MNC deficit which had reached $95,650 million.

INDUSTRY TRADE ROLES

This section is based on the trade data shown in Tables 7.1, 7.2, and 7.3 for 1975, 1982, and 1989, respectively. The trade role of each affiliate industry group is discussed on the basis of affiliate related trade.

Petroleum Affiliates

Affiliate related trade was $19,589 million in 1975, adjusted for the affiliate trade overlap. This figure represented a 9.5% share of total trade and a 17.0% share of MNC-related trade. Overall, the industry category ranked third and was

Table 7.3: Multinational Companies and
U.S. Total Geographic Trade in 1989

	MERCHANDISE TRADE (Millions of Dollars)			TOTAL TRADE (Percent Share)			ALL MNCs TRADE (Percent Share)		
	EXPORTS	IMPORTS	BALANCE	EXP	IMP	AVG	EXP	IMP	AVG
Affiliate Related Trade									
Total	363812	473211	-109399	100.0	100.0	100.0	NA	NA	NA
Non-MNCs	180925	211638	-30714	49.7	44.7	46.9	NA	NA	NA
All MNCs	182888	261573	-78686	50.3	55.3	53.1	100.0	100.0	100.0
USA MNCs	102558	97394	5164	28.2	20.6	23.9	56.1	37.2	45.0
ROW MNCs	86316	171847	-85531	23.7	36.3	30.8	47.2	65.7	58.1
Petro MNCs	4362	23281	-18919	1.2	4.9	3.3	2.4	8.9	6.2
USA MNCs	2512	10079	-7567	0.7	2.1	1.5	1.4	3.9	2.8
ROW MNCs	2014	14145	-12131	0.6	3.0	1.9	1.1	5.4	3.6
Manu MNCs	98142	114679	-16537	27.0	24.2	25.4	53.7	43.8	47.9
USA MNCs	70187	77372	-7185	19.3	16.4	17.6	38.4	29.6	33.2
ROW MNCs	31873	40871	-8998	8.8	8.6	8.7	17.4	15.6	16.4
Whole MNCs	75359	118878	-43520	20.7	25.1	23.2	41.2	45.4	43.7
USA MNCs	27886	7675	20211	7.7	1.6	4.2	15.2	2.9	8.0
ROW MNCs	49096	114049	-64953	13.5	24.1	19.5	26.8	43.6	36.7
Other MNCs	5025	4735	290	1.4	1.0	1.2	2.7	1.8	2.2
USA MNCs	1973	2268	-295	0.5	0.5	0.5	1.1	0.9	1.0
ROW MNCs	3333	2782	551	0.9	0.6	0.7	1.8	1.1	1.4
Intrafirm Related Trade									
Total	363812	473211	-109399	100.0	100.0	100.0	NA	NA	NA
Non-MNCs	239997	265978	-25981	66.0	56.2	60.4	NA	NA	NA
All MNCs	123815	207233	-83418	34.0	43.8	39.6	100.0	100.0	100.0
USA MNCs	89539	77307	12232	24.6	16.3	19.9	72.3	37.3	50.4
ROW MNCs	34276	129926	-95650	9.4	27.5	19.6	27.7	62.7	49.6
Petro MNCs	2665	15260	-12595	0.7	3.2	2.1	2.2	7.4	5.4
USA MNCs	1914	7332	-5418	0.5	1.5	1.1	1.5	3.5	2.8
ROW MNCs	751	7928	-7177	0.2	1.7	1.0	0.6	3.8	2.6
Manu MNCs	67988	90362	-22374	18.7	19.1	18.9	54.9	43.6	47.8
USA MNCs	60062	62775	-2713	16.5	13.3	14.7	48.5	30.3	37.1
ROW MNCs	7926	27587	-19661	2.2	5.8	4.2	6.4	13.3	10.7
Whole MNCs	51065	99383	-48318	14.0	21.0	18.0	41.2	48.0	45.4
USA MNCs	26283	6140	20143	7.2	1.3	3.9	21.2	3.0	9.8
ROW MNCs	24782	93243	-68461	6.8	19.7	14.1	20.0	45.0	35.7
Other MNCs	2097	2228	-131	0.6	0.5	0.5	1.7	1.1	1.3
USA MNCs	1280	1060	220	0.4	0.2	0.3	1.0	0.5	0.7
ROW MNCs	817	1168	-351	0.2	0.2	0.2	0.7	0.6	0.6

dominated by U.S.-based firms. The industry trade balance was a deficit of $11,502 million, compared to a total merchandise surplus of $12,684 million.

By 1982, industry trade had increased 44% to $28,106 million. This figure represented a 6.1% share of total trade (down 3.4 share points), and a 11.5% share of MNC-related trade (down 5.5 share points). The industry category ranked third, behind wholesale and manufacturing affiliates. The trade balance was a deficit of $18,949 million (up $7,347 million), compared to a total merchandise deficit of $27,510 million (a swing of $40,194 million).

Industry related trade decreased by 2.0% to $27,643 million in 1989. This figure represented a 3.3% share of total trade (down 2.8 share points), and a 6.2% share of MNC-related trade (down 5.3 share points). The industry category still ranked third, and continued to be dominated by U.S.-based firms. The trade balance was a deficit of $18,919 million (up $70 million), compared to a total merchandise deficit of $109,399 million (up $81,889 million).

Manufacturing Affiliates

Affiliate related trade was $42,074 million in 1975, adjusted for the affiliate trade overlap. This figure represented a 20.4% share of total trade and a 36.4% share of MNC-related trade. The industry category ranked second and was dominated by U.S.-based firms. The industry trade balance was a surplus of $11,237 million, compared to a total merchandise surplus of $12,684 million.

By 1982, industry trade had increased 115% to $90,438 million. This figure represented a 19.6% share of total trade (down 0.8 share points), and a 37.0% share of MNC-related trade (up 0.5 share points). The industry category ranked second, behind wholesale affiliates. The trade balance was a surplus of $5,954 million (down $5,283 million), compared to a total merchandise deficit of $27,510 million (a swing of $40,194 million).

Industry related trade increased by 135% to $212,821 million in 1989. This figure represented a 25.4% share of total trade (up 5.8 share points), and a 47.9% share of MNC-related trade (up 10.9 share points). The industry category now ranked first, and continued to be dominated by U.S.-based firms. The trade balance was a deficit of $16,537 million (a swing of $22,492 million), compared to a total merchandise deficit of $109,399 million (up $81,889 million).

Wholesale Trade Affiliates

Affiliate related trade was $49,496 million in 1975, adjusted for the affiliate trade overlap. This figure represented a 24.0% share of total trade and a 42.9% share of MNC-related trade. The industry category ranked first and was dominated by ROW-based firms. The industry trade balance was a surplus of $5,549 million, compared to a total merchandise surplus of $12,684 million.

By 1982, industry trade had increased 140% to $118,960 million. This figure represented a 25.8% share of total trade (up 1.8 share points), and a 48.6% share of MNC-related trade (up 5.8 share points). The industry category continued to rank first. The trade balance was a deficit of $6,336 million (a swing of $11,884 million), compared to a total merchandise deficit of $27,510 million (a swing of $40,194 million).

Industry related trade increased by 63% to $194,237 million in 1989. This

Table 7.4: Ultimate Beneficial Owners and U.S. Total Geographic Trade in 1975

	MERCHANDISE TRADE (Millions of Dollars)			TOTAL TRADE (Percent Share)			ALL MNCs TRADE (Percent Share)		
	EXPORTS	IMPORTS	BALANCE	EXP	IMP	AVG	EXP	IMP	AVG
Affiliate Related Trade									
Total	109254	96570	12684	100.0	100.0	100.0	NA	NA	NA
Non-MNCs	48651	41704	6947	44.5	43.2	43.9	NA	NA	NA
All MNCs	60604	54867	5737	55.5	56.8	56.1	100.0	100.0	100.0
USA MNCs	36181	27153	9028	33.1	28.1	30.8	59.7	49.5	54.8
ROW MNCs	26433	29367	-2934	24.2	30.4	27.1	43.6	53.5	48.3
CANADA	836	2602	-1766	0.8	2.7	1.7	1.4	4.7	3.0
EUROPE	10724	13213	-2489	9.8	13.7	11.6	17.7	24.1	20.7
JAPAN	11788	11213	575	10.8	11.6	11.2	19.5	20.4	19.9
OTHER	3085	2339	746	2.8	2.4	2.6	5.1	4.3	4.7
Intrafirm Related Trade									
Total	109254	96570	12684	100.0	100.0	100.0	NA	NA	NA
Non-MNCs	67688	54565	13123	62.0	56.5	59.4	NA	NA	NA
All MNCs	41566	42005	-439	38.0	43.5	40.6	100.0	100.0	100.0
USA MNCs	28739	21342	7397	26.3	22.1	24.3	69.1	50.8	59.9
ROW MNCs	12827	20663	-7836	11.7	21.4	16.3	30.9	49.2	40.1
CANADA	572	2257	-1685	0.5	2.3	1.4	1.4	5.4	3.4
EUROPE	3113	8695	-5582	2.8	9.0	5.7	7.5	20.7	14.1
JAPAN	8197	8110	87	7.5	8.4	7.9	19.7	19.3	19.5
OTHER	945	1601	-656	0.9	1.7	1.2	2.3	3.8	3.0

figure represented a 23.2% share of total trade (down 2.6 share points), and a 43.7% share of MNC-related trade (down 4.9 share points). The industry category now ranked second, behind manufacturing, and continued to be dominated by ROW-based firms. The trade balance was a deficit of $43,520 million (up $37,184 million), compared to a total merchandise deficit of $109,399 million (up $81,889 million).

Other Industry Affiliates

Affiliate related trade was $4,312 million in 1975, adjusted for the affiliate trade overlap. This figure represented a 2.1% share of total trade and a 3.7% share of MNC-related trade. The industry category ranked last and was dominated by U.S.-based firms. The industry trade balance was a surplus of $453 million, compared to a total merchandise surplus of $12,684 million.

By 1982, industry trade had increased 64% to $7,049 million. This figure represented a 1.5% share of total trade (down 0.6 share points), and a 2.9% share of MNC-related trade (down 0.9 share points). The industry category continued to rank last. The trade balance was a surplus of $282 million (down

Table 7.5: Ultimate Beneficial Owners and U.S. Total Geographic Trade in 1982

	MERCHANDISE TRADE (Millions of Dollars)			TOTAL TRADE (Percent Share)			ALL MNCs TRADE (Percent Share)		
	EXPORTS	IMPORTS	BALANCE	EXP	IMP	AVG	EXP	IMP	AVG
Affiliate Related Trade									
Total	216442	243952	-27510	100.0	100.0	100.0	NA	NA	NA
Non-MNCs	103641	112202	-8561	47.9	46.0	46.9	NA	NA	NA
All MNCs	112802	131751	-18949	52.1	54.0	53.1	100.0	100.0	100.0
USA MNCs	56718	51406	5312	26.2	21.1	23.5	50.3	39.0	44.2
ROW MNCs	60236	84290	-24054	27.8	34.6	31.4	53.4	64.0	59.1
CANADA	4162	6071	-1909	1.9	2.5	2.2	3.7	4.6	4.2
EUROPE	28734	32088	-3354	13.3	13.2	13.2	25.5	24.4	24.9
JAPAN	21514	35901	-14387	9.9	14.7	12.5	19.1	27.2	23.5
OTHER	5826	10230	-4404	2.7	4.2	3.5	5.2	7.8	6.6
Intrafirm Related Trade									
Total	216442	243952	-27510	100.0	100.0	100.0	NA	NA	NA
Non-MNCs	144859	150439	-5580	66.9	61.7	64.1	NA	NA	NA
All MNCs	71583	93513	-21930	33.1	38.3	35.9	100.0	100.0	100.0
USA MNCs	46559	41598	4961	21.5	17.1	19.1	65.0	44.5	53.4
ROW MNCs	25024	51915	-26891	11.6	21.3	16.7	35.0	55.5	46.6
CANADA	740	4218	-3478	0.3	1.7	1.1	1.0	4.5	3.0
EUROPE	8767	19005	-10238	4.1	7.8	6.0	12.2	20.3	16.8
JAPAN	13737	26931	-13194	6.3	11.0	8.8	19.2	28.8	24.6
OTHER	1780	1761	19	0.8	0.7	0.8	2.5	1.9	2.1

$171 million), compared to a total merchandise deficit of $27,510 million (a swing of $40,194 million).

Industry related trade increased by 38% to $9,759 million in 1989. This figure represented a 1.2% share of total trade (down 0.4 share points), and a 2.2% share of MNC-related trade (down 0.7 share points). The industry category still ranked last, and continued to be dominated by U.S.-based firms. The trade balance was a surplus of $290 million (up $8 million), compared to a total merchandise deficit of $109,399 million (up $81,889 million).

THE TRADE ROLE OF ULTIMATE BENEFICIAL OWNERS

This section is based on the trade data shown in Tables 7.4, 7.5, and 7.6 for 1975, 1982, and 1989, respectively. In the tables, four groups of Ultimate Beneficial Owners or "UBOs" are shown for ROW MNCs -- Canada, Europe, Japan, and Other Areas. U.S.-based MNCs are also a UBO group, and for analytical purposes, Non-MNC firms are treated as a UBO group. The UBO trade role is discussed for both affiliate and intrafirm related trade.

Table 7.6: Ultimate Beneficial Owners and
U.S. Total Geographic Trade in 1989

	MERCHANDISE TRADE (Millions of Dollars)			TOTAL TRADE (Percent Share)			ALL MNCs TRADE (Percent Share)		
	EXPORTS	IMPORTS	BALANCE	EXP	IMP	AVG	EXP	IMP	AVG
Affiliate Related Trade									
Total	363812	473211	-109399	100.0	100.0	100.0	NA	NA	NA
Non-MNCs	180925	211638	-30714	49.7	44.7	46.9	NA	NA	NA
All MNCs	182888	261573	-78686	50.3	55.3	53.1	100.0	100.0	100.0
USA MNCs	102558	97394	5164	28.2	20.6	23.9	56.1	37.2	45.0
ROW MNCs	86316	171847	-85531	23.7	36.3	30.8	47.2	65.7	58.1
CANADA	6020	10596	-4576	1.7	2.2	2.0	3.3	4.1	3.7
EUROPE	37975	59446	-21471	10.4	12.6	11.6	20.8	22.7	21.9
JAPAN	34076	84511	-50435	9.4	17.9	14.2	18.6	32.3	26.7
OTHER	8245	17294	-9049	2.3	3.7	3.1	4.5	6.6	5.7
Intrafirm Related Trade									
Total	363812	473211	-109399	100.0	100.0	100.0	NA	NA	NA
Non-MNCs	239997	265978	-25981	66.0	56.2	60.4	NA	NA	NA
All MNCs	123815	207233	-83418	34.0	43.8	39.6	100.0	100.0	100.0
USA MNCs	89539	77307	12232	24.6	16.3	19.9	72.3	37.3	50.4
ROW MNCs	34276	129926	-95650	9.4	27.5	19.6	27.7	62.7	49.6
CANADA	1502	7162	-5660	0.4	1.5	1.0	1.2	3.5	2.6
EUROPE	10543	39381	-28838	2.9	8.3	6.0	8.5	19.0	15.1
JAPAN	18856	70904	-52048	5.2	15.0	10.7	15.2	34.2	27.1
OTHER	3375	12479	-9104	0.9	2.6	1.9	2.7	6.0	4.8

Affiliate Related Trade

In 1975, Total Geographic trade was $205,824 million. Affiliates of multinational companies held a 56.1% share of total trade (adjusted for the trade overlap). From the UBO perspective, Non-MNC firms were the dominant group with a 43.9% share, followed by U.S. MNCs at a 30.8% share. European-based companies held a 11.6% share and Japanese-based firms a 11.2% share.

The Total Geographic trade balance in 1975 was a surplus of $12,684 million. By ranking, this reflected a U.S. MNC surplus of $9,028 million, a Non-MNC surplus of $6,947 million, a European MNC deficit of $2,489 million, and a Canadian MNC deficit of $1,766 million.

Between 1975 and 1982, Total Geographic trade grew to $460,394 million. The affiliate trade position decreased 3.0 share points to a 53.1% share. From the UBO perspective, Non-MNCs rose 3.0 share points to 46.9%, U.S. MNCs decreased 7.3 share points to 23.5%, European MNCs increased 1.6 share points to 13.2%, and Japanese MNCs were up 1.3 share points to 12.5%.

The Total Geographic trade balance in 1982 was a deficit of $27,510 million, a swing of $40,194 million. By ranking, this reflected a Japanese MNC deficit of $14,387 million (a swing of $14,962 million), a Non-MNC deficit of $8,561 million (a swing of $15,508 million), and a U.S. MNC surplus of $5,312 million (down $3,716 million).

Between 1982 and 1989, Total Geographic trade increased to $837,023 million. The affiliate trade position remained unchanged at a 53.1% share. From the UBO perspective, Non-MNCs held a 46.9% share, U.S. MNCs increased 0.4 share points to 23.9%, Japanese MNCs rose 1.7 share points to 14.2%, and European MNCs fell 1.6 share points to 11.6%.

The Total Geographic trade balance in 1989 was a deficit of $109,399 million, a increase of $81,889 million. By ranking, this reflected a Japanese MNC deficit of $50,435 million (up $36,048 million), a Non-MNC deficit of $30,714 million (up $22,153 million), a European MNC deficit of $21,471 million (up $18,117 million), a Other Areas MNC deficit of $9,049 million (up $4,645 million), and a U.S. MNC surplus of $5,164 million (down $148 million).

Intrafirm Related Trade

In 1975, Total Geographic trade was $205,824 million. Intrafirm trade by multinational companies accounted for a 40.6% share of total trade. From the UBO perspective, Non-MNC firms were the dominant group with a 59.4% share, followed by U.S. MNCs at a 24.3% share. Japanese-based companies held a 7.9% share and European-based firms a 5.7% share.

The Total Geographic trade balance in 1975 was a surplus of $12,684 million. By ranking, this reflected a Non-MNC surplus of $13,123 million, a U.S. MNC surplus of $7,397 million, and a European MNC deficit of $5,582 million.

Between 1975 and 1982, Total Geographic trade grew to $460,394 million. The intrafirm trade position decreased 4.7 share points to a 35.9% share. From the UBO perspective, Non-MNCs increased 4.7 share points to 64.1%, U.S. MNCs decreased 5.2 share points to 19.1%, Japanese MNCs gained 0.9 share points to 8.8%, and European MNCs increased 0.3 share points to 6.0%.

The Total Geographic trade balance in 1982 was a deficit of $27,510 million, a decline of $40,194 million. By ranking, this reflected a Japanese MNC deficit of $13,194 million (a decline of $13,281 million), a European MNC deficit of $10,238 million (up $4,656 million), a Non-MNC deficit of $5,580 million (a decline of $18,703 million), and a U.S. MNC surplus of $4,961 million (down $2,436 million).

Between 1982 and 1989, Total Geographic trade increased to $837,023 million. The intrafirm trade position rose 3.7 share points to a 39.6% share. From the UBO perspective, Non-MNCs fell 3.7 share points to 60.4%, U.S. MNCs rose 0.8 share points to 19.9%, Japanese MNCs increased 1.9 share points to 10.7%, and European MNCs decreased 0.1 points to 6.0%.

Table 7.7: Geographic Structure of
"Total" Merchandise Trade in
U.S. Total Geographic Trade

	MERCHANDISE TRADE (Millions of Dollars)			TOTAL TRADE (Percent Share)			ALL MNCs TRADE (Percent Share)		
	EXPORTS	IMPORTS	BALANCE	EXP	IMP	AVG	EXP	IMP	AVG
1975									
Total	109254	96570	12684	100.0	100.0	100.0	NA	NA	NA
Canada	22948	21747	1201	21.0	22.5	21.7	NA	NA	NA
Europe	32727	21466	11261	30.0	22.2	26.3	NA	NA	NA
Japan	9563	11268	-1705	8.8	11.7	10.1	NA	NA	NA
Other	44016	42089	1927	40.3	43.6	41.8	NA	NA	NA
1982									
Total	216442	243952	-27510	100.0	100.0	100.0	NA	NA	NA
Canada	37887	46477	-8590	17.5	19.1	18.3	NA	NA	NA
Europe	63664	53413	10251	29.4	21.9	25.4	NA	NA	NA
Japan	20966	37744	-16778	9.7	15.5	12.8	NA	NA	NA
Other	93925	106318	-12393	43.4	43.6	43.5	NA	NA	NA
1989									
Total	363812	473211	-109399	100.0	100.0	100.0	NA	NA	NA
Canada	78809	87953	-9144	21.7	18.6	19.9	NA	NA	NA
Europe	105472	103828	1644	29.0	21.9	25.0	NA	NA	NA
Japan	44494	93586	-49092	12.2	19.8	16.5	NA	NA	NA
Other	135037	187844	-52807	37.1	39.7	38.6	NA	NA	NA

The Total Geographic trade balance in 1989 was a deficit of $109,399 million, a decrease of $81,889 million. By ranking, this reflected a Japanese MNC deficit of $52,048 million (up $38,854 million), a European MNC deficit of $28,838 million (up $18,600 million), a Non-MNC deficit of $25,981 million (up $20,401 million), and a U.S. MNC surplus of $12,232 million (up $7,271 million).

STRUCTURE OF TOTAL GEOGRAPHIC TRADE

The three tables on geographic structure are a bridge between the trade tables in this chapter on "Total Geographic Trade" and the trade tables in the individual geographic trade chapters. Tables 7.7 to 7.9 provide direct linkages between Tables 7.1 to 7.3 -- the trade tables for 1975, 1982, and 1989 -- and the related trade tables in the chapters which follow. There are three geographic structure bridges or links: "Total" merchandise trade, affiliate related "All MNCs" trade, and intrafirm related "All MNCs" trade.

Table 7.8: Geographic Structure of
Affiliate Related "All MNCs" Trade in
U.S. Total Geographic Trade

	MERCHANDISE TRADE (Millions of Dollars)			TOTAL TRADE (Percent Share)			ALL MNCs TRADE (Percent Share)		
	EXPORTS	IMPORTS	BALANCE	EXP	IMP	AVG	EXP	IMP	AVG
1975									
Total	60604	54867	5737	55.5	56.8	56.1	100.0	100.0	100.0
Canada	15646	13816	1831	14.3	14.3	14.3	25.8	25.2	25.5
Europe	19521	12401	7120	17.9	12.8	15.5	32.2	22.6	27.6
Japan	9290	10637	-1347	8.5	11.0	9.7	15.3	19.4	17.3
Other	16147	18014	-1867	14.8	18.7	16.6	26.6	32.8	29.6
1982									
Total	112802	131751	-18949	52.1	54.0	53.1	100.0	100.0	100.0
Canada	22408	28029	-5622	10.4	11.5	11.0	19.9	21.3	20.6
Europe	35095	31296	3799	16.2	12.8	14.4	31.1	23.8	27.1
Japan	20192	35011	-14819	9.3	14.4	12.0	17.9	26.6	22.6
Other	35107	37415	-2308	16.2	15.3	15.8	31.1	28.4	29.7
1989									
Total	182888	261573	-78686	50.3	55.3	53.1	100.0	100.0	100.0
Canada	42878	51801	-8923	11.8	10.9	11.3	23.4	19.8	21.3
Europe	49261	58976	-9715	13.5	12.5	12.9	26.9	22.5	24.4
Japan	42142	83881	-41739	11.6	17.7	15.1	23.0	32.1	28.4
Other	48607	66916	-18309	13.4	14.1	13.8	26.6	25.6	26.0

"Total" Merchandise Trade

Table 7.7 covers the structure of "Total" merchandise exports and imports for 1975, 1982, and 1989. The term "Total" refers to the first data line in the affiliate and intrafirm related trade sections of Tables 7.1 to 7.3. These figures are total U.S. merchandise trade.

The table covers "Total" merchandise trade (the "Total" line in the table) and the four geographic trade categories for all three comparison years. Dollar values are shown for exports, imports, and trade balances. Trade shares are shown on the "Total Trade" basis; that is, the trade category is divided by total merchandise trade. Trade shares on the "All MNCs" basis are not applicable in these tables.

The leading category of geographic trade was Other Areas with an average 41.3% share of total merchandise trade. This area is primarily the less developed countries. Trade with the other three regions -- all advanced countries -- averaged a 58.7% share. The leading trade partner was Europe (25.6%), followed by Canada (20.0%) and Japan (13.1%). The most significant shift in this trade structure was the growing market share of Japan.

Table 7.9: Geographic Structure of
Intrafirm Related "All MNCs" Trade in
U.S. Total Geographic Trade

	MERCHANDISE TRADE (Millions of Dollars)			TOTAL TRADE (Percent Share)			ALL MNCs TRADE (Percent Share)		
	EXPORTS	IMPORTS	BALANCE	EXP	IMP	AVG	EXP	IMP	AVG
				1975					
Total	41566	42005	-439	38.0	43.5	40.6	100.0	100.0	100.0
Canada	11658	10443	1215	10.7	10.8	10.7	28.0	24.9	26.4
Europe	14112	10216	3896	12.9	10.6	11.8	34.0	24.3	29.1
Japan	6811	8454	-1643	6.2	8.8	7.4	16.4	20.1	18.3
Other	8985	12892	-3907	8.2	13.3	10.6	21.6	30.7	26.2
				1982					
Total	71583	93513	-21930	33.1	38.3	35.9	100.0	100.0	100.0
Canada	17348	22254	-4906	8.0	9.1	8.6	24.2	23.8	24.0
Europe	21342	20854	488	9.9	8.5	9.2	29.8	22.3	25.6
Japan	15231	27979	-12748	7.0	11.5	9.4	21.3	29.9	26.2
Other	17662	22426	-4764	8.2	9.2	8.7	24.7	24.0	24.3
				1989					
Total	123815	207233	-83418	34.0	43.8	39.6	100.0	100.0	100.0
Canada	34584	43531	-8947	9.5	9.2	9.3	27.9	21.0	23.6
Europe	35289	51312	-16023	9.7	10.8	10.3	28.5	24.8	26.2
Japan	27652	68763	-41111	7.6	14.5	11.5	22.3	33.2	29.1
Other	26290	43627	-17337	7.2	9.2	8.4	21.2	21.1	21.1

Affiliate Related "All MNCs" Trade

Table 7.8 covers the structure of affiliate related "All MNCs" trade for 1975, 1982, and 1989. The term "All MNCs" refers to the third data line in the affiliate related trade section of Tables 7.1 to 7.3. These figures are total MNC-related trade under the affiliate trade definition.

The table covers affiliate related "All MNCs" trade (the "Total" line in the table) and the four geographic trade categories for all three comparison years. Dollar values are shown for exports, imports, and trade balances. Trade shares are shown on two bases. The "Total Trade" basis is the trade category divided by total merchandise trade. The "All MNCs" basis is the trade category divided by affiliate related All MNCs trade.

The leading category of geographic trade was Other Areas with an average 28.4% share of affiliate related All MNCs trade. This area is primarily the less developed countries.

Trade with the other three regions -- all advanced countries -- averaged a 71.6% share. The leading trade partner was Europe (26.4%), followed by Japan (22.7%) and Canada (22.5%). The most significant shift in this trade structure was the growing market share of Japan. By 1989, Japan had emerged as the leading trade area, surpassing even Other Areas.

Intrafirm Related "All MNCs" Trade

Table 7.9 covers the structure of intrafirm related "All MNCs" trade for 1975, 1982, and 1989. The term "All MNCs" refers to the third data line in the intrafirm related trade section of Tables 7.1 to 7.3. These figures are total MNC-related trade under the intrafirm trade definition.

The table covers intrafirm related "All MNCs" trade (the "Total" line in the table) and the four geographic trade categories for all three comparison years. Dollar values are shown for exports, imports, and the trade balance. Trade shares are shown on two bases. The "Total Trade" basis is the trade category divided by total merchandise trade. The "All MNCs" basis is the trade category divided by intrafirm related All MNCs trade.

The leading category of geographic trade was Europe with an average 26.9% share of intrafirm related All MNCs trade, followed by Canada (24.7%), Japan (24.5%), and Other Areas (23.9%). Other Areas is primarily the less developed countries; trade with the other three regions -- all advanced countries -- averaged a 76.1% share. The most significant shift in this trade structure was the growing market share of Japan. By 1989, Japan had emerged as the leading trade area.

DERIVATION OF THE DATA

Total Geographic trade, Total Merchandise trade, and Total Product trade provide three different perspectives on the MNC role in total trade. Total Geographic trade is an aggregate of merchandise trade with four geographic areas.

Total Geographic data are generally identical to the trade data for Total Merchandise trade and Total Product trade. The exception is affiliate related trade where different procedures are used to estimate the trade overlap.

This section will discuss the data used in the five chapters comprising Part III of the book "Geographic Patterns of MNC-Related Trade." Three steps are needed to derive the geographic data on MNC-related trade.

First, the benchmark source tables must be restored by developing estimates for suppressed data cells. There are two sets of benchmark source tables for geographic trade and Ultimate Beneficial Owners. Second, all of the MNC-related trade data must be time shifted to common time periods for comparison. And third, estimates must be derived for the trade overlap in affiliate related trade.

The Benchmark Source Tables for Geographic Trade

The basic data for geographic trade come from the six foreign direct investment surveys conducted by the U.S. Government over the past two decades. The benchmark years are 1974, 1977, 1980, 1982, 1987, and 1989, and are referred to as BM74, BM77, etc. (Full citations are shown in the Selected Bibliography.) The 1974, 1980, and 1987 benchmarks cover foreign direct investment in the United States ("reverse investment"). The 1977, 1982, and 1989 benchmarks cover U.S. direct investment abroad ("outward investment").

The benchmark tables used as sources for geographic trade data are listed below. For each benchmark, export and import source tables are shown for affiliate related trade and intrafirm related trade. There are a total of twenty-four tables listed. (The BM74 trade data are organized by the four affiliate industry groups, so four source tables are cited in each of the four cases listed under that benchmark heading.)

The format used in the source tables was industry rows with geographic columns. The industry rows were collapsed into Petroleum, Manufacturing, Wholesale, and Other Industry categories. This structure was dictated by the set of affiliate industry data available in the 1974 benchmark. The geographic columns were collapsed into Canada, Europe, Japan, and Other Areas. This structure was dictated by analytical interest and the availability of data.

Even after the row and column compression, many of the source tables have data cells left empty to avoid disclosure of firm specific data. The figure in parenthesis shows the percent of the total trade covered by the table which is not allocated to specific data cells (the "table residual"). For example, under BM77, total affiliate imports are $41,525 million, while the unallocated trade is $1,008 million, or 2.4% of the total trade covered in Table II.I.20.

BM74: Foreign Direct Investment in the United States
    Affiliate Related Trade
        Exports: Tables E-2, E-6, E-7, E-8 (6.9%)
        Imports: Tables E-2, E-6, E-7, E-8 (0.0%)
    Intrafirm Related Trade
        Exports: Tables E-2, E-6, E-7, E-8 (11.5%)
        Imports: Tables E-2, E-6, E-7, E-8 (6.3%)

BM77: U.S. Direct Investment Abroad
    Affiliate Related Trade
        Exports: Table II.I.4 (0.0%)
        Imports: Table II.I.20 (2.4%)
    Intrafirm Related Trade
        Exports: Table II.I.7 (28.7%)

Imports: Table II.I.23 (6.3%)

BM80: Foreign Direct Investment in the United States
    Affiliate Related Trade
        Exports: Table G-18 (0.9%)
        Imports: Table G-32 (0.0%)
    Intrafirm Related Trade
        Exports: Table G-20 (1.9%)
        Imports: Table G-34 (2.6%)

BM82: U.S. Direct Investment Abroad
    Affiliate Related Trade
        Exports: Table II.G.3 (0.0%)
        Imports: Table II.G.20 (1.4%)
    Intrafirm Related Trade
        Exports: Table II.G.7 (4.9%)
        Imports: Table II.G.24 (12.2%)

BM87: Foreign Direct Investment in the United States
    Affiliate Related Trade
        Exports: Table G-23 (0.0%)
        Imports: Table G-29 (0.4%)
    Intrafirm Related Trade
        Exports: Table G-25 (0.0%)
        Imports: Table G-31 (0.2%)

BM89: U.S. Direct Investment Abroad
    Affiliate Related Trade
        Exports: Table II.H.5 (0.6%)
        Imports: Table II.H.22 (8.7%)
    Intrafirm Related Trade
        Exports: Table II.H.9 (1.0%)
        Imports: Table II.H.26 (13.8%)

The mean level of unallocated trade is 4.6%, but this figure masks a wide range. The table residuals range from a low of 0.0% in several source tables, to a high of 28.7% in BM77 intrafirm exports. The level of unallocated trade tends to be lower in the outward investment benchmarks, and lower in affiliate related trade.

The relationship between the table residuals for affiliate and intrafirm trade is important. The mean level of unallocated trade for affiliate related trade is 1.8%, with a range of 0.0% to 8.7%. The figures for intrafirm related trade are much higher -- an average of 7.5% and a range of 0.0% to 28.7%. The allocation process is driven by affiliate related trade, however, so the unallocated amounts for the intrafirm tables are actually identical with the companion affiliate tables. That is, the unallocated trade for any source table does not exceed 8.7%, and averages 1.8%.

The derivation process begins with affiliate related trade. Each of these source tables is a trade matrix where affiliate industry trade forms the rows and geographic category trade forms the columns. The row and column totals are known, but empty detail cells exist within the matrix. The total unallocated trade for the matrix is equal to the sum of the row or column residuals.

The row and column residuals are used in a joint probability procedure to provide initial estimates for each empty detail cell. These estimates represent a maximum probability estimate for each empty cell based upon the known information content within the row and column residuals.

The initial estimates usually do not provide a perfect "fit" with the row and column totals -- small row and column residuals will remain. Beginning with the rows with the smallest number of estimated cells, the detail cell estimates are adjusted to force all remaining row and column residuals to equal zero. These adjustments involve a minimum alteration of the initial estimated values. This last step "balances" the trade matrix and provides estimates for each empty cell that are consistent with the row and column totals.

The affiliate trade tables can now be used to allocate the row and column residuals in the intrafirm trade tables. Each data cell in an affiliate trade table is a constraint on the maximum value that can be assumed by the related data cell in an intrafirm trade table. Accordingly, the affiliate trade values are used to initially allocate the row and column residuals into empty cells in the intrafirm trade matrix. Then the intrafirm trade table can be balanced, forcing all row and column residuals to zero. The estimates for each empty cell are consistent with intrafirm row and column totals and with the related affiliate trade values.

The Benchmark Source Tables for Ultimate Beneficial Owners

The Ultimate Beneficial Owner, or UBO, is the location of the parent firm. In outward investment, the UBO is always the United States, thus the identity of the UBO is pertinent only to reverse investment. The format used in the source tables was UBO rows with geographic columns. The UBO rows were collapsed into Canada, Europe, Japan and Other Areas UBOs. The geographic columns were collapsed into the same four categories. These data are derived from the following source tables in the reverse investment benchmarks using the procedures discussed above.

BM74: Foreign Direct Investment in the United States
    Affiliate Related Trade
        Exports: Tables E-2, E-15, E-16, E-17, E-19 (0.0%)
        Imports: Tables E-2, E-15, E-16, E-17, E-19 (0.0%)

Intrafirm Related Trade
        Exports: Tables E-2, E-15, E-16, E-17, E-19 (70.2%)
        Imports: Tables E-2, E-15, E-16, E-17, E-19 (2.9%)

BM80: Foreign Direct Investment in the United States
    Affiliate Related Trade
        Exports: Table G-19 (0.0%)
        Imports: Table G-33 (1.8%)
    Intrafirm Related Trade
        Exports: Table G-21 (4.1%)
        Imports: Table G-35 (46.9%)

BM87: Foreign Direct Investment in the United States
    Affiliate Related Trade
        Exports: Table G-24 (0.0%)
        Imports: Table G-30 (0.0%)
    Intrafirm Related Trade
        Exports: Table G-26 (0.0%)
        Imports: Table G-32 (0.0%)

As previously noted, the appropriate figures for unallocated trade are from the affiliate related source tables. Here, the mean value is 0.3% with a range of 0.0% to 1.8%.

Conversion to Comparison Years for Geographic Trade

The common time periods for the trade data comparisons are 1975, 1982, and 1989. The time shifting of the benchmark data to these comparison years is accomplished by using information from two sources. In the late 1970s, the Bureau of Economic Analysis began a series of annual reports on foreign direct investment activities. These studies do not provide trade data by geographic category, but do provide trade data by affiliate industry groups. The second source is U.S. annual trade data by geographic category.

The BEA annual reports on multinational companies are linked to the previous benchmark surveys. Thus the annual reports on reverse investment for 1988 and 1989 are based on the 1987 benchmark. The reports on outward investment for 1987 and 1988, however, are still based on the 1982 benchmark. The comparison year of 1989 can draw upon the 1989 benchmark for outward investment, and the 1987 benchmark on reverse investment timeshifted by the 1989 annual report on reverse investment. The same situation holds for the 1980 to 1982 period.

There are no BEA annual FDI reports for the 1974 to 1977 period, so any year in that interval could be selected as the comparison year. Since the time period between 1982 and 1989 is seven years, it is convenient to select 1975 for the initial comparison year.

The time shifting process also uses U.S. annual trade data from *Business Statistics 1963-91*. This source provides time series data for total merchandise trade and geographic trade patterns for the entire period.

The conversion to comparison years involves the following time shifts and sources.

BM74: Foreign Direct Investment in the United States
    One-year time shift forward to 1975
        Exports: BS6391, 76-78
        Imports: BS6391, 79-81

BM77: U.S. Direct Investment Abroad
    Two-year time shift backward to 1975
        Exports: BS6391, 76-78
        Imports: BS6391, 79-81

BM80: Foreign Direct Investment in the United States
    Two-year time shift forward to 1980
        Exports: FDIUS82, G-3; BS6391, 76-78
        Imports: FDIUS82, G-3; BS6391, 79-81

BM82: U.S. Direct Investment Abroad
    No time shift

BM87: Foreign Direct Investment in the United States
    Two-year time shift forward to 1989
        Exports: FDIUS89, G-1; BS6391, 76-78
        Imports: FDIUS89, G-1; BS6391, 79-81

BM89: U.S. Direct Investment Abroad
    No time shift

The change in U.S. exports and imports by geographic category is used to initially convert the benchmark year geographic data to the comparison year. For example, affiliate imports from Canada were $6,771 million in BM80. Between 1980 and 1982, U.S. imports from Canada increased from $41,455 million to $46,477 million. Affiliate Canadian imports are increased by the same proportion to a 1982 level of $7,591 million. The assumption is that the MNC role in each geographic category remained unchanged during the time shift.

This geographic conversion, however, will produce affiliate industry group and trade totals that are different from the actual figures in the comparison year.

In the 1982 example, converted affiliate imports totaled $82,368 million, while the actual level of affiliate imports was $84,290 million.

A scalar adjustment is used to force the converted geographic data to generate the actual affiliate industry group and trade totals for the comparison year. In the example, affiliate imports from Canada were increased from the initial value of $7,591 million to a final value of $7,923 million.

In matrix terms, the initial geographic category time shift is a column conversion. The affiliate industry group totals for the comparison year are a row constraint on the values assumed by the detail trade cells in the matrix. The scalar adjustment is a row conversion, which generates new column totals for the geographic categories. The time shift conversion process thus captures changes both in the geographic (column) structure of trade and in the affiliate industry (row) structure of trade.

As noted above, industry trade totals are available for 1982 and 1989 from the annual BEA reverse investment reports. For 1975, however, these data must be generated by multiplying the BM74 and BM77 industry trade levels by the change in total merchandise exports or imports.

Conversion to Comparison Years for Ultimate Beneficial Owners

The conversion process for UBO data is based upon two data sources. The first is the geographic trade data developed above for the comparison years. The ROW MNC related trade by trading partner -- Canada, Europe, Japan, and Other Areas -- is a column constraint on the UBO table conversion. The second source is the aggregate UBO data from the annual BEA reports on reverse FDI. This data serves as a row constraint on the UBO table conversion.

The detail cell UBO data from the benchmark year is placed into a matrix with the known row and column totals from the comparison year. The resulting row and column residuals are allocated to the detail cells using the benchmark data as the allocation weights. Thus the UBO structure from the benchmark is preserved while being converted to comparison year row and column totals.

As noted before, aggregate UBO data are available for 1982 and 1989 from the annual BEA reverse investment reports. For 1975, however, these data must be generated by multiplying the BM74 UBO data by the change in total merchandise exports or imports.

The Overlap in Affiliate Related Trade

Two sets of comparable MNC-related trade data now exist -- affiliate related trade and intrafirm related trade. Intrafirm trade can be directly aggregated, but affiliate related trade must be adjusted for a trade overlap.

Intrafirm related trade is "closed trade" in the sense that the transactors on both sides are fully known, and there is no overlapping trade between the U.S.-based firms and the ROW-based firms. The export and import figures for U.S.

MNCs and ROW MNCs can be directly aggregated to find totals. For example, in Table 7.1, under the "All MNCs" heading, U.S. MNC exports were $28,739 million while ROW MNC exports were $12,827 million. These figures are added to find the All MNC export figure of $41,566 million. The related import and balance figures and trade shares are also sums of the U.S. MNCs and ROW MNCs data.

Affiliate related trade is "open" in the sense that the transactors beyond intrafirm trade are not known. Affiliates do trade with each other, and this overlap must be estimated to avoid overstating the significance of affiliate related trade. Returning to "All MNCs" related exports in Table 7.1, the trade level of U.S. MNCs was $36,181 million and ROW-based MNCs was $26,433 million. The level of All MNCs trade is not the sum of these figures or $62,614 million. Using the procedure described in Chapter 5, the trade overlap between the two groups of affiliates is estimated to be $2,010 million. This gives an All MNCs export figure of $60,604 million. The related import and balance figures and trade shares are also adjusted for the affiliate trade overlap.

The All MNCs affiliate trade overlap is the sum of the overlaps from the affiliate industry groups. For example, the export overlap for Wholesale MNCs is $1,264 million which accounts for over half of the All MNCs overlap.

As mentioned earlier, the values shown in the tables in this chapter are the sum of the values in the four geographic chapters. Thus the trade data shown in Table 7.1 for affiliate related trade in any industry group is the sum from the companion tables in subsequent chapters. This includes the dollar value of the affiliate trade overlap.

As discussed in Chapter 5, the value of the trade overlap must be calculated within a closed system, and at a disaggregated level. Accordingly, the dollar value of the affiliate trade overlap is calculated in the geographic chapters for All MNCs trade. This overlap is then allocated to the industry level subsets within each chapter. The industry subsets are then summed to derive the trade tables shown in this chapter.

CHAPTER 8

TRADE WITH CANADA

Trade with Canada includes one-fifth of total merchandise trade. Multinational companies dominate U.S.-Canadian trade. MNC affiliate trade accounts for a 61% share of total trade and MNC intrafirm trade has a 48% share. The equivalent figures for Total Geographic trade are 54% and 39%. Manufacturing affiliates are the dominant industry group, accounting for nearly half of all trade.

DEFINITION OF TRADE WITH CANADA

Trade with Canada consists of movements of merchandise between the United States and Canada. The two nations occupy the continent of North America and possess a long land frontier. Subsequently, most trade with Canada is land trade.

TRENDS IN TRADE WITH CANADA

In 1975, total trade with Canada was $44,695 million. Exports were $22,948 million and imports were $21,747 million, yielding a surplus of $1,201 million. In 1982, total trade reached a level of $84,364 million, an increase of 89% or $39,669 million. Both exports and imports recorded strong growth over the period, but with imports growing nearly twice as fast. This major imbalance converted the trade balance to a deficit of $8,590 by 1982. The deterioration in the trade balance was $9,791 million.

Between 1982 and 1989, total trade with Canada grew 98% or $82,398 million to reach $166,762 million. In a structural change, exports now increased slightly faster than imports. This held down the growth in the deficit, which increased only $554 million to reach $9,144 million by 1989.

THE TRADE ROLE OF MULTINATIONAL COMPANIES

This section is based on the trade data shown in Tables 8.1, 8.2, and 8.3 for 1975, 1982, and 1989, respectively. The overall trade role of multinational companies ("All MNCs" in the tables) is discussed for both affiliate related trade and intrafirm related trade.

Affiliate Related Trade

Trade with Canada totaled $44,695 million in 1975. Adjusted for the trade overlap, MNC affiliates were involved in a 65.9% share of the trade. The MNC-related trade position reflected a 68.2% share of export trade and a 63.5% share of import trade. The dominant MNC group was U.S.-based firms with a 57.3% share of total trade. Canadian-based firms had a 5.7% share. ROW-based firms held a 9.7% share. U.S. multinational companies had a much larger share of exports and imports.

The Canadian trade balance in 1975 was a modest surplus of $1,201 million. This reflected a $1,831 million surplus in MNC-related trade and a $630 million deficit in Non-MNC trade. Thus the overall trade surplus position with Canada was due to MNC-related trade. In turn, the MNC-related surplus was based on a surplus position of U.S.-based multinationals which offset a deficit position of ROW-based firms.

Between 1975 and 1982, Canadian trade grew 89% or $39,669 million to reach $84,364 million. In comparison, affiliate related trade increased $20,975 million or 71% to a level of $50,437 million (adjusted for the trade overlap). Accordingly, the overall affiliate position decreased from a 65.9% to a 59.8% share and Non-MNC trade rose to a 40.2% share. Within the affiliate trade structure, the export share fell to 59.1% and the import share to 60.3%. These changes reflected a decline in the U.S. MNC shares which offset a rise in ROW MNC shares.

The Canadian trade balance in 1982 had changed into a deficit of $8,590 million, a deterioration of $9,791 million from 1975. The affiliate related trade position had converted into a deficit of $5,622 million, a swing of $7,452 million; the Non-MNC trade deficit had risen $2,339 million to $2,969 million. Thus the change in the Canadian trade balance was due to unfavorable trends in both components. The conversion of MNC-related trade into a deficit was caused by a change in U.S. MNC trade balance.

In the 1982 to 1989 period, trade with Canada grew 98% or $82,398 million to reach $166,762 million. In comparison, affiliate related trade rose $44,243 million or 88% to a level of $94,679 million (adjusted for the trade overlap). As a result, the overall affiliate position decreased from a 59.8% to a 56.8% share and Non-MNC trade rose to a 43.2% share. Within the affiliate trade structure, the export share decreased to 54.4% and the import share to 58.9%. The export change reflected declines in trade shares of both U.S. and

Table 8.1: Multinational Companies and
U.S.-Canadian Trade in 1975

	MERCHANDISE TRADE (Millions of Dollars)			TOTAL TRADE (Percent Share)			ALL MNCs TRADE (Percent Share)		
	EXPORTS	IMPORTS	BALANCE	EXP	IMP	AVG	EXP	IMP	AVG
Affiliate Related Trade									
Total	22948	21747	1201	100.0	100.0	100.0	NA	NA	NA
Non-MNCs	7302	7932	-630	31.8	36.5	34.1	NA	NA	NA
All MNCs	15646	13816	1831	68.2	63.5	65.9	100.0	100.0	100.0
USA MNCs	14713	10877	3836	64.1	50.0	57.3	94.0	78.7	86.9
ROW MNCs	1122	3228	-2106	4.9	14.8	9.7	7.2	23.4	14.8
Petro MNCs	428	2050	-1622	1.9	9.4	5.5	2.7	14.8	8.4
USA MNCs	113	1522	-1409	0.5	7.0	3.7	0.7	11.0	5.5
ROW MNCs	317	606	-289	1.4	2.8	2.1	2.0	4.4	3.1
Manu MNCs	13104	9359	3746	57.1	43.0	50.3	83.8	67.7	76.2
USA MNCs	12838	8632	4206	55.9	39.7	48.0	82.1	62.5	72.9
ROW MNCs	431	894	-463	1.9	4.1	3.0	2.8	6.5	4.5
Whole MNCs	1680	1844	-165	7.3	8.5	7.9	10.7	13.4	12.0
USA MNCs	1410	228	1182	6.1	1.0	3.7	9.0	1.7	5.6
ROW MNCs	283	1642	-1359	1.2	7.6	4.3	1.8	11.9	6.5
Other MNCs	434	563	-129	1.9	2.6	2.2	2.8	4.1	3.4
USA MNCs	352	495	-143	1.5	2.3	1.9	2.2	3.6	2.9
ROW MNCs	91	86	5	0.4	0.4	0.4	0.6	0.6	0.6
Intrafirm Related Trade									
Total	22948	21747	1201	100.0	100.0	100.0	NA	NA	NA
Non-MNCs	11290	11304	-14	49.2	52.0	50.6	NA	NA	NA
All MNCs	11658	10443	1215	50.8	48.0	49.4	100.0	100.0	100.0
USA MNCs	10914	7794	3120	47.6	35.8	41.9	93.6	74.6	84.6
ROW MNCs	744	2649	-1905	3.2	12.2	7.6	6.4	25.4	15.4
Petro MNCs	387	1136	-749	1.7	5.2	3.4	3.3	10.9	6.9
USA MNCs	86	738	-652	0.4	3.4	1.8	0.7	7.1	3.7
ROW MNCs	301	398	-97	1.3	1.8	1.6	2.6	3.8	3.2
Manu MNCs	9632	7409	2223	42.0	34.1	38.1	82.6	70.9	77.1
USA MNCs	9419	6584	2835	41.0	30.3	35.8	80.8	63.0	72.4
ROW MNCs	213	825	-612	0.9	3.8	2.3	1.8	7.9	4.7
Whole MNCs	1404	1547	-143	6.1	7.1	6.6	12.0	14.8	13.4
USA MNCs	1228	169	1059	5.4	0.8	3.1	10.5	1.6	6.3
ROW MNCs	176	1378	-1202	0.8	6.3	3.5	1.5	13.2	7.0
Other MNCs	235	351	-116	1.0	1.6	1.3	2.0	3.4	2.7
USA MNCs	181	303	-122	0.8	1.4	1.1	1.6	2.9	2.2
ROW MNCs	54	48	6	0.2	0.2	0.2	0.5	0.5	0.5

ROW MNCs; the import change was due to a decline in the trade share of ROW MNCs. Compared to 1975, the U.S. MNC share of total trade had fallen from 57.3% to 47.4%; the ROW MNC share had risen from 9.7% to 11.5%.

The Canadian trade balance in 1989 was a deficit of $9,144 million, only $554 million above 1982. The affiliate trade deficit was $8,923 million, an increase of $3,302 million. In contrast, the Non-MNC trade deficit had fallen

$2,748 million to only $221 million. Thus the deterioration in the Canadian trade balance reflected trends in MNC-related trade. The MNC-related deficit was rooted in growing trade deficits of U.S. and ROW MNCs.

Intrafirm Related Trade

Canadian trade totaled $44,695 million in 1975. Intrafirm related trade was $22,101 million for a 49.4% share (compared to a 65.9% share for affiliate related trade). Arms-length or Non-MNC trade was $22,594 million for a 50.6% share. The MNC-related trade position reflected a 50.8% share of export trade and a 48.0% share of import trade. The dominant MNC group was U.S.-based firms with a 41.9% share of total trade; ROW-based firms held a 7.6% share. U.S. multinationals had the much larger share of exports and imports.

The Canadian trade balance in 1975 was a surplus of $1,201 million. This reflected a $1,215 million surplus in MNC-related trade and a tiny $14 million deficit in Non-MNC trade. The favorable balance in Canadian trade was due to MNC-related trade. In turn, the MNC-related surplus was linked to a surplus in U.S. MNC trade which offset a deficit in ROW MNC trade.

Between 1975 and 1982, Canadian trade grew $39,669 million or 89% to reach $84,364 million. In comparison, intrafirm related trade increased $17,501 million or 79% to a level of $39,602 million. Accordingly, the overall intrafirm position decreased from a 49.4% to a 46.9% share (compared to a 65.9% to 59.8% share change for affiliate related trade). The Non-MNC trade component rose to a 53.1% share. Within the intrafirm trade structure, the export share dropped to 45.8% and the import share remained at 47.9%. The export change reflected a decline in the share of U.S.-based MNCs which was partially offset by an increase in the share of ROW-based MNCs.

The Canadian trade balance in 1982 had changed into a deficit of $8,590 million, a swing of $9,791 million from 1975. Intrafirm related trade had dropped into a deficit of $4,906 million, a deterioration of $6,121 million; the Non-MNC trade deficit had risen $3,670 million to $3,684 million. Thus the decline in the Canadian trade balance resulted from adverse trends in both trade components. The MNC-related deficit emerged due to a deterioration in U.S. MNC trade performance.

In the 1982 to 1989 period, Canadian trade grew $82,398 million or 98% to $166,762 million. In comparison, intrafirm related trade increased $38,513 million or 97% to a level of $43,531 million. As a result, the overall intrafirm position remained at a 46.8% share (compared to a 59.8% to 56.8% share change for affiliate related trade). Non-MNC trade held a 53.2% share. Within the intrafirm trade structure, the export share fell to 43.9% and the import share rose to 49.5%. The export change reflected a decrease in the trade share of ROW MNCs; the import change was due to a rise in the trade share of U.S. MNCs. Compared to 1975, the U.S. MNC share of total trade had fallen from

Table 8.2: Multinational Companies and
U.S.-Canadian Trade in 1982

	MERCHANDISE TRADE (Millions of Dollars)			TOTAL TRADE (Percent Share)			ALL MNCs TRADE (Percent Share)		
	EXPORTS	IMPORTS	BALANCE	EXP	IMP	AVG	EXP	IMP	AVG
Affiliate Related Trade									
Total	37887	46477	-8590	100.0	100.0	100.0	NA	NA	NA
Non-MNCs	15480	18448	-2969	40.9	39.7	40.2	NA	NA	NA
All MNCs	22408	28029	-5622	59.1	60.3	59.8	100.0	100.0	100.0
USA MNCs	19505	21392	-1887	51.5	46.0	48.5	87.0	76.3	81.1
ROW MNCs	3971	7923	-3952	10.5	17.0	14.1	17.7	28.3	23.6
Petro MNCs	479	4467	-3988	1.3	9.6	5.9	2.1	15.9	9.8
USA MNCs	255	3844	-3589	0.7	8.3	4.9	1.1	13.7	8.1
ROW MNCs	256	824	-568	0.7	1.8	1.3	1.1	2.9	2.1
Manu MNCs	17873	19309	-1436	47.2	41.5	44.1	79.8	68.9	73.7
USA MNCs	16509	16429	80	43.6	35.3	39.0	73.7	58.6	65.3
ROW MNCs	2278	3662	-1384	6.0	7.9	7.0	10.2	13.1	11.8
Whole MNCs	3377	3469	-91	8.9	7.5	8.1	15.1	12.4	13.6
USA MNCs	2431	444	1987	6.4	1.0	3.4	10.8	1.6	5.7
ROW MNCs	1027	3258	-2231	2.7	7.0	5.1	4.6	11.6	8.5
Other MNCs	679	785	-106	1.8	1.7	1.7	3.0	2.8	2.9
USA MNCs	310	675	-365	0.8	1.5	1.2	1.4	2.4	2.0
ROW MNCs	410	179	231	1.1	0.4	0.7	1.8	0.6	1.2
Intrafirm Related Trade									
Total	37887	46477	-8590	100.0	100.0	100.0	NA	NA	NA
Non-MNCs	20539	24223	-3684	54.2	52.1	53.1	NA	NA	NA
All MNCs	17348	22254	-4906	45.8	47.9	46.9	100.0	100.0	100.0
USA MNCs	15514	16903	-1389	40.9	36.4	38.4	89.4	76.0	81.9
ROW MNCs	1834	5351	-3517	4.8	11.5	8.5	10.6	24.0	18.1
Petro MNCs	325	3563	-3238	0.9	7.7	4.6	1.9	16.0	9.8
USA MNCs	216	2782	-2566	0.6	6.0	3.6	1.2	12.5	7.6
ROW MNCs	109	781	-672	0.3	1.7	1.1	0.6	3.5	2.2
Manu MNCs	13543	15796	-2253	35.7	34.0	34.8	78.1	71.0	74.1
USA MNCs	12811	13402	-591	33.8	28.8	31.1	73.8	60.2	66.2
ROW MNCs	732	2394	-1662	1.9	5.2	3.7	4.2	10.8	7.9
Whole MNCs	2996	2422	574	7.9	5.2	6.4	17.3	10.9	13.7
USA MNCs	2257	333	1924	6.0	0.7	3.1	13.0	1.5	6.5
ROW MNCs	739	2089	-1350	2.0	4.5	3.4	4.3	9.4	7.1
Other MNCs	484	473	11	1.3	1.0	1.1	2.8	2.1	2.4
USA MNCs	230	386	-156	0.6	0.8	0.7	1.3	1.7	1.6
ROW MNCs	254	87	167	0.7	0.2	0.4	1.5	0.4	0.9

41.9% to 39.6%, and the ROW MNC share from 7.6% to 7.2%.

The Canadian trade deficit in 1989 was $9,144 million, a deterioration of only $554 million from 1982. The intrafirm related trade deficit was $8,947 million, an increase of $4,041 million; the Non-MNC trade deficit had declined $3,847 million to a level of only $197 million. Thus the deterioration in the Canadian trade balance was due to unfavorable trends in MNC trade. The

MNC-related trade deficit was based growing deficits in both U.S. and ROW MNC trade, especially the latter.

INDUSTRY TRADE ROLES

This section is based on the trade data shown in Tables 8.1, 8.2, and 8.3 for 1975, 1982, and 1989, respectively. The trade role of each affiliate industry group is discussed on the basis of affiliate related trade.

Petroleum Affiliates

Affiliate related trade was $2,478 million in 1975, adjusted for the affiliate trade overlap. This figure represented a 5.5% share of total trade and a 8.4% share of MNC-related trade. The industry category ranked third and was dominated by U.S.-based firms. The industry trade balance was a deficit of $1,622 million, compared to a total merchandise surplus of $1,201 million.

By 1982, industry trade had increased 100% to $4,945 million. This figure represented a 5.9% share of total trade (up 0.3 share points), and a 9.8% share of MNC-related trade (up 1.4 share points). The industry category ranked third, behind manufacturing and wholesale affiliates. The trade balance was a deficit of $3,988 million (up $2,367 million), compared to a total merchandise deficit of $8,590 million (a swing of $9,791 million).

Industry related trade increased by 4.0% to $5,135 million in 1989. This figure represented a 3.1% share of total trade (down 2.8 share points), and a 5.4% share of MNC-related trade (down 4.4 share points). The industry category still ranked third, and continued to be dominated by U.S.-based firms. The trade balance was a deficit of $4,165 million (up $176 million), compared to a total merchandise deficit of $9,144 million (up $554 million).

Manufacturing Affiliates

Affiliate related trade was $22,463 million in 1975, adjusted for the affiliate trade overlap. This figure represented a 50.3% share of total trade and a 76.2% share of MNC-related trade. The industry category ranked first and was dominated by U.S.-based firms. The industry trade balance was a surplus of $3,746 million, compared to a total merchandise surplus of $1,201 million.

By 1982, industry trade had increased 66% to $37,181 million. This figure represented a 44.1% share of total trade (down 6.2 share points), and a 73.7% share of MNC-related trade (down 2.5 share points). The industry category ranked first. The trade balance was a deficit of $1,436 million (a swing of $5,182 million), compared to a total merchandise deficit of $8,590 million (a swing of $9,791 million).

Industry related trade increased by 108% to 77,455 million in 1989. This

Table 8.3: Multinational Companies and
U.S.-Canadian Trade in 1989

	MERCHANDISE TRADE (Millions of Dollars)			TOTAL TRADE (Percent Share)			ALL MNCs TRADE (Percent Share)		
	EXPORTS	IMPORTS	BALANCE	EXP	IMP	AVG	EXP	IMP	AVG
Affiliate Related Trade									
Total	78809	87953	-9144	100.0	100.0	100.0	NA	NA	NA
Non-MNCs	35931	36152	-221	45.6	41.1	43.2	NA	NA	NA
All MNCs	42878	51801	-8923	54.4	58.9	56.8	100.0	100.0	100.0
USA MNCs	38173	40865	-2692	48.4	46.5	47.4	89.0	78.9	83.5
ROW MNCs	7121	12109	-4988	9.0	13.8	11.5	16.6	23.4	20.3
Petro MNCs	485	4650	-4165	0.6	5.3	3.1	1.1	9.0	5.4
USA MNCs	379	3893	-3514	0.5	4.4	2.6	0.9	7.5	4.5
ROW MNCs	130	855	-725	0.2	1.0	0.6	0.3	1.7	1.0
Manu MNCs	35875	41580	-5705	45.5	47.3	46.4	83.7	80.3	81.8
USA MNCs	33007	35347	-2340	41.9	40.2	41.0	77.0	68.2	72.2
ROW MNCs	4879	7185	-2306	6.2	8.2	7.2	11.4	13.9	12.7
Whole MNCs	5365	4500	865	6.8	5.1	5.9	12.5	8.7	10.4
USA MNCs	4209	767	3442	5.3	0.9	3.0	9.8	1.5	5.3
ROW MNCs	1387	3795	-2408	1.8	4.3	3.1	3.2	7.3	5.5
Other MNCs	1153	1071	82	1.5	1.2	1.3	2.7	2.1	2.3
USA MNCs	578	858	-280	0.7	1.0	0.9	1.3	1.7	1.5
ROW MNCs	725	274	451	0.9	0.3	0.6	1.7	0.5	1.1
Intrafirm Related Trade									
Total	78809	87953	-9144	100.0	100.0	100.0	NA	NA	NA
Non-MNCs	44225	44422	-197	56.1	50.5	53.2	NA	NA	NA
All MNCs	34584	43531	-8947	43.9	49.5	46.8	100.0	100.0	100.0
USA MNCs	32295	33768	-1473	41.0	38.4	39.6	93.4	77.6	84.6
ROW MNCs	2289	9763	-7474	2.9	11.1	7.2	6.6	22.4	15.4
Petro MNCs	403	3957	-3554	0.5	4.5	2.6	1.2	9.1	5.6
USA MNCs	346	3102	-2756	0.4	3.5	2.1	1.0	7.1	4.4
ROW MNCs	57	855	-798	0.1	1.0	0.5	0.2	2.0	1.2
Manu MNCs	28971	34870	-5899	36.8	39.6	38.3	83.8	80.1	81.7
USA MNCs	27770	29643	-1873	35.2	33.7	34.4	80.3	68.1	73.5
ROW MNCs	1201	5227	-4026	1.5	5.9	3.9	3.5	12.0	8.2
Whole MNCs	4571	4064	507	5.8	4.6	5.2	13.2	9.3	11.1
USA MNCs	3884	586	3298	4.9	0.7	2.7	11.2	1.3	5.7
ROW MNCs	687	3478	-2791	0.9	4.0	2.5	2.0	8.0	5.3
Other MNCs	639	640	-1	0.8	0.7	0.8	1.8	1.5	1.6
USA MNCs	295	437	-142	0.4	0.5	0.4	0.9	1.0	0.9
ROW MNCs	344	203	141	0.4	0.2	0.3	1.0	0.5	0.7

figure represented a 46.4% share of total trade (up 2.4 share points), and a 81.8% share of MNC-related trade (up 8.1 share points). The industry category still ranked first, and continued to be dominated by U.S.-based firms. The trade balance was a deficit of $5,705 million (up $4,269 million), compared to a total merchandise deficit of $9,144 million (up $554 million).

Wholesale Trade Affiliates

Affiliate related trade was $3,524 million in 1975, adjusted for the affiliate trade overlap. This figure represented a 7.9% share of total trade and a 12.0% share of MNC-related trade. The industry category ranked second and was dominated by ROW-based firms. The industry trade balance was a deficit of $165 million, compared to total merchandise trade which was in surplus by $1,201 million.

By 1982, industry trade had increased 94% to $6,846 million. This figure represented a 8.1% share of total trade (up 0.2 share points), and a 13.6% share of MNC-related trade (up 1.6 share points). The industry category ranked second, behind manufacturing. The trade balance was a deficit of $91 million (down $73 million), compared to a total merchandise deficit of $8,590 million (a swing of $9,791 million).

Industry related trade increased by 44% to 9,865 million in 1989, adjusted for the affiliate trade overlap. This figure represented a 5.9% share of total trade (down 2.2 share points), and a 10.4% share of MNC-related trade (down 3.2 share points). The industry category still ranked second, but was now more evenly divided between U.S.-based and ROW-based firms. The trade balance was a surplus of $865 million (a swing of $956 million), compared to total merchandise trade which continued to have a deficit balance of $9,144 million (up $554 million).

Other Industry Affiliates

Affiliate related trade was $996 million in 1975, adjusted for the affiliate trade overlap. This figure represented a 2.2% share of total trade and a 3.4% share of MNC-related trade. The industry category ranked last and was dominated by U.S.-based firms. The industry trade balance was a deficit of $129 million, compared to a total merchandise trade which was in surplus by $1,201 million.

By 1982, industry trade had increased 47% to $1,463 million. This figure represented a 1.7% share of total trade (down 0.5 share points), and a 2.9% share of MNC-related trade (down 0.5 share points). The industry category ranked last. The trade balance was a deficit of $106 million (down $23 million), compared to a total merchandise deficit of $8,590 million (a swing of $9,791 million).

Industry related trade increased by 52% to 2,224 million in 1989, adjusted for the affiliate trade overlap. This figure represented a 1.3% share of total trade (down 0.4 share points), and a 2.3% share of MNC-related trade (down 0.6 share points). The industry category ranked last, and was still dominated by U.S.-based firms. The trade balance was a surplus of $82 million (a swing of $188 million), compared to a total merchandise deficit of $9,144 million (up $554 million).

Table 8.4: Ultimate Beneficial Owners and U.S.-Canadian Trade in 1975

	MERCHANDISE TRADE (Millions of Dollars)			TOTAL TRADE (Percent Share)			ALL MNCs TRADE (Percent Share)		
	EXPORTS	IMPORTS	BALANCE	EXP	IMP	AVG	EXP	IMP	AVG
Affiliate Related Trade									
Total	22948	21747	1201	100.0	100.0	100.0	NA	NA	NA
Non-MNCs	7302	7932	-630	31.8	36.5	34.1	NA	NA	NA
All MNCs	15646	13816	1831	68.2	63.5	65.9	100.0	100.0	100.0
USA MNCs	14713	10877	3836	64.1	50.0	57.3	94.0	78.7	86.9
ROW MNCs	1122	3228	-2106	4.9	14.8	9.7	7.2	23.4	14.8
CANADA	507	2061	-1554	2.2	9.5	5.7	3.2	14.9	8.7
EUROPE	346	992	-646	1.5	4.6	3.0	2.2	7.2	4.5
JAPAN	176	106	70	0.8	0.5	0.6	1.1	0.8	1.0
OTHER	93	69	24	0.4	0.3	0.4	0.6	0.5	0.5
Intrafirm Related Trade									
Total	22948	21747	1201	100.0	100.0	100.0	NA	NA	NA
Non-MNCs	11290	11304	-14	49.2	52.0	50.6	NA	NA	NA
All MNCs	11658	10443	1215	50.8	48.0	49.4	100.0	100.0	100.0
USA MNCs	10914	7794	3120	47.6	35.8	41.9	93.6	74.6	84.6
ROW MNCs	744	2649	-1905	3.2	12.2	7.6	6.4	25.4	15.4
CANADA	446	1972	-1526	1.9	9.1	5.4	3.8	18.9	10.9
EUROPE	98	600	-502	0.4	2.8	1.6	0.8	5.7	3.2
JAPAN	158	27	131	0.7	0.1	0.4	1.4	0.3	0.8
OTHER	42	50	-8	0.2	0.2	0.2	0.4	0.5	0.4

THE TRADE ROLE OF ULTIMATE BENEFICIAL OWNERS

This section is based on the trade data shown in Tables 8.4, 8.5, and 8.6 for 1975, 1982, and 1989, respectively. In the tables, four groups of Ultimate Beneficial Owners or "UBOs" are shown for ROW MNCs -- Canada, Europe, Japan, and Other Areas. U.S.-based MNCs are also a UBO group, and for analytical purposes, Non-MNC firms are treated as a UBO group. The trade role of UBOs in MNC-related trade is discussed for both affiliate related trade and intrafirm related trade.

Affiliate Related Trade

In 1975, trade with Canada was $44,695 million. Affiliates of multinational companies held a 65.9% share of trade with Canada (adjusted for the trade overlap). From the UBO perspective, U.S.-based firms were the dominant group with a 57.3% share, followed by Non-MNCs at a 34.1% share. Canadian-based companies were third with a 5.7% share.

Table 8.5: Ultimate Beneficial Owners and
U.S.-Canadian Trade in 1982

	MERCHANDISE TRADE (Millions of Dollars)			TOTAL TRADE (Percent Share)			ALL MNCs TRADE (Percent Share)		
	EXPORTS	IMPORTS	BALANCE	EXP	IMP	AVG	EXP	IMP	AVG
Affiliate Related Trade									
Total	37887	46477	-8590	100.0	100.0	100.0	NA	NA	NA
Non-MNCs	15480	18448	-2969	40.9	39.7	40.2	NA	NA	NA
All MNCs	22408	28029	-5622	59.1	60.3	59.8	100.0	100.0	100.0
USA MNCs	19505	21392	-1887	51.5	46.0	48.5	87.0	76.3	81.1
ROW MNCs	3971	7923	-3952	10.5	17.0	14.1	17.7	28.3	23.6
CANADA	1127	4708	-3581	3.0	10.1	6.9	5.0	16.8	11.6
EUROPE	2195	1613	582	5.8	3.5	4.5	9.8	5.8	7.6
JAPAN	457	1025	-568	1.2	2.2	1.8	2.0	3.7	2.9
OTHER	192	577	-385	0.5	1.2	0.9	0.9	2.1	1.5
Intrafirm Related Trade									
Total	37887	46477	-8590	100.0	100.0	100.0	NA	NA	NA
Non-MNCs	20539	24223	-3684	54.2	52.1	53.1	NA	NA	NA
All MNCs	17348	22254	-4906	45.8	47.9	46.9	100.0	100.0	100.0
USA MNCs	15514	16903	-1389	40.9	36.4	38.4	89.4	76.0	81.9
ROW MNCs	1834	5351	-3517	4.8	11.5	8.5	10.6	24.0	18.1
CANADA	612	3868	-3256	1.6	8.3	5.3	3.5	17.4	11.3
EUROPE	1053	830	223	2.8	1.8	2.2	6.1	3.7	4.8
JAPAN	37	548	-511	0.1	1.2	0.7	0.2	2.5	1.5
OTHER	132	105	27	0.3	0.2	0.3	0.8	0.5	0.6

The Canadian trade balance in 1975 was a modest surplus of $1,201 million. By ranking, this reflected a U.S. MNC surplus of $3,836 million, a Canadian MNC deficit of $1,554 million, a European MNC deficit of $646 million, and a Non-MNC deficit of $630 million.

Between 1975 and 1982, Canadian trade grew to $84,364 million. The affiliate trade position decreased 6.1 share points to a 59.8% share. From the UBO perspective, U.S. MNCs fell 8.8 share points to 48.5%, Non-MNCs rose 6.1 share points to 40.2%, and Canadian MNCs increased 1.2 share points to 6.9%.

The Canadian trade balance in 1982 was a deficit of $8,590 million, a swing of $9,791 million. By ranking, this reflected a Canadian MNC deficit of $3,581 million (up $2,027 million), a Non-MNC deficit of $2,969 million (up $2,339 million), and a U.S. MNC deficit of $1,887 million (a swing of $5,723 million).

Between 1982 and 1989, Canadian trade increased to $166,762 million. The affiliate trade position decreased 3.0 share points to a 56.8% share. From the UBO perspective, U.S. MNCs fell 1.1 share points to 47.4%, Non-MNCs rose 3.0 share points to 43.2%, and Canadian MNCs decreased 2.2 share points to 4.7%.

Table 8.6: Ultimate Beneficial Owners and
U.S.-Canadian Trade in 1989

	MERCHANDISE TRADE (Millions of Dollars)			TOTAL TRADE (Percent Share)			ALL MNCs TRADE (Percent Share)		
	EXPORTS	IMPORTS	BALANCE	EXP	IMP	AVG	EXP	IMP	AVG
Affiliate Related Trade									
Total	78809	87953	-9144	100.0	100.0	100.0	NA	NA	NA
Non-MNCs	35931	36152	-221	45.6	41.1	43.2	NA	NA	NA
All MNCs	42878	51801	-8923	54.4	58.9	56.8	100.0	100.0	100.0
USA MNCs	38173	40865	-2692	48.4	46.5	47.4	89.0	78.9	83.5
ROW MNCs	7121	12109	-4988	9.0	13.8	11.5	16.6	23.4	20.3
CANADA	1604	6274	-4670	2.0	7.1	4.7	3.7	12.1	8.3
EUROPE	3523	2927	596	4.5	3.3	3.9	8.2	5.7	6.8
JAPAN	1547	1933	-386	2.0	2.2	2.1	3.6	3.7	3.7
OTHER	447	975	-528	0.6	1.1	0.9	1.0	1.9	1.5
Intrafirm Related Trade									
Total	78809	87953	-9144	100.0	100.0	100.0	NA	NA	NA
Non-MNCs	44225	44422	-197	56.1	50.5	53.2	NA	NA	NA
All MNCs	34584	43531	-8947	43.9	49.5	46.8	100.0	100.0	100.0
USA MNCs	32295	33768	-1473	41.0	38.4	39.6	93.4	77.6	84.6
ROW MNCs	2289	9763	-7474	2.9	11.1	7.2	6.6	22.4	15.4
CANADA	817	5695	-4878	1.0	6.5	3.9	2.4	13.1	8.3
EUROPE	848	1503	-655	1.1	1.7	1.4	2.5	3.5	3.0
JAPAN	540	1622	-1082	0.7	1.8	1.3	1.6	3.7	2.8
OTHER	84	943	-859	0.1	1.1	0.6	0.2	2.2	1.3

The Canadian trade balance in 1989 was a deficit of $9,144 million, an increase of $554 million. By ranking, this reflected a Canadian MNC deficit of $4,670 million (up $1,089 million), a U.S. MNC deficit of $2,692 million (up $805 million), and a Other MNC deficit of $528 million (up $143 million).

Intrafirm Related Trade

In 1975, trade with Canada was $44,695 million. Intrafirm trade by multinational companies accounted for a 49.4% share of trade with Canada. From the UBO perspective, Non-MNC firms were the dominant group with a 50.6% share, followed by U.S. MNCs at a 41.9% share. Canadian-based companies were third with a 5.4% share.

The Canadian trade balance in 1975 was a modest surplus of $1,201 million. By ranking, this reflected a U.S. MNC surplus of $3,120 million, a Canadian MNC deficit of $1,526 million, and a European MNC deficit of $502 million.

Between 1975 and 1982, Canadian trade grew to $84,364 million. The intrafirm trade position decreased 2.5 share points to a 46.9% share. From the

UBO perspective, Non-MNCs increased 2.5 share points to 53.1%, U.S. MNCs fell 3.4 share points to 38.4%, and Canadian MNCs decreased 0.1 share points to 5.3%.

The Canadian trade balance in 1982 was a deficit of $8,590 million, a swing of $9,791 million. By ranking, this reflected a Non-MNC deficit of $3,684 million (up $3,670 million), a Canadian MNC deficit of $3,256 million (up $1,730 million), and a U.S. MNC deficit of $1,389 million (a swing of $4,509 million).

Between 1982 and 1989, Canadian trade increased to $166,762 million. The intrafirm trade position decreased 0.1 share points to a 46.8% share. From the UBO perspective, Non-MNCs rose 0.1 share points to 53.2%, U.S. MNCs rose 1.2 share points to 39.6%, and Canadian MNCs decreased 1.4 share points to 3.9%.

The Canadian trade balance in 1989 was a deficit of $9,144 million, an increase of $554 million. By ranking, this reflected a Canadian MNC deficit of $4,878 million (up $1,622 million), a U.S. MNC deficit of $1,473 million (up $84 million), and a Japanese MNC deficit of $1,082 million (up $571 million).

DERIVATION OF THE DATA

The derivation of the MNC-related geographic trade data is discussed at length in Chapter 7 on "Total Geographic Trade."

CHAPTER 9

TRADE WITH EUROPE

Trade with Europe includes one-fourth of total merchandise trade. Multinational companies are important in U.S.-European trade. MNC affiliate trade accounts for a 56% share of total trade and MNC intrafirm trade has a 41% share. The equivalent figures for Total Geographic trade are 54% and 39%. Wholesale affiliates are the dominant industry group, followed by manufacturing affiliates.

DEFINITION OF TRADE WITH EUROPE

Trade with Europe consists of movements of merchandise between the United States and Europe. The two areas are separated by the Atlantic Ocean. Subsequently, most trade with Europe is waterborne trade.

Europe, as defined by the Bureau of Economic Analysis, consists of the market economies of Western Europe. The major nations are France, Germany, Italy, and the United Kingdom. Europe is dominated by the European Union, formerly the European Economic Community.

TRENDS IN TRADE WITH EUROPE

In 1975, total trade with Europe was $54,193 million. Exports were $32,727 million and imports were $21,466 million, yielding a surplus of $11,261 million. In 1982, total trade reached a level of $117,077 million, an increase of 116% or $62,884 million. Both exports and imports enjoyed strong growth over the period, but with imports growing over 50% faster. As a result, the trade balance declined by $1,010 million, falling to a surplus of $10,251 by 1982.

Between 1982 and 1989, the growth in trade with Europe slowed. Total trade grew 79% or $92,223 million to reach $209,300 million. Imports still outpaced export growth by a factor of one-third. This imbalance reduced the trade surplus even further. The surplus was only $1,644 million in 1989, a decline of $8,607 million.

THE TRADE ROLE OF MULTINATIONAL COMPANIES

This section is based on the trade data shown in Tables 9.1, 9.2, and 9.3 for 1975, 1982, and 1989, respectively. The overall trade role of multinational companies ("All MNCs" in the tables) is discussed for both affiliate related trade and intrafirm related trade.

Affiliate Related Trade

Trade with Europe totaled $54,193 million in 1975. Adjusted for the trade overlap, affiliate related trade was $31,921 million for a 58.9% share; Non-MNC trade was $22,272 million for a 41.1% share. The MNC-related trade position reflected a 59.6% share of export trade and a 57.8% share of import trade. The dominant MNC group was ROW-based firms with a 33.5% share of total trade; U.S.-based firms held a 27.9% share. ROW multinational companies had a larger share of imports; U.S.-based firms had the larger share of exports.

The European trade balance in 1975 was a surplus of $11,261 million. This reflected a $7,120 million surplus in MNC-related trade and a $4,141 million surplus in Non-MNC trade. Thus the overall trade surplus position with Europe was due to both components. In turn, the MNC-related surplus was based on a surplus position of U.S.-based multinationals which offset a small deficit position of ROW-based firms.

Between 1975 and 1982, European trade grew 116% or $62,884 million to reach $117,077 million. In comparison, affiliate related trade increased $34,470 million or 108% to a level of $66,391 million (adjusted for the trade overlap). Accordingly, the overall affiliate position decreased from a 58.9% to a 56.7% share and Non-MNC trade rose to a 43.3% share. Within the affiliate trade structure, the export share fell to 55.1% and the import share rose slightly to 58.6%. The export change reflected a decline in the U.S. MNC share; the import change was due to a rise in the ROW MNC share which barely offset a decline in the U.S. MNC share.

The European trade balance in 1982 remained at a surplus of $10,251 million, a decrease of $1,010 million from 1975. The affiliate related trade surplus had dipped to $3,799 million, a change of $3,321 million; the Non-MNC trade surplus had risen $2,311 million to $6,452 million. Thus the decline in the European trade balance was due to an unfavorable trend in MNC-related trade. The reduction in the MNC-related surplus was caused by a jump

Table 9.1: Multinational Companies and U.S.-European Trade in 1975

	MERCHANDISE TRADE (Millions of Dollars)			TOTAL TRADE (Percent Share)			ALL MNCs TRADE (Percent Share)		
	EXPORTS	IMPORTS	BALANCE	EXP	IMP	AVG	EXP	IMP	AVG
Affiliate Related Trade									
Total	32727	21466	11261	100.0	100.0	100.0	NA	NA	NA
Non-MNCs	13207	9066	4141	40.4	42.2	41.1	NA	NA	NA
All MNCs	19521	12401	7120	59.6	57.8	58.9	100.0	100.0	100.0
USA MNCs	11344	3768	7576	34.7	17.6	27.9	58.1	30.4	47.3
ROW MNCs	9001	9171	-170	27.5	42.7	33.5	46.1	74.0	56.9
Petro MNCs	819	1498	-679	2.5	7.0	4.3	4.2	12.1	7.3
USA MNCs	355	1463	-1108	1.1	6.8	3.4	1.8	11.8	5.7
ROW MNCs	477	173	304	1.5	0.8	1.2	2.4	1.4	2.0
Manu MNCs	6950	3074	3876	21.2	14.3	18.5	35.6	24.8	31.4
USA MNCs	6288	1758	4530	19.2	8.2	14.8	32.2	14.2	25.2
ROW MNCs	866	1433	-567	2.6	6.7	4.2	4.4	11.6	7.2
Whole MNCs	11166	7568	3598	34.1	35.3	34.6	57.2	61.0	58.7
USA MNCs	4413	502	3911	13.5	2.3	9.1	22.6	4.0	15.4
ROW MNCs	7316	7326	-10	22.4	34.1	27.0	37.5	59.1	45.9
Other MNCs	585	260	325	1.8	1.2	1.6	3.0	2.1	2.6
USA MNCs	288	45	243	0.9	0.2	0.6	1.5	0.4	1.0
ROW MNCs	342	239	103	1.0	1.1	1.1	1.8	1.9	1.8
Intrafirm Related Trade									
Total	32727	21466	11261	100.0	100.0	100.0	NA	NA	NA
Non-MNCs	18615	11250	7365	56.9	52.4	55.1	NA	NA	NA
All MNCs	14112	10216	3896	43.1	47.6	44.9	100.0	100.0	100.0
USA MNCs	9695	2691	7004	29.6	12.5	22.9	68.7	26.3	50.9
ROW MNCs	4417	7525	-3108	13.5	35.1	22.0	31.3	73.7	49.1
Petro MNCs	735	938	-203	2.2	4.4	3.1	5.2	9.2	6.9
USA MNCs	289	791	-502	0.9	3.7	2.0	2.0	7.7	4.4
ROW MNCs	446	147	299	1.4	0.7	1.1	3.2	1.4	2.4
Manu MNCs	5615	2601	3014	17.2	12.1	15.2	39.8	25.5	33.8
USA MNCs	5294	1539	3755	16.2	7.2	12.6	37.5	15.1	28.1
ROW MNCs	321	1062	-741	1.0	4.9	2.6	2.3	10.4	5.7
Whole MNCs	7470	6512	958	22.8	30.3	25.8	52.9	63.7	57.5
USA MNCs	3911	325	3586	12.0	1.5	7.8	27.7	3.2	17.4
ROW MNCs	3559	6187	-2628	10.9	28.8	18.0	25.2	60.6	40.1
Other MNCs	292	165	127	0.9	0.8	0.8	2.1	1.6	1.9
USA MNCs	201	36	165	0.6	0.2	0.4	1.4	0.4	1.0
ROW MNCs	91	129	-38	0.3	0.6	0.4	0.6	1.3	0.9

in the ROW MNC trade deficit which offset a larger U.S. MNC surplus.

In the 1982 to 1989 period, trade with Europe grew 79% or $92,223 million to reach $209,300 million. In comparison, affiliate related trade rose $41,846 million or 63% to a level of $108,237 million (adjusted for the trade overlap). As a result, the overall affiliate position decreased from a 56.7% to a 51.7% share and Non-MNC trade rose to a 48.3% share. Within the affiliate trade structure the export share decreased to 46.7% and the import share to 56.8%. The export change reflected a decline in the trade share of ROW MNCs; the small import change was due to a decline in the trade share of ROW MNCs which offset a higher share of U.S. MNCs. Compared to 1975, the U.S. MNC share of total trade had fallen from 27.9% to 21.6%, the ROW MNC share from 33.5% to 31.3%.

The European trade balance in 1989 was a surplus of only $1,644 million, down $8,607 million from 1982. The affiliate trade balance had changed into a deficit of $9,715 million, a swing of $13,514 million. In contrast, the Non-MNC trade balance had risen $4,907 million to a surplus of $11,359 million. Thus the deterioration in the European trade balance reflected trends in MNC-related trade. The conversion of MNC-related trade into a deficit was caused by a $17,440 million increase in the ROW MNC deficit position.

Intrafirm Related Trade

European trade totaled $54,193 million in 1975. Intrafirm related trade was $24,328 million for a 44.9% share (compared to a 58.9% share for affiliate related trade). Arms-length or Non-MNC trade was $29,865 million for a 55.1% share. The MNC-related trade position reflected a 43.1% share of export trade and a 47.6% share of import trade. U.S.-based firms held a 22.9% share of total trade; ROW-based firms held a 22.0% share. U.S. multinationals had the larger share of exports; foreign-based firms had the larger share of imports.

The European trade balance in 1975 was a surplus of $11,261 million. This reflected a $3,896 million surplus in MNC-related trade and a $7,365 million surplus in Non-MNC trade. The favorable balance in European trade was due to both components. In turn, the MNC-related surplus was linked to a surplus in U.S. MNC trade which offset a deficit in ROW MNC trade.

Between 1975 and 1982, European trade grew $62,884 million or 116% to reach $117,077 million. In comparison, intrafirm related trade increased $17,868 million or 73% to a level of $42,196 million. Accordingly, the overall intrafirm position decreased from a 44.9% to a 36.0% share (compared to a 58.9% to 56.7% share change for affiliate related trade). The Non-MNC trade component rose to a 64.0% share. Within the intrafirm trade structure, the export share dropped to 33.5% and the import share to 39.0%. These changes reflected declines in the trade shares of both U.S. and ROW MNCs.

The European trade surplus in 1982 was $10,251 million, a drop of $1,010 million from 1975. The intrafirm trade surplus had fallen to $488 million, a change of $3,408 million; the Non-MNC trade surplus had risen $2,398 million to $9,763 million. Thus the modest decline in the European trade balance resulted from changes in MNC-related trade. The smaller MNC-related surplus was due to a larger deficit in ROW MNC trade which offset a rise in the U.S. MNC surplus.

Table 9.2: Multinational Companies and U.S.-European Trade in 1982

	MERCHANDISE TRADE (Millions of Dollars)			TOTAL TRADE (Percent Share)			ALL MNCs TRADE (Percent Share)		
	EXPORTS	IMPORTS	BALANCE	EXP	IMP	AVG	EXP	IMP	AVG
Affiliate Related Trade									
Total	63664	53413	10251	100.0	100.0	100.0	NA	NA	NA
Non-MNCs	28569	22117	6452	44.9	41.4	43.3	NA	NA	NA
All MNCs	35095	31296	3799	55.1	58.6	56.7	100.0	100.0	100.0
USA MNCs	18091	6112	11979	28.4	11.4	20.7	51.5	19.5	36.5
ROW MNCs	18258	26170	-7912	28.7	49.0	37.9	52.0	83.6	66.9
Petro MNCs	1031	3092	-2061	1.6	5.8	3.5	2.9	9.9	6.2
USA MNCs	612	1912	-1300	1.0	3.6	2.2	1.7	6.1	3.8
ROW MNCs	452	1347	-895	0.7	2.5	1.5	1.3	4.3	2.7
Manu MNCs	13355	9137	4217	21.0	17.1	19.2	38.1	29.2	33.9
USA MNCs	9708	3225	6483	15.2	6.0	11.0	27.7	10.3	19.5
ROW MNCs	4001	6120	-2119	6.3	11.5	8.6	11.4	19.6	15.2
Whole MNCs	19639	18229	1409	30.8	34.1	32.3	56.0	58.2	57.0
USA MNCs	7533	950	6583	11.8	1.8	7.2	21.5	3.0	12.8
ROW MNCs	12919	17841	-4922	20.3	33.4	26.3	36.8	57.0	46.3
Other MNCs	1070	837	234	1.7	1.6	1.6	3.1	2.7	2.9
USA MNCs	238	25	213	0.4	0.0	0.2	0.7	0.1	0.4
ROW MNCs	886	862	24	1.4	1.6	1.5	2.5	2.8	2.6
Intrafirm Related Trade									
Total	63664	53413	10251	100.0	100.0	100.0	NA	NA	NA
Non-MNCs	42322	32559	9763	66.5	61.0	64.0	NA	NA	NA
All MNCs	21342	20854	488	33.5	39.0	36.0	100.0	100.0	100.0
USA MNCs	15583	4140	11443	24.5	7.8	16.8	73.0	19.9	46.7
ROW MNCs	5759	16714	-10955	9.0	31.3	19.2	27.0	80.1	53.3
Petro MNCs	665	1325	-660	1.0	2.5	1.7	3.1	6.4	4.7
USA MNCs	422	718	-296	0.7	1.3	1.0	2.0	3.4	2.7
ROW MNCs	243	607	-364	0.4	1.1	0.7	1.1	2.9	2.0
Manu MNCs	9472	6940	2532	14.9	13.0	14.0	44.4	33.3	38.9
USA MNCs	8236	2690	5546	12.9	5.0	9.3	38.6	12.9	25.9
ROW MNCs	1236	4250	-3014	1.9	8.0	4.7	5.8	20.4	13.0
Whole MNCs	10722	12283	-1561	16.8	23.0	19.6	50.2	58.9	54.5
USA MNCs	6723	713	6010	10.6	1.3	6.4	31.5	3.4	17.6
ROW MNCs	3999	11570	-7571	6.3	21.7	13.3	18.7	55.5	36.9
Other MNCs	483	306	177	0.8	0.6	0.7	2.3	1.5	1.9
USA MNCs	202	19	183	0.3	0.0	0.2	0.9	0.1	0.5
ROW MNCs	281	287	-6	0.4	0.5	0.5	1.3	1.4	1.3

In the 1982 to 1989 period, European trade grew $92,223 million or 79% to $209,300 million. In comparison, intrafirm related trade increased $44,405 million or 105% to a level of $86,601 million. As a result, the overall intrafirm position increased from a 36.0% to a 41.4% share (compared to a 56.7% to 51.7% share change for affiliate related trade). Non-MNC trade fell to a 58.6% share. Within the intrafirm trade structure, the export share remained at 33.5%

while the import share jumped to 49.4%. The import change was due to a rise in the trade shares of both MNC groups. Compared to 1975, the U.S. MNC share of total trade had fallen from 22.9% to 19.2%, while the ROW MNC changed from 22.0% to 22.2%.

The European trade surplus in 1989 had fallen to $1,644 million, a decrease of $8,607 million from 1982. Intrafirm related trade had changed into a deficit of $16,023 million, a swing of $16,511 million; the Non-MNC trade surplus had risen $7,904 million to a level of $17,667 million. Thus the deterioration in the European trade balance was due to unfavorable trends in MNC-related trade. The conversion of MNC-related trade into a deficit was caused by a $20,785 million increase in the ROW MNC deficit.

INDUSTRY TRADE ROLES

This section is based on the trade data shown in Tables 9.1, 9.2, and 9.3 for 1975, 1982, and 1989, respectively. The trade role of each affiliate industry group is discussed on the basis of affiliate related trade.

Petroleum Affiliates

Affiliate related trade was $2,317 million in 1975, adjusted for the affiliate trade overlap. This figure represented a 4.3% share of total trade and a 7.3% share of MNC-related trade. The industry category ranked third and was dominated by U.S.-based firms. The industry trade balance was a deficit of $679 million, compared to a total merchandise surplus of $11,261 million.

By 1982, industry trade had increased 78% to $4,123 million. This figure represented a 3.5% share of total trade (down 0.8 share points), and a 6.2% share of MNC-related trade (down 1.0 share points). The industry category ranked third, behind wholesale and manufacturing affiliates. The trade balance was a deficit of $2,061 million (up $1,383 million), compared to a total merchandise surplus of $10,251 million (down $1,010 million).

Industry related trade increased by 10% to $4,540 million in 1989. This figure represented a 2.2% share of total trade (down 1.4 share points), and a 4.2% share of MNC-related trade (down 2.0 share points). The industry category still ranked third, but was now dominated by ROW-based firms. The trade balance was a deficit of $2,188 million (up $126 million), compared to a total merchandise surplus of $1,644 million (down $8,607 million).

Manufacturing Affiliates

Affiliate related trade was $10,025 million in 1975, adjusted for the affiliate trade overlap. This figure represented a 18.5% share of total trade and a 31.4% share of MNC-related trade. Overall, the industry category ranked second and

Table 9.3: Multinational Companies and U.S.-European Trade in 1989

	MERCHANDISE TRADE (Millions of Dollars)			TOTAL TRADE (Percent Share)			ALL MNCs TRADE (Percent Share)		
	EXPORTS	IMPORTS	BALANCE	EXP	IMP	AVG	EXP	IMP	AVG
Affiliate Related Trade									
Total	105472	103828	1644	100.0	100.0	100.0	NA	NA	NA
Non-MNCs	56211	44852	11359	53.3	43.2	48.3	NA	NA	NA
All MNCs	49261	58976	-9715	46.7	56.8	51.7	100.0	100.0	100.0
USA MNCs	30435	14878	15557	28.9	14.3	21.6	61.8	25.2	41.9
ROW MNCs	20079	45431	-25352	19.0	43.8	31.3	40.8	77.0	60.5
Petro MNCs	1176	3364	-2188	1.1	3.2	2.2	2.4	5.7	4.2
USA MNCs	505	1602	-1097	0.5	1.5	1.0	1.0	2.7	1.9
ROW MNCs	703	2008	-1305	0.7	1.9	1.3	1.4	3.4	2.5
Manu MNCs	27770	27330	440	26.3	26.3	26.3	56.4	46.3	50.9
USA MNCs	17063	10620	6443	16.2	10.2	13.2	34.6	18.0	25.6
ROW MNCs	11467	17468	-6001	10.9	16.8	13.8	23.3	29.6	26.7
Whole MNCs	19378	26919	-7542	18.4	25.9	22.1	39.3	45.6	42.8
USA MNCs	12395	2328	10067	11.8	2.2	7.0	25.2	3.9	13.6
ROW MNCs	7408	24819	-17411	7.0	23.9	15.4	15.0	42.1	29.8
Other MNCs	937	1363	-426	0.9	1.3	1.1	1.9	2.3	2.1
USA MNCs	472	328	144	0.4	0.3	0.4	1.0	0.6	0.7
ROW MNCs	501	1136	-635	0.5	1.1	0.8	1.0	1.9	1.5
Intrafirm Related Trade									
Total	105472	103828	1644	100.0	100.0	100.0	NA	NA	NA
Non-MNCs	70183	52516	17667	66.5	50.6	58.6	NA	NA	NA
All MNCs	35289	51312	-16023	33.5	49.4	41.4	100.0	100.0	100.0
USA MNCs	27929	12212	15717	26.5	11.8	19.2	79.1	23.8	46.4
ROW MNCs	7360	39100	-31740	7.0	37.7	22.2	20.9	76.2	53.6
Petro MNCs	821	1949	-1128	0.8	1.9	1.3	2.3	3.8	3.2
USA MNCs	487	679	-192	0.5	0.7	0.6	1.4	1.3	1.3
ROW MNCs	334	1270	-936	0.3	1.2	0.8	0.9	2.5	1.9
Manu MNCs	19295	22972	-3677	18.3	22.1	20.2	54.7	44.8	48.8
USA MNCs	15256	9300	5956	14.5	9.0	11.7	43.2	18.1	28.4
ROW MNCs	4039	13672	-9633	3.8	13.2	8.5	11.4	26.6	20.5
Whole MNCs	14636	25610	-10974	13.9	24.7	19.2	41.5	49.9	46.5
USA MNCs	11862	2143	9719	11.2	2.1	6.7	33.6	4.2	16.2
ROW MNCs	2774	23467	-20693	2.6	22.6	12.5	7.9	45.7	30.3
Other MNCs	537	781	-244	0.5	0.8	0.6	1.5	1.5	1.5
USA MNCs	324	90	234	0.3	0.1	0.2	0.9	0.2	0.5
ROW MNCs	213	691	-478	0.2	0.7	0.4	0.6	1.3	1.0

was dominated by U.S.-based firms. The industry trade balance was a surplus of $3,876 million, compared to a total merchandise surplus of $11,261 million.

By 1982, industry trade had increased 124% to $22,492 million. This figure represented a 19.2% share of total trade (up 0.7 share points), and a 33.9% share of MNC-related trade (up 2.5 share points). The industry category ranked second, behind wholesale affiliates. The trade balance was a surplus of

$4,217 million (up $341 million), compared to a total merchandise surplus of $10,251 million (down $1,010 million).

Industry related trade increased by 145% to $55,100 million in 1989. This figure represented a 26.3% share of total trade (up 7.1 share points), and a 50.9% share of MNC-related trade (up 17.0 share points). The industry category now ranked first, ahead of wholesaling, and was now more evenly divided between U.S.-based and ROW-based firms. The trade balance was a surplus of $440 million (down $3,777 million), compared to a total merchandise surplus of $1,644 million (down $8,607 million).

Wholesale Trade Affiliates

Affiliate related trade was $18,733 million in 1975, adjusted for the affiliate trade overlap. This figure represented a 34.6% share of total trade and a 58.7% share of MNC-related trade. The industry category ranked first and was dominated by ROW-based firms. The industry trade balance was a surplus of $3,598 million, compared to a total merchandise surplus of $11,261 million.

By 1982, industry trade had increased 102% to $37,868 million. This figure represented a 32.3% share of total trade (down 2.2 share points), and a 57.0% share of MNC-related trade (down 1.6 share points). The industry category ranked first, ahead of manufacturing affiliates. The trade balance was a surplus of $1,409 million (down $2,188 million), compared to a total merchandise surplus of $10,251 million (down $1,010 million).

Industry related trade increased by 22% to $46,297 million in 1989. This figure represented a 22.1% share of total trade (down 10.2 share points), and a 42.8% share of MNC-related trade (down 14.3 share points). The industry category now ranked second, behind manufacturing, and was still dominated by ROW-based firms. The trade balance was a deficit of $7,542 million (a swing of $8,951 million), compared to a total merchandise surplus of $1,644 million (down $8,607 million).

Other Industry Affiliates

Affiliate related trade was $846 million in 1975, adjusted for the affiliate trade overlap. This figure represented a 1.6% share of total trade and a 2.6% share of MNC-related trade. The industry category ranked last and was dominated by ROW-based firms. The industry trade balance was a surplus of $325 million, compared to a total merchandise surplus of $11,261 million.

By 1982, industry trade had increased 126% to $1,907 million. This figure represented a 1.6% share of total trade (unchanged from 1975), and a 2.9% share of MNC-related trade (up 0.2 share points). The industry category ranked last, behind wholesale, manufacturing, and petroleum affiliates. The trade balance was a surplus of $234 million (down $91 million), compared to a total merchandise surplus of $10,251 million (down $1,010 million).

Table 9.4: Ultimate Beneficial Owners and U.S.-European Trade in 1975

	MERCHANDISE TRADE (Millions of Dollars)			TOTAL TRADE (Percent Share)			ALL MNCs TRADE (Percent Share)		
	EXPORTS	IMPORTS	BALANCE	EXP	IMP	AVG	EXP	IMP	AVG
Affiliate Related Trade									
Total	32727	21466	11261	100.0	100.0	100.0	NA	NA	NA
Non-MNCs	13207	9066	4141	40.4	42.2	41.1	NA	NA	NA
All MNCs	19521	12401	7120	59.6	57.8	58.9	100.0	100.0	100.0
USA MNCs	11344	3768	7576	34.7	17.6	27.9	58.1	30.4	47.3
ROW MNCs	9001	9171	-170	27.5	42.7	33.5	46.1	74.0	56.9
CANADA	170	360	-190	0.5	1.7	1.0	0.9	2.9	1.7
EUROPE	5568	7461	-1893	17.0	34.8	24.0	28.5	60.2	40.8
JAPAN	1990	187	1803	6.1	0.9	4.0	10.2	1.5	6.8
OTHER	1273	1163	110	3.9	5.4	4.5	6.5	9.4	7.6
Intrafirm Related Trade									
Total	32727	21466	11261	100.0	100.0	100.0	NA	NA	NA
Non-MNCs	18615	11250	7365	56.9	52.4	55.1	NA	NA	NA
All MNCs	14112	10216	3896	43.1	47.6	44.9	100.0	100.0	100.0
USA MNCs	9695	2691	7004	29.6	12.5	22.9	68.7	26.3	50.9
ROW MNCs	4417	7525	-3108	13.5	35.1	22.0	31.3	73.7	49.1
CANADA	90	260	-170	0.3	1.2	0.6	0.6	2.5	1.4
EUROPE	2102	6239	-4137	6.4	29.1	15.4	14.9	61.1	34.3
JAPAN	1721	19	1702	5.3	0.1	3.2	12.2	0.2	7.2
OTHER	504	1007	-503	1.5	4.7	2.8	3.6	9.9	6.2

Industry related trade increased by 21% to $2,300 million in 1989. This figure represented a 1.1% share of total trade (down 0.5 share points), and a 2.1% share of MNC-related trade (down 0.7 share points). The industry category still ranked last, and continued to be dominated by ROW-based firms. The trade balance was a deficit of $426 million (a swing of $659 million), compared to a total merchandise surplus of $1,644 million (down $8,607 million).

THE TRADE ROLE OF ULTIMATE BENEFICIAL OWNERS

This section is based on the trade data shown in Tables 9.4, 9.5, and 9.6 for 1975, 1982, and 1989 respectively. In the tables, four groups of Ultimate Beneficial Owners or "UBOs" are shown for ROW MNCs -- Canada, Europe, Japan, and Other Areas. U.S.-based MNCs are also a UBO group, and for analytical purposes, Non-MNC firms are treated as a UBO group. The trade role of UBOs in MNC-related trade is discussed for both affiliate related trade and intrafirm related trade.

Table 9.5: Ultimate Beneficial Owners and U.S.-European Trade in 1982

	MERCHANDISE TRADE (Millions of Dollars)			TOTAL TRADE (Percent Share)			ALL MNCs TRADE (Percent Share)		
	EXPORTS	IMPORTS	BALANCE	EXP	IMP	AVG	EXP	IMP	AVG
Affiliate Related Trade									
Total	63664	53413	10251	100.0	100.0	100.0	NA	NA	NA
Non-MNCs	28569	22117	6452	44.9	41.4	43.3	NA	NA	NA
All MNCs	35095	31296	3799	55.1	58.6	56.7	100.0	100.0	100.0
USA MNCs	18091	6112	11979	28.4	11.4	20.7	51.5	19.5	36.5
ROW MNCs	18258	26170	-7912	28.7	49.0	37.9	52.0	83.6	66.9
CANADA	1156	684	472	1.8	1.3	1.6	3.3	2.2	2.8
EUROPE	13006	17906	-4900	20.4	33.5	26.4	37.1	57.2	46.6
JAPAN	2409	3087	-678	3.8	5.8	4.7	6.9	9.9	8.3
OTHER	1687	4493	-2806	2.6	8.4	5.3	4.8	14.4	9.3
Intrafirm Related Trade									
Total	63664	53413	10251	100.0	100.0	100.0	NA	NA	NA
Non-MNCs	42322	32559	9763	66.5	61.0	64.0	NA	NA	NA
All MNCs	21342	20854	488	33.5	39.0	36.0	100.0	100.0	100.0
USA MNCs	15583	4140	11443	24.5	7.8	16.8	73.0	19.9	46.7
ROW MNCs	5759	16714	-10955	9.0	31.3	19.2	27.0	80.1	53.3
CANADA	85	316	-231	0.1	0.6	0.3	0.4	1.5	1.0
EUROPE	4822	15142	-10320	7.6	28.3	17.1	22.6	72.6	47.3
JAPAN	546	1094	-548	0.9	2.0	1.4	2.6	5.2	3.9
OTHER	306	162	144	0.5	0.3	0.4	1.4	0.8	1.1

Affiliate Related Trade

In 1975, trade with Europe was $54,193 million. Affiliates of multinational companies held a 58.9% share of trade with Europe (adjusted for the trade overlap). From the UBO perspective, Non-MNC firms were the dominant group with a 41.1% share, followed by U.S. MNCs at a 27.9% share. European-based companies were third with a 24.0% share.

The European trade balance in 1975 was a surplus of $11,261 million. By ranking, this reflected a U.S. MNC surplus of $7,576 million, a Non-MNC surplus of $4,141 million, a European MNC deficit of $1,893 million, and a Japanese MNC surplus of $1,803 million.

Between 1975 and 1982, European trade grew to $117,077 million. The affiliate trade position decreased 2.2 share points to a 56.7% share. From the UBO perspective, Non-MNCs rose 2.2 share points to 43.3%, European MNCs increased 2.4 share points to 26.4%, and U.S. MNCs decreased 7.2 share points to 20.7%.

The European trade balance in 1982 was a surplus of $10,251 million, a decrease of $1,010 million. By ranking, this reflected a U.S. MNC surplus of

Table 9.6: Ultimate Beneficial Owners and
U.S.-European Trade in 1989

	MERCHANDISE TRADE (Millions of Dollars)			TOTAL TRADE (Percent Share)			ALL MNCs TRADE (Percent Share)		
	EXPORTS	IMPORTS	BALANCE	EXP	IMP	AVG	EXP	IMP	AVG
Affiliate Related Trade									
Total	105472	103828	1644	100.0	100.0	100.0	NA	NA	NA
Non-MNCs	56211	44852	11359	53.3	43.2	48.3	NA	NA	NA
All MNCs	49261	58976	-9715	46.7	56.8	51.7	100.0	100.0	100.0
USA MNCs	30435	14878	15557	28.9	14.3	21.6	61.8	25.2	41.9
ROW MNCs	20079	45431	-25352	19.0	43.8	31.3	40.8	77.0	60.5
CANADA	1885	1419	466	1.8	1.4	1.6	3.8	2.4	3.1
EUROPE	11983	37725	-25742	11.4	36.3	23.7	24.3	64.0	45.9
JAPAN	4750	3688	1062	4.5	3.6	4.0	9.6	6.3	7.8
OTHER	1461	2599	-1138	1.4	2.5	1.9	3.0	4.4	3.8
Intrafirm Related Trade									
Total	105472	103828	1644	100.0	100.0	100.0	NA	NA	NA
Non-MNCs	70183	52516	17667	66.5	50.6	58.6	NA	NA	NA
All MNCs	35289	51312	-16023	33.5	49.4	41.4	100.0	100.0	100.0
USA MNCs	27929	12212	15717	26.5	11.8	19.2	79.1	23.8	46.4
ROW MNCs	7360	39100	-31740	7.0	37.7	22.2	20.9	76.2	53.6
CANADA	200	806	-606	0.2	0.8	0.5	0.6	1.6	1.2
EUROPE	4932	33389	-28457	4.7	32.2	18.3	14.0	65.1	44.3
JAPAN	1810	3094	-1284	1.7	3.0	2.3	5.1	6.0	5.7
OTHER	418	1811	-1393	0.4	1.7	1.1	1.2	3.5	2.6

$11,979 million (up $4,403 million), a Non-MNC surplus of $6,452 million (up $2,311 million), and a European MNC deficit of $4,900 million (up $3,007 million).

Between 1982 and 1989, European trade increased to $209,300 million. The affiliate trade position decreased 5.0 share points to a 51.7% share. From the UBO perspective, Non-MNCs rose 5.0 share points to 48.3%, European MNCs decreased 2.7 share points to 23.7%, and U.S. MNCs rose 1.0 share points to 21.6%.

The European trade balance in 1989 was a small surplus of $1,644 million, a decrease of $8,607 million. By ranking, this reflected a European MNC deficit of $25,742 million (up $20,842 million), a U.S. MNC surplus of $15,557 million (up $3,578 million), and a Non-MNC surplus of $11,359 million (up $4,907 million).

Intrafirm Related Trade

In 1975, trade with Europe was $54,193 million. Intrafirm trade by multinational companies accounted for a 44.9% share of trade with Europe.

From the UBO perspective, Non-MNC firms were the dominant group with a 55.1% share, followed by U.S. MNCs at a 22.9% share. European-based companies were third with a 15.4% share.

The European trade balance in 1975 was a surplus of $11,261 million. By ranking, this reflected a Non-MNC surplus of $7,365 million, a U.S. MNC surplus of $7,004 million, and a European MNC deficit of $4,137 million.

Between 1975 and 1982, European trade grew to $117,077 million. The intrafirm trade position decreased 8.9 share points to a 36.0% share. From the UBO perspective, Non-MNCs increased 8.9 share points to 64.0%, European MNCs increased 1.7 share points to 17.1%, and U.S. MNCs decreased 6.0 share points to 16.8%.

The European trade balance in 1982 was a surplus of $10,251 million, a decrease of $1,010 million. By ranking, this reflected a U.S. MNC surplus of $11,443 million (up $4,439 million), a European MNC deficit of $10,320 million (up $6,183 million), and a Non-MNC surplus of $9,763 million (up $2,398 million).

Between 1982 and 1989, European trade increased to $209,300 million. The intrafirm trade position increased 5.3 share points to a 41.4% share. From the UBO perspective, Non-MNCs fell 5.3 share points to 58.6%, U.S. MNCs rose 2.3 share points to 19.2%, and European MNCs increased 1.3 share points to 18.3%.

The European trade balance in 1989 was a surplus of $1,644 million, a decrease of $8,607 million. By ranking, this reflected a European MNC deficit of $28,457 million (up $18,137 million), a Non-MNC surplus of $17,667 million (up $7,904 million), and a U.S. MNC surplus of $15,717 million (up $4,274 million).

DERIVATION OF THE DATA

The derivation of the MNC-related geographic trade data is discussed at length in Chapter 7 on "Total Geographic Trade."

CHAPTER 10

TRADE WITH JAPAN

Trade with Japan includes one-eighth of total merchandise trade. Multinational companies, for practical purposes, are U.S.-Japanese trade. MNC affiliate trade accounts for a 94% share of total trade and MNC intrafirm trade has a 72% share. The equivalent figures for Total Geographic trade are 54% and 39%. Wholesale affiliates are the dominant industry group, accounting for over three-fourths of total trade.

DEFINITION OF TRADE WITH JAPAN

Trade with Japan consists of movements of merchandise between the United States and Japan. The two nations are separated by the Pacific Ocean. Subsequently, most trade with Japan is waterborne trade.

TRENDS IN TRADE WITH JAPAN

In 1975, total trade with Japan was $20,831 million. Exports were $9,563 million and imports were $11,268 million, yielding a deficit of $1,705 million. In 1982, total trade reached a level of $58,710 million, an increase of 182% or $37,879 million. Both exports and imports enjoyed robust growth over the period, but with imports growing nearly twice as fast. As a result, the trade deficit increased by $15,073 million to reach $16,778 by 1982.

Between 1982 and 1989, the growth in trade with Japan declined slightly. Total trade grew 148% or $79,370 million to reach $138,080 million. Imports continued to exceed export growth, but only by a factor of one-fourth. Nevertheless, the trade deficit increased by $32,314 million, to reach $49,092 million by 1989.

THE TRADE ROLE OF MULTINATIONAL COMPANIES

This section is based on the trade data shown in Tables 10.1, 10.2, and 10.3 for 1975, 1982, and 1989 respectively. The overall trade role of multinational companies ("All MNCs" in the tables) is discussed for both affiliate related trade and intrafirm related trade.

Affiliate Related Trade

Trade with Japan totaled $20,831 million in 1975. Adjusted for the trade overlap, affiliate related trade was $19,927 million for a 95.7% share; Non-MNC trade was $905 million for a 4.3% share. The MNC-related trade position reflected a 97.1% share of export trade and a 94.4% share of import trade. The dominant MNC group was ROW-based firms with a 88.3% share of total trade; U.S.-based firms held only a 7.9% share. ROW multinational companies had a much larger share of exports and imports.

The Japanese trade balance in 1975 was a modest deficit of $1,705 million. This reflected a $1,347 million deficit in MNC-related trade and a $359 million deficit in Non-MNC trade. Thus the overall trade position with Japan was due to both components. In turn, the MNC-related deficit was based on a deficit position of ROW-based multinationals which offset a deficit position of U.S.-based firms.

Between 1975 and 1982, Japanese trade grew 182% or $37,879 million to reach $58,710 million. In comparison, affiliate related trade increased $35,277 million or 177% to a level of $55,203 million (adjusted for the trade overlap). Accordingly, the overall affiliate position decreased slightly from a 95.7% to a 94.0% share and Non-MNC trade rose to a 6.0% share. Within the affiliate trade structure, the export share fell to 96.3% and the import share to 92.8%. These changes reflected a decline in the ROW MNC shares which offset a rise in U.S. MNC shares.

The Japanese trade deficit in 1982 was $16,778 million, an increase of $15,073 million from 1975. The affiliate trade deficit had risen to $14,819 million, a change of $13,473 million; the Non-MNC trade deficit had increased $1,601 million to $1,959 million. Thus the change in the Japanese trade balance was due to unfavorable trends in both components. The growth in the MNC-related deficit was caused by a larger deficit in ROW MNC trade, and a conversion of the U.S. MNC trade to a deficit position.

In the 1982 to 1989 period, trade with Japan grew 135% or $79,370 million to reach $138,080 million. In comparison, affiliate related trade rose $70,820 million or 128% to a level of $126,023 million (adjusted for the trade overlap). As a result, the overall affiliate position decreased from a 94.0% to a 91.3% share and Non-MNC trade rose to a 8.7% share. Within the affiliate trade structure the export share decreased to 94.7% and the import share to 89.6%. These changes reflected a decrease in the trade shares of the ROW MNCs which

Table 10.1: Multinational Companies and
U.S.-Japanese Trade in 1975

	MERCHANDISE TRADE (Millions of Dollars)			TOTAL TRADE (Percent Share)			ALL MNCs TRADE (Percent Share)		
	EXPORTS	IMPORTS	BALANCE	EXP	IMP	AVG	EXP	IMP	AVG
Affiliate Related Trade									
Total	9563	11268	-1705	100.0	100.0	100.0	NA	NA	NA
Non-MNCs	273	632	-359	2.9	5.6	4.3	NA	NA	NA
All MNCs	9290	10637	-1347	97.1	94.4	95.7	100.0	100.0	100.0
USA MNCs	966	678	288	10.1	6.0	7.9	10.4	6.4	8.3
ROW MNCs	8352	10035	-1683	87.3	89.1	88.3	89.9	94.3	92.3
Petro MNCs	883	979	-97	9.2	8.7	8.9	9.5	9.2	9.3
USA MNCs	15	67	-52	0.2	0.6	0.4	0.2	0.6	0.4
ROW MNCs	869	919	-50	9.1	8.2	8.6	9.4	8.6	9.0
Manu MNCs	635	534	100	6.6	4.7	5.6	6.8	5.0	5.9
USA MNCs	479	358	121	5.0	3.2	4.0	5.2	3.4	4.2
ROW MNCs	157	181	-24	1.6	1.6	1.6	1.7	1.7	1.7
Whole MNCs	7492	8894	-1402	78.3	78.9	78.7	80.6	83.6	82.2
USA MNCs	446	101	345	4.7	0.9	2.6	4.8	0.9	2.7
ROW MNCs	7070	8856	-1786	73.9	78.6	76.5	76.1	83.3	79.9
Other MNCs	281	229	52	2.9	2.0	2.4	3.0	2.2	2.6
USA MNCs	26	152	-126	0.3	1.3	0.9	0.3	1.4	0.9
ROW MNCs	256	79	177	2.7	0.7	1.6	2.8	0.7	1.7
Intrafirm Related Trade									
Total	9563	11268	-1705	100.0	100.0	100.0	NA	NA	NA
Non-MNCs	2752	2814	-62	28.8	25.0	26.7	NA	NA	NA
All MNCs	6811	8454	-1643	71.2	75.0	73.3	100.0	100.0	100.0
USA MNCs	910	525	385	9.5	4.7	6.9	13.4	6.2	9.4
ROW MNCs	5901	7929	-2028	61.7	70.4	66.4	86.6	93.8	90.6
Petro MNCs	753	785	-32	7.9	7.0	7.4	11.1	9.3	10.1
USA MNCs	15	15	0	0.2	0.1	0.1	0.2	0.2	0.2
ROW MNCs	738	770	-32	7.7	6.8	7.2	10.8	9.1	9.9
Manu MNCs	538	406	132	5.6	3.6	4.5	7.9	4.8	6.2
USA MNCs	444	314	130	4.6	2.8	3.6	6.5	3.7	5.0
ROW MNCs	94	92	2	1.0	0.8	0.9	1.4	1.1	1.2
Whole MNCs	5358	7097	-1739	56.0	63.0	59.8	78.7	83.9	81.6
USA MNCs	431	85	346	4.5	0.8	2.5	6.3	1.0	3.4
ROW MNCs	4927	7012	-2085	51.5	62.2	57.3	72.3	82.9	78.2
Other MNCs	162	166	-4	1.7	1.5	1.6	2.4	2.0	2.1
USA MNCs	20	111	-91	0.2	1.0	0.6	0.3	1.3	0.9
ROW MNCs	142	55	87	1.5	0.5	0.9	2.1	0.7	1.3

offset an increase in the trade shares of U.S. MNCs. Compared to 1975, the U.S. MNC share of total trade had risen from 7.9% to 14.1%; the ROW MNC share had fallen from 88.3% to 79.4%.

The Japanese trade deficit in 1989 ballooned to $49,092 million, a jump of $32,314 million above 1982. The affiliate trade deficit was $41,739 million, an increase of $26,920 million. The Non-MNC trade deficit had risen $5,395 million to $7,354 million. Thus the deterioration in the Japanese trade balance reflected trends in both components. The MNC-related deficit was rooted in growing trade deficits of U.S. and ROW MNCs.

Intrafirm Related Trade

Japanese trade totaled $20,831 million in 1975. Intrafirm related trade was $15,265 million for a 73.3% share (compared to a 95.7% share for affiliate related trade). Arms-length or Non-MNC trade was $5,566 million for a 26.7% share. The MNC-related trade position reflected a 71.2% share of export trade and a 75.0% share of import trade. The dominant MNC group was ROW-based firms with a 66.4% share of total trade; U.S.-based firms held a mere 6.9% share. ROW multinationals had the much larger share of exports and imports.

The Japanese trade balance in 1975 was a deficit of $1,705 million. This reflected a $1,643 million deficit in MNC-related trade and a small $62 million deficit in Non-MNC trade. The balance in Japanese trade was due to MNC-related trade. In turn, the MNC-related deficit was linked to a deficit in ROW MNC trade which offset a surplus in U.S. MNC trade.

Between 1975 and 1982, Japanese trade grew $37,879 million or 182% to reach $58,710 million. In comparison, intrafirm related trade increased $27,945 million or 183% to a level of $43,210 million. Accordingly, the overall intrafirm position changed very little, going from 73.3% to a 73.6% share (compared to a 95.7% to 94.0% share change for affiliate related trade). The Non-MNC trade component was a 26.4% share. Within the intrafirm trade structure, the export share rose to 72.6% and the import share decreased to 74.1%. The export change reflected a higher share of U.S.-based MNCs; the import change was due to a decrease in the share of ROW-based MNCs which was only partially offset by an increase in the U.S. MNC share.

The Japanese trade deficit in 1982 had grown to $16,778 million, a change of $15,073 million. The intrafirm related trade deficit reached $12,748 million, a rise of $11,105 million; the Non-MNC trade deficit had increased $3,968 million to $4,030 million. Thus the decline in the Japanese trade balance resulted from adverse trends in both trade components. The MNC-related balance was due to higher deficits in both MNC groups.

In the 1982 to 1989 period, trade with Japan grew $79,370 million or 135% to $138,080 million. In comparison, intrafirm related trade increased $53,205 million or 123% to a level of $96,415 million. As a result, the overall intrafirm position fell from a 73.6% to a 69.8% share (compared to a 94.0% to 91.3% share change for affiliate related trade). The Non-MNC trade component rose to a 30.2% share. Within the intrafirm trade structure, the export share fell to 62.1% and the import share to 73.5%. The drop in export share reflected a large decrease in the share of ROW MNCs which offset an increase in the U.S. MNC share. The small import change was due to a decline in the trade share of the U.S. MNCs. Compared to 1975, the U.S. MNC share of total trade had

Table 10.2: Multinational Companies and U.S.-Japanese Trade in 1982

	MERCHANDISE TRADE (Millions of Dollars)			TOTAL TRADE (Percent Share)			ALL MNCs TRADE (Percent Share)		
	EXPORTS	IMPORTS	BALANCE	EXP	IMP	AVG	EXP	IMP	AVG
Affiliate Related Trade									
Total	20966	37744	-16778	100.0	100.0	100.0	NA	NA	NA
Non-MNCs	774	2733	-1959	3.7	7.2	6.0	NA	NA	NA
All MNCs	20192	35011	-14819	96.3	92.8	94.0	100.0	100.0	100.0
USA MNCs	2516	3934	-1418	12.0	10.4	11.0	12.5	11.2	11.7
ROW MNCs	17770	31642	-13872	84.8	83.8	84.2	88.0	90.4	89.5
Petro MNCs	214	198	16	1.0	0.5	0.7	1.1	0.6	0.7
USA MNCs	104	144	-40	0.5	0.4	0.4	0.5	0.4	0.4
ROW MNCs	113	56	57	0.5	0.1	0.3	0.6	0.2	0.3
Manu MNCs	2212	4304	-2091	10.6	11.4	11.1	11.0	12.3	11.8
USA MNCs	1150	3288	-2138	5.5	8.7	7.6	5.7	9.4	8.0
ROW MNCs	1074	1141	-67	5.1	3.0	3.8	5.3	3.3	4.0
Whole MNCs	17421	30218	-12798	83.1	80.1	81.1	86.3	86.3	86.3
USA MNCs	1253	502	751	6.0	1.3	3.0	6.2	1.4	3.2
ROW MNCs	16243	30140	-13897	77.5	79.9	79.0	80.4	86.1	84.0
Other MNCs	345	291	54	1.6	0.8	1.1	1.7	0.8	1.2
USA MNCs	9	0	9	0.0	0.0	0.0	0.0	0.0	0.0
ROW MNCs	340	305	35	1.6	0.8	1.1	1.7	0.9	1.2
Intrafirm Related Trade									
Total	20966	37744	-16778	100.0	100.0	100.0	NA	NA	NA
Non-MNCs	5735	9765	-4030	27.4	25.9	26.4	NA	NA	NA
All MNCs	15231	27979	-12748	72.6	74.1	73.6	100.0	100.0	100.0
USA MNCs	2328	2804	-476	11.1	7.4	8.7	15.3	10.0	11.9
ROW MNCs	12903	25175	-12272	61.5	66.7	64.9	84.7	90.0	88.1
Petro MNCs	82	174	-92	0.4	0.5	0.4	0.5	0.6	0.6
USA MNCs	53	143	-90	0.3	0.4	0.3	0.3	0.5	0.5
ROW MNCs	29	31	-2	0.1	0.1	0.1	0.2	0.1	0.1
Manu MNCs	1587	2743	-1156	7.6	7.3	7.4	10.4	9.8	10.0
USA MNCs	1085	2162	-1077	5.2	5.7	5.5	7.1	7.7	7.5
ROW MNCs	502	581	-79	2.4	1.5	1.8	3.3	2.1	2.5
Whole MNCs	13437	24942	-11505	64.1	66.1	65.4	88.2	89.1	88.8
USA MNCs	1185	499	686	5.7	1.3	2.9	7.8	1.8	3.9
ROW MNCs	12252	24443	-12191	58.4	64.8	62.5	80.4	87.4	84.9
Other MNCs	125	120	5	0.6	0.3	0.4	0.8	0.4	0.6
USA MNCs	5	0	5	0.0	0.0	0.0	0.0	0.0	0.0
ROW MNCs	120	120	0	0.6	0.3	0.4	0.8	0.4	0.6

risen from 6.9% to 9.7%; the ROW MNC share fell from 66.4% to 60.1%.

The Japanese trade deficit in 1989 was $49,092 million, some $32,314 million above 1982. The intrafirm trade deficit was $41,111 million, an increase of $28,363 million; the Non-MNC trade deficit had risen $3,951 million to a level of $7,981 million. Thus the deterioration in the Japanese trade balance was due to unfavorable trends in both trade components. The MNC-

trade components. The larger MNC-related trade deficit was based on a growing deficit in ROW MNC trade.

INDUSTRY TRADE ROLES

This section is based on the trade data shown in Tables 10.1, 10.2, and 10.3 for 1975, 1982, and 1989, respectively. The trade role of each affiliate industry group is discussed on the basis of affiliate related trade.

Petroleum Affiliates

Affiliate related trade was $1,862 million in 1975, adjusted for the affiliate trade overlap. This figure represented a 8.9% share of total trade and a 9.3% share of MNC-related trade. The industry category ranked second and was dominated by ROW-based firms. The industry trade balance was a deficit of $97 million, compared to a total merchandise deficit of $1,705 million.

By 1982, industry trade had decreased 78% to $413 million. This figure represented a 0.7% share of total trade (down 8.2 share points), and a 0.7% share of MNC-related trade (down 8.6 share points). The industry category now ranked last, behind wholesale, manufacturing, and other industry affiliates. The trade balance was a surplus of $16 million (a swing of $113 million), compared to a total merchandise deficit of $16,778 million (up 15,073 million).

Industry related trade decreased by 22% to $322 million in 1989. This figure represented a 0.2% share of total trade (down 0.5 share points), and a 0.3% share of MNC-related trade (down 0.5 share points). The industry category still ranked last, and continued to be dominated by ROW-based firms. The trade balance was a surplus of $51 million (up $35 million), compared to a total merchandise deficit of $49,092 million (up $32,314 million).

Manufacturing Affiliates

Affiliate related trade was $1,169 million in 1975, adjusted for the affiliate trade overlap. This figure represented a 5.6% share of total trade and a 5.9% share of MNC-related trade. The industry category ranked third and was dominated by U.S.-based firms. The industry trade balance was a surplus of $100 million, compared to a total merchandise deficit of $1,705 million.

By 1982, industry trade had increased 458% to $6,516 million. This figure represented a 11.1% share of total trade (up 5.5 share points), and a 11.8% share of MNC-related trade (up 5.9 share points). The industry category now ranked second, behind wholesale affiliates. The trade balance was a deficit of $2,091 million (a swing of $2,192 million), compared to a total merchandise deficit of $16,778 million (up 15,073 million).

Industry related trade increased by 269% to $24,060 million in 1989. This

Table 10.3: Multinational Companies and U.S.-Japanese Trade in 1989

	MERCHANDISE TRADE (Millions of Dollars)			TOTAL TRADE (Percent Share)			ALL MNCs TRADE (Percent Share)		
	EXPORTS	IMPORTS	BALANCE	EXP	IMP	AVG	EXP	IMP	AVG
Affiliate Related Trade									
Total	44494	93586	-49092	100.0	100.0	100.0	NA	NA	NA
Non-MNCs	2352	9706	-7354	5.3	10.4	8.7	NA	NA	NA
All MNCs	42142	83881	-41739	94.7	89.6	91.3	100.0	100.0	100.0
USA MNCs	8395	11116	-2721	18.9	11.9	14.1	19.9	13.3	15.5
ROW MNCs	33988	75590	-41602	76.4	80.8	79.4	80.7	90.1	87.0
Petro MNCs	187	136	51	0.4	0.1	0.2	0.4	0.2	0.3
USA MNCs	72	10	62	0.2	0.0	0.1	0.2	0.0	0.1
ROW MNCs	117	137	-20	0.3	0.1	0.2	0.3	0.2	0.2
Manu MNCs	7281	16778	-9497	16.4	17.9	17.4	17.3	20.0	19.1
USA MNCs	3384	10286	-6902	7.6	11.0	9.9	8.0	12.3	10.8
ROW MNCs	3947	7626	-3679	8.9	8.1	8.4	9.4	9.1	9.2
Whole MNCs	33370	66805	-33436	75.0	71.4	72.5	79.2	79.6	79.5
USA MNCs	4873	818	4055	11.0	0.9	4.1	11.6	1.0	4.5
ROW MNCs	28666	67661	-38995	64.4	72.3	69.8	68.0	80.7	76.4
Other MNCs	1304	161	1143	2.9	0.2	1.1	3.1	0.2	1.2
USA MNCs	66	2	64	0.1	0.0	0.0	0.2	0.0	0.1
ROW MNCs	1258	166	1092	2.8	0.2	1.0	3.0	0.2	1.1
Intrafirm Related Trade									
Total	44494	93586	-49092	100.0	100.0	100.0	NA	NA	NA
Non-MNCs	16842	24823	-7981	37.9	26.5	30.2	NA	NA	NA
All MNCs	27652	68763	-41111	62.1	73.5	69.8	100.0	100.0	100.0
USA MNCs	7913	5465	2448	17.8	5.8	9.7	28.6	7.9	13.9
ROW MNCs	19739	63298	-43559	44.4	67.6	60.1	71.4	92.1	86.1
Petro MNCs	63	74	-11	0.1	0.1	0.1	0.2	0.1	0.1
USA MNCs	40	6	34	0.1	0.0	0.0	0.1	0.0	0.0
ROW MNCs	23	68	-45	0.1	0.1	0.1	0.1	0.1	0.1
Manu MNCs	4304	10713	-6409	9.7	11.4	10.9	15.6	15.6	15.6
USA MNCs	3114	4875	-1761	7.0	5.2	5.8	11.3	7.1	8.3
ROW MNCs	1190	5838	-4648	2.7	6.2	5.1	4.3	8.5	7.3
Whole MNCs	23181	57851	-34670	52.1	61.8	58.7	83.8	84.1	84.0
USA MNCs	4717	583	4134	10.6	0.6	3.8	17.1	0.8	5.5
ROW MNCs	18464	57268	-38804	41.5	61.2	54.8	66.8	83.3	78.5
Other MNCs	104	125	-21	0.2	0.1	0.2	0.4	0.2	0.2
USA MNCs	42	1	41	0.1	0.0	0.0	0.2	0.0	0.0
ROW MNCs	62	124	-62	0.1	0.1	0.1	0.2	0.2	0.2

figure represented a 17.4% share of total trade (up 6.3 share points), and a 19.1% share of MNC-related trade (up 7.3 share points). The industry category ranked second, and was more evenly divided between U.S.-based and ROW-based firms. The trade balance was a deficit of $9,497 million (up $7,405 million), compared to the deficit in total merchandise trade of $49,092 million (up $32,314 million).

Wholesale Trade Affiliates

Affiliate related trade was $16,386 million in 1975, adjusted for the affiliate trade overlap. This figure represented a 78.7% share of total trade and a 82.2% share of MNC-related trade. The industry category ranked first and was completely dominated by ROW-based firms. The industry trade balance was a deficit of $1,402 million, compared to a total merchandise deficit of $1,705 million.

By 1982, industry trade had increased 190% to $47,639 million. This figure represented a 81.1% share of total trade (up 2.5 share points), and a 86.3% share of MNC-related trade (up 4.1 share points). The industry category ranked first, ahead of manufacturing affiliates. The trade balance was a deficit of $12,798 million (up $11,395 million), compared to a total merchandise deficit of $16,778 million (up 15,073 million).

Industry related trade increased by 110% to $100,175 million in 1989, adjusted for the affiliate trade overlap. This figure represented a 72.5% share of total trade (down 8.6 share points), and a 79.5% share of MNC-related trade (down 6.8 share points). The industry category still ranked first, and remained dominated by ROW-based firms. The trade balance was a deficit of $33,436 million (up $20,638 million), compared to a total merchandise deficit of $49,092 million (up $32,314 million).

Other Industry Affiliates

Affiliate related trade was $509 million in 1975, adjusted for the affiliate trade overlap. This figure represented a 2.4% share of total trade and a 2.6% share of MNC-related trade. The industry category ranked last and was dominated by ROW-based firms. The industry trade balance was a small surplus of $52 million, compared to the total merchandise balance which was in deficit by $1,705 million.

By 1982, industry trade had increased 25% to $636 million. This figure represented a 1.1% share of total trade (down 1.4 share points), and a 1.2% share of MNC-related trade (down 1.4 share points). The industry category now ranked third, ahead of petroleum affiliates and behind wholesale and manufacturing affiliates. The trade balance remained in a surplus of $54 million (up $2 million), in contrast to the total merchandise deficit of $16,778 million (up $15,073 million).

Industry related trade increased by 130% to $1,465 million in 1989, adjusted for the affiliate trade overlap. This figure represented a 1.1% share of total trade (unchanged from 1982), and a 1.2% share of MNC-related trade (also unchanged). The industry category ranked third, and remained dominated by ROW-based firms. The trade balance surplus reached $1,143 million (up $1,089 million), compared to a total merchandise deficit of $49,092 million (up $32,314 million).

Table 10.4: Ultimate Beneficial Owners and
U.S.-Japanese Trade in 1975

	MERCHANDISE TRADE (Millions of Dollars)			TOTAL TRADE (Percent Share)			ALL MNCs TRADE (Percent Share)		
	EXPORTS	IMPORTS	BALANCE	EXP	IMP	AVG	EXP	IMP	AVG
Affiliate Related Trade									
Total	9563	11268	-1705	100.0	100.0	100.0	NA	NA	NA
Non-MNCs	273	632	-359	2.9	5.6	4.3	NA	NA	NA
All MNCs	9290	10637	-1347	97.1	94.4	95.7	100.0	100.0	100.0
USA MNCs	966	678	288	10.1	6.0	7.9	10.4	6.4	8.3
ROW MNCs	8352	10035	-1683	87.3	89.1	88.3	89.9	94.3	92.3
CANADA	23	41	-18	0.2	0.4	0.3	0.2	0.4	0.3
EUROPE	514	406	108	5.4	3.6	4.4	5.5	3.8	4.6
JAPAN	7431	9529	-2098	77.7	84.6	81.4	80.0	89.6	85.1
OTHER	384	59	325	4.0	0.5	2.1	4.1	0.6	2.2
Intrafirm Related Trade									
Total	9563	11268	-1705	100.0	100.0	100.0	NA	NA	NA
Non-MNCs	2752	2814	-62	28.8	25.0	26.7	NA	NA	NA
All MNCs	6811	8454	-1643	71.2	75.0	73.3	100.0	100.0	100.0
USA MNCs	910	525	385	9.5	4.7	6.9	13.4	6.2	9.4
ROW MNCs	5901	7929	-2028	61.7	70.4	66.4	86.6	93.8	90.6
CANADA	12	4	8	0.1	0.0	0.1	0.2	0.0	0.1
EUROPE	84	11	73	0.9	0.1	0.5	1.2	0.1	0.6
JAPAN	5589	7879	-2290	58.4	69.9	64.7	82.1	93.2	88.2
OTHER	216	35	181	2.3	0.3	1.2	3.2	0.4	1.6

THE TRADE ROLE OF ULTIMATE BENEFICIAL OWNERS

This section is based on the trade data shown in Tables 10.4, 10.5, and 10.6 for 1975, 1982, and 1989, respectively. In the tables, four groups of Ultimate Beneficial Owners or "UBOs" are shown for ROW MNCs -- Canada, Europe, Japan, and Other Areas. U.S.-based MNCs are also a UBO group, and for analytical purposes, Non-MNC firms are treated as a UBO group. The trade role of UBOs in MNC-related trade is discussed for both affiliate related trade and intrafirm related trade.

Affiliate Related Trade

In 1975, trade with Japan was $20,831 million. Affiliates of multinational companies held a 95.7% share of trade with Japan (adjusted for the trade overlap). From the UBO perspective, Japanese-based firms were the dominant group with a 81.4% share, followed by U.S. MNCs at a 7.9% share. European MNCs held a 4.4% share and Non-MNCs a 4.3% share.

Table 10.5: Ultimate Beneficial Owners and U.S.-Japanese Trade in 1982

	MERCHANDISE TRADE (Millions of Dollars)			TOTAL TRADE (Percent Share)			ALL MNCs TRADE (Percent Share)		
	EXPORTS	IMPORTS	BALANCE	EXP	IMP	AVG	EXP	IMP	AVG
Affiliate Related Trade									
Total	20966	37744	-16778	100.0	100.0	100.0	NA	NA	NA
Non-MNCs	774	2733	-1959	3.7	7.2	6.0	NA	NA	NA
All MNCs	20192	35011	-14819	96.3	92.8	94.0	100.0	100.0	100.0
USA MNCs	2516	3934	-1418	12.0	10.4	11.0	12.5	11.2	11.7
ROW MNCs	17770	31642	-13872	84.8	83.8	84.2	88.0	90.4	89.5
CANADA	74	379	-305	0.4	1.0	0.8	0.4	1.1	0.8
EUROPE	2171	1071	1100	10.4	2.8	5.5	10.8	3.1	5.9
JAPAN	14062	29156	-15094	67.1	77.2	73.6	69.6	83.3	78.3
OTHER	1463	1036	427	7.0	2.7	4.3	7.2	3.0	4.5
Intrafirm Related Trade									
Total	20966	37744	-16778	100.0	100.0	100.0	NA	NA	NA
Non-MNCs	5735	9765	-4030	27.4	25.9	26.4	NA	NA	NA
All MNCs	15231	27979	-12748	72.6	74.1	73.6	100.0	100.0	100.0
USA MNCs	2328	2804	-476	11.1	7.4	8.7	15.3	10.0	11.9
ROW MNCs	12903	25175	-12272	61.5	66.7	64.9	84.7	90.0	88.1
CANADA	1	5	-4	0.0	0.0	0.0	0.0	0.0	0.0
EUROPE	222	538	-316	1.1	1.4	1.3	1.5	1.9	1.8
JAPAN	12649	24361	-11712	60.3	64.5	63.0	83.0	87.1	85.7
OTHER	31	271	-240	0.1	0.7	0.5	0.2	1.0	0.7

The Japanese trade balance in 1975 was a modest deficit of $1,705 million. By ranking, this reflected a Japanese MNC deficit of $2,098 million, a Non-MNC deficit of $359 million, a Other Area MNC surplus of $325 million, and a U.S. MNC surplus of $288 million.

Between 1975 and 1982, Japanese trade grew to $58,710 million. The affiliate trade position decreased 1.6 share points to a 94.0% share. From the UBO perspective, Japanese MNCs fell 7.8 share points to 73.6%, U.S. MNCs rose 3.1 share points to 11.0%, Non-MNCs increased 1.6 share points to 6.0%, and European MNCs were up 1.1 share points to 5.5%.

The Japanese trade balance in 1982 was a deficit of $16,778 million, a jump of $15,073 million. By ranking, this reflected a Japanese MNC deficit of $15,094 million (up $12,996 million), a Non-MNC deficit of $1,959 million (up $1,601 million), and a U.S. MNC deficit of $1,418 million (up $1,706 million).

Between 1982 and 1989, Japanese trade increased to $138,080 million. The affiliate trade position decreased 2.8 share points to a 91.3% share. From the UBO perspective, Japanese MNCs fell 7.4 share points to 66.2%, U.S. MNCs rose 3.1 share points to 14.1%, European MNCs increased 3.7 share points to 9.2%, and Non-MNCs rose 2.8 share points to 8.7%.

Table 10.6: Ultimate Beneficial Owners and
U.S.-Japanese Trade in 1989

	MERCHANDISE TRADE (Millions of Dollars)			TOTAL TRADE (Percent Share)			ALL MNCs TRADE (Percent Share)		
	EXPORTS	IMPORTS	BALANCE	EXP	IMP	AVG	EXP	IMP	AVG
Affiliate Related Trade									
Total	44494	93586	-49092	100.0	100.0	100.0	NA	NA	NA
Non-MNCs	2352	9706	-7354	5.3	10.4	8.7	NA	NA	NA
All MNCs	42142	83881	-41739	94.7	89.6	91.3	100.0	100.0	100.0
USA MNCs	8395	11116	-2721	18.9	11.9	14.1	19.9	13.3	15.5
ROW MNCs	33988	75590	-41602	76.4	80.8	79.4	80.7	90.1	87.0
CANADA	877	788	89	2.0	0.8	1.2	2.1	0.9	1.3
EUROPE	9510	3220	6290	21.4	3.4	9.2	22.6	3.8	10.1
JAPAN	21136	70249	-49113	47.5	75.1	66.2	50.2	83.7	72.5
OTHER	2465	1333	1132	5.5	1.4	2.8	5.8	1.6	3.0
Intrafirm Related Trade									
Total	44494	93586	-49092	100.0	100.0	100.0	NA	NA	NA
Non-MNCs	16842	24823	-7981	37.9	26.5	30.2	NA	NA	NA
All MNCs	27652	68763	-41111	62.1	73.5	69.8	100.0	100.0	100.0
USA MNCs	7913	5465	2448	17.8	5.8	9.7	28.6	7.9	13.9
ROW MNCs	19739	63298	-43559	44.4	67.6	60.1	71.4	92.1	86.1
CANADA	386	273	113	0.9	0.3	0.5	1.4	0.4	0.7
EUROPE	3274	672	2602	7.4	0.7	2.9	11.8	1.0	4.1
JAPAN	15123	61584	-46461	34.0	65.8	55.6	54.7	89.6	79.6
OTHER	956	769	187	2.1	0.8	1.2	3.5	1.1	1.8

The Japanese trade balance in 1989 was a deficit of $49,092 million, an increase of $32,314 million. By ranking, this reflected a Japanese MNC deficit of $49,113 million (up $34,019 million), a Non-MNC deficit of $7,354 million (up $5,395 million), a European MNC surplus of $6,290 million (up $5,190 million), and a U.S. MNC deficit of $2,721 million (up $1,303 million).

Intrafirm Related Trade

In 1975, trade with Japan was $20,831 million. Intrafirm trade by multinational companies accounted for a 73.3% share of trade with Japan. From the UBO perspective, Japanese-based firms were the dominant group with a 64.7% share, followed by Non-MNCs at a 26.7% share. U.S. MNCs were third with a 6.9% share.

The Japanese trade balance in 1975 was a modest deficit of $1,705 million. By ranking, this reflected a Japanese MNC deficit of $2,290 million and a U.S. MNC surplus of $385 million.

Between 1975 and 1982, Japanese trade grew to $58,710 million. The intrafirm trade position increased 0.3 share points to a 73.6% share. From the

UBO perspective, Japanese MNCs fell 1.6 share points to 63.0%, Non-MNCs declined 0.3 share points to 26.4%, and U.S. MNCs increased 1.9 share points to 8.7%.

The Japanese trade balance in 1982 was a deficit of $16,778 million, a jump of $15,073 million. By ranking, this reflected a Japanese MNC deficit of $11,712 million (up $9,422 million), a Non-MNC deficit of $4,030 million (up $3,968 million), and a U.S. MNC deficit of $476 million (a swing of $861 million).

Between 1982 and 1989, Japanese trade increased to $138,080 million. The intrafirm trade position decreased 3.8 share points to a 69.8% share. From the UBO perspective, Japanese MNCs fell 7.5 share points to 55.6%, Non-MNCs rose 3.8 share points to 30.2%, and U.S. MNCs rose 0.9 share points to 9.7%.

The Japanese trade balance in 1989 was a deficit of $49,092 million, an increase of $32,314 million. By ranking, this reflected a Japanese MNC deficit of $46,461 million (up $34,749 million), a Non-MNC deficit of $7,981 million (up $3,951 million), a European MNC surplus of $2,602 million (a swing of $2,918 million), and a U.S. MNC surplus of $2,448 million (a swing of $2,924 million).

DERIVATION OF THE DATA

The derivation of the MNC-related geographic trade data is discussed at length in Chapter 7 on "Total Geographic Trade."

CHAPTER 11

TRADE WITH OTHER AREAS

Trade with Other Areas includes two-fifths of total merchandise trade. Multinational companies are least important in U.S.-Other Areas trade. MNC affiliate trade accounts for a 37% share of total trade and MNC intrafirm trade has a 22% share. The equivalent figures for Total Geographic trade are 54% and 39%. Wholesale and manufacturing affiliates are the dominant industry groups.

DEFINITION OF TRADE WITH OTHER AREAS

Trade with Other Areas consists of movements of merchandise between the United States and Other Areas. The two areas are mostly separated by water. Subsequently, most trade with Other Areas is waterborne trade.

Other Areas is the remainder of the world not covered in the preceding geographic trade chapters on Canada, Europe, and Japan. Other Areas consists of the Less Developed Countries, the former Soviet Bloc (including China), and Australia and New Zealand. Most trade in the Other Areas category is trade with the Third World.

TRENDS IN TRADE WITH OTHER AREAS

In 1975, total trade with Other Areas was $86,105 million. Exports were $44,016 million and imports were $42,089 million, yielding a surplus of $1,927 million. In 1982, total trade reached a level of $200,243 million, an increase of 133% or $114,138 million. Both exports and imports enjoyed strong growth over the period, but with imports growing slightly faster. This imbalance converted the trade balance to a deficit of $12,393 by 1982. The deterioration in the trade balance was $14,320 million.

Between 1982 and 1989, the growth in trade with Other Areas slowed markedly. Total trade grew 61% or $122,638 million to reach $322,881 million. Imports continued to outpace export growth. As a result, the trade deficit increased by $40,414 million to a level of $52,807 in 1989.

THE TRADE ROLE OF MULTINATIONAL COMPANIES

This section is based on the trade data shown in Tables 11.1, 11.2, and 11.3 for 1975, 1982, and 1989 respectively. The overall trade role of multinational companies ("All MNCs" in the tables) is discussed for both affiliate related trade and intrafirm related trade.

Affiliate Related Trade

Trade with Other Areas totaled $86,105 million in 1975. Adjusted for the trade overlap, affiliate related trade was $34,161 million for a 39.7% share; Non-MNC trade was $51,944 million for a 60.3% share. The MNC-related trade position reflected a 36.7% share of export trade and a 42.8% share of import trade. The dominant MNC group was U.S.-based firms with a 24.4% share of total trade; ROW-based firms held a 17.3% share. U.S. multinational companies had the larger share of exports and imports.

The Other Areas trade balance in 1975 was a modest surplus of $1,927 million. This reflected a $1,867 million deficit in MNC-related trade and a $3,794 million surplus in Non-MNC trade. Thus the overall trade surplus position with Other Areas was due to Non-MNC trade. The MNC-related deficit was based on a deficit position of U.S.-based multinationals which offset a surplus position of ROW-based firms.

Between 1975 and 1982, Other Areas trade grew 133% or $114,138 million to reach $200,243 million. In comparison, affiliate related trade increased $38,361 million or 112% to a level of $72,522 million (adjusted for the trade overlap). Accordingly, the overall affiliate position decreased from a 39.7% to a 36.2% share and Non-MNC trade rose to a 63.8% share. Within the affiliate trade structure, the export share rose slightly to 37.4% and the import share fell to 35.2%. The export change reflected a higher ROW MNC share which offset a decline in the U.S. MNC share. The import change was due to a drop in the U.S. MNC share.

The Other Areas trade balance in 1982 had changed into a deficit of $12,393 million, a deterioration of $14,320 million from 1975. The affiliate trade deficit was $2,308 million, a rise of only $441 million. The Non-MNC trade balance was now a deficit of $10,086 million, a swing of $13,880 million. Thus the change in the Other Areas trade balance was due to unfavorable trends in both components, especially Non-MNC trade. The MNC-related trade deficit

Table 11.1: Multinational Companies and U.S.-Other Areas Trade in 1975

	MERCHANDISE TRADE (Millions of Dollars)			TOTAL TRADE (Percent Share)			ALL MNCs TRADE (Percent Share)		
	EXPORTS	IMPORTS	BALANCE	EXP	IMP	AVG	EXP	IMP	AVG
Affiliate Related Trade									
Total	44016	42089	1927	100.0	100.0	100.0	NA	NA	NA
Non-MNCs	27869	24075	3794	63.3	57.2	60.3	NA	NA	NA
All MNCs	16147	18014	-1867	36.7	42.8	39.7	100.0	100.0	100.0
USA MNCs	9158	11830	-2672	20.8	28.1	24.4	56.7	65.7	61.4
ROW MNCs	7958	6933	1025	18.1	16.5	17.3	49.3	38.5	43.6
Petro MNCs	1914	11019	-9105	4.3	26.2	15.0	11.9	61.2	37.9
USA MNCs	1322	8608	-7286	3.0	20.5	11.5	8.2	47.8	29.1
ROW MNCs	658	2719	-2061	1.5	6.5	3.9	4.1	15.1	9.9
Manu MNCs	5966	2451	3515	13.6	5.8	9.8	36.9	13.6	24.6
USA MNCs	5379	2075	3304	12.2	4.9	8.7	33.3	11.5	21.8
ROW MNCs	763	439	324	1.7	1.0	1.4	4.7	2.4	3.5
Whole MNCs	7185	3667	3517	16.3	8.7	12.6	44.5	20.4	31.8
USA MNCs	1539	335	1204	3.5	0.8	2.2	9.5	1.9	5.5
ROW MNCs	6309	3690	2619	14.3	8.8	11.6	39.1	20.5	29.3
Other MNCs	1083	877	206	2.5	2.1	2.3	6.7	4.9	5.7
USA MNCs	918	812	106	2.1	1.9	2.0	5.7	4.5	5.1
ROW MNCs	228	85	143	0.5	0.2	0.4	1.4	0.5	0.9
Intrafirm Related Trade									
Total	44016	42089	1927	100.0	100.0	100.0	NA	NA	NA
Non-MNCs	35031	29197	5834	79.6	69.4	74.6	NA	NA	NA
All MNCs	8985	12892	-3907	20.4	30.6	25.4	100.0	100.0	100.0
USA MNCs	7220	10332	-3112	16.4	24.5	20.4	80.4	80.1	80.2
ROW MNCs	1765	2560	-795	4.0	6.1	5.0	19.6	19.9	19.8
Petro MNCs	1424	8911	-7487	3.2	21.2	12.0	15.8	69.1	47.2
USA MNCs	1083	7476	-6393	2.5	17.8	9.9	12.1	58.0	39.1
ROW MNCs	341	1435	-1094	0.8	3.4	2.1	3.8	11.1	8.1
Manu MNCs	4663	2017	2646	10.6	4.8	7.8	51.9	15.6	30.5
USA MNCs	4490	1810	2680	10.2	4.3	7.3	50.0	14.0	28.8
ROW MNCs	173	207	-34	0.4	0.5	0.4	1.9	1.6	1.7
Whole MNCs	2281	1221	1060	5.2	2.9	4.1	25.4	9.5	16.0
USA MNCs	1099	317	782	2.5	0.8	1.6	12.2	2.5	6.5
ROW MNCs	1182	904	278	2.7	2.1	2.4	13.2	7.0	9.5
Other MNCs	617	743	-126	1.4	1.8	1.6	6.9	5.8	6.2
USA MNCs	548	729	-181	1.2	1.7	1.5	6.1	5.7	5.8
ROW MNCs	69	14	55	0.2	0.0	0.1	0.8	0.1	0.4

reflected a U.S. MNC deficit which exceeded a ROW MNC surplus.

In the 1982 to 1989 period, trade with Other Areas grew 61% or $122,638 million to reach $322,881 million. In comparison, affiliate related trade rose $43,001 million or 59% to a level of $115,522 million (adjusted for the trade overlap). As a result, the overall affiliate position decreased slightly from a 36.2% to a 35.8% share and Non-MNC trade rose to a 64.2% share. Within the affiliate trade structure the export share decreased to 36.0% and the import share rose to 35.6%. The export change reflected a decline in the trade share of ROW MNCs which offset a rise in the U.S. MNC share. The import change was due to a rise in the ROW MNC share which exceeded a fall in the U.S. MNC share. Compared to 1975, the U.S. MNC share of total trade had fallen from 24.4% to 17.4%; the ROW MNC share had risen from 17.3% to 19.8%. Foreign-based firms had become the dominant MNC group in Other Areas trade.

The Other Areas trade balance in 1989 was a deficit of $52,807 million, some $40,414 million above 1982. The affiliate trade deficit was $18,309 million, an increase of $16,002 million. The Non-MNC trade deficit had risen $24,413 million to $34,498 million. Thus the deterioration in the Other Areas trade balance reflected unfavorable trends in both components. The MNC-related deficit was caused by growing trade deficits in both U.S. and ROW MNC trade.

Intrafirm Related Trade

Other Areas trade totaled $86,105 million in 1975. Intrafirm related trade was $21,877 million for a 25.4% share (compared to a 39.7% share for affiliate related trade). Arms-length or Non-MNC trade was $64,228 million for a 74.6% share. The MNC-related trade position reflected a 20.4% share of export trade and a 30.6% share of import trade. The dominant MNC group was U.S.-based firms with a 20.4% share of total trade; ROW-based firms held a 5.0% share. U.S. multinationals had the larger share of exports and imports.

The Other Areas trade balance in 1975 was a surplus of $1,927 million. This reflected a $3,907 million deficit in MNC-related trade and a $5,834 million surplus in Non-MNC trade. The favorable balance in Other Areas trade was due to Non-MNC trade. The MNC-related deficit was linked to deficit positions in both U.S. and ROW MNC trade.

Between 1975 and 1982, Other Areas trade grew $114,138 million or 133% to reach $200,243 million. In comparison, intrafirm related trade increased $18,211 million or 83% to a level of $40,088 million. Accordingly, the overall intrafirm position decreased from a 25.4% to a 20.0% share (compared to a 39.7% to 36.2% share change for affiliate related trade). The Non-MNC trade component rose to a 80.0% share. Within the intrafirm trade structure, the export share decreased slightly to 18.8%; the import share dropped to 21.1%. These changes reflected a decline in the trade shares of U.S.-based MNCs.

The Other Areas trade balance in 1982 had changed into a deficit of $12,393 million, a swing of $14,320 million from 1975. The intrafirm trade deficit had increased $857 million to $4,764 million. The Non-MNC trade balance had shifted to a deficit of $7,629 million, a decline of $13,463 million. The decline in the Other Areas trade balance resulted from adverse trends in both trade components, especially Non-MNC trade. The MNC-related deficit

Table 11.2: Multinational Companies and U.S.-Other Areas Trade in 1982

	MERCHANDISE TRADE (Millions of Dollars)			TOTAL TRADE (Percent Share)			ALL MNCs TRADE (Percent Share)		
	EXPORTS	IMPORTS	BALANCE	EXP	IMP	AVG	EXP	IMP	AVG
Affiliate Related Trade									
Total	93925	106318	-12393	100.0	100.0	100.0	NA	NA	NA
Non-MNCs	58818	68904	-10086	62.6	64.8	63.8	NA	NA	NA
All MNCs	35107	37415	-2308	37.4	35.2	36.2	100.0	100.0	100.0
USA MNCs	16606	19968	-3362	17.7	18.8	18.3	47.3	53.4	50.4
ROW MNCs	20237	18555	1682	21.5	17.5	19.4	57.6	49.6	53.5
Petro MNCs	2905	15720	-12816	3.1	14.8	9.3	8.3	42.0	25.7
USA MNCs	2333	9871	-7538	2.5	9.3	6.1	6.6	26.4	16.8
ROW MNCs	710	6259	-5549	0.8	5.9	3.5	2.0	16.7	9.6
Manu MNCs	14756	9492	5265	15.7	8.9	12.1	42.0	25.4	33.4
USA MNCs	9813	8165	1648	10.4	7.7	9.0	28.0	21.8	24.8
ROW MNCs	5530	1463	4067	5.9	1.4	3.5	15.8	3.9	9.6
Whole MNCs	15875	10731	5144	16.9	10.1	13.3	45.2	28.7	36.7
USA MNCs	3649	810	2839	3.9	0.8	2.2	10.4	2.2	6.1
ROW MNCs	13147	10440	2707	14.0	9.8	11.8	37.4	27.9	32.5
Other MNCs	1571	1471	100	1.7	1.4	1.5	4.5	3.9	4.2
USA MNCs	811	1122	-311	0.9	1.1	1.0	2.3	3.0	2.7
ROW MNCs	850	393	457	0.9	0.4	0.6	2.4	1.1	1.7
Intrafirm Related Trade									
Total	93925	106318	-12393	100.0	100.0	100.0	NA	NA	NA
Non-MNCs	76263	83892	-7629	81.2	78.9	80.0	NA	NA	NA
All MNCs	17662	22426	-4764	18.8	21.1	20.0	100.0	100.0	100.0
USA MNCs	13134	17751	-4617	14.0	16.7	15.4	74.4	79.2	77.0
ROW MNCs	4528	4675	-147	4.8	4.4	4.6	25.6	20.8	23.0
Petro MNCs	1513	10181	-8668	1.6	9.6	5.8	8.6	45.4	29.2
USA MNCs	1224	9003	-7779	1.3	8.5	5.1	6.9	40.1	25.5
ROW MNCs	289	1178	-889	0.3	1.1	0.7	1.6	5.3	3.7
Manu MNCs	8860	7649	1211	9.4	7.2	8.2	50.2	34.1	41.2
USA MNCs	8218	7194	1024	8.7	6.8	7.7	46.5	32.1	38.4
ROW MNCs	642	455	187	0.7	0.4	0.5	3.6	2.0	2.7
Whole MNCs	6619	3718	2901	7.0	3.5	5.2	37.5	16.6	25.8
USA MNCs	3268	737	2531	3.5	0.7	2.0	18.5	3.3	10.0
ROW MNCs	3351	2981	370	3.6	2.8	3.2	19.0	13.3	15.8
Other MNCs	670	878	-208	0.7	0.8	0.8	3.8	3.9	3.9
USA MNCs	424	817	-393	0.5	0.8	0.6	2.4	3.6	3.1
ROW MNCs	246	61	185	0.3	0.1	0.2	1.4	0.3	0.8

reflected a growing imbalance in U.S. MNC trade.

In the 1982 to 1989 period, Other Areas trade grew $122,638 million or 61% to $322,881 million. In comparison, intrafirm related trade increased $29,829 million or 74% to a level of $69,917 million. As a result, the overall intrafirm position increased from 20.0% to a 21.7% share (compared to a 36.2% to 35.8% share change for affiliate related trade). Non-MNC trade rose to a 78.3% share. Within the intrafirm trade structure, the export share increased slightly to 19.5% and the import share to 23.2%. The export change reflected an increase in the trade share of U.S. MNCs which offset a decline in the ROW MNC share. The import change was due to a rise in the ROW MNC share which exceeded a fall in the U.S. MNC share. Compared to 1975, the U.S. MNC share of total trade had declined from 20.4% to 14.6%; the ROW MNC share increased from 5.0% to 7.0%.

The Other Areas trade deficit in 1989 was $52,807 million, a large increase of $40,414 million over 1982. The intrafirm related trade deficit was $17,337 million, an increase of $12,573 million; the Non-MNC trade deficit had risen $27,841 million to a level of $35,470 million. Thus the deterioration in the Other Areas trade balance was due to unfavorable trends in both components. The increase in the MNC-related deficit was linked to a large deficit in ROW MNC trade.

INDUSTRY TRADE ROLES

This section is based on the trade data shown in Tables 11.1, 11.2, and 11.3 for 1975, 1982, and 1989, respectively. The trade role of each affiliate industry group is discussed on the basis of affiliate related trade.

Petroleum Affiliates

Affiliate related trade was $12,933 million in 1975, adjusted for the affiliate trade overlap. This figure represented a 15.0% share of total trade and a 37.9% share of MNC-related trade. The industry category ranked first and was dominated by U.S.-based firms, reflecting U.S. imports of petroleum from Third World sources. The industry trade balance was a deficit of $9,105 million, compared to a total merchandise surplus of $1,927 million.

By 1982, industry trade had increased 44% to $18,625 million. This figure represented a 9.3% share of total trade (down 5.7 share points), and a 25.7% share of MNC-related trade (down 12.2 share points). The petroleum affiliates category now ranked third, behind wholesale and manufacturing affiliates. The industry trade balance was a deficit of $12,816 million (up $3,711 million), compared to a total merchandise deficit of $12,393 million (a swing of $14,320 million).

Industry related trade decreased by 5.0% to $17,646 million in 1989, adjusted for the affiliate trade overlap. This figure represented a 5.5% share of total trade (down 3.8 share points), and a 15.3% share of MNC-related trade (down 10.4 share points). The industry category still ranked third, but was now dominated by ROW-based firms. The trade balance was a deficit of $12,618 million (down $198 million), compared to a total merchandise deficit in Other Areas trade of $52,807 million (up $40,414 million).

Table 11.3: Multinational Companies and U.S.-Other Areas Trade in 1989

	MERCHANDISE TRADE (Millions of Dollars)			TOTAL TRADE (Percent Share)			ALL MNCs TRADE (Percent Share)		
	EXPORTS	IMPORTS	BALANCE	EXP	IMP	AVG	EXP	IMP	AVG
Affiliate Related Trade									
Total	135037	187844	-52807	100.0	100.0	100.0	NA	NA	NA
Non-MNCs	86431	120929	-34498	64.0	64.4	64.2	NA	NA	NA
All MNCs	48607	66916	-18309	36.0	35.6	35.8	100.0	100.0	100.0
USA MNCs	25555	30535	-4980	18.9	16.3	17.4	52.6	45.6	48.6
ROW MNCs	25128	38717	-13589	18.6	20.6	19.8	51.7	57.9	55.3
Petro MNCs	2514	15132	-12618	1.9	8.1	5.5	5.2	22.6	15.3
USA MNCs	1556	4574	-3018	1.2	2.4	1.9	3.2	6.8	5.3
ROW MNCs	1064	11145	-10081	0.8	5.9	3.8	2.2	16.7	10.6
Manu MNCs	27215	28990	-1775	20.2	15.4	17.4	56.0	43.3	48.7
USA MNCs	16733	21119	-4386	12.4	11.2	11.7	34.4	31.6	32.8
ROW MNCs	11580	8592	2988	8.6	4.6	6.2	23.8	12.8	17.5
Whole MNCs	17247	20654	-3407	12.8	11.0	11.7	35.5	30.9	32.8
USA MNCs	6409	3762	2647	4.7	2.0	3.2	13.2	5.6	8.8
ROW MNCs	11635	17774	-6139	8.6	9.5	9.1	23.9	26.6	25.5
Other MNCs	1630	2140	-509	1.2	1.1	1.2	3.4	3.2	3.3
USA MNCs	857	1080	-223	0.6	0.6	0.6	1.8	1.6	1.7
ROW MNCs	849	1206	-357	0.6	0.6	0.6	1.7	1.8	1.8
Intrafirm Related Trade									
Total	135037	187844	-52807	100.0	100.0	100.0	NA	NA	NA
Non-MNCs	108747	144217	-35470	80.5	76.8	78.3	NA	NA	NA
All MNCs	26290	43627	-17337	19.5	23.2	21.7	100.0	100.0	100.0
USA MNCs	21402	25862	-4460	15.8	13.8	14.6	81.4	59.3	67.6
ROW MNCs	4888	17765	-12877	3.6	9.5	7.0	18.6	40.7	32.4
Petro MNCs	1378	9280	-7902	1.0	4.9	3.3	5.2	21.3	15.2
USA MNCs	1041	3545	-2504	0.8	1.9	1.4	4.0	8.1	6.6
ROW MNCs	337	5735	-5398	0.2	3.1	1.9	1.3	13.1	8.7
Manu MNCs	15418	21807	-6389	11.4	11.6	11.5	58.6	50.0	53.2
USA MNCs	13922	18957	-5035	10.3	10.1	10.2	53.0	43.5	47.0
ROW MNCs	1496	2850	-1354	1.1	1.5	1.3	5.7	6.5	6.2
Whole MNCs	8677	11858	-3181	6.4	6.3	6.4	33.0	27.2	29.4
USA MNCs	5820	2828	2992	4.3	1.5	2.7	22.1	6.5	12.4
ROW MNCs	2857	9030	-6173	2.1	4.8	3.7	10.9	20.7	17.0
Other MNCs	817	682	135	0.6	0.4	0.5	3.1	1.6	2.1
USA MNCs	619	532	87	0.5	0.3	0.4	2.4	1.2	1.6
ROW MNCs	198	150	48	0.1	0.1	0.1	0.8	0.3	0.5

Manufacturing Affiliates

Affiliate related trade was $8,416 million in 1975, adjusted for the affiliate trade overlap. This figure represented a 9.8% share of total trade and a 24.6% share of MNC-related trade. The industry category ranked third and was dominated by U.S.-based firms. The industry trade balance was a surplus of

$3,515 million, compared to a total merchandise surplus of $1,927 million.

By 1982, industry trade had increased 188% to $24,248 million. This figure represented a 12.1% share of total trade (up 2.3 share points), and a 33.4% share of MNC-related trade (up 8.8 share points). The industry category now ranked second, behind wholesale affiliates and ahead of petroleum affiliates. The trade balance was a surplus of $5,265 million (up $1,749 million), compared to a total merchandise deficit of $12,393 million (a swing of $14,320 million).

Industry related trade increased by 132% to $56,206 million in 1989. This figure represented a 17.4% share of total trade (up 5.3 share points), and a 48.7% share of MNC-related trade (up 15.2 share points). The industry category now ranked first, ahead of wholesale affiliates, and was still dominated by U.S.-based firms. The trade balance was a deficit of $1,775 million (a swing of $7,040 million), compared to a total merchandise deficit of $52,807 million (up $40,414 million).

Wholesale Trade Affiliates

Affiliate related trade was $10,852 million in 1975, adjusted for the affiliate trade overlap. This figure represented a 12.6% share of total trade and a 31.8% share of MNC-related trade. The industry category ranked second and was dominated by ROW-based firms. The industry trade balance was a surplus of $3,517 million, compared to a total merchandise surplus of $1,927 million.

By 1982, industry trade had increased 145% to $26,606 million. This figure represented a 13.3% share of total trade (up 0.7 share points), and a 36.7% share of MNC-related trade (up 4.9 share points). The industry category now ranked first, ahead of manufacturing and petroleum affiliates. The trade balance was a surplus of $5,144 million (up $1,626 million), compared to a total merchandise deficit of $12,393 million (a swing of $14,320 million).

Industry related trade increased by 42% to $37,900 million in 1989. This figure represented a 11.7% share of total trade (down 1.5 share points), and a 32.8% share of MNC-related trade (down 3.9 share points). The industry category now ranked second, behind manufacturing affiliates, and remained dominated by ROW-based firms. The trade balance was a deficit of $3,407 million (a swing of $8,551 million), compared to a total merchandise deficit of $52,807 million (up $40,414 million).

Other Industry Affiliates

Affiliate related trade was $1,960 million in 1975, adjusted for the affiliate trade overlap. This figure represented a 2.3% share of total trade and a 5.7% share of MNC-related trade. The industry category ranked last and was dominated by U.S.-based firms. The industry trade balance was a surplus of $206 million, compared to a total merchandise surplus of $1,927 million.

Table 11.4: Ultimate Beneficial Owners and U.S.-Other Areas Trade in 1975

	MERCHANDISE TRADE (Millions of Dollars)			TOTAL TRADE (Percent Share)			ALL MNCs TRADE (Percent Share)		
	EXPORTS	IMPORTS	BALANCE	EXP	IMP	AVG	EXP	IMP	AVG
Affiliate Related Trade									
Total	44016	42089	1927	100.0	100.0	100.0	NA	NA	NA
Non-MNCs	27869	24075	3794	63.3	57.2	60.3	NA	NA	NA
All MNCs	16147	18014	-1867	36.7	42.8	39.7	100.0	100.0	100.0
USA MNCs	9158	11830	-2672	20.8	28.1	24.4	56.7	65.7	61.4
ROW MNCs	7958	6933	1025	18.1	16.5	17.3	49.3	38.5	43.6
CANADA	136	140	-4	0.3	0.3	0.3	0.8	0.8	0.8
EUROPE	4296	4354	-58	9.8	10.3	10.0	26.6	24.2	25.3
JAPAN	2191	1391	800	5.0	3.3	4.2	13.6	7.7	10.5
OTHER	1335	1048	287	3.0	2.5	2.8	8.3	5.8	7.0
Intrafirm Related Trade									
Total	44016	42089	1927	100.0	100.0	100.0	NA	NA	NA
Non-MNCs	35031	29197	5834	79.6	69.4	74.6	NA	NA	NA
All MNCs	8985	12892	-3907	20.4	30.6	25.4	100.0	100.0	100.0
USA MNCs	7220	10332	-3112	16.4	24.5	20.4	80.4	80.1	80.2
ROW MNCs	1765	2560	-795	4.0	6.1	5.0	19.6	19.9	19.8
CANADA	24	21	3	0.1	0.0	0.1	0.3	0.2	0.2
EUROPE	829	1845	-1016	1.9	4.4	3.1	9.2	14.3	12.2
JAPAN	729	185	544	1.7	0.4	1.1	8.1	1.4	4.2
OTHER	183	509	-326	0.4	1.2	0.8	2.0	3.9	3.2

By 1982, industry trade had increased 55% to $3,042 million. This figure represented a 1.5% share of total trade (down 0.8 share points), and a 4.2% share of MNC-related trade (down 1.5 share points). The industry category ranked last, behind wholesale, manufacturing, and petroleum affiliates. The trade balance was a surplus of $100 million (down $105 million), compared to a total merchandise deficit of $12,393 million (a swing of $14,320 million).

Industry related trade increased by 24% to $3,770 million in 1989, for a 1.2% share of total trade (down 0.4 share points), and a 3.3% share of MNC-related trade (down 0.9 share points). The industry category still ranked last, but was now more evenly divided between U.S.-based and ROW-based firms. The trade balance was a deficit of $509 million (a swing of $610 million), compared to the total deficit of $52,807 million (up $40,414 million).

THE TRADE ROLE OF ULTIMATE BENEFICIAL OWNERS

This section is based on the trade data shown in Tables 11.4, 11.5, and 11.6 for 1975, 1982, and 1989, respectively. In these tables, four groups of Ultimate

Table 11.5: Ultimate Beneficial Owners and U.S.-Other Areas Trade in 1982

	MERCHANDISE TRADE (Millions of Dollars)			TOTAL TRADE (Percent Share)			ALL MNCs TRADE (Percent Share)		
	EXPORTS	IMPORTS	BALANCE	EXP	IMP	AVG	EXP	IMP	AVG
Affiliate Related Trade									
Total	93925	106318	-12393	100.0	100.0	100.0	NA	NA	NA
Non-MNCs	58818	68904	-10086	62.6	64.8	63.8	NA	NA	NA
All MNCs	35107	37415	-2308	37.4	35.2	36.2	100.0	100.0	100.0
USA MNCs	16606	19968	-3362	17.7	18.8	18.3	47.3	53.4	50.4
ROW MNCs	20237	18555	1682	21.5	17.5	19.4	57.6	49.6	53.5
CANADA	1805	300	1505	1.9	0.3	1.1	5.1	0.8	2.9
EUROPE	11362	11498	-136	12.1	10.8	11.4	32.4	30.7	31.5
JAPAN	4586	2633	1953	4.9	2.5	3.6	13.1	7.0	10.0
OTHER	2484	4124	-1640	2.6	3.9	3.3	7.1	11.0	9.1
Intrafirm Related Trade									
Total	93925	106318	-12393	100.0	100.0	100.0	NA	NA	NA
Non-MNCs	76263	83892	-7629	81.2	78.9	80.0	NA	NA	NA
All MNCs	17662	22426	-4764	18.8	21.1	20.0	100.0	100.0	100.0
USA MNCs	13134	17751	-4617	14.0	16.7	15.4	74.4	79.2	77.0
ROW MNCs	4528	4675	-147	4.8	4.4	4.6	25.6	20.8	23.0
CANADA	42	29	13	0.0	0.0	0.0	0.2	0.1	0.2
EUROPE	2670	2495	175	2.8	2.3	2.6	15.1	11.1	12.9
JAPAN	505	928	-423	0.5	0.9	0.7	2.9	4.1	3.6
OTHER	1311	1223	88	1.4	1.2	1.3	7.4	5.5	6.3

Beneficial Owners or "UBOs" are shown for ROW MNCs -- Canada, Europe, Japan, and Other Areas. U.S.-based MNCs are also a UBO group, and for analytical purposes, Non-MNC firms are treated as a UBO group. The trade role of UBOs in MNC-related trade is discussed for both affiliate related trade and intrafirm related trade.

Affiliate Related Trade

In 1975, trade with Other Areas was $86,105 million. Affiliates of multinational companies held a 39.7% share of trade with Other Areas (adjusted for the trade overlap). From the UBO perspective, Non-MNC firms were the dominant group with a 60.3% share, followed by U.S. MNCs at a 24.4% share. European MNCs held a 10.0 % share and Japanese MNCs a 4.2% share. Other Areas MNCs were fifth with a small 2.8% share.

The Other Areas trade balance in 1975 was a modest surplus of $1,927 million. By ranking, this reflected a Non-MNC surplus of $3,794 million, a U.S. MNC deficit of $2,672 million, a Japanese MNC surplus of $800 million, and a Other Areas surplus of $287 million.

Table 11.6: Ultimate Beneficial Owners and
U.S.-Other Areas Trade in 1989

	MERCHANDISE TRADE (Millions of Dollars)			TOTAL TRADE (Percent Share)			ALL MNCs TRADE (Percent Share)		
	EXPORTS	IMPORTS	BALANCE	EXP	IMP	AVG	EXP	IMP	AVG
Affiliate Related Trade									
Total	135037	187844	-52807	100.0	100.0	100.0	NA	NA	NA
Non-MNCs	86431	120929	-34498	64.0	64.4	64.2	NA	NA	NA
All MNCs	48607	66916	-18309	36.0	35.6	35.8	100.0	100.0	100.0
USA MNCs	25555	30535	-4980	18.9	16.3	17.4	52.6	45.6	48.6
ROW MNCs	25128	38717	-13589	18.6	20.6	19.8	51.7	57.9	55.3
CANADA	1654	2115	-461	1.2	1.1	1.2	3.4	3.2	3.3
EUROPE	12959	15574	-2615	9.6	8.3	8.8	26.7	23.3	24.7
JAPAN	6643	8641	-1998	4.9	4.6	4.7	13.7	12.9	13.2
OTHER	3872	12387	-8515	2.9	6.6	5.0	8.0	18.5	14.1
Intrafirm Related Trade									
Total	135037	187844	-52807	100.0	100.0	100.0	NA	NA	NA
Non-MNCs	108747	144217	-35470	80.5	76.8	78.3	NA	NA	NA
All MNCs	26290	43627	-17337	19.5	23.2	21.7	100.0	100.0	100.0
USA MNCs	21402	25862	-4460	15.8	13.8	14.6	81.4	59.3	67.6
ROW MNCs	4888	17765	-12877	3.6	9.5	7.0	18.6	40.7	32.4
CANADA	99	388	-289	0.1	0.2	0.2	0.4	0.9	0.7
EUROPE	1489	3817	-2328	1.1	2.0	1.6	5.7	8.7	7.6
JAPAN	1383	4604	-3221	1.0	2.5	1.9	5.3	10.6	8.6
OTHER	1917	8956	-7039	1.4	4.8	3.4	7.3	20.5	15.6

Between 1975 and 1982, Other Areas trade grew to $200,243 million. The affiliate trade position decreased 3.5 share points to a 36.2% share. From the UBO perspective, Non-MNCs rose 3.5 share points to 63.8%, U.S. MNCs fell 6.1 share points to 18.3%, European MNCs increased 1.4 share points to 11.4%, Japanese MNCs declined 0.6 share points to 3.6%, and Other Areas MNCs increased 0.5 share points to 3.3%.

The Other Areas trade balance in 1982 was a deficit of $12,393 million, a swing of $14,320 million. This reflected a Non-MNC deficit of $10,086 million (a swing of $13,880 million), a U.S. MNC deficit of $3,362 million (up $690 million), a Japanese MNC surplus of $1,953 million (up $1,153 million), and a Other Areas MNC deficit of $1,640 million (a swing of $1,927 million).

Between 1982 and 1989, Other Areas trade increased to $322,881 million. The affiliate trade position decreased 0.4 share points to a 35.8% share. From the UBO perspective, Non-MNCs rose 0.4 share points to 64.2%, U.S. MNCs fell 0.9 share points to 17.4%, and European MNCs declined 2.6 share points to 8.8%. Other Areas MNCs increased 1.7 share points to 5.0%, passing Japanese MNCs which rose 1.1 share points to 4.7%.

The Other Areas trade balance in 1989 was a large deficit of $52,807 million, an increase of $40,414 million. By ranking, this reflected a Non-MNC deficit of $34,498 million (up $24,413 million), a Other Areas MNC deficit of $8,515 million (up $6,875 million), and a U.S. MNC deficit of $4,980 million (up $1,618 million).

Intrafirm Related Trade

In 1975, trade with Other Areas was $86,105 million. Intrafirm trade by multinational companies accounted for a 25.4% share of trade with Other Areas. From the UBO perspective, Non-MNC firms were the dominant group with a 74.6% share, followed by U.S. MNCs at a 20.4% share. European MNCs held a 3.1% share and Japanese MNCs a 1.1% share. Other Areas-based companies were fifth with only a 0.8% share.

The Other Areas trade balance in 1975 was a modest surplus of $1,927 million. This reflected a Non-MNC surplus of $5,834 million, a U.S. MNC deficit of $3,112 million, a European MNC deficit of $1,016 million, a Japanese MNC surplus of $544 million, and a Other Areas deficit of $326 million.

Between 1975 and 1982, Other Areas trade grew to $200,243 million. The intrafirm trade position decreased 5.4 share points to a 20.0% share. From the UBO perspective, Non-MNCs increased 5.4 share points to 80.0%, U.S. MNCs fell 5.0 share points to 15.4%, European MNCs decreased 0.5 share points to 2.6%, and Other Areas MNCs increased 0.5 share points to 1.3%.

The Other Areas trade balance in 1982 was a deficit of $12,393 million, a swing of $14,320 million. This reflected a Non-MNC deficit of $7,629 million (a swing of $13,463 million), a U.S. MNC deficit of $4,617 million (up $1,505 million), a Japanese MNC deficit of $423 million (a swing of $967 million), a European MNC surplus of $175 million (a swing of $1,191 million), and a Other Areas MNC surplus of $88 million (a swing of $414 million).

Between 1982 and 1989, Other Areas trade increased to $322,881 million. The intrafirm trade position increased 1.6 share points to a 21.7% share. Non-MNCs fell 1.6 share points to 78.3%, U.S. MNCs declined 0.8 share points to 14.6%, and Other Areas MNCs increased 2.1 share points to 3.4%.

The Other Areas trade balance in 1989 was a deficit of $52,807 million, an increase of $40,414 million. By ranking, this reflected a Non-MNC deficit of $35,470 million (up $27,841 million), a Other Areas MNC deficit of $7,039 million (a swing of $7,127 million), and a U.S. MNC deficit of $4,460 million (down $157 million).

DERIVATION OF THE DATA

The derivation of the MNC-related geographic trade data is discussed at length in Chapter 7 on "Total Geographic Trade."

PART IV

PRODUCT PATTERNS OF MNC-RELATED TRADE

CHAPTER 12

TOTAL PRODUCT TRADE

Total Product trade provides the third overview of the trade role of multinational companies. From this perspective, MNC affiliate trade accounts for a 54% share of total trade, and MNC intrafirm trade has a 39% share. Wholesale affiliates are the dominant industry group, followed by manufacturing affiliates.

DEFINITION OF TOTAL PRODUCT TRADE

Total Product trade, along with Total Merchandise trade and Total Geographic trade, provide three different perspectives on the role of multinational companies in total trade. Total Product trade is an aggregate of twelve individual categories of product trade.

For its trade categories, the Bureau of Economic Analysis employs product groups based on the Standard International Trade Classification (SITC) system [BEA 1990 21-24]. The twelve BEA product groups are inclusive, thus Total Product trade consists of all SITC 0-9 categories.

Food (Raw and Prepared) and Live Animals Chiefly for Food
(SITC code 0)

Beverages and Tobacco
(SITC code 1)

Crude Materials, Inedible, Except Fuels
(SITC code 2)

Petroleum and Products, Mineral Waxes, Natural and Manufactured Gas
(SITC codes 33-34)

Coal, Coke, and Briquets
(SITC code 32)

Animal and Vegetable Oils, Fats, and Waxes, and Commodities N.E.C.
(SITC codes 4 and 9)

Chemicals and Related Products
(SITC code 5)

Machinery, Electrical and Nonelectrical, except Transportation Equipment
(SITC codes 71-77)

Road Vehicles (Including Air Cushion Vehicles) and Parts
(SITC code 78)

Other Transport Equipment
(SITC code 79)

Metal Manufactures
(SITC codes 67-69)

Other Manufactures
(SITC codes 61-66, and 8)

The twelve BEA product groups serve as the basis for the product trade chapters in Part IV of the book "Product Patterns of MNC-Related Trade." These chapters provide the core of the analysis of MNC-related trade from the perspective of product categories. Each chapter includes a detailed listing of the items that constitute the BEA product group, and shows the affiliate and intrafirm related trade for the three comparison years of 1975, 1982, and 1989.

This chapter on "Total Product Trade" summarizes the MNC-related trade which is covered in the individual product chapters. The trade data shown in the following tables represents the aggregate dollar value of all the product categories combined.

Further, these product categories can be combined into Non-Manufactured Goods trade and Manufactured Goods trade. These two trade aggregate chapters are placed at the front of the related group of product trade chapters.

TRENDS IN TOTAL PRODUCT TRADE

In 1975, Total Product trade was $205,824 million. Exports were $109,254 million and imports were $96,570 million yielding a surplus of $12,684 million. Between 1975 and 1982, total trade increased 124% or $254,570 million to reach $460,394 million. Both exports and imports enjoyed strong growth, but with imports growing one-third faster. This growth imbalance converted the modest 1975 trade surplus into a 1982 deficit of $27,510 million. The total swing in the trade balance was 317% or a decline of $40,194 million.

Between 1982 and 1989, the growth rates slowed in Total Product trade. Total trade grew 82% or $376,629 million to reach $837,023 million. Imports still continued to grow one-third faster than exports. This resulted in another 298% deterioration in the trade balance of $81,889 million, pushing the deficit to $109,399 million by 1989.

THE TRADE ROLE OF MULTINATIONAL COMPANIES

This section is based on the trade data shown in Tables 12.1, 12.2, and 12.3 for 1975, 1982, and 1989, respectively. The overall trade role of multinational companies ("All MNCs" in the tables) is discussed for both affiliate related trade and intrafirm related trade.

The affiliate related data for Total Product trade are different from Total Merchandise and Total Geographic trade data due to differing estimates of the affiliate trade overlap. The intrafirm trade data are identical in all three instances.

Affiliate Related Trade

Total Product trade totaled $205,824 million in 1975. Adjusted for the trade overlap, affiliate related trade was $114,964 million for a 55.9% share; Non-MNC trade was $90,860 million for a 44.1% share. The MNC-related trade position reflected a 55.4% share of export trade and a 56.4% share of import trade. The dominant MNC group was U.S.-based firms with a 30.8% share of total trade; ROW-based firms held a 27.1% share. U.S. multinational companies had a larger share of exports; ROW MNCs held the larger share of imports.

The Total Product trade balance in 1975 was a surplus of $12,684 million. This reflected a $6,041 million surplus in MNC-related trade and a $6,643 million surplus in Non-MNC trade. Thus the overall trade surplus position in Total Product was due to both components. In turn, the MNC-related surplus was based on a surplus position of U.S.-based multinationals which offset a small deficit position of ROW-based firms.

Between 1975 and 1982, Total Product trade grew 124% or $254,570 million to reach $460,394 million. In comparison, affiliate related trade increased $128,340 million or 112% to a level of $243,304 million (adjusted for the trade overlap). Accordingly, the overall affiliate position decreased slightly from a 55.9% to a 52.8% share and Non-MNC trade rose to a 47.2% share. Within the affiliate trade structure, the export share fell to 51.9% and the import share to 53.7%. These changes reflected a decline in the U.S. MNC shares which offset a rise in ROW MNC shares.

The Total Product trade balance in 1982 had changed to a deficit of $27,510 million, a $40,194 deterioration from 1975. The affiliate related trade position had changed into a deficit of $18,480 million, a swing of $24,521 million; the Non-MNC trade balance had also become a deficit of $9,030 million, a change of $15,673 million. Thus the deterioration in the Total Product trade balance was due to unfavorable trends in both components. The conversion of MNC-related trade into a deficit was caused by the growing deficit position of ROW multinationals, linked to a decline in the size of the U.S. MNC surplus.

In the 1982 to 1989 period, Total Product trade grew 82% or $376,629 million to $837,023 million. In comparison, affiliate related trade rose $200,044 million or 82% to a level of $443,348 million (adjusted for the trade overlap). The overall affiliate position was little changed, increasing from a 52.8% share to a 53.0% share; Non-MNC trade had a 47.0% share. Within the affiliate trade structure the export share decreased to 50.4% and the import share increased to 54.9%. The export change reflected a decline in the trade share of ROW MNCs which offset an increased share of U.S. MNCs. The import change was due to a higher trade share of ROW MNCs which offset a lower U.S. MNC share. Compared to 1975, the U.S. MNC share of total trade had fallen from 30.8% to 23.9%; the ROW MNC share had risen from 27.1% to 30.8%. ROW-based firms had supplanted U.S.-based firms as the dominant MNC group in Total Product trade.

The Total Product trade deficit in 1989 was $109,399 million, a rise of $81,889 million over 1982. The affiliate related trade deficit was $76,459 million, an increase of $57,979 million; the Non-MNC trade deficit was $32,940 million, an increase of $23,910 million. Thus the deterioration in the Total Product trade balance reflected trends in both components. The MNC-related deficit was based on the growing trade deficit of ROW MNCs which had reached $85,531 million.

Intrafirm Related Trade

Total Product trade totaled $205,824 million in 1975. Intrafirm related trade was $83,571 million for a 40.6% share (compared to a 54.7% share for affiliate related trade). Arms-length or Non-MNC trade was $122,253 million for a 59.4% share. The MNC-related trade position reflected a 38.0% share of export trade and a 43.5% share of import trade. The dominant MNC group was U.S.-based firms with a 24.3% share while ROW-based firms held a 16.3% share. U.S. multinationals had the larger share of exports and imports.

The Total Product trade balance in 1975 was a surplus of $12,684 million. This reflected a $439 million deficit in MNC-related trade and a $13,123 million surplus in Non-MNC trade. Thus the trade surplus was due to Non-MNC trade. The MNC-related deficit was linked to a deficit in ROW MNC trade which offset a surplus in U.S. MNC trade.

Table 12.1: Multinational Companies and U.S. Total Product Trade (SITC 0-9) in 1975

	MERCHANDISE TRADE (Millions of Dollars)			TOTAL TRADE (Percent Share)			ALL MNCs TRADE (Percent Share)		
	EXPORTS	IMPORTS	BALANCE	EXP	IMP	AVG	EXP	IMP	AVG
Affiliate Related Trade									
Total	109254	96570	12684	100.0	100.0	100.0	NA	NA	NA
Non-MNCs	48752	42109	6643	44.6	43.6	44.1	NA	NA	NA
All MNCs	60503	54462	6041	55.4	56.4	55.9	100.0	100.0	100.0
USA MNCs	36181	27153	9028	33.1	28.1	30.8	59.8	49.9	55.1
ROW MNCs	26433	29367	-2934	24.2	30.4	27.1	43.7	53.9	48.5
Petro MNCs	4000	15384	-11384	3.7	15.9	9.4	6.6	28.2	16.9
USA MNCs	1805	11660	-9855	1.7	12.1	6.5	3.0	21.4	11.7
ROW MNCs	2321	4417	-2096	2.1	4.6	3.3	3.8	8.1	5.9
Manu MNCs	26407	15187	11220	24.2	15.7	20.2	43.6	27.9	36.2
USA MNCs	24984	12823	12161	22.9	13.3	18.4	41.3	23.5	32.9
ROW MNCs	2217	2947	-730	2.0	3.1	2.5	3.7	5.4	4.5
Whole MNCs	27771	21984	5788	25.4	22.8	24.2	45.9	40.4	43.3
USA MNCs	7808	1166	6642	7.1	1.2	4.4	12.9	2.1	7.8
ROW MNCs	20978	21514	-536	19.2	22.3	20.6	34.7	39.5	37.0
Other MNCs	2324	1907	417	2.1	2.0	2.1	3.8	3.5	3.7
USA MNCs	1584	1504	80	1.4	1.6	1.5	2.6	2.8	2.7
ROW MNCs	917	489	428	0.8	0.5	0.7	1.5	0.9	1.2
Intrafirm Related Trade									
Total	109254	96570	12684	100.0	100.0	100.0	NA	NA	NA
Non-MNCs	67688	54565	13123	62.0	56.5	59.4	NA	NA	NA
All MNCs	41566	42005	-439	38.0	43.5	40.6	100.0	100.0	100.0
USA MNCs	28739	21342	7397	26.3	22.1	24.3	69.1	50.8	59.9
ROW MNCs	12827	20663	-7836	11.7	21.4	16.3	30.9	49.2	40.1
Petro MNCs	3299	11770	-8471	3.0	12.2	7.3	7.9	28.0	18.0
USA MNCs	1473	9020	-7547	1.3	9.3	5.1	3.5	21.5	12.6
ROW MNCs	1826	2750	-924	1.7	2.8	2.2	4.4	6.5	5.5
Manu MNCs	20448	12433	8015	18.7	12.9	16.0	49.2	29.6	39.3
USA MNCs	19647	10247	9400	18.0	10.6	14.5	47.3	24.4	35.8
ROW MNCs	801	2186	-1385	0.7	2.3	1.5	1.9	5.2	3.6
Whole MNCs	16513	16377	136	15.1	17.0	16.0	39.7	39.0	39.4
USA MNCs	6669	896	5773	6.1	0.9	3.7	16.0	2.1	9.1
ROW MNCs	9844	15481	-5637	9.0	16.0	12.3	23.7	36.9	30.3
Other MNCs	1306	1425	-119	1.2	1.5	1.3	3.1	3.4	3.3
USA MNCs	950	1179	-229	0.9	1.2	1.0	2.3	2.8	2.5
ROW MNCs	356	246	110	0.3	0.3	0.3	0.9	0.6	0.7

Between 1975 and 1982, Total Product trade grew $254,570 million or 124% to reach $460,394 million. In comparison, intrafirm related trade increased $81,525 million or 98% to a level of $165,096 million. Accordingly, the overall intrafirm position decreased from a 40.6% to a 35.9% share (compared to a 54.7% to 52.7% share change for affiliate related trade). Non-MNC trade rose to a 64.1% share. Within the intrafirm trade structure, the export share dropped to 33.1% and the import share to 38.3%. These changes reflected a decline in the shares of U.S.-based MNCs; the shares of ROW-based MNCs were largely unchanged.

The Total Product trade balance in 1982 had changed to a deficit of $27,510 million, a deterioration of $40,194 million from 1975. The intrafirm related trade deficit had increased $21,491 to a level of $21,930 million. The Non-MNC trade surplus had become a deficit of $5,580 million, a decline of $18,703 million. Thus the decline in the Total Product trade balance resulted from unfavorable trends in both components. The MNC-related deficit emerged due to a growing deficit in ROW MNC trade and a shrinking surplus in U.S. MNC trade.

In the 1982 to 1989 period, Total Product trade grew $376,629 million or 82% to $837,023 million. In comparison, intrafirm related trade increased $165,952 million or 101% to a level of $331,048 million. As a result, the overall intrafirm position increased from a 35.9% to a 39.6% share (compared to a 52.7% to 52.8% share change for affiliate related trade). Non-MNC trade fell to a 60.4% share. Within the intrafirm trade structure, the export share rose slightly to 34.0% and the import share pushed up to 43.8%. The export change reflected an increase in the trade share of U.S. MNCs which offset a decline in the ROW MNC share. The import change was due to a jump in the trade share of ROW MNCs. Compared to 1975, the U.S. MNC share of total trade had fallen from 24.3% to 19.9%; the ROW MNC share had risen from 16.3% to 19.6%. U.S.-based firms remained the dominant MNC group by a mere 0.3% share.

The Total Product trade deficit in 1989 had increased to $109,399 million, a deterioration of $81,889 million from 1982. The intrafirm related trade deficit was $83,418 million, an increase of $61,488 million; the Non-MNC trade deficit had risen $20,401 million to reach $25,981 million. Thus the growth in the Total Product trade deficit was due to unfavorable trends in both components, especially in MNC-related trade. The MNC-related deficit was based on the ballooning ROW MNC deficit which had reached $95,650 million.

INDUSTRY TRADE ROLES

This section is based on the trade data shown in Tables 12.1, 12.2, and 12.3 for 1975, 1982, and 1989, respectively. The trade role of each affiliate industry group is discussed on the basis of affiliate related trade.

Petroleum Affiliates

Affiliate related trade was $19,385 million in 1975, adjusted for the affiliate trade overlap. This figure represented a 9.4% share of total trade and a 16.9% share of MNC-related trade. Overall, the industry category ranked third and was

Table 12.2: Multinational Companies and U.S. Total Product Trade (SITC 0-9) in 1982

	MERCHANDISE TRADE (Millions of Dollars)			TOTAL TRADE (Percent Share)			ALL MNCs TRADE (Percent Share)		
	EXPORTS	IMPORTS	BALANCE	EXP	IMP	AVG	EXP	IMP	AVG
Affiliate Related Trade									
Total	216442	243952	-27510	100.0	100.0	100.0	NA	NA	NA
Non-MNCs	104030	113060	-9030	48.1	46.3	47.2	NA	NA	NA
All MNCs	112412	130892	-18480	51.9	53.7	52.8	100.0	100.0	100.0
USA MNCs	56718	51406	5312	26.2	21.1	23.5	50.5	39.3	44.4
ROW MNCs	60236	84290	-24054	27.8	34.6	31.4	53.6	64.4	59.4
Petro MNCs	4556	22878	-18322	2.1	9.4	6.0	4.1	17.5	11.3
USA MNCs	3304	15771	-12467	1.5	6.5	4.1	2.9	12.0	7.8
ROW MNCs	1531	8486	-6955	0.7	3.5	2.2	1.4	6.5	4.1
Manu MNCs	47495	42118	5377	21.9	17.3	19.5	42.3	32.2	36.8
USA MNCs	37180	31107	6073	17.2	12.8	14.8	33.1	23.8	28.1
ROW MNCs	12883	12386	497	6.0	5.1	5.5	11.5	9.5	10.4
Whole MNCs	56707	62515	-5808	26.2	25.6	25.9	50.4	47.8	49.0
USA MNCs	14866	2706	12160	6.9	1.1	3.8	13.2	2.1	7.2
ROW MNCs	43336	61679	-18343	20.0	25.3	22.8	38.6	47.1	43.2
Other MNCs	3654	3381	272	1.7	1.4	1.5	3.3	2.6	2.9
USA MNCs	1368	1822	-454	0.6	0.7	0.7	1.2	1.4	1.3
ROW MNCs	2486	1739	747	1.1	0.7	0.9	2.2	1.3	1.7
Intrafirm Related Trade									
Total	216442	243952	-27510	100.0	100.0	100.0	NA	NA	NA
Non-MNCs	144859	150439	-5580	66.9	61.7	64.1	NA	NA	NA
All MNCs	71583	93513	-21930	33.1	38.3	35.9	100.0	100.0	100.0
USA MNCs	46559	41598	4961	21.5	17.1	19.1	65.0	44.5	53.4
ROW MNCs	25024	51915	-26891	11.6	21.3	16.7	35.0	55.5	46.6
Petro MNCs	2585	15243	-12658	1.2	6.2	3.9	3.6	16.3	10.8
USA MNCs	1915	12646	-10731	0.9	5.2	3.2	2.7	13.5	8.8
ROW MNCs	670	2597	-1927	0.3	1.1	0.7	0.9	2.8	2.0
Manu MNCs	33462	33128	334	15.5	13.6	14.5	46.7	35.4	40.3
USA MNCs	30350	25448	4902	14.0	10.4	12.1	42.4	27.2	33.8
ROW MNCs	3112	7680	-4568	1.4	3.1	2.3	4.3	8.2	6.5
Whole MNCs	33774	43365	-9591	15.6	17.8	16.8	47.2	46.4	46.7
USA MNCs	13433	2282	11151	6.2	0.9	3.4	18.8	2.4	9.5
ROW MNCs	20341	41083	-20742	9.4	16.8	13.3	28.4	43.9	37.2
Other MNCs	1762	1777	-15	0.8	0.7	0.8	2.5	1.9	2.1
USA MNCs	861	1222	-361	0.4	0.5	0.5	1.2	1.3	1.3
ROW MNCs	901	555	346	0.4	0.2	0.3	1.3	0.6	0.9

dominated by U.S.-based firms. The industry trade balance was a deficit of $11,384 million, compared to a total merchandise surplus of $12,684 million.

By 1982, industry trade had increased 42% to $27,434 million. This figure represented a 6.0% share of total trade (down 3.5 share points), and a 11.3% share of MNC-related trade (down 5.6 share points). The industry category ranked third, behind wholesale and manufacturing affiliates. The trade balance was a deficit of $18,322 million (up $6,938 million), compared to a total merchandise deficit of $27,510 million (a swing of $40,194 million).

Industry related trade was $27,433 million in 1989, unchanged from 1982 levels. This figure represented a 3.3% share of total trade (down 2.7 share points), and a 6.2% share of MNC-related trade (down 5.1 share points). The industry category still ranked third, and continued to be dominated by U.S.-based firms. The trade balance was a deficit of $18,685 million (up $363 million), compared to a total merchandise deficit of $109,399 million (up $81,889 million).

Manufacturing Affiliates

Affiliate related trade was $41,594 million in 1975, adjusted for the affiliate trade overlap. This figure represented a 20.2% share of total trade and a 36.2% share of MNC-related trade. The industry category ranked second and was dominated by U.S.-based firms. The industry trade balance was a surplus of $11,220 million, compared to a total merchandise surplus of $12,684 million.

By 1982, industry trade had increased 115% to $89,613 million. This figure represented a 19.5% share of total trade (down 0.7 share points), and a 36.8% share of MNC-related trade (up 0.7 share points). The industry category ranked second, behind wholesale affiliates. The trade balance was a surplus of $5,377 million (down $5,842 million), compared to a total merchandise deficit of $27,510 million (a swing of $40,194 million).

Industry related trade increased by 136% to $211,860 million in 1989. This figure represented a 25.3% share of total trade (up 5.8 share points), and a 47.8% share of MNC-related trade (up 11.0 share points). The industry category now ranked first, and continued to be dominated by U.S.-based firms. The trade balance was a deficit of $14,944 million (a swing of $20,321 million), compared to a total merchandise deficit of $109,399 million (up $81,889 million).

Wholesale Trade Affiliates

Affiliate related trade was $49,755 million in 1975, adjusted for the affiliate trade overlap. This figure represented a 24.2% share of total trade and a 43.3% share of MNC-related trade. The industry category ranked first and was dominated by ROW-based firms. The industry trade balance was a surplus of $5,788 million, compared to a total merchandise surplus of $12,684 million.

By 1982, industry trade had increased 140% to $119,221 million. This figure represented a 25.9% share of total trade (up 1.7 share points), and a 49.0% share of MNC-related trade (up 5.7 share points). The industry category continued to rank first. The trade balance was a deficit of $5,808 million (a swing of $11,596 million), compared to a total merchandise deficit of $27,510 million (a swing of $40,194 million).

Table 12.3: Multinational Companies and
U.S. Total Product Trade (SITC 0-9) in 1989

	MERCHANDISE TRADE (Millions of Dollars)			TOTAL TRADE (Percent Share)			ALL MNCs TRADE (Percent Share)		
	EXPORTS	IMPORTS	BALANCE	EXP	IMP	AVG	EXP	IMP	AVG
Affiliate Related Trade									
Total	363812	473211	-109399	100.0	100.0	100.0	NA	NA	NA
Non-MNCs	180368	213308	-32940	49.6	45.1	47.0	NA	NA	NA
All MNCs	183445	259904	-76459	50.4	54.9	53.0	100.0	100.0	100.0
USA MNCs	102558	97394	5164	28.2	20.6	23.9	55.9	37.5	45.1
ROW MNCs	86316	171847	-85531	23.7	36.3	30.8	47.1	66.1	58.2
Petro MNCs	4374	23059	-18685	1.2	4.9	3.3	2.4	8.9	6.2
USA MNCs	2512	10079	-7567	0.7	2.1	1.5	1.4	3.9	2.8
ROW MNCs	2014	14145	-12131	0.6	3.0	1.9	1.1	5.4	3.6
Manu MNCs	98458	113402	-14944	27.1	24.0	25.3	53.7	43.6	47.8
USA MNCs	70187	77372	-7185	19.3	16.4	17.6	38.3	29.8	33.3
ROW MNCs	31873	40871	-8998	8.8	8.6	8.7	17.4	15.7	16.4
Whole MNCs	75539	118827	-43288	20.8	25.1	23.2	41.2	45.7	43.8
USA MNCs	27886	7675	20211	7.7	1.6	4.2	15.2	3.0	8.0
ROW MNCs	49096	114049	-64953	13.5	24.1	19.5	26.8	43.9	36.8
Other MNCs	5074	4615	458	1.4	1.0	1.2	2.8	1.8	2.2
USA MNCs	1973	2268	-295	0.5	0.5	0.5	1.1	0.9	1.0
ROW MNCs	3333	2782	551	0.9	0.6	0.7	1.8	1.1	1.4
Intrafirm Related Trade									
Total	363812	473211	-109399	100.0	100.0	100.0	NA	NA	NA
Non-MNCs	239997	265978	-25981	66.0	56.2	60.4	NA	NA	NA
All MNCs	123815	207233	-83418	34.0	43.8	39.6	100.0	100.0	100.0
USA MNCs	89539	77307	12232	24.6	16.3	19.9	72.3	37.3	50.4
ROW MNCs	34276	129926	-95650	9.4	27.5	19.6	27.7	62.7	49.6
Petro MNCs	2665	15260	-12595	0.7	3.2	2.1	2.2	7.4	5.4
USA MNCs	1914	7332	-5418	0.5	1.5	1.1	1.5	3.5	2.8
ROW MNCs	751	7928	-7177	0.2	1.7	1.0	0.6	3.8	2.6
Manu MNCs	67988	90362	-22374	18.7	19.1	18.9	54.9	43.6	47.8
USA MNCs	60062	62775	-2713	16.5	13.3	14.7	48.5	30.3	37.1
ROW MNCs	7926	27587	-19661	2.2	5.8	4.2	6.4	13.3	10.7
Whole MNCs	51065	99383	-48318	14.0	21.0	18.0	41.2	48.0	45.4
USA MNCs	26283	6140	20143	7.2	1.3	3.9	21.2	3.0	9.8
ROW MNCs	24782	93243	-68461	6.8	19.7	14.1	20.0	45.0	35.7
Other MNCs	2097	2228	-131	0.6	0.5	0.5	1.7	1.1	1.3
USA MNCs	1280	1060	220	0.4	0.2	0.3	1.0	0.5	0.7
ROW MNCs	817	1168	-351	0.2	0.2	0.2	0.7	0.6	0.6

Industry related trade increased by 63% to $194,366 million in 1989 -- a 23.2% share of total trade (down 2.7 share points), and a 43.8% share of MNC-related trade (down 5.2 share points). The industry category now ranked second, behind manufacturing, and continued to be dominated by ROW-based firms. The trade balance was a deficit of $43,288 million (up $37,481 million), compared to a total deficit of $109,399 million (up $81,889 million).

Other Industry Affiliates

Affiliate related trade was $4,231 million in 1975, adjusted for the affiliate trade overlap. This figure represented a 2.1% share of total trade and a 3.7% share of MNC-related trade. The industry category ranked last and was dominated by U.S.-based firms. The industry trade balance was a surplus of $417 million, compared to a total merchandise surplus of $12,684 million.

By 1982, industry trade had increased 66% to $7,035 million. This figure represented a 1.5% share of total trade (down 0.5 share points), and a 2.9% share of MNC-related trade (down 0.8 share points). The industry category continued to rank last. The trade balance was a surplus of $272 million (down $145 million), compared to a total merchandise deficit of $27,510 million (a swing of $40,194 million).

Industry related trade increased by 38% to $9,689 million in 1989. This figure represented a 1.2% share of total trade (down 0.4 share points), and a 2.2% share of MNC-related trade (down 0.7 share points). The industry category still ranked last, and continued to be dominated by U.S.-based firms. The trade balance was a surplus of $458 million (up $186 million), compared to a total merchandise deficit of $109,399 million (up $81,889 million).

STRUCTURE OF TOTAL PRODUCT TRADE

The nine tables on product structure are a bridge between the trade tables in this chapter on "Total Product Trade" and the trade tables in the individual product trade chapters. Tables 12.4 to 12.12 provide direct linkages between Tables 12.1 to 12.3 -- the trade tables for 1975, 1982, and 1989 -- and the related trade tables in the chapters which follow. There are three product structure bridges or links: "Total" merchandise trade, affiliate related "All MNCs" trade, and intrafirm related "All MNCs" trade.

"Total" Merchandise Trade

Tables 12.4 to 12.6 cover the structure of "Total" merchandise exports and imports for 1975, 1982, and 1989. The term "Total" refers to the first data line in the affiliate and intrafirm related trade sections of Tables 12.1 to 12.3 respectively. These figures are total U.S. merchandise trade.

Each table covers "Total" merchandise trade (the "Total" line in the table), the twelve product trade categories, and the two product groupings of Non-Manufactures trade and Manufactures trade. Dollar values are shown for exports, imports, and trade balances. Trade shares are shown on the "Total Trade" basis; that is, the trade category is divided by total merchandise trade. Trade shares on the "All MNCs" basis are not applicable in these tables.

Manufactured goods trade accounted for an average 65.9% share of total

Table 12.4: Product Structure of
"Total" Merchandise Trade in
U.S. Total Product Trade (SITC 0-9) in 1975

	MERCHANDISE TRADE (Millions of Dollars)			TOTAL TRADE (Percent Share)			ALL MNCs TRADE (Percent Share)		
	EXPORTS	IMPORTS	BALANCE	EXP	IMP	AVG	EXP	IMP	AVG
TOTAL	109254	96570	12684	100.0	100.0	100.0	NA	NA	NA
NonManuf	36510	45249	-8739	33.4	46.9	39.7	NA	NA	NA
Food	15875	8543	7332	14.5	8.8	11.9	NA	NA	NA
Bev&Tob	1341	1426	-85	1.2	1.5	1.3	NA	NA	NA
CrdMatl	10031	5592	4439	9.2	5.8	7.6	NA	NA	NA
Petro	1242	26017	-24775	1.1	26.9	13.2	NA	NA	NA
Coal	3341	584	2757	3.1	0.6	1.9	NA	NA	NA
OtherProd	4680	3087	1593	4.3	3.2	3.8	NA	NA	NA
Manufact	72744	51321	21423	66.6	53.1	60.3	NA	NA	NA
Chem	8911	3713	5198	8.2	3.8	6.1	NA	NA	NA
Machnry	29954	12027	17927	27.4	12.5	20.4	NA	NA	NA
Veh&Pts	9525	9968	-443	8.7	10.3	9.5	NA	NA	NA
OtherTrans	7343	1573	5770	6.7	1.6	4.3	NA	NA	NA
MetManu	5804	8986	-3182	5.3	9.3	7.2	NA	NA	NA
OtherManu	11207	15054	-3847	10.3	15.6	12.8	NA	NA	NA

Table 12.5: Product Structure of
"Total" Merchandise Trade in
U.S. Total Product Trade (SITC 0-9) in 1982

	MERCHANDISE TRADE (Millions of Dollars)			TOTAL TRADE (Percent Share)			ALL MNCs TRADE (Percent Share)		
	EXPORTS	IMPORTS	BALANCE	EXP	IMP	AVG	EXP	IMP	AVG
TOTAL	216442	243952	-27510	100.0	100.0	100.0	NA	NA	NA
NonManuf	70665	99930	-29265	32.6	41.0	37.1	NA	NA	NA
Food	25103	14453	10650	11.6	5.9	8.6	NA	NA	NA
Bev&Tob	3172	3364	-192	1.5	1.4	1.4	NA	NA	NA
CrdMatl	20175	8589	11586	9.3	3.5	6.2	NA	NA	NA
Petro	7067	65331	-58264	3.3	26.8	15.7	NA	NA	NA
Coal	6275	79	6196	2.9	0.0	1.4	NA	NA	NA
OtherProd	8873	8114	759	4.1	3.3	3.7	NA	NA	NA
Manufact	145777	144022	1755	67.4	59.0	62.9	NA	NA	NA
Chem	20848	9493	11355	9.6	3.9	6.6	NA	NA	NA
Machnry	62702	39457	23245	29.0	16.2	22.2	NA	NA	NA
Veh&Pts	13365	29218	-15853	6.2	12.0	9.2	NA	NA	NA
OtherTrans	14587	4645	9942	6.7	1.9	4.2	NA	NA	NA
MetManu	8640	19227	-10587	4.0	7.9	6.1	NA	NA	NA
OtherManu	25635	41982	-16347	11.8	17.2	14.7	NA	NA	NA

Table 12.6: Product Structure of
"Total" Merchandise Trade in
U.S. Total Product Trade (SITC 0-9) in 1989

	MERCHANDISE TRADE (Millions of Dollars)			TOTAL TRADE (Percent Share)			ALL MNCs TRADE (Percent Share)		
	EXPORTS	IMPORTS	BALANCE	EXP	IMP	AVG	EXP	IMP	AVG
TOTAL	363812	473211	-109399	100.0	100.0	100.0	NA	NA	NA
NonManuf	105329	108210	-2881	29.0	22.9	25.5	NA	NA	NA
Food	30026	20677	9349	8.3	4.4	6.1	NA	NA	NA
Bev&Tob	5566	4362	1204	1.5	0.9	1.2	NA	NA	NA
CrdMatl	27221	15364	11857	7.5	3.2	5.1	NA	NA	NA
Petro	5636	50882	-45246	1.5	10.8	6.8	NA	NA	NA
Coal	4330	1746	2584	1.2	0.4	0.7	NA	NA	NA
OtherProd	32550	15179	17371	8.9	3.2	5.7	NA	NA	NA
Manufact	258483	365001	-106518	71.0	77.1	74.5	NA	NA	NA
Chem	36856	20744	16112	10.1	4.4	6.9	NA	NA	NA
Machnry	110902	126708	-15806	30.5	26.8	28.4	NA	NA	NA
Veh&Pts	24334	70282	-45948	6.7	14.9	11.3	NA	NA	NA
OtherTrans	25902	8691	17211	7.1	1.8	4.1	NA	NA	NA
MetManu	12721	30449	-17728	3.5	6.4	5.2	NA	NA	NA
OtherManu	47768	108127	-60359	13.1	22.8	18.6	NA	NA	NA

Table 12.7: Product Structure of
Affiliate Related "All MNCs" Trade in
U.S. Total Product Trade (SITC 0-9) in 1975

	MERCHANDISE TRADE (Millions of Dollars)			TOTAL TRADE (Percent Share)			ALL MNCs TRADE (Percent Share)		
	EXPORTS	IMPORTS	BALANCE	EXP	IMP	AVG	EXP	IMP	AVG
TOTAL	60503	54462	6041	55.4	56.4	55.9	100.0	100.0	100.0
NonManuf	24427	23281	1146	22.4	24.1	23.2	40.4	42.7	41.5
Food	15532	3051	12482	14.2	3.2	9.0	25.7	5.6	16.2
Bev&Tob	515	612	-97	0.5	0.6	0.5	0.9	1.1	1.0
CrdMatl	4629	3203	1427	4.2	3.3	3.8	7.7	5.9	6.8
Petro	938	14145	-13208	0.9	14.6	7.3	1.5	26.0	13.1
Coal	472	38	435	0.4	0.0	0.2	0.8	0.1	0.4
OtherProd	2341	2234	108	2.1	2.3	2.2	3.9	4.1	4.0
Manufact	36076	31181	4895	33.0	32.3	32.7	59.6	57.3	58.5
Chem	4627	1822	2805	4.2	1.9	3.1	7.6	3.3	5.6
Machnry	14107	7907	6200	12.9	8.2	10.7	23.3	14.5	19.1
Veh&Pts	8013	9389	-1377	7.3	9.7	8.5	13.2	17.2	15.1
OtherTrans	570	636	-66	0.5	0.7	0.6	0.9	1.2	1.0
MetManu	2786	6080	-3294	2.6	6.3	4.3	4.6	11.2	7.7
OtherManu	5974	5348	626	5.5	5.5	5.5	9.9	9.8	9.8

Table 12.8: Product Structure of
Affiliate Related "All MNCs" Trade in
U.S. Total Product Trade (SITC 0-9) in 1982

	MERCHANDISE TRADE (Millions of Dollars)			TOTAL TRADE (Percent Share)			ALL MNCs TRADE (Percent Share)		
	EXPORTS	IMPORTS	BALANCE	EXP	IMP	AVG	EXP	IMP	AVG
TOTAL	112412	130892	-18480	51.9	53.7	52.8	100.0	100.0	100.0
NonManuf	45258	42443	2815	20.9	17.4	19.0	40.3	32.4	36.0
Food	21492	7405	14088	9.9	3.0	6.3	19.1	5.7	11.9
Bev&Tob	1010	1433	-423	0.5	0.6	0.5	0.9	1.1	1.0
CrdMatl	10610	5235	5375	4.9	2.1	3.4	9.4	4.0	6.5
Petro	6434	23413	-16979	3.0	9.6	6.5	5.7	17.9	12.3
Coal	3547	59	3488	1.6	0.0	0.8	3.2	0.0	1.5
OtherProd	2165	4900	-2735	1.0	2.0	1.5	1.9	3.7	2.9
Manufact	67155	88449	-21295	31.0	36.3	33.8	59.7	67.6	64.0
Chem	11541	5318	6224	5.3	2.2	3.7	10.3	4.1	6.9
Machnry	30648	29299	1349	14.2	12.0	13.0	27.3	22.4	24.6
Veh&Pts	11381	24650	-13269	5.3	10.1	7.8	10.1	18.8	14.8
OtherTrans	1690	2082	-392	0.8	0.9	0.8	1.5	1.6	1.6
MetManu	4686	15088	-10402	2.2	6.2	4.3	4.2	11.5	8.1
OtherManu	7210	12014	-4805	3.3	4.9	4.2	6.4	9.2	7.9

Table 12.9: Product Structure of
Affiliate Related "All MNCs" Trade in
U.S. Total Product Trade (SITC 0-9) in 1989

	MERCHANDISE TRADE (Millions of Dollars)			TOTAL TRADE (Percent Share)			ALL MNCs TRADE (Percent Share)		
	EXPORTS	IMPORTS	BALANCE	EXP	IMP	AVG	EXP	IMP	AVG
TOTAL	183445	259904	-76459	50.4	54.9	53.0	100.0	100.0	100.0
NonManuf	46821	51997	-5176	12.9	11.0	11.8	25.5	20.0	22.3
Food	19502	7883	11619	5.4	1.7	3.3	10.6	3.0	6.2
Bev&Tob	2465	2576	-112	0.7	0.5	0.6	1.3	1.0	1.1
CrdMatl	10501	8887	1614	2.9	1.9	2.3	5.7	3.4	4.4
Petro	5179	24877	-19698	1.4	5.3	3.6	2.8	9.6	6.8
Coal	2089	257	1832	0.6	0.1	0.3	1.1	0.1	0.5
OtherProd	7086	7517	-431	1.9	1.6	1.7	3.9	2.9	3.3
Manufact	136624	207907	-71284	37.6	43.9	41.2	74.5	80.0	77.7
Chem	26931	15455	11477	7.4	3.3	5.1	14.7	5.9	9.6
Machnry	55753	86027	-30274	15.3	18.2	16.9	30.4	33.1	32.0
Veh&Pts	21541	56778	-35237	5.9	12.0	9.4	11.7	21.8	17.7
OtherTrans	2097	4513	-2416	0.6	1.0	0.8	1.1	1.7	1.5
MetManu	10420	17752	-7332	2.9	3.8	3.4	5.7	6.8	6.4
OtherManu	19882	27384	-7502	5.5	5.8	5.6	10.8	10.5	10.7

Table 12.10: Product Structure of
Intrafirm Related "All MNCs" Trade in
U.S. Total Product Trade (SITC 0-9) in 1975

	MERCHANDISE TRADE (Millions of Dollars)			TOTAL TRADE (Percent Share)			ALL MNCs TRADE (Percent Share)		
	EXPORTS	IMPORTS	BALANCE	EXP	IMP	AVG	EXP	IMP	AVG
TOTAL	41566	42005	-439	38.0	43.5	40.6	100.0	100.0	100.0
NonManuf	13400	15931	-2531	12.3	16.5	14.3	32.2	37.9	35.1
Food	7592	1265	6327	6.9	1.3	4.3	18.3	3.0	10.6
Bev&Tob	401	469	-68	0.4	0.5	0.4	1.0	1.1	1.0
CrdMatl	3401	1865	1536	3.1	1.9	2.6	8.2	4.4	6.3
Petro	648	10894	-10246	0.6	11.3	5.6	1.6	25.9	13.8
Coal	371	21	350	0.3	0.0	0.2	0.9	0.0	0.5
OtherProd	987	1417	-430	0.9	1.5	1.2	2.4	3.4	2.9
Manufact	28166	26074	2092	25.8	27.0	26.4	67.8	62.1	64.9
Chem	3626	1387	2239	3.3	1.4	2.4	8.7	3.3	6.0
Machnry	11552	7366	4186	10.6	7.6	9.2	27.8	17.5	22.6
Veh&Pts	6208	8457	-2249	5.7	8.8	7.1	14.9	20.1	17.5
OtherTrans	455	446	9	0.4	0.5	0.4	1.1	1.1	1.1
MetManu	1613	4410	-2797	1.5	4.6	2.9	3.9	10.5	7.2
OtherManu	4712	4008	704	4.3	4.2	4.2	11.3	9.5	10.4

Table 12.11: Product Structure of
Intrafirm Related "All MNCs" Trade in
U.S. Total Product Trade (SITC 0-9) in 1982

	MERCHANDISE TRADE (Millions of Dollars)			TOTAL TRADE (Percent Share)			ALL MNCs TRADE (Percent Share)		
	EXPORTS	IMPORTS	BALANCE	EXP	IMP	AVG	EXP	IMP	AVG
TOTAL	71583	93513	-21930	33.1	38.3	35.9	100.0	100.0	100.0
NonManuf	21412	23586	-2174	9.9	9.7	9.8	29.9	25.2	27.3
Food	8752	2749	6003	4.0	1.1	2.5	12.2	2.9	7.0
Bev&Tob	660	933	-273	0.3	0.4	0.3	0.9	1.0	1.0
CrdMatl	5668	2526	3142	2.6	1.0	1.8	7.9	2.7	5.0
Petro	2767	14859	-12092	1.3	6.1	3.8	3.9	15.9	10.7
Coal	2638	22	2616	1.2	0.0	0.6	3.7	0.0	1.6
OtherProd	927	2497	-1570	0.4	1.0	0.7	1.3	2.7	2.1
Manufact	50171	69927	-19756	23.2	28.7	26.1	70.1	74.8	72.7
Chem	7636	3785	3851	3.5	1.6	2.5	10.7	4.0	6.9
Machnry	24600	25699	-1099	11.4	10.5	10.9	34.4	27.5	30.5
Veh&Pts	8689	20548	-11859	4.0	8.4	6.4	12.1	22.0	17.7
OtherTrans	968	1348	-380	0.4	0.6	0.5	1.4	1.4	1.4
MetManu	2769	10303	-7534	1.3	4.2	2.8	3.9	11.0	7.9
OtherManu	5509	8244	-2735	2.5	3.4	3.0	7.7	8.8	8.3

Table 12.12: Product Structure of
Intrafirm Related "All MNCs" Trade in
U.S. Total Product Trade (SITC 0-9) in 1989

	MERCHANDISE TRADE (Millions of Dollars)			TOTAL TRADE (Percent Share)			ALL MNCs TRADE (Percent Share)		
	EXPORTS	IMPORTS	BALANCE	EXP	IMP	AVG	EXP	IMP	AVG
TOTAL	123815	207233	-83418	34.0	43.8	39.6	100.0	100.0	100.0
NonManuf	23022	30503	-7481	6.3	6.4	6.4	18.6	14.7	16.2
Food	9465	3749	5716	2.6	0.8	1.6	7.6	1.8	4.0
Bev&Tob	1047	1536	-489	0.3	0.3	0.3	0.8	0.7	0.8
CrdMatl	6539	4563	1976	1.8	1.0	1.3	5.3	2.2	3.4
Petro	2612	15621	-13009	0.7	3.3	2.2	2.1	7.5	5.5
Coal	820	142	678	0.2	0.0	0.1	0.7	0.1	0.3
OtherProd	2539	4892	-2353	0.7	1.0	0.9	2.1	2.4	2.2
Manufact	100793	176730	-75937	27.7	37.3	33.2	81.4	85.3	83.8
Chem	16469	11436	5033	4.5	2.4	3.3	13.3	5.5	8.4
Machnry	45241	78321	-33080	12.4	16.6	14.8	36.5	37.8	37.3
Veh&Pts	18454	51465	-33011	5.1	10.9	8.4	14.9	24.8	21.1
OtherTrans	1361	3063	-1702	0.4	0.6	0.5	1.1	1.5	1.3
MetManu	4513	11309	-6796	1.2	2.4	1.9	3.6	5.5	4.8
OtherManu	14755	21136	-6381	4.1	4.5	4.3	11.9	10.2	10.8

merchandise trade, while Non-Manufactured goods trade averaged a 34.1% share. These averages masked a significant shift in the structural composition of trade. In 1975 the Manufactures share was 60.3%; in 1989 the share had risen to 74.5%. The Non-Manufactures share fell from 39.7% to 25.5%. The major factor in the share shift was the large drop in Petroleum and Products imports between 1982 and 1989.

The four leading product categories accounted for 60% of total trade. They were Machinery (23.7%), Other Manufactures (15.4%), Petroleum and Products (11.9%), and Vehicles and Parts (10.0%). The other categories gained share after 1982 as Petroleum trade declined.

The four intermediate product categories included less than 30% of merchandise trade. They were Food (8.8%), Chemicals (6.5%), Crude Materials (6.3%), and Metal Manufactures (6.1%).

The four smallest product categories amounted to little more than 10% of total exports and imports. These categories were Other Products (4.4%), Other Transportation Equipment (4.2%), Beverages and Tobacco (1.3%), and Coal and Coke (1.3%).

Affiliate Related "All MNCs" Trade

Tables 12.7 to 12.9 cover the structure of affiliate related "All MNCs" trade for 1975, 1982, and 1989. The term "All MNCs" refers to the third data line in the affiliate related trade section of Tables 12.1 to 12.3 respectively. These figures are total MNC-related trade under the affiliate trade definition.

Each table covers affiliate related "All MNCs" trade (the "Total" line in the table), the twelve product trade categories, and the two product groupings of Non-Manufactures trade and Manufactures trade. Dollar values are shown for exports, imports, and trade balances. Trade shares are shown on two bases. The "Total Trade" basis is the trade category divided by total merchandise trade. The "All MNCs" basis is the trade category divided by affiliate related All MNCs trade.

Manufactured goods trade accounted for an average 66.7% of affiliate related All MNCs trade, while Non-Manufactured goods trade averaged 33.3%. These averages masked a significant shift in the structural composition of MNC-related trade. In 1975 the Manufactures share was 58.5%; in 1989 the share had risen to 77.7%. The Non-Manufactures share fell from 41.5% to 22.3%. The major factor in the share shift was the large drop in Petroleum and Products imports between 1982 and 1989.

The four leading product categories accounted for more than 60% of affiliate related All MNCs trade. They were Machinery (25.3%), Vehicles and Parts (15.9%), Food (11.4%), and Petroleum and Products (10.7%).

The four intermediate product categories included less than 30% of the foreign trade. They were Other Manufactures (9.5%), Chemicals (7.4%), Metal Manufactures (7.4%), and Crude Materials (5.9%). The four smallest product categories amounted to little more than 10% of affiliate related All MNCs trade. These categories were Other Products (3.4%), Other Transportation Equipment (1.4%), Beverages and Tobacco (1.0%), and Coal and Coke (0.8%).

Intrafirm Related "All MNCs" Trade

Tables 12.10 to 12.12 cover the structure of intrafirm related "All MNCs" trade for 1975, 1982, and 1989. The term "All MNCs" refers to the third data line in the intrafirm related trade section of Tables 12.1 to 12.3 respectively. These figures are total MNC-related trade under the intrafirm trade definition.

Each table covers intrafirm related "All MNCs" trade (the "Total" line in the table), the twelve product trade categories, and the two product groupings of Non-Manufactures trade and Manufactures trade. Dollar values are shown for exports, imports, and the trade balance. Trade shares are shown on two bases. The "Total Trade" basis is the trade category divided by total merchandise trade. The "All MNCs" basis is the trade category divided by intrafirm related All MNCs trade.

Manufactured goods trade accounted for an average 73.8% of intrafirm related All MNCs trade, while Non-Manufactured goods trade averaged 26.2%. These averages masked a significant shift in the structural composition of MNC-related trade. In 1975 the Manufactures share was 64.9%; in 1989 the share had risen to 83.8%. The Non-Manufactures share was halved, falling from

35.1% to 16.2%. The major factor in the share shift was the large drop in Petroleum and Products imports between 1982 and 1989.

The four leading product categories accounted for nearly 70% of intrafirm related All MNCs trade. They were Machinery (30.1%), Vehicles and Parts (18.8%), Petroleum and Products (10.0%), and Other Manufactures (9.9%).

The four intermediate product categories included less than 30% of the foreign trade. They were Food (7.2%), Chemicals (7.1%), Metal Manufactures (6.6%), and Crude Materials (4.9%).

The four smallest product categories amounted to little more than 5% of intrafirm related All MNCs trade. These categories were Other Products (2.4%), Other Transportation Equipment (1.3%), Beverages and Tobacco (0.9%), and Coal and Coke (0.8%).

DERIVATION OF THE DATA

Total Product trade, Total Merchandise trade, and Total Geographic trade provide three different perspectives on the MNC role in total trade. Total Product trade is an aggregate of twelve categories of product trade based on the SITC foreign trade classification system. Total Product trade data is generally identical to the trade data for Total Merchandise trade and Total Product trade. The exception is affiliate related trade where different procedures are used to estimate the trade overlap.

This section will discuss the data used in the fifteen chapters comprising Part IV of the book "Product Patterns of MNC-Related Trade." Five steps are needed to derive the product data on MNC-related trade. First, the benchmark source tables must be restored by developing estimates for suppressed data cells. Second, the product categories in the six benchmark surveys must be converted to a common format. Third, the benchmark source tables must be converted to a common affiliate basis. Fourth, all of the MNC-related trade data must be time shifted to common time periods for comparison. And fifth, estimates must be derived for the trade overlap in affiliate related trade.

The Benchmark Source Tables

The basic data for product trade come from the six foreign direct investment surveys conducted by the U.S. Government over the past two decades. The benchmark years are 1974, 1977, 1980, 1982, 1987, and 1989, and are referred to as BM74, BM77, etc. (Full citations are shown in Selected Bibliography.) The 1974, 1980, and 1987 benchmarks cover foreign direct investment in the United States ("reverse investment"). The 1977, 1982, and 1989 benchmarks cover U.S. direct investment abroad ("outward investment").

The benchmark tables used as sources for geographic trade data are listed below. For each benchmark, export and import source tables are shown for affiliate related trade and intrafirm related trade. There are a total of twenty-four source tables. (The BM74 trade data are organized by the four affiliate industry groups, so four source tables are cited in each of the four cases listed under that benchmark heading.)

The source tables for the reverse investment benchmarks show the trade conducted by all affiliates (10% equity interest or more). The source tables for the outward investment benchmarks show the trade conducted by majority-owned affiliates (MOFA -- 50% equity interest or more).

The format used in the source tables was industry rows with product columns. The industry rows were collapsed into Petroleum, Manufacturing, Wholesale, and Other Industry categories. This structure was dictated by the set of affiliate industry data available in the 1974 benchmark. All product columns were retained. However, no consistent product format was used in the various benchmark surveys.

Even after the row compression, many of the source tables have data cells left empty to avoid disclosure of firm specific data. The figures in parentheses show the percent of the total trade covered by the table which is not allocated to specific data cells (the "table residual"). For example, under BM77, total affiliate exports are $35,813 million, while the unallocated trade is $1,539 million, or 4.3% of the total trade covered in Table III.I.2.

BM74: Foreign Direct Investment in the United States
    Affiliate Related Trade
        Exports: Tables E-1, E-3, E-4, E-5 (6.4%)
        Imports: Tables E-1, E-3, E-4, E-5 (4.8%)
    Intrafirm Related Trade
        Exports: Tables E-1, E-3, E-4, E-5 (10.4%)
        Imports: Tables E-1, E-3, E-4, E-5 (39.7%)

BM77: U.S. Direct Investment Abroad
    Affiliate Related Trade
        Exports: Table III.I.2 (4.3%)
        Imports: Table III.I.18 (2.4%)
    Intrafirm Related Trade
        Exports: Table III.I.6 (3.6%)
        Imports: Table III.I.22 (4.9%)

BM80: Foreign Direct Investment in the United States
    Affiliate Related Trade
        Exports: Table G-12 (3.8%)
        Imports: Table G-24 (1.7%)
    Intrafirm Related Trade
        Exports: Table G-14 (9.1%)
        Imports: Table G-26 (28.5%)

BM82: U.S. Direct Investment Abroad
   Affiliate Related Trade
      Exports: Table III.G.2 (0.3%)
      Imports: Table III.G.19 (0.8%)
   Intrafirm Related Trade
      Exports: Table III.G.6 (0.2%)
      Imports: Table III.G.23 (0.9%)

BM87: Foreign Direct Investment in the United States
   Affiliate Related Trade
      Exports: Table G-10 (5.5%)
      Imports: Table G-16 (6.7%)
   Intrafirm Related Trade
      Exports: Table G-12 (3.8%)
      Imports: Table G-18 (6.7%)

BM89: U.S. Direct Investment Abroad
   Affiliate Related Trade
      Exports: Table III.H.4 (1.1%)
      Imports: Table III.H.21 (0.8%)
   Intrafirm Related Trade
      Exports: Table III.H.8 (1.2%)
      Imports: Table III.H.25 (1.1%)

The mean level of unallocated trade is 6.2%, but this figure masks a wide range. The table residuals range from a low of 0.2% in BM82 intrafirm exports, to a high of 39.7% in BM74 intrafirm imports. The level of unallocated trade tends to be lower in the later benchmarks, lower in the outward investment benchmarks, and lower in affiliate related trade.

The relationship between the table residuals for affiliate and intrafirm trade is important. The mean level of unallocated trade for affiliate related trade is 1.6%, with a range of 0.3% to 6.4%. The figures for intrafirm related trade are much higher -- an average of 4.6% and a range of 0.2% to 39.7%. The allocation process is driven by affiliate related trade, however, so the unallocated amounts for the intrafirm tables are actually identical with the companion affiliate tables. That is, the unallocated trade for any source table does not exceed 6.4%, and averages 1.6%.

The derivation process begins with affiliate related trade. Each of these source tables is a trade matrix where affiliate industry trade forms the rows and product category trade forms the columns. The row and column totals are known, but empty detail cells exist within the matrix. The total unallocated trade for the matrix is equal to the sum of the row or column residuals.

The row and column residuals are used in a joint probability procedure to provide initial estimates for each empty detail cell. These estimates represent a maximum probability estimate for each empty cell based upon the known information content within the row and column residuals.

The initial estimates usually do not provide a perfect "fit" with the row and column totals -- small row and column residuals will remain. Beginning with the rows with the smallest number of estimated cells, the detail cell estimates are adjusted to force all remaining row and column residuals to equal zero. These adjustments involve a minimum alteration of the initial estimated values. This last step "balances" the trade matrix and provides estimates for each empty cell that are consistent with the row and column totals.

The affiliate trade tables can now be used to allocate the row and column residuals in the intrafirm trade tables. Each data cell in an affiliate trade table is a constraint on the maximum value that can be assumed by the related data cell in an intrafirm trade table. Accordingly, the affiliate trade values are used to initially allocate the row and column residuals into empty cells in the intrafirm trade matrix. Then the intrafirm trade table can be balanced, forcing all row and column residuals to zero. The estimates for each empty cell are consistent with intrafirm row and column totals and with the related affiliate trade values.

Common Product Trade Format

The product trade format was dictated by the need to show manufactured goods trade (SITC 5-8) and non-manufactured goods trade (SITC 0-4,9). This is the narrow definition of manufactured goods [Bailey and Bowden 57-59]. The necessary detail is found in the twelve product groups used in the 1982 and 1989 benchmark surveys of U.S. direct investment abroad. These product groups are summarized in the definition section above, and serve as the basis of the twelve specific product chapters which follow.

The 1977 benchmark on outward investment and all of the three reverse investment benchmarks show less detail regarding product trade. The trade categories are consistent, but fewer in number. All four of these benchmarks contain combined groupings of product trade.

BM74: Foreign Direct Investment in the United States
    Food (#0) combined with Beverages and Tobacco (#1)
    Coal and Coke (#32) combined with Other Products (#4,9)

BM77: U.S. Direct Investment Abroad
    Food (#0) combined with Beverages and Tobacco (#1)
    Petroleum and Products (#33-34) combined with Coal and Coke (#32)

BM80: Foreign Direct Investment in the United States
    Other Manufactures (#61-66,8) combined with Other Products (#4,9)

BM87: Foreign Direct Investment in the United States
Other Manufactures (#61-66,8) combined with Other Products (#4,9)

For example, in the 1974 and 1977 benchmarks, Food (SITC 0) and Beverages
and Tobacco (SITC 1) were combined into a single category. These combined
categories must be split into their component parts to derive consistent product
trade data.

The most difficult problem was due to the combining of Other Manufactures
with Other Products in the 1980 and 1987 reverse investment surveys to form
a large residual "other" grouping (SITC 4,61-66,8,9). The Other Manufactures
(SITC 61-66,8) category had to be broken out to complete the definition of
Manufactured Goods trade (SITC 5-8). These operations are discussed in the
data derivation sections of the product chapters.

Common Affiliate Basis

The source trade tables are not on a common affiliate basis. The reverse
investment benchmarks show the trade conducted on an all-affiliate basis (a 10%
equity interest or more). In contrast, the trade tables from the outward
investment benchmarks show the trade conducted on a majority-owned foreign
affiliate basis (MOFA -- a 50% equity interest or more).

Due to a lack of data, the reverse investment tables cannot be converted to
a majority-owned basis. However, the outward investment benchmark surveys
do provide trade data by affiliate industry groups on an all affiliate basis. These
tables can be used to convert the MOFA basis product trade data to a consistent
all-affiliate basis. The conversion procedure is a simple scalar multiplication.
The benchmark source tables used for the conversion are shown below.

BM77: U.S. Direct Investment Abroad
    Affiliate Related Trade
        Exports: Table II.I.4
        Imports: Table II.I.20
    Intrafirm Related Trade
        Exports: Table II.I.7
        Imports: Table II.I.23

BM82: U.S. Direct Investment Abroad
    Affiliate Related Trade
        Exports: Table II.G.4
        Imports: Table II.G.21
    Intrafirm Related Trade
        Exports: Table II.G.7
        Imports: Table II.G.24

BM89: U.S. Direct Investment Abroad
    Affiliate Related Trade
        Exports: Table II.H.2
        Imports: Table II.H.2
    Intrafirm Related Trade
        Exports: Table II.H.2
        Imports: Table II.H.2

Conversion to Comparison Years

The common time periods for the trade data comparisons are 1975, 1982, and 1989. The time shifting of the benchmark data to these comparison years is accomplished by using information from two sources. In the late 1970s, the Bureau of Economic Analysis began a series of annual reports on foreign direct investment activities. These studies do not provide trade data by product category, but do provide trade data by affiliate industry groups. The second source is United States annual trade data by product category.

The BEA annual reports on multinational companies are linked to the previous benchmark surveys. Thus the annual reports on reverse investment for 1988 and 1989 are based on the 1987 benchmark. The reports on outward investment for 1987 and 1988, however, are still based on the 1982 benchmark. The comparison year of 1989 can draw on the 1989 benchmark for outward investment, and the 1987 benchmark on reverse investment timeshifted by the 1989 annual report on reverse foreign direct investment. The same situation holds for the 1980 to 1982 period.

There are no BEA annual FDI reports for the 1974 to 1977 period, so any year in that interval could be selected as the comparison year. Since the time period between 1982 and 1989 is seven years, it is convenient to select 1975 for the initial comparison year.

The time shifting process also uses U.S. annual trade data by product category. The trade data reported in standard statistical sources is compatible with the twelve product categories used for the benchmark surveys. The most detailed and consistent source of product trade data is *The Statistical Abstract of the United States*. Several issues had to be used to develop time series covering the period under study. A second source, *Business Statistics 1963-91* provides time series data for total merchandise trade for the entire period. The product trade data in this latter source, however, is less detailed.

The product trade data in the *Abstract* was used to develop annual time series for the twelve product groups for the period 1974 to 1989. In most cases, this data was identical to the available *Business Statistics* trade data. The total of the product data, however, was not equal to the level of total merchandise exports and imports. Total merchandise trade includes revisions and errors that are not allocated to the product categories. Exports also include re-exports. In a perfect world, there would be no revision or error categories. Further, as shown by the benchmark survey questionnaires, exports reported by respondents includes re-exports.

Accordingly, the revisions, errors, and re-export categories were proportionally allocated among the twelve product groups to force the sum of the parts to be equal to the whole. These adjusted product trade series were used in time shifting the benchmark source tables to the comparison years. These adjusted series are also used as a basis for the trade shares shown in the tables that appear in the product trade chapters.

The conversion to comparison years involves the following time shifts and sources. The conversions from MOFA basis to all-affiliate basis are also noted.

BM74: Foreign Direct Investment in the United States
    One-year time shift forward to 1975
        Exports: ABUS79, 867-868; BS6391, 76-78
        Imports: ABUS79, 869-870; BS6391, 79-81

BM77: U.S. Direct Investment Abroad
    Two-year time shift backward to 1975, MOFA conversion
        Exports: ABUS79, 867-868; BS6391, 76-78
        Imports: ABUS79, 869-870; BS6391, 79-81

BM80: Foreign Direct Investment in the United States
    Two-year time shift forward to 1980
        Exports: FDIUS82, G-3; ABUS85, 820-821; BS6391, 76-78
        Imports: FDIUS82, G-3; ABUS85, 822-823; BS6391, 79-81

BM82: U.S. Direct Investment Abroad
    No time shift, MOFA conversion

BM87: Foreign Direct Investment in the United States
    Two-year time shift forward to 1989
        Exports: FDIUS89, G-1; ABUS91, 811-812; BS6391, 76-78
        Imports: FDIUS89, G-1; ABUS91, 813-814; BS6391, 79-81

BM89: U.S. Direct Investment Abroad
    No time shift, MOFA conversion

The change in U.S. exports and imports by product group is used to initially convert the benchmark year product data to the comparison year. For example, affiliate imports of food were $6,452 million in BM80. Between 1980 and 1982, U.S. imports of food declined from $15,507 million to $14,453 million. Affiliate food imports are reduced by the same proportion to a 1982 level of $6,013 million. The assumption is that the MNC role in each product category remained unchanged during the time shift.

This product conversion, however, will produce affiliate industry group and trade totals that are different from the actual figures in the comparison year. In the 1982 example, converted affiliate imports totaled $81,314 million, while the actual level of affiliate imports was $84,290 million.

A scalar adjustment is used to force the converted product data to generate the actual affiliate industry group and trade totals for the comparison year. In the example, affiliate imports of food were increased from the initial value of $6,013 million to a final value of $6,271 million.

In matrix terms, the initial product group time shift is a column conversion. The affiliate industry group totals for the comparison year are a row constraint on the values assumed by the detail trade cells in the matrix. The scalar adjustment is a row conversion, which generates new column totals for the specific product categories. The time shift conversion process thus captures changes both in the product (column) structure of trade and in the affiliate industry (row) structure of trade.

As noted above, industry and affiliate trade totals are available for 1982 and 1989 from the annual BEA reverse investment reports. For 1975, however, these data must be generated by multiplying the BM74 and BM77 industry and affiliate trade levels by the change in total merchandise exports or imports.

The Overlap in Affiliate Related Trade

Two sets of comparable MNC-related trade data now exist -- affiliate related trade and intrafirm related trade. Intrafirm trade can be directly aggregated, but affiliate related trade must be adjusted for a trade overlap.

Intrafirm related trade is "closed trade" in the sense that the transactors on both sides are fully known, and there is no overlapping trade between the U.S.-based firms and the ROW-based firms. The export and import figures for U.S. MNCs and ROW MNCs can be directly aggregated to find totals. For example, in Table 12.1, under the "All MNCs" heading, U.S. MNC exports were $28,739 million while ROW MNCs exports were $12,827 million. These figures are added to find the All MNC export figure of $41,566 million.

Affiliate related trade is "open" in the sense that the transactors beyond intrafirm trade are not known. Affiliates do trade with each other, and this overlap must be estimated to avoid overstating the significance of affiliate related trade. Returning to All MNCs related exports in Table 12.1, the trade level of U.S. MNCs is $36,181 million and ROW-based MNCs is $26,433 million. The level of All MNCs trade is not the sum of these figures or $62,614 million. Using the procedure described in Chapter 4, the trade overlap between the two groups of affiliates is estimated to be $2,111 million. This gives an All MNCs export figure of $60,503 million. The related import and balance figures and trade shares are also adjusted for the affiliate trade overlap.

The All MNCs affiliate trade overlap is the sum of the overlaps from the affiliate industry groups. For example, the export overlap for Wholesale MNCs is $1,015 million which accounts for nearly half of the All MNCs overlap.

As mentioned earlier, the values shown in the tables in this chapter are the sum of the values in the twelve product chapters. Thus the trade data shown in Table 12.1 for affiliate related trade in any industry group is the sum from the companion tables in subsequent chapters. This includes the dollar value of the affiliate trade overlap.

As discussed in Chapter 5, the value of the trade overlap must be calculated within a closed system, and at a disaggregated level. Accordingly, the dollar value of the affiliate trade overlap is calculated in the product chapters for All MNCs trade. This overlap is then allocated to the industry level subsets within each chapter. The industry subsets are then summed to derive the trade tables shown in this chapter and in Chapter 13 on "Non-Manufactured Goods Trade" and Chapter 20 on "Manufactured Goods Trade."

NON-MANUFACTURED GOODS TRADE

Non-Manufactured Goods trade includes some 34.1% of Total Product trade. Multinational companies are involved in 52% of trade on an affiliate basis and 29% on an intrafirm basis. Wholesale affiliates are the dominant industry group, followed by petroleum affiliates.

DEFINITION OF NON-MANUFACTURED GOODS PRODUCTS

Non-Manufactured Goods and Manufactured Goods are two trade aggregates within Total Product trade. Non-Manufactured Goods trade is composed of six BEA product trade groups.

As defined by the Bureau of Economic Analysis, the "Non-Manufactured Goods" foreign trade classification consists of products in the SITC 0-4 and 9 categories. This definition of non-manufactured goods trade corresponds to the narrow definition (SITC 5-8) of manufactured goods trade [Bailey and Bowden 57-59]. Non-Manufactured Goods trade includes the following six product groups [BEA 1990 21-24]:

Food (Raw and Prepared) and Live Animals Chiefly for Food
(SITC code 0)

Beverages and Tobacco
(SITC code 1)

Crude Materials, Inedible, Except Fuels
(SITC code 2)

Petroleum and Products, Mineral Waxes, Natural and Manufactured Gas
(SITC codes 33-34)

Coal, Coke, and Briquets
(SITC code 32)

Animal and Vegetable Oils, Fats, and Waxes, and Commodities N.E.C.
(SITC codes 4 and 9)

These BEA product groups serve as the basis for the following six product trade chapters. These chapters provide the core of the analysis of MNC-related trade in non-manufactured goods. Each chapter includes a detailed product listing of the items that constitute the trade category, and shows the affiliate and intrafirm related trade for the three comparison years of 1975, 1982, and 1989.

This chapter on "Non-Manufactured Goods Trade" is the summary chapter on the MNC-related trade which is covered in the individual product chapters. The trade data shown in the following tables represents the aggregate dollar value of all non-manufactured goods trade combined.

TRENDS IN NON-MANUFACTURED GOODS TRADE

In 1975, total Non-Manufactures trade was $81,759 million. Exports were $36,510 million and imports were $45,249 million yielding a deficit of $8,739 million. Between 1975 and 1982, total trade increased 109% or $88,836 million to reach $170,595 million. Imports increased slightly faster than exports, increasing the deficit by 235% or $20,526 million and putting the overall trade imbalance at $29,265 in 1982.

Between 1982 and 1989, the growth in Non-Manufactures trade declined significantly. Total trade increased 25% or $42,944 million to reach $213,539 million. Imports were up only 8%; Petroleum and Products imports actually declined over the seven-year period, offsetting the growth in the other trade categories. Subsequently, the trade balance improved 90% or $26,384 million, dropping the deficit to only $2,881 million.

THE TRADE ROLE OF MULTINATIONAL COMPANIES

This section is based on the trade data shown in Tables 13.1, 13.2, and 13.3 for 1975, 1982, and 1989, respectively. The overall trade role of multinational companies ("All MNCs" in the tables) is discussed for both affiliate related trade and intrafirm related trade.

Affiliate Related Trade

Non-Manufactured Goods trade totaled $81,759 million in 1975. Adjusted for the trade overlap, the affiliate related trade was $47,707 million for a 58.4%

Table 13.1: Multinational Companies and
U.S. Non-Manufactures Trade (SITC 0-4,9) in 1975

	MERCHANDISE TRADE (Millions of Dollars)			TOTAL TRADE (Percent Share)			ALL MNCs TRADE (Percent Share)		
	EXPORTS	IMPORTS	BALANCE	EXP	IMP	AVG	EXP	IMP	AVG
Affiliate Related Trade									
Total	36510	45249	-8739	100.0	100.0	100.0	NA	NA	NA
Non-MNCs	12084	21969	-9885	33.1	48.6	41.6	NA	NA	NA
All MNCs	24427	23281	1146	66.9	51.4	58.4	100.0	100.0	100.0
USA MNCs	4623	13854	-9231	12.7	30.6	22.6	18.9	59.5	38.7
ROW MNCs	20563	10456	10107	56.3	23.1	37.9	84.2	44.9	65.0
Petro MNCs	1967	14675	-12709	5.4	32.4	20.4	8.1	63.0	34.9
USA MNCs	460	11564	-11104	1.3	25.6	14.7	1.9	49.7	25.2
ROW MNCs	1548	3762	-2214	4.2	8.3	6.5	6.3	16.2	11.1
Manu MNCs	2191	1527	664	6.0	3.4	4.5	9.0	6.6	7.8
USA MNCs	1891	877	1014	5.2	1.9	3.4	7.7	3.8	5.8
ROW MNCs	381	728	-347	1.0	1.6	1.4	1.6	3.1	2.3
Whole MNCs	19508	6033	13475	53.4	13.3	31.2	79.9	25.9	53.5
USA MNCs	2013	498	1515	5.5	1.1	3.1	8.2	2.1	5.3
ROW MNCs	18106	5782	12324	49.6	12.8	29.2	74.1	24.8	50.1
Other MNCs	761	1046	-285	2.1	2.3	2.2	3.1	4.5	3.8
USA MNCs	259	915	-656	0.7	2.0	1.4	1.1	3.9	2.5
ROW MNCs	528	184	344	1.4	0.4	0.9	2.2	0.8	1.5
Intrafirm Related Trade									
Total	36510	45249	-8739	100.0	100.0	100.0	NA	NA	NA
Non-MNCs	23110	29318	-6208	63.3	64.8	64.1	NA	NA	NA
All MNCs	13400	15931	-2531	36.7	35.2	35.9	100.0	100.0	100.0
USA MNCs	3104	10467	-7363	8.5	23.1	16.6	23.2	65.7	46.3
ROW MNCs	10296	5464	4832	28.2	12.1	19.3	76.8	34.3	53.7
Petro MNCs	1649	11254	-9605	4.5	24.9	15.8	12.3	70.6	44.0
USA MNCs	378	8967	-8589	1.0	19.8	11.4	2.8	56.3	31.9
ROW MNCs	1271	2287	-1016	3.5	5.1	4.4	9.5	14.4	12.1
Manu MNCs	1245	1007	238	3.4	2.2	2.8	9.3	6.3	7.7
USA MNCs	1095	580	515	3.0	1.3	2.0	8.2	3.6	5.7
ROW MNCs	150	427	-277	0.4	0.9	0.7	1.1	2.7	2.0
Whole MNCs	10069	2957	7112	27.6	6.5	15.9	75.1	18.6	44.4
USA MNCs	1469	287	1182	4.0	0.6	2.1	11.0	1.8	6.0
ROW MNCs	8600	2670	5930	23.6	5.9	13.8	64.2	16.8	38.4
Other MNCs	437	713	-276	1.2	1.6	1.4	3.3	4.5	3.9
USA MNCs	162	633	-471	0.4	1.4	1.0	1.2	4.0	2.7
ROW MNCs	275	80	195	0.8	0.2	0.4	2.1	0.5	1.2

share while Non-MNC trade was $34,052 million for a 41.6% share. The MNC-related trade position reflected a 66.9% share of export trade and a 51.4% share of import trade. The dominant MNC group was foreign-based firms with a 37.9% share of total trade; U.S.-based firms held a 22.6% share. ROW multinational companies had a much larger share of export trade; U.S. MNCs had a larger share of import trade.

The Non-Manufactured Goods trade balance in 1975 was a deficit of $8,739 million. This reflected a $1,146 million surplus in MNC-related trade and a $9,885 million deficit in Non-MNC trade. Thus the overall deficit in Non-Manufactured Goods was due to Non-MNC trade. The MNC-related surplus reflected a surplus position of ROW multinationals offsetting a deficit in U.S. MNC trade.

Between 1975 and 1982, Non-Manufactured Goods trade grew 109% or $88,836 million to reach $170,595 million. In comparison, affiliate related trade increased $39,994 million or 84% to a level of $87,701 million (adjusted for the trade overlap). Accordingly, the overall affiliate position decreased from a 58.4% to a 51.4% share and Non-MNC trade rose to a 48.6% share.

Within the affiliate trade structure, the export share dropped to 64.0% and the import share to 42.5%. These changes reflected declines in the export shares of U.S.-based MNCs and an increase in the import share of foreign multinationals.

The Non-Manufactured Goods trade balance in 1982 was a deficit of $29,265 million, up $20,526 million from 1975. The affiliate related trade surplus was $2,815 million, an increase of $1,669 million; the Non-MNC trade deficit had increased $22,195 million to $32,080 million. Thus the deterioration in the Non-Manufactured Goods trade balance was due to unfavorable trends in Non-MNC trade. The MNC-related surplus continued to reflect a ROW MNC surplus which exceeded a U.S. MNC deficit.

In the 1982 to 1989 period, Non-Manufactured Goods trade grew 25% or $42,944 million to $213,539 million. In comparison, affiliate related trade rose $11,117 million or 13% percent to a level of $98,818 million. As a result, the overall affiliate position dropped from a 51.4% to a 46.3% share and Non-MNC trade rose to a 53.7% share.

Within the affiliate trade structure, the export share plummeted to 44.5% and the import share increased to 48.1%. The export change reflected declines in the trade shares of both MNC groups, especially foreign-based MNCs. The import change was due to an increase in ROW MNC share offsetting a decline in the U.S. MNC share. Compared to 1975, the U.S. MNC share of total trade had decreased by half from 22.6% to 11.2%; the ROW MNC share had changed from 37.9% to 36.9%.

The Non-Manufactured Goods trade deficit in 1989 was only $2,881 million and represented an improvement of $26,384 million from 1982. However, the affiliate related trade balance changed to a deficit of $5,176 million, a swing of $7,990 million. In contrast, the Non-MNC trade balance converted to a surplus of $2,295 million, an improvement of $34,374 million.

The significant decline in the Non-Manufactured Goods deficit between 1982 and 1989 reflected favorable trends in Non-MNC related trade. Within MNC-related trade, both of the MNC groups recorded a trade deficit. Of note is that the ROW MNC trade balance deteriorated by $13,079 million and changed into a deficit.

Table 13.2: Multinational Companies and
U.S. Non-Manufactures Trade (SITC 0-4,9) in 1982

	MERCHANDISE TRADE (Millions of Dollars)			TOTAL TRADE (Percent Share)			ALL MNCs TRADE (Percent Share)		
	EXPORTS	IMPORTS	BALANCE	EXP	IMP	AVG	EXP	IMP	AVG
Affiliate Related Trade									
Total	70665	99930	-29265	100.0	100.0	100.0	NA	NA	NA
Non-MNCs	25408	57487	-32080	36.0	57.5	48.6	NA	NA	NA
All MNCs	45258	42443	2815	64.0	42.5	51.4	100.0	100.0	100.0
USA MNCs	6733	19745	-13012	9.5	19.8	15.5	14.9	46.5	30.2
ROW MNCs	39568	24765	14803	56.0	24.8	37.7	87.4	58.3	73.4
Petro MNCs	2058	22163	-20105	2.9	22.2	14.2	4.5	52.2	27.6
USA MNCs	1081	15642	-14561	1.5	15.7	9.8	2.4	36.9	19.1
ROW MNCs	1012	7882	-6870	1.4	7.9	5.2	2.2	18.6	10.1
Manu MNCs	4714	3503	1211	6.7	3.5	4.8	10.4	8.3	9.4
USA MNCs	3380	1627	1753	4.8	1.6	2.9	7.5	3.8	5.7
ROW MNCs	1452	1971	-519	2.1	2.0	2.0	3.2	4.6	3.9
Whole MNCs	36564	14542	22023	51.7	14.6	30.0	80.8	34.3	58.3
USA MNCs	2032	854	1178	2.9	0.9	1.7	4.5	2.0	3.3
ROW MNCs	35388	14216	21172	50.1	14.2	29.1	78.2	33.5	56.6
Other MNCs	1921	2235	-314	2.7	2.2	2.4	4.2	5.3	4.7
USA MNCs	240	1622	-1382	0.3	1.6	1.1	0.5	3.8	2.1
ROW MNCs	1716	696	1020	2.4	0.7	1.4	3.8	1.6	2.8
Intrafirm Related Trade									
Total	70665	99930	-29265	100.0	100.0	100.0	NA	NA	NA
Non-MNCs	49253	76344	-27091	69.7	76.4	73.6	NA	NA	NA
All MNCs	21412	23586	-2174	30.3	23.6	26.4	100.0	100.0	100.0
USA MNCs	4646	15611	-10965	6.6	15.6	11.9	21.7	66.2	45.0
ROW MNCs	16766	7975	8791	23.7	8.0	14.5	78.3	33.8	55.0
Petro MNCs	1194	14636	-13442	1.7	14.6	9.3	5.6	62.1	35.2
USA MNCs	885	12552	-11667	1.3	12.6	7.9	4.1	53.2	29.9
ROW MNCs	309	2084	-1775	0.4	2.1	1.4	1.4	8.8	5.3
Manu MNCs	2346	2120	226	3.3	2.1	2.6	11.0	9.0	9.9
USA MNCs	1894	1300	594	2.7	1.3	1.9	8.8	5.5	7.1
ROW MNCs	452	820	-368	0.6	0.8	0.7	2.1	3.5	2.8
Whole MNCs	16974	5607	11367	24.0	5.6	13.2	79.3	23.8	50.2
USA MNCs	1673	692	981	2.4	0.7	1.4	7.8	2.9	5.3
ROW MNCs	15301	4915	10386	21.7	4.9	11.9	71.5	20.8	44.9
Other MNCs	898	1223	-325	1.3	1.2	1.2	4.2	5.2	4.7
USA MNCs	194	1067	-873	0.3	1.1	0.7	0.9	4.5	2.8
ROW MNCs	704	156	548	1.0	0.2	0.5	3.3	0.7	1.9

Intrafirm Related Trade

Non-Manufactured Goods trade totaled $81,759 million in 1975. Intrafirm related trade was $29,331 million for a 35.9% share (compared to a 58.4% share for affiliate related trade). Arms-length or Non-MNC trade was $52,428 million for a 64.1% share. The MNC-related trade position reflected a 36.7%

share of export trade and a 35.2% share of import trade. The dominant MNC group was foreign-based firms with a 19.3% share of total trade; U.S.-based firms held a 16.6% share. ROW multinationals had a larger share of export trade; U.S. firms had a larger share of import trade.

The Non-Manufactured Goods trade balance in 1975 was a deficit of $8,739 million. This reflected a $2,531 million deficit in MNC-related trade and a $6,208 million deficit in Non-MNC trade. Thus the overall trade balance was due to deficits in both components. The MNC-related deficit reflected a deficit position of U.S. multinationals which offset a surplus of foreign-based MNCs.

Between 1975 and 1982, Non-Manufactured Goods trade grew $88,836 million or 109% to reach $170,595 million. In comparison, intrafirm related trade increased $15,667 million or 53% to a level of $44,998 million. Accordingly, the overall intrafirm position decreased from a 35.9% to a 26.4% share (compared to a 58.4% to 51.4% share change for affiliate related trade). Non-MNC trade rose to a 73.6% share. Within the intrafirm trade structure, the export share dropped to 30.3% and the import share to 23.6%. These changes reflected declines in the trade shares of both MNC groups.

The Non-Manufactured Goods trade balance in 1982 was a deficit of $29,265 million, up $20,526 million from 1975. The intrafirm related trade deficit was $2,174 million, a decrease of $357 million; the Non-MNC trade deficit had risen $20,883 million to $27,091 million. Thus the increase in the Non-Manufactured Goods trade deficit resulted from unfavorable trends in arms-length transactions. The modest MNC-related surplus was created by a ROW MNC surplus which exceeded a U.S. MNC deficit.

In the 1982 to 1989 period, Non-Manufactured Goods trade grew $42,944 million or 25% to $213,539 million. In comparison, intrafirm related trade increased $8,527 million or 19% to a level of $53,525 million. As a result, the overall intrafirm position dropped slightly from a 26.4% to a 25.1% share (compared to a 51.4% to 46.3% share change for affiliate related trade). Non-MNC trade rose to a 74.9% share. Within the intrafirm trade structure, the export share dropped to 21.9% and the import share increased to 28.2%. The export change reflected declines in the export shares of both U.S. and ROW MNCs. The import change was due to a jump in ROW MNC share which offset a drop in the U.S. MNC share. Since 1975, the U.S. MNC share had fallen from 16.6% to 7.6% and the ROW MNC share had decreased from 19.3% to 17.4%.

The Non-Manufactured Goods trade balance in 1989 was a modest deficit of $2,881 million, down $26,384 million from 1982. The intrafirm related trade deficit was $7,481 million, an increase of $5,307 million. In contrast, the Non-MNC trade balance had switched to a surplus of $4,600 million, a positive swing of $31,691 million. Thus the Non-Manufactured Goods trade balance reflected a positive trend in the Non-MNC component. Within MNC-related trade, both groups recorded a deficit. Notably, the ROW MNC trade balance had deteriorated $11,316 million and changed into a deficit.

Table 13.3: Multinational Companies and
U.S. Non-Manufactures Trade (SITC 0-4,9) in 1989

	MERCHANDISE TRADE (Millions of Dollars)			TOTAL TRADE (Percent Share)			ALL MNCs TRADE (Percent Share)		
	EXPORTS	IMPORTS	BALANCE	EXP	IMP	AVG	EXP	IMP	AVG
Affiliate Related Trade									
Total	105329	108210	-2881	100.0	100.0	100.0	NA	NA	NA
Non-MNCs	58508	56214	2295	55.5	51.9	53.7	NA	NA	NA
All MNCs	46821	51997	-5176	44.5	48.1	46.3	100.0	100.0	100.0
USA MNCs	7493	16336	-8843	7.1	15.1	11.2	16.0	31.4	24.1
ROW MNCs	40244	38520	1724	38.2	35.6	36.9	86.0	74.1	79.7
Petro MNCs	1866	22707	-20841	1.8	21.0	11.5	4.0	43.7	24.9
USA MNCs	1398	10061	-8663	1.3	9.3	5.4	3.0	19.3	11.6
ROW MNCs	491	13787	-13296	0.5	12.7	6.7	1.0	26.5	14.4
Manu MNCs	8488	9553	-1065	8.1	8.8	8.4	18.1	18.4	18.3
USA MNCs	3312	3332	-20	3.1	3.1	3.1	7.1	6.4	6.7
ROW MNCs	5360	6972	-1612	5.1	6.4	5.8	11.4	13.4	12.5
Whole MNCs	33418	16686	16732	31.7	15.4	23.5	71.4	32.1	50.7
USA MNCs	2188	1214	974	2.1	1.1	1.6	4.7	2.3	3.4
ROW MNCs	31860	16152	15708	30.2	14.9	22.5	68.0	31.1	48.6
Other MNCs	3049	3050	-1	2.9	2.8	2.9	6.5	5.9	6.2
USA MNCs	595	1729	-1134	0.6	1.6	1.1	1.3	3.3	2.4
ROW MNCs	2533	1609	924	2.4	1.5	1.9	5.4	3.1	4.2
Intrafirm Related Trade									
Total	105329	108210	-2881	100.0	100.0	100.0	NA	NA	NA
Non-MNCs	82307	77707	4600	78.1	71.8	74.9	NA	NA	NA
All MNCs	23022	30503	-7481	21.9	28.2	25.1	100.0	100.0	100.0
USA MNCs	5661	10617	-4956	5.4	9.8	7.6	24.6	34.8	30.4
ROW MNCs	17361	19886	-2525	16.5	18.4	17.4	75.4	65.2	69.6
Petro MNCs	1349	15018	-13669	1.3	13.9	7.7	5.9	49.2	30.6
USA MNCs	1180	7317	-6137	1.1	6.8	4.0	5.1	24.0	15.9
ROW MNCs	169	7701	-7532	0.2	7.1	3.7	0.7	25.2	14.7
Manu MNCs	3498	4674	-1176	3.3	4.3	3.8	15.2	15.3	15.3
USA MNCs	2309	1691	618	2.2	1.6	1.9	10.0	5.5	7.5
ROW MNCs	1189	2983	-1794	1.1	2.8	2.0	5.2	9.8	7.8
Whole MNCs	17271	9503	7768	16.4	8.8	12.5	75.0	31.2	50.0
USA MNCs	1896	863	1033	1.8	0.8	1.3	8.2	2.8	5.2
ROW MNCs	15375	8640	6735	14.6	8.0	11.2	66.8	28.3	44.9
Other MNCs	904	1308	-404	0.9	1.2	1.0	3.9	4.3	4.1
USA MNCs	276	746	-470	0.3	0.7	0.5	1.2	2.4	1.9
ROW MNCs	628	562	66	0.6	0.5	0.6	2.7	1.8	2.2

INDUSTRY TRADE ROLES

This section is based on the trade data shown in Tables 13.1, 13.2, and 13.3 for 1975, 1982, and 1989, respectively. The trade role of each affiliate industry group is discussed on the basis of affiliate related trade.

Petroleum Affiliates

Affiliate related trade was $16,642 million in 1975, adjusted for the affiliate trade overlap. This figure represented a 20.4% share of total trade and a 34.9% share of MNC-related trade. The industry category ranked second and was dominated by U.S.-based firms. The industry trade balance was a deficit of $12,709 million, compared to a total merchandise deficit of $8,739 million.

By 1982, industry trade had increased 46% to $24,222 million. This figure represented a 14.2% share of total trade (down 6.2 share points), and a 27.6% share of MNC-related trade (down 7.3 share points). The industry category ranked second behind wholesale affiliates. The trade balance was a deficit of $20,105 million (up $7,397 million), compared to a total merchandise deficit of $29,265 million (up $20,526 million).

Industry related trade increased by 2.0% to $24,573 million in 1989. This figure represented a 11.5% share of total trade (down 2.7 share points), and a 24.9% share of MNC-related trade (down 2.8 share points). The industry category still ranked second, but was now dominated by ROW-based firms. The trade balance was a deficit of $20,841 million (up $736 million), compared to a total merchandise deficit of $2,881 million (down $26,384 million).

Manufacturing Affiliates

Affiliate related trade was $3,718 million in 1975, adjusted for the affiliate trade overlap. This figure represented a 4.5% share of total trade and a 7.8% share of MNC-related trade. The industry category ranked third and was dominated by U.S.-based firms. The industry trade balance was a surplus of $664 million, compared to a total merchandise deficit of $8,739 million.

By 1982, industry trade had increased 121% to $8,217 million. This figure represented a 4.8% share of total trade (up 0.3 share points), and a 9.4% share of MNC-related trade (up 1.6 share points). The industry category ranked third behind wholesale and petroleum affiliates. The trade balance was a surplus of $1,211 million (up $547 million), compared to a total merchandise deficit of $29,265 million (up $20,526 million).

Industry related trade increased by 120% to $18,041 million in 1989. This figure represented a 8.4% share of total trade (up 3.6 share points), and a 18.3% share of MNC-related trade (up 8.9 share points). The industry category still ranked second, but was now dominated by ROW-based firms. The trade balance was a deficit of $1,065 million (a swing of $2,277 million), compared to a total merchandise deficit of $2,881 million (down $26,384 million).

Wholesale Trade Affiliates

Affiliate related trade was $25,541 million in 1975, adjusted for the affiliate trade overlap. This figure represented a 31.2% share of total trade and a 53.5%

Table 13.4: Product Structure of
"Total" Merchandise Trade in
U.S. Non-Manufactures Trade (SITC 0-4,9)

	MERCHANDISE TRADE (Millions of Dollars)			TOTAL TRADE (Percent Share)			ALL MNCs TRADE (Percent Share)		
	EXPORTS	IMPORTS	BALANCE	EXP	IMP	AVG	EXP	IMP	AVG
1975									
NonManuf	36510	45249	-8739	100.0	100.0	100.0	NA	NA	NA
Food	15875	8543	7332	43.5	18.9	29.9	NA	NA	NA
Bev&Tob	1341	1426	-85	3.7	3.2	3.4	NA	NA	NA
CrdMatl	10031	5592	4439	27.5	12.4	19.1	NA	NA	NA
Petro	1242	26017	-24775	3.4	57.5	33.3	NA	NA	NA
Coal	3341	584	2757	9.2	1.3	4.8	NA	NA	NA
OtherProd	4680	3087	1593	12.8	6.8	9.5	NA	NA	NA
1982									
NonManuf	70665	99930	-29265	100.0	100.0	100.0	NA	NA	NA
Food	25103	14453	10650	35.5	14.5	23.2	NA	NA	NA
Bev&Tob	3172	3364	-192	4.5	3.4	3.8	NA	NA	NA
CrdMatl	20175	8589	11586	28.6	8.6	16.9	NA	NA	NA
Petro	7067	65331	-58264	10.0	65.4	42.4	NA	NA	NA
Coal	6275	79	6196	8.9	0.1	3.7	NA	NA	NA
OtherProd	8873	8114	759	12.6	8.1	10.0	NA	NA	NA
1989									
NonManuf	105329	108210	-2881	100.0	100.0	100.0	NA	NA	NA
Food	30026	20677	9349	28.5	19.1	23.7	NA	NA	NA
Bev&Tob	5566	4362	1204	5.3	4.0	4.6	NA	NA	NA
CrdMatl	27221	15364	11857	25.8	14.2	19.9	NA	NA	NA
Petro	5636	50882	-45246	5.4	47.0	26.5	NA	NA	NA
Coal	4330	1746	2584	4.1	1.6	2.8	NA	NA	NA
OtherProd	32550	15179	17371	30.9	14.0	22.4	NA	NA	NA

share of MNC-related trade. The industry category ranked first and was dominated by ROW-based firms. The industry trade balance was a surplus of $13,475 million, compared to a total merchandise deficit of $8,739 million.

By 1982, industry trade had increased 100% to $51,106 million. This figure represented a 30.0% share of total trade (down 1.3 share points), and a 58.3% share of MNC-related trade (up 4.7 share points). The industry category ranked first, ahead of petroleum and manufacturing affiliates. The trade balance was a surplus of $22,023 million (up $8,547 million), compared to a total merchandise deficit of $29,265 million (up $20,526 million).

Industry related trade decreased by 2.0% to $50,103 million in 1989, adjusted for the affiliate trade overlap. This figure represented a 23.5% share of total trade (down 6.5 share points), and a 50.7% share of MNC-related trade (down 7.6 share points). The industry category still ranked first, and continued

Table 13.5: Product Structure of
Affiliate Related "All MNCs" Trade in
U.S. Non-Manufactures Trade (SITC 0-4,9)

	MERCHANDISE TRADE (Millions of Dollars)			TOTAL TRADE (Percent Share)			ALL MNCs TRADE (Percent Share)		
	EXPORTS	IMPORTS	BALANCE	EXP	IMP	AVG	EXP	IMP	AVG
1975									
NonManuf	24427	23281	1146	66.9	51.4	58.4	100.0	100.0	100.0
Food	15532	3051	12482	42.5	6.7	22.7	63.6	13.1	39.0
Bev&Tob	515	612	-97	1.4	1.4	1.4	2.1	2.6	2.4
CrdMatl	4629	3203	1427	12.7	7.1	9.6	19.0	13.8	16.4
Petro	938	14145	-13208	2.6	31.3	18.4	3.8	60.8	31.6
Coal	472	38	435	1.3	0.1	0.6	1.9	0.2	1.1
OtherProd	2341	2234	108	6.4	4.9	5.6	9.6	9.6	9.6
1982									
NonManuf	45258	42443	2815	64.0	42.5	51.4	100.0	100.0	100.0
Food	21492	7405	14088	30.4	7.4	16.9	47.5	17.4	32.9
Bev&Tob	1010	1433	-423	1.4	1.4	1.4	2.2	3.4	2.8
CrdMatl	10610	5235	5375	15.0	5.2	9.3	23.4	12.3	18.1
Petro	6434	23413	-16979	9.1	23.4	17.5	14.2	55.2	34.0
Coal	3547	59	3488	5.0	0.1	2.1	7.8	0.1	4.1
OtherProd	2165	4900	-2735	3.1	4.9	4.1	4.8	11.5	8.1
1989									
NonManuf	46821	51997	-5176	44.5	48.1	46.3	100.0	100.0	100.0
Food	19502	7883	11619	18.5	7.3	12.8	41.7	15.2	27.7
Bev&Tob	2465	2576	-112	2.3	2.4	2.4	5.3	5.0	5.1
CrdMatl	10501	8887	1614	10.0	8.2	9.1	22.4	17.1	19.6
Petro	5179	24877	-19698	4.9	23.0	14.1	11.1	47.8	30.4
Coal	2089	257	1832	2.0	0.2	1.1	4.5	0.5	2.4
OtherProd	7086	7517	-431	6.7	6.9	6.8	15.1	14.5	14.8

to be dominated by ROW-based firms. The trade balance was a surplus of $16,732 million (down $5,291 million), compared to a total merchandise deficit of $2,881 million (down $26,384 million).

Other Industry Affiliates

Affiliate related trade was $1,806 million in 1975, adjusted for the affiliate trade overlap. This figure represented a 2.2% share of total trade and a 3.8% share of MNC-related trade. The industry category ranked last and was dominated by U.S.-based firms. The industry trade balance was a deficit of $285 million, compared to a total merchandise deficit of $8,739 million.

By 1982, industry trade had increased 130% to $4,155 million. This figure represented a 2.4% share of total trade (up 0.2 share points), and a 4.7% share

Table 13.6: Product Structure of
Intrafirm Related "All MNCs" Trade in
U.S. Non-Manufactures Trade (SITC 0-4,9)

	MERCHANDISE TRADE (Millions of Dollars)			TOTAL TRADE (Percent Share)			ALL MNCs TRADE (Percent Share)		
	EXPORTS	IMPORTS	BALANCE	EXP	IMP	AVG	EXP	IMP	AVG
1975									
NonManuf	13400	15931	-2531	36.7	35.2	35.9	100.0	100.0	100.0
Food	7592	1265	6327	20.8	2.8	10.8	56.7	7.9	30.2
Bev&Tob	401	469	-68	1.1	1.0	1.1	3.0	2.9	3.0
CrdMatl	3401	1865	1536	9.3	4.1	6.4	25.4	11.7	18.0
Petro	648	10894	-10246	1.8	24.1	14.1	4.8	68.4	39.4
Coal	371	21	350	1.0	0.0	0.5	2.8	0.1	1.3
OtherProd	987	1417	-430	2.7	3.1	2.9	7.4	8.9	8.2
1982									
NonManuf	21412	23586	-2174	30.3	23.6	26.4	100.0	100.0	100.0
Food	8752	2749	6003	12.4	2.8	6.7	40.9	11.7	25.6
Bev&Tob	660	933	-273	0.9	0.9	0.9	3.1	4.0	3.5
CrdMatl	5668	2526	3142	8.0	2.5	4.8	26.5	10.7	18.2
Petro	2767	14859	-12092	3.9	14.9	10.3	12.9	63.0	39.2
Coal	2638	22	2616	3.7	0.0	1.6	12.3	0.1	5.9
OtherProd	927	2497	-1570	1.3	2.5	2.0	4.3	10.6	7.6
1989									
NonManuf	23022	30503	-7481	21.9	28.2	25.1	100.0	100.0	100.0
Food	9465	3749	5716	9.0	3.5	6.2	41.1	12.3	24.7
Bev&Tob	1047	1536	-489	1.0	1.4	1.2	4.5	5.0	4.8
CrdMatl	6539	4563	1976	6.2	4.2	5.2	28.4	15.0	20.7
Petro	2612	15621	-13009	2.5	14.4	8.5	11.3	51.2	34.1
Coal	820	142	678	0.8	0.1	0.5	3.6	0.5	1.8
OtherProd	2539	4892	-2353	2.4	4.5	3.5	11.0	16.0	13.9

of MNC-related trade (up 1.0 share points). The industry category ranked last, behind wholesale, petroleum, and manufacturing affiliates. The trade balance was a deficit of $314 million (up $30 million), compared to a total merchandise deficit of $29,265 million (up $20,526 million).

Industry related trade increased by 47% to $6,100 million in 1989, adjusted for the affiliate trade overlap. This figure represented a 2.9% share of total trade (up 0.4 share points), and a 6.2% share of MNC-related trade (up 1.4 share points).

The industry category still ranked last, but was now dominated by ROW-based firms. The trade balance deficit was $1 million (down $314 million), compared to total merchandise trade where the deficit was $2,881 million (down $26,384 million).

THE STRUCTURE OF NON-MANUFACTURED GOODS TRADE

The three tables on product structure are a bridge between the trade tables in this chapter on "Non-Manufactured Goods Trade" and the trade tables in the subsequent six product trade chapters. Tables 13.4 to 13.6 provide direct linkages between Tables 13.1 to 13.3 -- the trade tables for 1975, 1982, and 1989 -- and the related trade tables in the chapters which follow. There are three product structure bridges or links: "Total" merchandise trade, affiliate related "All MNCs" trade, and intrafirm related "All MNCs" trade.

"Total" Merchandise Trade

Table 13.4 covers the structure of "Total" Non-Manufactures merchandise trade for 1975, 1982, and 1989. The term "Total" refers to the first data line in the affiliate and intrafirm related trade sections of Tables 13.1 to 13.3. These figures are total U.S. merchandise trade in Non-Manufactured Goods.

The table covers "Total" Non-Manufactures trade (the "Total" line in the table) and the six product trade categories. Dollar values are shown for exports, imports, and trade balances. Trade shares are shown on the "Total Trade" basis; that is, the trade category is divided by total Non-Manufactures trade. Trade shares on the "All MNCs" basis are not applicable in this table.

The two leading product categories accounted for 60% of total trade. They were Petroleum and Products (34.9%) and Food (25.9%). The two intermediate product categories included just over 30% of Non-Manufactures trade. They were Crude Materials (18.5%), and Other Products (12.9%). The two smallest product categories amounted to less than 10% of total exports and imports. These were Beverages and Tobacco (3.9%) and Coal and Coke (3.9%).

Affiliate Related "All MNCs" Trade

Table 13.5 covers the structure of affiliate related "All MNCs" Non-Manufactures trade for 1975, 1982, and 1989. The term "All MNCs" refers to the third data line in the affiliate related trade section of Tables 13.1 to 13.3. These figures are total MNC-related trade under the affiliate trade definition.

The table covers affiliate related "All MNCs" Non-Manufactures trade (the "Total" line in the table) and the six product trade categories. Dollar values are shown for exports, imports, and trade balances. Trade shares are shown on two bases. The "Total Trade" basis is the trade category divided by total Non-Manufactures trade. The "All MNCs" basis is the trade category divided by affiliate related All MNCs Non-Manufactures trade.

The two leading product categories accounted for nearly 70% of total trade. They were Food (34.3%) and Petroleum and Products (32.2%). The two intermediate product categories included over 25% of Non-Manufactures trade. They were Crude Materials (17.7%), and Other Products (10.2%). The two smallest product categories barely exceeded 5% of total exports and imports. These were Beverages and Tobacco (3.1%) and Coal and Coke (2.5%).

Intrafirm Related "All MNCs" Trade

Table 13.6 covers the structure of intrafirm related "All MNCs" Non-Manufactures trade for 1975, 1982, and 1989. The term "All MNCs" refers to the third data line in the intrafirm related trade section of Tables 13.1 to 13.3. These figures are total MNC-related trade under the intrafirm trade definition.

The table covers intrafirm related "All MNCs" Non-Manufactures trade (the "Total" line in the table) and the six product trade categories. Dollar values are shown for exports, imports, and trade balances. Trade shares are shown on two bases. The "Total Trade" basis is the trade category divided by total Non-Manufactures trade. The "All MNCs" basis is the trade category divided by intrafirm related All MNCs Non-Manufactures trade.

The two leading product categories accounted for 65% of total trade. They were Petroleum and Products (38.2%) and Food (27.5%). The two intermediate product categories included nearly 30% of Non-Manufactures trade. They were Crude Materials (18.6%), and Other Products (9.2%). The two smallest product categories slightly exceeded 5% of total exports and imports. These categories were Beverages and Tobacco (3.5%) and Coal and Coke (3.0%).

DERIVATION OF THE DATA

The derivation of the MNC-related product trade data is covered at length in Chapter 12 on "Total Product Trade." As noted in that discussion, trade categories were combined in certain benchmark surveys. For example, in the 1974 and 1977 benchmarks, Food (SITC 0) and Beverages and Tobacco (SITC 1) were combined into a single category. These combined categories must be split into their component parts to derive consistent product trade data. These operations are discussed in the data derivation sections of the affected product chapters.

As mentioned earlier, the values shown in the tables in this chapter are the aggregate values taken from the next six chapters. Thus the trade data shown in Table 13.1 for 1975 are the sum of the companion tables in Chapters 14 to 19. This includes the dollar value of the affiliate trade overlap.

CHAPTER 14

FOOD TRADE

Food exports and imports include one-fourth of all Non-Manufactures trade, second only to Petroleum and Products. The product category accounts for 8.8% of total merchandise trade, ranking fifth. In affiliate related trade, multinational companies are involved in 68% of Food trade, compared to 52% for all Non-Manufactures. This level of MNC-related trade is among the highest of all product categories. Wholesale affiliates are the dominant industry group, accounting for more than one-half of all Food trade.

DEFINITION OF FOOD PRODUCTS

As defined by the Bureau of Economic Analysis, the "Food" foreign trade classification consists of products in the SITC 0 category. Food trade includes the following specific products [BEA 1990 21]:

Food (Raw and Prepared) and Live Animals Chiefly for Food
(SITC code 0)

Live animals chiefly for food (exclude zoo animals, insects, dogs, cats, etc.)

Meat and meat preparations (fresh, concentrated, or preserved)

Dairy products and bird's eggs (fresh, concentrated, or preserved)

Fish, crustaceans and mollusks, and preparations thereof (fresh, frozen, or preserved)

Cereals and cereal preparations (unmilled, cereal meals and flours, "prepared breakfast" foods, bakery products, etc.)

Vegetables and fruits (fresh, frozen, preserved or prepared; include edible beans and nuts, except soybeans and other oil seeds)

Sugar, sugar preparations, and honey

Coffee, tea, cocoa, spices and manufactures thereof (include coffee and tea substitutes)

Animal feeding stuffs

Margarine, shortening, and prepared edible fats, excluding all other fats and oils

Miscellaneous edible products and preparations

TRENDS IN FOOD TRADE

In 1975, Food trade totaled $24,418 million. Exports were $15,875 million and imports were $8,543 million yielding a surplus of $7,332 million. Between 1975 and 1982, total trade increased 62% or $15,138 million to reach $39,556 million. Both exports and imports enjoyed strong growth, with imports growing slightly faster. The trade surplus increased $3,318 million or 45% to a 1982 level of $10,650 million.

Between 1982 and 1989, the growth rates slowed in Food trade, especially in exports. Total trade increased 28% or $11,147 million to reach $50,703 million. Imports jumped 43% while exports rose only 20%. This resulted in a 12% deterioration in the trade balance of $1,301 million, dropping the trade surplus to $9,349 million in 1989.

THE TRADE ROLE OF MULTINATIONAL COMPANIES

This section is based on the trade data shown in Tables 14.1, 14.2, and 14.3 for 1975, 1982, and 1989, respectively. The overall trade role of multinational companies ("All MNCs" in the tables) is discussed for both affiliate related trade and intrafirm related trade.

Affiliate Related Trade

Food trade totaled $24,418 million in 1975. Adjusted for the trade overlap, affiliate related trade was $18,583 million for a 76.1% share; Non-MNC trade was $5,836 million for a 23.9% share. The MNC-related trade position primarily reflected a 97.8% share of export trade, the dominant trade component; the import share was only 35.7%. The dominant MNC group was foreign-based firms with a 65.5% share of total trade; U.S.-based firms held a

Table 14.1: Multinational Companies and U.S. Food Trade (SITC 0) in 1975

	MERCHANDISE TRADE (Millions of Dollars)			TOTAL TRADE (Percent Share)			ALL MNCs TRADE (Percent Share)		
	EXPORTS	IMPORTS	BALANCE	EXP	IMP	AVG	EXP	IMP	AVG
Affiliate Related Trade									
Total	15875	8543	7332	100.0	100.0	100.0	NA	NA	NA
Non-MNCs	343	5493	-5150	2.2	64.3	23.9	NA	NA	NA
All MNCs	15532	3051	12482	97.8	35.7	76.1	100.0	100.0	100.0
USA MNCs	2632	525	2107	16.6	6.1	12.9	16.9	17.2	17.0
ROW MNCs	13392	2599	10793	84.4	30.4	65.5	86.2	85.2	86.1
Petro MNCs	653	149	504	4.1	1.7	3.3	4.2	4.9	4.3
USA MNCs	5	0	5	0.0	0.0	0.0	0.0	0.0	0.0
ROW MNCs	657	152	505	4.1	1.8	3.3	4.2	5.0	4.4
Manu MNCs	876	367	510	5.5	4.3	5.1	5.6	12.0	6.7
USA MNCs	799	171	628	5.0	2.0	4.0	5.1	5.6	5.2
ROW MNCs	107	199	-92	0.7	2.3	1.3	0.7	6.5	1.6
Whole MNCs	13775	2301	11474	86.8	26.9	65.8	88.7	75.4	86.5
USA MNCs	1644	165	1479	10.4	1.9	7.4	10.6	5.4	9.7
ROW MNCs	12579	2201	10378	79.2	25.8	60.5	81.0	72.2	79.5
Other MNCs	228	234	-6	1.4	2.7	1.9	1.5	7.7	2.5
USA MNCs	184	189	-5	1.2	2.2	1.5	1.2	6.2	2.0
ROW MNCs	49	47	2	0.3	0.6	0.4	0.3	1.5	0.5
Intrafirm Related Trade									
Total	15875	8543	7332	100.0	100.0	100.0	NA	NA	NA
Non-MNCs	8283	7278	1005	52.2	85.2	63.7	NA	NA	NA
All MNCs	7592	1265	6327	47.8	14.8	36.3	100.0	100.0	100.0
USA MNCs	1648	378	1270	10.4	4.4	8.3	21.7	29.9	22.9
ROW MNCs	5944	887	5057	37.4	10.4	28.0	78.3	70.1	77.1
Petro MNCs	503	64	439	3.2	0.7	2.3	6.6	5.1	6.4
USA MNCs	2	0	2	0.0	0.0	0.0	0.0	0.0	0.0
ROW MNCs	501	64	437	3.2	0.7	2.3	6.6	5.1	6.4
Manu MNCs	396	282	114	2.5	3.3	2.8	5.2	22.3	7.7
USA MNCs	362	129	233	2.3	1.5	2.0	4.8	10.2	5.5
ROW MNCs	34	153	-119	0.2	1.8	0.8	0.4	12.1	2.1
Whole MNCs	6551	731	5820	41.3	8.6	29.8	86.3	57.8	82.2
USA MNCs	1161	71	1090	7.3	0.8	5.0	15.3	5.6	13.9
ROW MNCs	5390	660	4730	34.0	7.7	24.8	71.0	52.2	68.3
Other MNCs	142	188	-46	0.9	2.2	1.4	1.9	14.9	3.7
USA MNCs	123	178	-55	0.8	2.1	1.2	1.6	14.1	3.4
ROW MNCs	19	10	9	0.1	0.1	0.1	0.3	0.8	0.3

12.9% share. ROW multinational companies had a larger share of both export and import trade. Notably, these firms held a 84.4% share of all Food export trade.

The Food trade balance in 1975 was a surplus of $7,332 million. This reflected a $12,482 million surplus in MNC-related trade and a $5,150 million deficit in Non-MNC trade. The MNC-related surplus reflected a surplus position of both U.S. and ROW multinationals, primarily the foreign-based MNCs. Thus the overall surplus in Food was due to MNC-related trade.

Between 1975 and 1982, Food trade grew 62% or $15,138 million to reach $39,556 million. In comparison, affiliate related trade increased $10,314 million or 56% to a level of $28,897 million (adjusted for the trade overlap). Accordingly, the overall affiliate position decreased slightly from a 76.1% to a 73.1% share and Non-MNC trade rose to a 26.9% share. Within the affiliate trade structure, the export share dropped to 85.6% and the import share increased to 51.2%. This structural change reflected declines in the export shares of U.S.-based and ROW-based MNCs; and an increase in the import share of foreign multinationals.

The Food trade balance in 1982 was a surplus of $10,650 million, up $3,318 million from 1975. The affiliate related trade surplus was $14,088 million, an increase of $1,606 million; the Non-MNC trade deficit had fallen $1,712 million to $3,438 million. Thus the improvement in the Food trade balance was due to favorable trends in both components. The MNC-related surplus continued to reflect surplus positions of both U.S. and ROW multinationals. The improvement in the surplus was due entirely to a larger surplus in ROW MNC trade; the surplus in U.S. MNC trade actually declined.

In the 1982 to 1989 period, Food trade grew 28% or $11,147 million to $50,703 million. In comparison, affiliate related trade fell $1,512 million or 5% to a level of $27,385 million (adjusted for the trade overlap). As a result, the overall affiliate position dropped from a 73.1% to a 54.0% share and Non-MNC trade rose to a 46.0% share. The affiliate trade structure continued to change. The export share dropped further to 64.9% and the import share decreased to 38.1%. These structural changes reflected declines in the export and import shares of foreign-based MNCs, the dominant MNC group. Compared to 1975, the ROW MNC share of total trade had fallen from 65.5% to 46.7%; the U.S. MNC share had fallen from 12.9% to 8.3%. Foreign-based MNCs still held 57.4% of export trade but their import share had fallen to the 31.2% level.

The Food trade balance in 1989 was a surplus of $9,349 million, down $1,301 million from 1982. The affiliate related trade surplus was $11,619 million, a decrease of $2,469 million; the Non-MNC trade deficit had improved $1,168 million to $2,270 million. Thus the deterioration in the Food trade balance reflected trends in MNC-related trade. The MNC-related surplus was the result of continuing surplus positions of both U.S. and ROW multinationals. The decline in the surplus was linked to smaller positive balances in both MNC groups.

Intrafirm Related Trade

Food trade totaled $24,418 million in 1975. Intrafirm related trade was $8,857 million for a 36.3% share (compared to a 76.1% share for affiliate related trade). The arms-length or Non-MNC trade was $15,561 million for a

Table 14.2: Multinational Companies and
U.S. Food Trade (SITC 0) in 1982

	MERCHANDISE TRADE (Millions of Dollars)			TOTAL TRADE (Percent Share)			ALL MNCs TRADE (Percent Share)		
	EXPORTS	IMPORTS	BALANCE	EXP	IMP	AVG	EXP	IMP	AVG
Affiliate Related Trade									
Total	25103	14453	10650	100.0	100.0	100.0	NA	NA	NA
Non-MNCs	3611	7049	-3438	14.4	48.8	26.9	NA	NA	NA
All MNCs	21492	7405	14088	85.6	51.2	73.1	100.0	100.0	100.0
USA MNCs	2652	1226	1426	10.6	8.5	9.8	12.3	16.6	13.4
ROW MNCs	19258	6271	12987	76.7	43.4	64.5	89.6	84.7	88.3
Petro MNCs	6	0	6	0.0	0.0	0.0	0.0	0.0	0.0
USA MNCs	6	0	6	0.0	0.0	0.0	0.0	0.0	0.0
ROW MNCs	0	0	0	0.0	0.0	0.0	0.0	0.0	0.0
Manu MNCs	1359	863	497	5.4	6.0	5.6	6.3	11.7	7.7
USA MNCs	844	287	557	3.4	2.0	2.9	3.9	3.9	3.9
ROW MNCs	544	586	-42	2.2	4.1	2.9	2.5	7.9	3.9
Whole MNCs	19901	5841	14060	79.3	40.4	65.1	92.6	78.9	89.1
USA MNCs	1665	402	1263	6.6	2.8	5.2	7.7	5.4	7.2
ROW MNCs	18623	5518	13105	74.2	38.2	61.0	86.7	74.5	83.5
Other MNCs	225	701	-476	0.9	4.8	2.3	1.0	9.5	3.2
USA MNCs	137	537	-400	0.5	3.7	1.7	0.6	7.3	2.3
ROW MNCs	91	167	-76	0.4	1.2	0.7	0.4	2.3	0.9
Intrafirm Related Trade									
Total	25103	14453	10650	100.0	100.0	100.0	NA	NA	NA
Non-MNCs	16351	11704	4647	65.1	81.0	70.9	NA	NA	NA
All MNCs	8752	2749	6003	34.9	19.0	29.1	100.0	100.0	100.0
USA MNCs	1816	1041	775	7.2	7.2	7.2	20.7	37.9	24.8
ROW MNCs	6936	1708	5228	27.6	11.8	21.9	79.3	62.1	75.2
Petro MNCs	5	0	5	0.0	0.0	0.0	0.1	0.0	0.0
USA MNCs	5	0	5	0.0	0.0	0.0	0.1	0.0	0.0
ROW MNCs	0	0	0	0.0	0.0	0.0	0.0	0.0	0.0
Manu MNCs	487	342	145	1.9	2.4	2.1	5.6	12.4	7.2
USA MNCs	363	207	156	1.4	1.4	1.4	4.1	7.5	5.0
ROW MNCs	124	135	-11	0.5	0.9	0.7	1.4	4.9	2.3
Whole MNCs	8118	1863	6255	32.3	12.9	25.2	92.8	67.8	86.8
USA MNCs	1335	309	1026	5.3	2.1	4.2	15.3	11.2	14.3
ROW MNCs	6783	1554	5229	27.0	10.8	21.1	77.5	56.5	72.5
Other MNCs	142	544	-402	0.6	3.8	1.7	1.6	19.8	6.0
USA MNCs	113	525	-412	0.5	3.6	1.6	1.3	19.1	5.5
ROW MNCs	29	19	10	0.1	0.1	0.1	0.3	0.7	0.4

63.7% share. The MNC-related trade position primarily reflected a 47.8% share of export trade, the dominant trade component; the import share was only 14.8%. The dominant MNC group was foreign-based firms with a 28.0% share of total trade; U.S.-based firms held a 8.3% share. ROW multinationals had a larger share of both export and import trade.

The Food trade balance in 1975 was a surplus of $7,332 million. This reflected a $6,327 million surplus in MNC-related trade and a $1,005 million surplus in Non-MNC trade. The MNC-related surplus reflected a surplus position of both U.S. and ROW multinationals, especially foreign-based MNCs.

Between 1975 and 1982, Food trade grew $15,138 million or 62% to reach $39,556 million. In comparison, intrafirm related trade increased $2,644 million or 30% to a level of $11,501 million. Accordingly, the overall intrafirm position decreased slightly from a 36.3% to a 29.1% share (compared to a 76.1% to 73.1% share change for affiliate related trade). Non-MNC trade rose to a 70.9% share. Within the intrafirm trade structure, the export share dropped to 34.9% and the import share increased to 19.0%, reflecting changes in the trade shares of ROW MNCs and U.S. MNCs, respectively.

The Food trade balance in 1982 was a surplus of $10,650 million, up $3,318 million from 1975. The intrafirm related trade surplus was $6,003 million, a decrease of $324 million; the Non-MNC trade surplus had risen $3,642 million to $4,647 million. Thus the improvement in the Food trade balance resulted from favorable trends in arms-length transactions. The MNC-related surplus continued to reflect surplus positions of both U.S. and ROW multinationals. The decline in the surplus was due entirely to a smaller surplus in U.S. MNC trade; the surplus in ROW MNC trade actually increased.

In the 1982 to 1989 period, Food trade grew $11,147 million or 28% to $50,703 million. In comparison, intrafirm related trade increased $1,713 million or 15% to a level of $13,214 million. As a result, the overall intrafirm position dropped from a 29.1% to a 26.1% share (compared to a 73.1% to 54.0% share change for affiliate related trade). Non-MNC trade rose to a 73.9% share. Within the intrafirm trade structure, the export share dropped further to 31.5% and the import share decreased to 18.1%. This structural change reflected declines in the export shares of U.S. and ROW MNCs, and a drop in the import share of U.S.-based firms. Compared to 1975, the ROW MNC share of total trade had fallen from 28.0% to 19.8%; the U.S. MNC share had fallen from 8.3% to 6.3%.

The Food trade balance in 1989 was a surplus of $9,349 million, down $1,301 million from 1982. The intrafirm related trade surplus was $5,716 million, a decrease of $287 million; the Non-MNC trade surplus had fallen $1,014 million to $3,633 million. Thus the deterioration in the Food trade balance reflected trends in both components. The MNC-related surplus continued to reflect surplus positions of both U.S. and MNC multinationals. The decline in the surplus was linked to smaller balances in both MNC groups.

INDUSTRY TRADE ROLES

This section is based on the trade data shown in Tables 14.1, 14.2, and 14.3 for 1975, 1982, and 1989, respectively. The trade role of each affiliate industry group is discussed on the basis of affiliate related trade.

Table 14.3: Multinational Companies and
U.S. Food Trade (SITC 0) in 1989

	MERCHANDISE TRADE (Millions of Dollars)			TOTAL TRADE (Percent Share)			ALL MNCs TRADE (Percent Share)		
	EXPORTS	IMPORTS	BALANCE	EXP	IMP	AVG	EXP	IMP	AVG
Affiliate Related Trade									
Total	30026	20677	9349	100.0	100.0	100.0	NA	NA	NA
Non-MNCs	10525	12794	-2270	35.1	61.9	46.0	NA	NA	NA
All MNCs	19502	7883	11619	64.9	38.1	54.0	100.0	100.0	100.0
USA MNCs	2628	1598	1030	8.8	7.7	8.3	13.5	20.3	15.4
ROW MNCs	17231	6443	10788	57.4	31.2	46.7	88.4	81.7	86.5
Petro MNCs	0	0	0	0.0	0.0	0.0	0.0	0.0	0.0
USA MNCs	0	0	0	0.0	0.0	0.0	0.0	0.0	0.0
ROW MNCs	0	0	0	0.0	0.0	0.0	0.0	0.0	0.0
Manu MNCs	2451	1925	526	8.2	9.3	8.6	12.6	24.4	16.0
USA MNCs	1528	801	727	5.1	3.9	4.6	7.8	10.2	8.5
ROW MNCs	961	1151	-190	3.2	5.6	4.2	4.9	14.6	7.7
Whole MNCs	16677	5408	11270	55.5	26.2	43.6	85.5	68.6	80.6
USA MNCs	919	368	551	3.1	1.8	2.5	4.7	4.7	4.7
ROW MNCs	16069	5164	10905	53.5	25.0	41.9	82.4	65.5	77.5
Other MNCs	373	550	-177	1.2	2.7	1.8	1.9	7.0	3.4
USA MNCs	181	429	-248	0.6	2.1	1.2	0.9	5.4	2.2
ROW MNCs	201	128	73	0.7	0.6	0.6	1.0	1.6	1.2
Intrafirm Related Trade									
Total	30026	20677	9349	100.0	100.0	100.0	NA	NA	NA
Non-MNCs	20561	16928	3633	68.5	81.9	73.9	NA	NA	NA
All MNCs	9465	3749	5716	31.5	18.1	26.1	100.0	100.0	100.0
USA MNCs	1913	1282	631	6.4	6.2	6.3	20.2	34.2	24.2
ROW MNCs	7552	2467	5085	25.2	11.9	19.8	79.8	65.8	75.8
Petro MNCs	0	0	0	0.0	0.0	0.0	0.0	0.0	0.0
USA MNCs	0	0	0	0.0	0.0	0.0	0.0	0.0	0.0
ROW MNCs	0	0	0	0.0	0.0	0.0	0.0	0.0	0.0
Manu MNCs	1378	1226	152	4.6	5.9	5.1	14.6	32.7	19.7
USA MNCs	1032	639	393	3.4	3.1	3.3	10.9	17.0	12.6
ROW MNCs	346	587	-241	1.2	2.8	1.8	3.7	15.7	7.1
Whole MNCs	7956	2151	5805	26.5	10.4	19.9	84.1	57.4	76.5
USA MNCs	758	297	461	2.5	1.4	2.1	8.0	7.9	8.0
ROW MNCs	7198	1854	5344	24.0	9.0	17.9	76.0	49.5	68.5
Other MNCs	131	372	-241	0.4	1.8	1.0	1.4	9.9	3.8
USA MNCs	123	346	-223	0.4	1.7	0.9	1.3	9.2	3.5
ROW MNCs	8	26	-18	0.0	0.1	0.1	0.1	0.7	0.3

Petroleum Affiliates

Affiliate related trade was $801 million in 1975, adjusted for the affiliate trade overlap. This figure represented a 3.3% share of total trade and a 4.3% share of overall MNC-related trade. The industry category ranked third and was dominated by ROW-based firms. The industry recorded a trade balance in surplus by $504 million, compared to the total merchandise trade surplus of $7,332 million.

By 1982, industry trade had decreased 99% to $6 million. This figure represented a 0.0% share of total trade (down 3.3 share points), and a 0.0% share of MNC-related trade (down 4.3 share points). The industry category ranked last, behind wholesale, manufacturing, and other affiliates. The trade balance was a surplus of $6 million (down $498 million), compared to a total merchandise surplus of $10,650 million (up $3,318 million).

Industry related trade fell 100% to $0 million in 1989. This figure represented a 0.0% share of total trade, and a 0.0% share of MNC-related trade. The industry category still ranked last. The trade balance was $0 million (down $6 million), compared to a total merchandise surplus of $9,349 million (down $1,301 million).

Manufacturing Affiliates

Affiliate related trade was $1,243 million in 1975, adjusted for the affiliate trade overlap. This figure represented a 5.1% share of total trade and a 6.7% share of MNC-related trade. The industry category ranked second and was dominated by U.S.-based firms. The industry trade balance was a surplus of $510 million, compared to a total merchandise surplus of $7,332 million.

By 1982, industry trade had increased 79% to $2,222 million. This figure represented a 5.6% share of total trade (up 0.5 share points), and a 7.7% share of MNC-related trade (up 1.0 share points). The industry category ranked second, behind wholesale affiliates. The trade balance was a surplus of $497 million (down $13 million), compared to a total merchandise deficit of $10,650 million (up $3,318 million).

Industry related trade increased by 97% to $4,376 million in 1989. This figure represented a 8.6% share of total trade (up 3.0 share points), and a 16.0% share of MNC-related trade (up 8.3 share points). The industry category ranked second, behind wholesale affiliates, and remained dominated by U.S.-based firms. The trade balance was a surplus of $526 million (up $29 million), compared to a total merchandise surplus of $9,349 million (down $1,301 million).

Wholesale Trade Affiliates

Affiliate related trade was $16,077 million in 1975, adjusted for the affiliate trade overlap. This figure represented a 65.8% share of total trade and a 86.5% share of MNC-related trade. The industry category ranked first and was clearly dominated by ROW-based firms. The industry trade balance was a surplus of $11,474 million, compared to a total merchandise surplus of $7,332 million.

By 1982, industry trade had increased 60% to $25,742 million. This figure represented a 65.1% share of total trade (down 0.8 share points), and a 89.1%

share of MNC-related trade (up 2.6 share points). The industry category
continued to rank first. The trade balance was a surplus of $14,060 million (up
$2,586 million), compared to a total merchandise surplus of $10,650 million (up
$3,318 million).

Industry related trade decreased by 14% to $22,085 million in 1989. This
figure represented a 43.6% share of total trade (down 21.5 share points), and
a 80.6% share of MNC-related trade (down 8.4 share points). The industry
category still ranked first, and continued to be dominated by ROW-based firms.
The trade balance was a surplus of $11,270 million (down $2,791 million),
compared to a total merchandise surplus of $9,349 million (down $1,301
million).

Other Industry Affiliates

Affiliate related trade was $462 million in 1975, adjusted for the affiliate
trade overlap. This figure represented a 1.9% share of total trade and a 2.5%
share of MNC-related trade. The industry category ranked last and was
dominated by U.S.-based firms. The industry trade balance was a deficit of $6
million, compared to a total merchandise surplus of $7,332 million.

By 1982, industry trade had increased 101% to $926 million. This figure
represented a 2.3% share of total trade (up 0.5 share points), and a 3.2% share
of MNC-related trade (up 0.7 share points). The industry category ranked third,
ahead of petroleum. The trade balance was a deficit of $476 million (up $469
million), compared to a total merchandise surplus of $10,650 million (up $3,318
million).

Industry related trade decreased less than 1% to $924 million in 1989. This
figure represented a 1.8% share of total trade (down 0.5 share points), and a
3.4% share of MNC-related trade (up 0.2 share points). The industry category
still ranked third, and continued to be dominated by U.S.-based firms. The
trade balance was a deficit of $177 million (down $299 million), compared to
a total merchandise surplus of $9,349 million (down $1,301 million).

DERIVATION OF THE DATA

The derivation of the MNC-related product trade data is discussed at length
in Chapter 12 on "Total Product Trade." As noted in that discussion, trade
categories were combined in certain benchmark surveys. Food (SITC 0) was
combined with Beverages and Tobacco (SITC 1) in the reverse benchmark for
1974 and the outward benchmark for 1977. Separate data on Food trade have
been collected in all later FDI surveys.

The task was to allocate the combined trade groupings into their component
categories. As elsewhere, this was done with sets of allocation ratios. The
Food category was special since it had been combined with another product

classification in both a reverse survey and an outward survey. Since cross survey data were not usable for developing allocation ratios, each benchmark was treated separately.

In the 1974 benchmark, Food (SITC 0) trade was combined with Beverages and Tobacco (SITC 1) trade into a expanded "Edibles" category (SITC 0,1). Food trade and Beverages and Tobacco trade were separately reported in the 1980 and 1987 reverse investment benchmarks. The ratios were calculated for each benchmark year, and showed some variability. The BM87 ratios were discarded and the BM80 ratios, being the closest reverse benchmark to 1974, were used to allocate the Edibles trade into the Food category and the Beverages and Tobacco category for BM74.

In the 1977 benchmark, Food (SITC 0) trade was again combined with Beverages and Tobacco (SITC 1) into an "Edibles" category (SITC 0,1). Food trade and Beverages and Tobacco trade were separately reported in the 1982 and 1989 outward investment benchmarks. The ratios were calculated for each benchmark year, and showed some variability. The BM89 ratios were discarded and the BM82 ratios, being the closest outward benchmark to 1977, were used to allocate the Edibles trade into the Food category and the Beverages and Tobacco category for BM77.

These data for the 1974 reverse benchmark and the 1977 outward benchmark were used as the basis for the tables in this chapter.

CHAPTER 15

BEVERAGES AND TOBACCO TRADE

Beverages and Tobacco, along with Coal and Coke, are the smallest product groups in Non-Manufactures trade. The product category amounts to only 1.3 % of total merchandise trade, ranking last. In affiliate related trade, multinational companies are involved in 43 % of Beverages and Tobacco trade, compared to 52 % for all Non-Manufactures. Manufacturing affiliates are the dominant industry group, but account for less than one-fourth of the product trade.

DEFINITION OF BEVERAGES AND TOBACCO PRODUCTS

As defined by the Bureau of Economic Analysis, the "Beverages and Tobacco" trade classification consists of products in the SITC 1 category. Beverages and Tobacco trade includes the following products [BEA 1990 21]:

Beverages and Tobacco
(SITC code 1)

Bottled and canned soft drinks, mineral waters, and other nonalcoholic beverages

Alcoholic beverages

Unmanufactured and manufactured tobacco products

TRENDS IN BEVERAGES AND TOBACCO TRADE

In 1975, Beverages and Tobacco trade totaled $2,767 million. Exports were $1,341 million and imports were $1,426 million yielding a small deficit of $85 million. Between 1975 and 1982, total trade increased 136% or $3,769 million to reach $6,536 million. Both exports and imports enjoyed strong and nearly identical growth. The trade deficit remained and increased 126% or $107 million to a 1982 level of $192 million.

Between 1982 and 1989, the growth rates slowed in Beverages and Tobacco trade, especially in imports. Total trade increased 51.9% or $3,392 million to reach $9,928 million. Imports rose only 30% while exports jumped 75%. This resulted in a 727% improvement in the trade balance of $1,396 million, creating the trade surplus of $1,204 million in 1989.

THE TRADE ROLE OF MULTINATIONAL COMPANIES

This section is based on the trade data shown in Tables 15.1, 15.2, and 15.3 for 1975, 1982, and 1989, respectively. The overall trade role of multinational companies ("All MNCs" in the tables) is discussed for both affiliate related trade and intrafirm related trade.

Affiliate Related Trade

Beverages and Tobacco trade totaled $2,767 million in 1975. Adjusted for the trade overlap, affiliate related trade was $1,127 million for a 40.7% share; Non-MNC trade was $1,641 million for a 59.3% share. The MNC-related trade position reflected a 31.8% share of export trade and a 42.6% share of import trade. The dominant MNC group was foreign-based firms with a 24.9% share; U.S.-based firms held a 17.6% share. ROW multinational companies held slightly larger shares of both export and import trade.

The Beverages and Tobacco trade balance in 1975 was a deficit of only $85 million. This reflected a $97 million deficit in MNC-related trade and a $12 million surplus in Non-MNC trade. Thus the overall deficit in Beverages and Tobacco trade was linked to MNC-related trade. In turn, the MNC-related deficit reflected a deficit position of both U.S. and ROW multinationals.

Between 1975 and 1982, Beverages and Tobacco trade grew 136% or $3,769 million to reach $6,536 million. In comparison, affiliate related trade increased $1,316 million or 117% to a level of $2,443 million (adjusted for the trade overlap). Accordingly, the overall affiliate position decreased slightly from a 40.7% to a 37.4% share and Non-MNC trade rose to a 62.6% share. Within the affiliate trade structure, the export share dropped to 31.8% and the import share remained almost unchanged at 42.6%. This change reflected declines in the export shares of both U.S.-based and ROW-based MNCs, and offsetting decreases and increases in the import shares of U.S.-based and ROW-based multinationals.

The Beverages and Tobacco trade balance in 1982 was a another small deficit of $192 million, a deterioration of $107 million from 1975. The affiliate

Table 15.1: Multinational Companies and
U.S. Beverages and Tobacco Trade (SITC 1) in 1975

	MERCHANDISE TRADE (Millions of Dollars)			TOTAL TRADE (Percent Share)			ALL MNCs TRADE (Percent Share)		
	EXPORTS	IMPORTS	BALANCE	EXP	IMP	AVG	EXP	IMP	AVG
Affiliate Related Trade									
Total	1341	1426	-85	100.0	100.0	100.0	NA	NA	NA
Non-MNCs	826	815	12	61.6	57.1	59.3	NA	NA	NA
All MNCs	515	612	-97	38.4	42.9	40.7	100.0	100.0	100.0
USA MNCs	197	290	-93	14.7	20.3	17.6	38.3	47.4	43.2
ROW MNCs	327	362	-35	24.4	25.4	24.9	63.5	59.2	61.2
Petro MNCs	15	22	-7	1.1	1.5	1.3	2.9	3.6	3.3
USA MNCs	0	0	0	0.0	0.0	0.0	0.0	0.0	0.0
ROW MNCs	15	22	-7	1.1	1.5	1.3	2.9	3.6	3.3
Manu MNCs	170	391	-221	12.7	27.4	20.3	33.0	63.9	49.8
USA MNCs	167	247	-80	12.5	17.3	15.0	32.4	40.4	36.8
ROW MNCs	4	164	-160	0.3	11.5	6.1	0.8	26.8	14.9
Whole MNCs	245	162	83	18.2	11.3	14.7	47.5	26.4	36.1
USA MNCs	24	43	-19	1.8	3.0	2.4	4.7	7.0	5.9
ROW MNCs	223	135	88	16.6	9.5	12.9	43.3	22.1	31.8
Other MNCs	85	37	48	6.4	2.6	4.4	16.6	6.1	10.9
USA MNCs	6	0	6	0.4	0.0	0.2	1.2	0.0	0.5
ROW MNCs	85	41	44	6.3	2.9	4.6	16.5	6.7	11.2
Intrafirm Related Trade									
Total	1341	1426	-85	100.0	100.0	100.0	NA	NA	NA
Non-MNCs	940	957	-17	70.1	67.1	68.6	NA	NA	NA
All MNCs	401	469	-68	29.9	32.9	31.4	100.0	100.0	100.0
USA MNCs	179	209	-30	13.3	14.7	14.0	44.6	44.6	44.6
ROW MNCs	222	260	-38	16.6	18.2	17.4	55.4	55.4	55.4
Petro MNCs	12	22	-10	0.9	1.5	1.2	3.0	4.7	3.9
USA MNCs	0	0	0	0.0	0.0	0.0	0.0	0.0	0.0
ROW MNCs	12	22	-10	0.9	1.5	1.2	3.0	4.7	3.9
Manu MNCs	159	319	-160	11.9	22.4	17.3	39.7	68.0	54.9
USA MNCs	158	194	-36	11.8	13.6	12.7	39.4	41.4	40.5
ROW MNCs	1	125	-124	0.1	8.8	4.6	0.2	26.7	14.5
Whole MNCs	215	104	111	16.0	7.3	11.5	53.6	22.2	36.7
USA MNCs	19	15	4	1.4	1.1	1.2	4.7	3.2	3.9
ROW MNCs	196	89	107	14.6	6.2	10.3	48.9	19.0	32.8
Other MNCs	15	24	-9	1.1	1.7	1.4	3.7	5.1	4.5
USA MNCs	2	0	2	0.1	0.0	0.1	0.5	0.0	0.2
ROW MNCs	13	24	-11	1.0	1.7	1.3	3.2	5.1	4.3

related trade deficit was $423 million in 1982, an increase of $326 million; the Non-MNC trade surplus had risen $219 million to $231 million. Thus the deterioration in the Beverages and Tobacco trade balance was due to unfavorable trends in MNC-related trade. The MNC-related deficit reflected the deficit positions of ROW and U.S. multinationals. The increase in this deficit was due to a larger deficit in ROW MNC trade; the deficit in U.S. MNC trade was largely unchanged.

In the 1982 to 1989 period, Beverages and Tobacco trade grew 52% or $3,392 million to $9,928 million. In comparison, affiliate related trade rose $2,598 million or 106% percent to a level of $5,041 million (adjusted for the trade overlap). As a result, the overall affiliate position increased from a 37.4% to a 50.8% share and Non-MNC trade fell to a 49.2% share. Within the affiliate trade structure, the export share increased to 44.3% and the import share to 59.1%. This change reflected increases in the export shares of U.S. and ROW multinationals, and a large jump in the import share of ROW MNCs. Compared to 1975, the ROW MNC share of total trade had risen from 24.9% to 37.6%; the U.S. MNC share had fallen from 17.6% to 14.4%.

The Beverages and Tobacco trade balance in 1989 was a surplus of $1,204 million, an improvement of $1,396 million which reversed the 1982 deficit position. The affiliate related trade deficit was $112 million, an improvement of $311 million; the Non-MNC trade surplus had risen $1,085 million to $1,316 million. Thus the improvement in the Beverages and Tobacco trade balance reflected favorable trends in both components. The MNC-related deficit was due to a growing deficit in ROW MNC trade; U.S. MNC trade had moved to a comfortable surplus position.

Intrafirm Related Trade

Beverages and Tobacco trade totaled $2,767 million in 1975. Intrafirm related trade was $870 million for a 31.4% share (compared to a 40.7% share for affiliate related trade). Arms-length or Non-MNC trade was $1,897 million for a 68.6% share. The MNC-related trade position reflected a 29.9% share of export trade and a 32.9% share of import trade. The dominant MNC group was foreign-based firms with a 17.4% share of total trade; U.S.-based firms had a 14.0% share. ROW multinational companies held slightly larger shares of both export and import trade.

The Beverages and Tobacco trade balance in 1975 was a deficit of $85 million. This reflected a $68 million deficit in MNC-related trade and a $17 million deficit in Non-MNC trade. The MNC-related deficit reflected a negative balance for both U.S. and ROW multinationals.

Between 1975 and 1982, Beverages and Tobacco trade grew $3,769 million or 136% to reach $6,536 million. In comparison, intrafirm related trade increased $723 million or 83% to a level of $1,593 million. Accordingly, the overall intrafirm position decreased slightly from a 31.4% to a 24.4% share (compared to a 40.7% to 37.4% share change for affiliate related trade). Non-MNC trade rose to a 75.6% share. Within the intrafirm trade structure, the export share dropped to 20.8% and the import share to 27.7%. This structural change reflected declines in the export shares of U.S.-based and foreign-based MNCs, and a decrease in the import share of U.S.-based MNCs.

The Beverages and Tobacco trade balance for 1982 was in deficit by $192

Table 15.2: Multinational Companies and
U.S. Beverages and Tobacco Trade (SITC 1) in 1982

	MERCHANDISE TRADE (Millions of Dollars)			TOTAL TRADE (Percent Share)			ALL MNCs TRADE (Percent Share)		
	EXPORTS	IMPORTS	BALANCE	EXP	IMP	AVG	EXP	IMP	AVG
Affiliate Related Trade									
Total	3172	3364	-192	100.0	100.0	100.0	NA	NA	NA
Non-MNCs	2162	1932	231	68.2	57.4	62.6	NA	NA	NA
All MNCs	1010	1433	-423	31.8	42.6	37.4	100.0	100.0	100.0
USA MNCs	317	413	-96	10.0	12.3	11.2	31.4	28.8	29.9
ROW MNCs	711	1076	-365	22.4	32.0	27.3	70.4	75.1	73.2
Petro MNCs	0	0	0	0.0	0.0	0.0	0.0	0.0	0.0
USA MNCs	0	0	0	0.0	0.0	0.0	0.0	0.0	0.0
ROW MNCs	0	0	0	0.0	0.0	0.0	0.0	0.0	0.0
Manu MNCs	305	841	-536	9.6	25.0	17.5	30.2	58.7	46.9
USA MNCs	274	331	-57	8.6	9.8	9.3	27.1	23.1	24.8
ROW MNCs	34	537	-503	1.1	16.0	8.7	3.4	37.5	23.4
Whole MNCs	487	439	48	15.4	13.1	14.2	48.3	30.7	37.9
USA MNCs	37	82	-45	1.2	2.4	1.8	3.7	5.7	4.9
ROW MNCs	456	375	81	14.4	11.1	12.7	45.1	26.2	34.0
Other MNCs	217	152	65	6.9	4.5	5.7	21.5	10.6	15.1
USA MNCs	6	0	6	0.2	0.0	0.1	0.6	0.0	0.2
ROW MNCs	221	164	57	7.0	4.9	5.9	21.9	11.4	15.8
Intrafirm Related Trade									
Total	3172	3364	-192	100.0	100.0	100.0	NA	NA	NA
Non-MNCs	2512	2431	81	79.2	72.3	75.6	NA	NA	NA
All MNCs	660	933	-273	20.8	27.7	24.4	100.0	100.0	100.0
USA MNCs	281	300	-19	8.9	8.9	8.9	42.6	32.2	36.5
ROW MNCs	379	633	-254	11.9	18.8	15.5	57.4	67.8	63.5
Petro MNCs	0	0	0	0.0	0.0	0.0	0.0	0.0	0.0
USA MNCs	0	0	0	0.0	0.0	0.0	0.0	0.0	0.0
ROW MNCs	0	0	0	0.0	0.0	0.0	0.0	0.0	0.0
Manu MNCs	250	599	-349	7.9	17.8	13.0	37.9	64.2	53.3
USA MNCs	243	247	-4	7.7	7.3	7.5	36.8	26.5	30.8
ROW MNCs	7	352	-345	0.2	10.5	5.5	1.1	37.7	22.5
Whole MNCs	378	284	94	11.9	8.4	10.1	57.3	30.4	41.6
USA MNCs	35	53	-18	1.1	1.6	1.3	5.3	5.7	5.5
ROW MNCs	343	231	112	10.8	6.9	8.8	52.0	24.8	36.0
Other MNCs	32	50	-18	1.0	1.5	1.3	4.8	5.4	5.1
USA MNCs	3	0	3	0.1	0.0	0.0	0.5	0.0	0.2
ROW MNCs	29	50	-21	0.9	1.5	1.2	4.4	5.4	5.0

million, a deterioration of $107 million from 1975. The intrafirm related trade deficit was $273 million in 1982, an increase of $205 million; the Non-MNC trade position had changed by $98 million to a surplus of $81 million. Thus the deterioration in the Beverages and Tobacco trade balance reflected MNC-related trade. The MNC-related deficit continued to be linked to deficits in both ROW and U.S. MNC trade. However the growth in this deficit was caused by a growing negative imbalance in ROW MNC trade.

In the 1982 to 1989 period, Beverages and Tobacco trade grew $3,392 million or 52% to $9,928 million. In comparison, intrafirm related trade increased $990 million or 62% to a level of $2,583 million. As a result, the overall intrafirm position increased from a 24.4% to a 26.0% share (compared to a 37.4% to 50.8% share change for affiliate related trade). Non-MNC trade fell to a 74.0% share. Within the intrafirm trade structure, the export share dropped to 18.8% while the import share increased to 35.2%. This structural change reflected positive and negative shifts in the export shares of U.S. and ROW MNCs, and an increase in the import share of ROW-based firms. Compared to 1975, the ROW MNC share of total trade had fallen from 17.4% to 14.1%; the U.S. MNC share had decreased from 14.0% to 12.0%.

The Beverages and Tobacco trade balance in 1989 was a surplus of $1,204 million, up $1,396 million from 1982 and eliminating the small deficit position. The intrafirm related trade deficit was $489 million in 1989, a deterioration of $216 million; the Non-MNC trade surplus had risen $1,612 million to $1,693 million. Thus the improvement in the Beverages and Tobacco trade balance was due entirely to arms-length trade. The MNC-related deficit was now linked solely to the growing shortfall in ROW MNC trade; U.S.-based firms had moved to a trade surplus position.

INDUSTRY TRADE ROLES

This section is based on the trade data shown in Tables 15.1, 15.2, and 15.3 for 1975, 1982, and 1989, respectively. The trade role of each affiliate industry group is discussed on the basis of affiliate related trade.

Petroleum Affiliates

Affiliate related trade was $37 million in 1975, adjusted for the affiliate trade overlap. This figure represented a 1.3% share of total trade and a 3.3% share of MNC-related trade. The industry category ranked last and was dominated by ROW-based firms. The industry trade balance was a deficit of $7 million, compared to a total merchandise deficit of $85 million.

By 1982, industry trade had decreased 100% to $0. This figure represented a 0.0% share of total trade (down 1.3 share points), and a 0.0% share of MNC-related trade (down 3.3 share points). The industry category ranked last. The trade balance was $0 (up $7 million), compared to a total merchandise deficit of $192 million (up $107 million).

Industry related trade was $0 in 1989, unchanged from 1982 levels. This figure represented a 0.0% share of total trade (unchanged), and a 0.0% share of MNC-related trade (unchanged). The industry category still ranked last. The

Table 15.3: Multinational Companies and U.S. Beverages and Tobacco Trade (SITC 1) in 1989

	MERCHANDISE TRADE (Millions of Dollars)			TOTAL TRADE (Percent Share)			ALL MNCs TRADE (Percent Share)		
	EXPORTS	IMPORTS	BALANCE	EXP	IMP	AVG	EXP	IMP	AVG
Affiliate Related Trade									
Total	5566	4362	1204	100.0	100.0	100.0	NA	NA	NA
Non-MNCs	3102	1786	1316	55.7	40.9	49.2	NA	NA	NA
All MNCs	2465	2576	-112	44.3	59.1	50.8	100.0	100.0	100.0
USA MNCs	914	512	402	16.4	11.7	14.4	37.1	19.9	28.3
ROW MNCs	1609	2125	-516	28.9	48.7	37.6	65.3	82.5	74.1
Petro MNCs	0	0	0	0.0	0.0	0.0	0.0	0.0	0.0
USA MNCs	0	0	0	0.0	0.0	0.0	0.0	0.0	0.0
ROW MNCs	0	0	0	0.0	0.0	0.0	0.0	0.0	0.0
Manu MNCs	1229	1537	-308	22.1	35.2	27.9	49.9	59.7	54.9
USA MNCs	308	353	-45	5.5	8.1	6.7	12.5	13.7	13.1
ROW MNCs	954	1224	-270	17.1	28.1	21.9	38.7	47.5	43.2
Whole MNCs	879	981	-102	15.8	22.5	18.7	35.7	38.1	36.9
USA MNCs	599	136	463	10.8	3.1	7.4	24.3	5.3	14.6
ROW MNCs	291	863	-572	5.2	19.8	11.6	11.8	33.5	22.9
Other MNCs	357	58	299	6.4	1.3	4.2	14.5	2.3	8.2
USA MNCs	7	23	-16	0.1	0.5	0.3	0.3	0.9	0.6
ROW MNCs	364	38	326	6.5	0.9	4.0	14.8	1.5	8.0
Intrafirm Related Trade									
Total	5566	4362	1204	100.0	100.0	100.0	NA	NA	NA
Non-MNCs	4519	2826	1693	81.2	64.8	74.0	NA	NA	NA
All MNCs	1047	1536	-489	18.8	35.2	26.0	100.0	100.0	100.0
USA MNCs	797	390	407	14.3	8.9	12.0	76.1	25.4	46.0
ROW MNCs	250	1146	-896	4.5	26.3	14.1	23.9	74.6	54.0
Petro MNCs	0	0	0	0.0	0.0	0.0	0.0	0.0	0.0
USA MNCs	0	0	0	0.0	0.0	0.0	0.0	0.0	0.0
ROW MNCs	0	0	0	0.0	0.0	0.0	0.0	0.0	0.0
Manu MNCs	428	851	-423	7.7	19.5	12.9	40.9	55.4	49.5
USA MNCs	202	263	-61	3.6	6.0	4.7	19.3	17.1	18.0
ROW MNCs	226	588	-362	4.1	13.5	8.2	21.6	38.3	31.5
Whole MNCs	613	678	-65	11.0	15.5	13.0	58.5	44.1	50.0
USA MNCs	589	120	469	10.6	2.8	7.1	56.3	7.8	27.4
ROW MNCs	24	558	-534	0.4	12.8	5.9	2.3	36.3	22.5
Other MNCs	6	7	-1	0.1	0.2	0.1	0.6	0.5	0.5
USA MNCs	6	7	-1	0.1	0.2	0.1	0.6	0.5	0.5
ROW MNCs	0	0	0	0.0	0.0	0.0	0.0	0.0	0.0

Manufacturing Affiliates

Affiliate related trade was $561 million in 1975, adjusted for the affiliate trade overlap. This figure represented a 20.3% share of total trade and a 49.8% share of MNC-related trade. The industry category ranked first and was dominated by U.S.-based firms. The industry trade balance was a deficit of

$221 million, compared to a total merchandise deficit of $85 million.

By 1982, industry trade had increased 104% to $1,146 million. This figure represented a 17.5% share of total trade (down 2.7 share points), and a 46.9% share of MNC-related trade (down 2.9 share points). The industry category again ranked first. The trade balance was a deficit of $536 million (up $315 million), compared to a total merchandise deficit of $192 million (up $107 million).

Industry related trade increased by 141% to $2,766 million in 1989. This figure represented a 27.9% share of total trade (up 10.3 share points), and a 54.9% share of MNC-related trade (up 8.0 share points). The industry category still ranked first, but was now dominated by ROW-based firms. The trade balance was a deficit of $308 million (down $228 million), compared to a total merchandise surplus of $1,204 million (a swing of $1,396 million).

Wholesale Trade Affiliates

Affiliate related trade was $406 million in 1975, adjusted for the affiliate trade overlap. This figure represented a 14.7% share of total trade and a 36.1% share of MNC-related trade. The industry category ranked second and was dominated by ROW-based firms. The industry trade balance was a surplus of $83 million, compared to a total merchandise deficit of $85 million.

By 1982, industry trade had increased 128% to $927 million. This figure represented a 14.2% share of total trade (down 0.5 share points), and a 37.9% share of MNC-related trade (up 1.9 share points). The industry category continued to rank second. The trade balance was a surplus of $48 million (down $35 million), compared to a total merchandise deficit of $192 million (up $107 million).

Industry related trade increased by 101% to $1,860 million in 1989. This figure represented a 18.7% share of total trade (up 4.6 share points), and a 36.9% share of MNC-related trade (down 1.0 share points). The industry category still ranked second, behind manufacturing, and continued to be dominated by ROW-based firms. The trade balance was a deficit of $102 million (a swing of $150 million), compared to a total merchandise surplus of $1,204 million (a swing of $1,396 million).

Other Industry Affiliates

Affiliate related trade was $123 million in 1975, adjusted for the affiliate trade overlap. This figure represented a 4.4% share of total trade and a 10.9% share of MNC-related trade. The industry category ranked third and was dominated by ROW-based firms. The industry trade balance was a surplus of $48 million, compared to a total merchandise deficit of $85 million.

By 1982, industry trade had increased 202% to $370 million. This figure represented a 5.7% share of total trade (up 1.2 share points), and a 15.1% share of MNC-related trade (up 4.3 share points). The industry category continued to rank third. The trade balance was a surplus of $65 million (up $17 million), compared to a total merchandise deficit of $192 million (up $107 million).

Industry related trade increased by 12% to $415 million in 1989. This figure represented a 4.2% share of total trade (down 1.5 share points), and a 8.2% share of MNC-related trade (down 6.9 share points). The industry category still ranked third, and continued to be dominated by ROW-based firms. The trade balance was a surplus of $299 million (up $233 million), compared to a total merchandise surplus of $1,204 million (a swing of $1,396 million).

DERIVATION OF THE DATA

The derivation of the MNC-related product trade data is discussed at length in Chapter 12 on "Total Product Trade." As noted in that discussion, trade categories were combined in certain benchmark surveys. Beverages and Tobacco (SITC 1) were combined with Food (SITC 0) in the reverse benchmark for 1974 and again in the outward benchmark for 1977. Separate data on Beverages and Tobacco trade have been collected in all later FDI surveys.

The task was to allocate the combined trade groupings into their component categories. As elsewhere, this was done with sets of allocation ratios. The Beverages and Tobacco category is special since it was combined with another product classification in both a reverse survey and an outward survey. Since cross survey data were not usable for developing allocation ratios, each benchmark was treated separately.

The development of Beverages and Tobacco estimates for the 1974 and 1977 benchmarks is described in the data derivation section of Chapter 14 on "Food Trade." These data were used as the basis for the tables in this chapter.

CHAPTER 16

CRUDE MATERIALS TRADE

Crude Materials exports and imports includes one-sixth of all Non-Manufactures trade, and is the third largest category. The product group includes 6.3% of total merchandise trade, ranking seventh. In affiliate related trade, multinational companies are involved in 50% of Crude Materials trade, compared to 52% for all Non-Manufactures. Wholesale affiliates are the dominant industry group, accounting for nearly one-third of all Crude Materials trade.

DEFINITION OF CRUDE MATERIALS PRODUCTS

As defined by the Bureau of Economic Analysis, the "Crude Materials" foreign trade classification consists of products in the SITC 2 category. Crude Materials trade includes the following products [BEA 1990 21]:

Crude Materials, Inedible, Except Fuels
(SITC code 2)

Raw hides, skins, and furskins

Soybeans, other oil seeds, and oleaginous fruit

Crude rubber, natural, synthetic, and reclaimed (exclude compounded, semiprocessed, and finished rubber products)

Cork, natural, raw, and waste

Fuelwood and wood charcoal

Pulpwood (particles, chips, wood waste, logs and bolts, poles, pilings and posts)

Rough-sawed, dressed, and cut-stock lumber, except veneers

Pulp and waste paper

Textile fibers and their wastes (raw, natural and synthetic fiber; include scouring and combing mill products, manmade fiber, filament, staple and tow, and rags, but exclude yarn, thread, and fabric)

Crude natural fertilizers of animal or vegetable origin, and fertilizers of natural phosphates, nitrates, and potassic salts

Crude nonmetallic minerals, except coal, petroleum, and precious stones (include stone, sand and gravel, sulfur, industrial diamonds, natural abrasives, salt, asbestos, etc.)

Ferrous and nonferrous metal ores, concentrates, waste and scrap (include those of precious metals, but exclude gold waste and scrap)

Other crude inedible animal and vegetable materials such as seeds, nursery stock, natural resins and gums, etc.

TRENDS IN CRUDE MATERIALS TRADE

In 1975, Crude Materials trade totaled $15,623 million. Exports were $10,031 million and imports were $5,592 million yielding a surplus of $4,439 million. Between 1975 and 1982, total trade increased 84% or $13,141 million to reach $28,764 million. Both exports and imports enjoyed strong growth, with exports growing twice as fast as imports. Since exports already exceeded imports, the trade surplus grew 161% or $7,147 million to a 1982 level of $11,586 million.

Between 1982 and 1989, the growth patterns in Crude Materials changed, with imports now growing twice as fast as exports. Total trade increased 48% or $13,821 million to reach $42,585 million. Imports jumped 79% while exports rose only 35%. However, since exports continued to exceed imports, the trade balance actually improved by 2% or $271 million, keeping the trade surplus at $11,857 million in 1989.

THE TRADE ROLE OF MULTINATIONAL COMPANIES

This section is based on the trade data shown in Tables 16.1, 16.2, and 16.3 for 1975, 1982, and 1989, respectively. The overall trade role of multinational companies ("All MNCs" in the tables) is discussed for both affiliate related trade and intrafirm related trade.

Table 16.1: Multinational Companies and
U.S. Crude Materials Trade (SITC 2) in 1975

	MERCHANDISE TRADE (Millions of Dollars)			TOTAL TRADE (Percent Share)			ALL MNCs TRADE (Percent Share)		
	EXPORTS	IMPORTS	BALANCE	EXP	IMP	AVG	EXP	IMP	AVG
Affiliate Related Trade									
Total	10031	5592	4439	100.0	100.0	100.0	NA	NA	NA
Non-MNCs	5402	2390	3013	53.9	42.7	49.9	NA	NA	NA
All MNCs	4629	3203	1427	46.1	57.3	50.1	100.0	100.0	100.0
USA MNCs	1121	1406	-285	11.2	25.1	16.2	24.2	43.9	32.3
ROW MNCs	3681	2068	1613	36.7	37.0	36.8	79.5	64.6	73.4
Petro MNCs	485	327	158	4.8	5.8	5.2	10.5	10.2	10.4
USA MNCs	13	14	-1	0.1	0.3	0.2	0.3	0.4	0.3
ROW MNCs	475	329	146	4.7	5.9	5.1	10.3	10.3	10.3
Manu MNCs	780	527	253	7.8	9.4	8.4	16.8	16.5	16.7
USA MNCs	761	408	353	7.6	7.3	7.5	16.4	12.7	14.9
ROW MNCs	59	170	-111	0.6	3.0	1.5	1.3	5.3	2.9
Whole MNCs	3239	1669	1570	32.3	29.9	31.4	70.0	52.1	62.7
USA MNCs	310	274	36	3.1	4.9	3.7	6.7	8.6	7.5
ROW MNCs	3049	1553	1496	30.4	27.8	29.5	65.9	48.5	58.8
Other MNCs	125	679	-554	1.2	12.2	5.2	2.7	21.2	10.3
USA MNCs	37	710	-673	0.4	12.7	4.8	0.8	22.2	9.5
ROW MNCs	98	16	82	1.0	0.3	0.7	2.1	0.5	1.5
Intrafirm Related Trade									
Total	10031	5592	4439	100.0	100.0	100.0	NA	NA	NA
Non-MNCs	6630	3727	2903	66.1	66.6	66.3	NA	NA	NA
All MNCs	3401	1865	1536	33.9	33.4	33.7	100.0	100.0	100.0
USA MNCs	775	863	-88	7.7	15.4	10.5	22.8	46.3	31.1
ROW MNCs	2626	1002	1624	26.2	17.9	23.2	77.2	53.7	68.9
Petro MNCs	462	247	215	4.6	4.4	4.5	13.6	13.2	13.5
USA MNCs	12	14	-2	0.1	0.3	0.2	0.4	0.8	0.5
ROW MNCs	450	233	217	4.5	4.2	4.4	13.2	12.5	13.0
Manu MNCs	494	276	218	4.9	4.9	4.9	14.5	14.8	14.6
USA MNCs	474	220	254	4.7	3.9	4.4	13.9	11.8	13.2
ROW MNCs	20	56	-36	0.2	1.0	0.5	0.6	3.0	1.4
Whole MNCs	2389	892	1497	23.8	16.0	21.0	70.2	47.8	62.3
USA MNCs	266	189	77	2.7	3.4	2.9	7.8	10.1	8.6
ROW MNCs	2123	703	1420	21.2	12.6	18.1	62.4	37.7	53.7
Other MNCs	56	450	-394	0.6	8.0	3.2	1.6	24.1	9.6
USA MNCs	23	440	-417	0.2	7.9	3.0	0.7	23.6	8.8
ROW MNCs	33	10	23	0.3	0.2	0.3	1.0	0.5	0.8

Affiliate Related Trade

Crude Materials trade totaled $15,623 million in 1975. Adjusted for the trade overlap, affiliate related trade was $7,832 million for a 50.1% share; Non-MNC trade was $7,792 million for a 49.9% share. The MNC-related trade position reflected a 46.1% share of export trade and a 57.3% share of import trade. The dominant MNC group was foreign-based firms with a 36.8% share; U.S.-based firms held a 16.2% share. ROW multinational companies held larger shares of both export and import trade.

The Crude Materials trade balance in 1975 was a surplus of $4,439 million. This reflected a $1,427 million surplus in MNC-related trade and a $3,013 million surplus in Non-MNC trade. Thus the overall surplus in Crude Materials trade was linked to both components. In turn, the MNC-related surplus reflected the surplus position of ROW multinationals; U.S.-based firms incurred a small trade deficit.

Between 1975 and 1982, Crude Materials trade grew 84% or $13,141 million to reach $28,764 million. In comparison, affiliate related trade increased $8,014 million or 102% to a level of $15,845 million (adjusted for the trade overlap). Accordingly, the overall affiliate position increased from a 50.1% to a 55.1% share and Non-MNC trade fell to a 44.9% share. Within the affiliate trade structure, the export share rose to 52.6% and the import share to 61.0%. This change reflected increases in the export share of ROW-based MNCs and the import share of U.S.-based multinationals.

The Crude Materials trade balance in 1982 was a surplus of $11,586 million, an increase of $7,147 million from 1975. The affiliate related trade surplus was $5,375 million, an increase of $3,949 million; the Non-MNC trade surplus had risen $3,199 million to $6,211 million. Thus the improvement in the Crude Materials trade balance was due to favorable trends in both trade components. The MNC-related surplus again reflected the surplus position of ROW multinationals; the increase in this surplus was due to the larger surplus by foreign-based firms. U.S.-based MNCs continued to record a small deficit in Crude Materials trade.

In the 1982 to 1989 period, Crude Materials trade grew 48% or $13,821 million to $42,585 million. In comparison, affiliate related trade rose $3,543 million or 22% percent to a level of $19,388 million (adjusted for the trade overlap). As a result, the overall affiliate position decreased from a 55.1% to a 45.5% share and Non-MNC trade rose to a 54.5% share. Within the affiliate trade structure, the export share decreased to 38.6% and the import share to 57.8%. This change reflected decreases in the export and import shares of U.S. and ROW multinationals. Compared to 1975, the ROW MNC share of total trade had barely changed from 36.8% to 35.9%; the U.S. MNC share had fallen from 16.2% to 12.9%.

The Crude Materials trade balance in 1989 was a surplus of $11,857 million, a small improvement of $271 million over the 1982 position. The affiliate related trade surplus was down to $1,614 million, a large decline of $3,761 million; the Non-MNC trade surplus had risen $4,032 million to reach $10,243 million. Thus the trade surplus in Crude Materials trade reflected favorable trends in Non-NC trade. The MNC-related trade surplus was preserved only due to the surplus in ROW MNC trade; U.S. MNC trade had moved into a deeper deficit position.

Table 16.2: Multinational Companies and
U.S. Crude Materials Trade (SITC 2) in 1982

	MERCHANDISE TRADE (Millions of Dollars)			TOTAL TRADE (Percent Share)			ALL MNCs TRADE (Percent Share)		
	EXPORTS	IMPORTS	BALANCE	EXP	IMP	AVG	EXP	IMP	AVG
Affiliate Related Trade									
Total	20175	8589	11586	100.0	100.0	100.0	NA	NA	NA
Non-MNCs	9565	3354	6211	47.4	39.0	44.9	NA	NA	NA
All MNCs	10610	5235	5375	52.6	61.0	55.1	100.0	100.0	100.0
USA MNCs	2192	2387	-195	10.9	27.8	15.9	20.7	45.6	28.9
ROW MNCs	8818	3215	5603	43.7	37.4	41.8	83.1	61.4	75.9
Petro MNCs	33	65	-32	0.2	0.8	0.3	0.3	1.2	0.6
USA MNCs	12	12	0	0.1	0.1	0.1	0.1	0.2	0.2
ROW MNCs	23	59	-36	0.1	0.7	0.3	0.2	1.1	0.5
Manu MNCs	2155	1361	794	10.7	15.8	12.2	20.3	26.0	22.2
USA MNCs	1845	955	890	9.1	11.1	9.7	17.4	18.2	17.7
ROW MNCs	381	458	-77	1.9	5.3	2.9	3.6	8.7	5.3
Whole MNCs	8126	2773	5353	40.3	32.3	37.9	76.6	53.0	68.8
USA MNCs	256	342	-86	1.3	4.0	2.1	2.4	6.5	3.8
ROW MNCs	8186	2673	5513	40.6	31.1	37.8	77.2	51.1	68.5
Other MNCs	297	1036	-739	1.5	12.1	4.6	2.8	19.8	8.4
USA MNCs	79	1078	-999	0.4	12.6	4.0	0.7	20.6	7.3
ROW MNCs	228	25	203	1.1	0.3	0.9	2.1	0.5	1.6
Intrafirm Related Trade									
Total	20175	8589	11586	100.0	100.0	100.0	NA	NA	NA
Non-MNCs	14507	6063	8444	71.9	70.6	71.5	NA	NA	NA
All MNCs	5668	2526	3142	28.1	29.4	28.5	100.0	100.0	100.0
USA MNCs	1392	1653	-261	6.9	19.2	10.6	24.6	65.4	37.2
ROW MNCs	4276	873	3403	21.2	10.2	17.9	75.4	34.6	62.8
Petro MNCs	11	24	-13	0.1	0.3	0.1	0.2	1.0	0.4
USA MNCs	10	11	-1	0.0	0.1	0.1	0.2	0.4	0.3
ROW MNCs	1	13	-12	0.0	0.2	0.0	0.0	0.5	0.2
Manu MNCs	1272	976	296	6.3	11.4	7.8	22.4	38.6	27.4
USA MNCs	1074	803	271	5.3	9.3	6.5	18.9	31.8	22.9
ROW MNCs	198	173	25	1.0	2.0	1.3	3.5	6.8	4.5
Whole MNCs	4218	988	3230	20.9	11.5	18.1	74.4	39.1	63.5
USA MNCs	238	304	-66	1.2	3.5	1.9	4.2	12.0	6.6
ROW MNCs	3980	684	3296	19.7	8.0	16.2	70.2	27.1	56.9
Other MNCs	167	538	-371	0.8	6.3	2.5	2.9	21.3	8.6
USA MNCs	70	535	-465	0.3	6.2	2.1	1.2	21.2	7.4
ROW MNCs	97	3	94	0.5	0.0	0.3	1.7	0.1	1.2

Intrafirm Related Trade

Crude Materials trade totaled $15,623 million in 1975. Intrafirm related trade was $5,266 million for a 33.7% share (compared to a 50.1% share for affiliate related trade). Arms-length or Non-MNC trade was $10,357 million for a 66.3% share. The MNC-related trade position reflected a nearly identical

33.9% share of export trade and a 33.4% share of import trade. The dominant MNC group was foreign-based firms with a 23.2% share of total trade; U.S.-based firms had only a 10.5% share. ROW multinational companies held larger shares of both export and import trade.

The Crude Materials trade balance in 1975 was a surplus of $4,439 million. This reflected a $1,536 million surplus in MNC-related trade and a $2,903 million surplus in Non-MNC trade. The MNC-related surplus was based on the positive balance for ROW multinationals; U.S.-based firms recorded a small trade deficit.

Between 1975 and 1982, Crude Materials trade grew $13,141 million or 84% to reach $28,764 million. In comparison, intrafirm related trade increased $2,928 million or 56% to a level of $8,194 million. Accordingly, the overall intrafirm position decreased slightly from a 33.7% to a 28.5% share (compared to a 50.1% to 55.1% share change for affiliate related trade). Non-MNC trade rose to a 71.9% share. Within the intrafirm trade structure, the export share dropped to 28.1% and the import share to 29.4%. This structural change reflected declines in the export and import shares of foreign-based MNCs, and an increase in the import share of U.S.-based MNCs.

The Crude Materials trade balance in 1982 was a surplus of $11,586 million, an improvement of $7,147 million from 1975. The intrafirm related trade surplus was $3,142 million, an increase of $1,606 million; the Non-MNC surplus had grown by $5,541 million to a level of $8,444 million. Thus the improvement in the Crude Materials trade balance reflected both components. The MNC-related surplus continued to be linked to a growing positive balance in ROW MNC trade. U.S.-based firms again reported a small deficit in their Crude Materials trade.

In the 1982 to 1989 period, Crude Materials trade grew $13,821 million or 48% to $42,585 million. In comparison, intrafirm related trade increased $2,908 million or 36% to a level of $11,102 million. As a result, the overall intrafirm position decreased from a 28.5% to a 26.1% share (compared to a 55.1% to 45.5% share change for affiliate related trade). Non-MNC trade rose to a 73.9% share. Within the intrafirm trade structure, the export share dropped to 24.0% while the import share increased slightly to 29.7%. This structural change reflected small declines in export shares of both U.S. and ROW MNCs; and large but offsetting import share increases and decreases for U.S. and ROW MNCs. Compared to 1975, the ROW MNC share of total trade had fallen from 23.2% to 19.7%; the U.S. MNC share had decreased from 10.5% to 6.4%.

The Crude Materials trade balance in 1989 was a surplus of $11,857 million, up only $271 million. The intrafirm related trade surplus was $1,976 million, a decrease of $1,166 million; the Non-MNC trade surplus had risen $1,437 million to $9,881 million. Thus the improvement in the Crude Materials trade balance was due entirely to arms-length trade. The MNC-related surplus was again linked solely to the surplus in ROW MNC trade; U.S.-based firms saw their deficit position become deeper.

Table 16.3: Multinational Companies and
U.S. Crude Materials Trade (SITC 2) in 1989

	MERCHANDISE TRADE (Millions of Dollars)			TOTAL TRADE (Percent Share)			ALL MNCs TRADE (Percent Share)		
	EXPORTS	IMPORTS	BALANCE	EXP	IMP	AVG	EXP	IMP	AVG
Affiliate Related Trade									
Total	27221	15364	11857	100.0	100.0	100.0	NA	NA	NA
Non-MNCs	16720	6477	10243	61.4	42.2	54.5	NA	NA	NA
All MNCs	10501	8887	1614	38.6	57.8	45.5	100.0	100.0	100.0
USA MNCs	1465	4049	-2584	5.4	26.4	12.9	14.0	45.6	28.4
ROW MNCs	9207	6068	3139	33.8	39.5	35.9	87.7	68.3	78.8
Petro MNCs	32	65	-33	0.1	0.4	0.2	0.3	0.7	0.5
USA MNCs	0	0	0	0.0	0.0	0.0	0.0	0.0	0.0
ROW MNCs	33	82	-49	0.1	0.5	0.3	0.3	0.9	0.6
Manu MNCs	1934	3929	-1995	7.1	25.6	13.8	18.4	44.2	30.2
USA MNCs	853	2123	-1270	3.1	13.8	7.0	8.1	23.9	15.3
ROW MNCs	1131	2434	-1303	4.2	15.8	8.4	10.8	27.4	18.4
Whole MNCs	8026	3787	4239	29.5	24.6	27.7	76.4	42.6	60.9
USA MNCs	439	656	-217	1.6	4.3	2.6	4.2	7.4	5.6
ROW MNCs	7699	3517	4182	28.3	22.9	26.3	73.3	39.6	57.9
Other MNCs	509	1106	-597	1.9	7.2	3.8	4.8	12.4	8.3
USA MNCs	173	1270	-1097	0.6	8.3	3.4	1.6	14.3	7.4
ROW MNCs	344	35	309	1.3	0.2	0.9	3.3	0.4	2.0
Intrafirm Related Trade									
Total	27221	15364	11857	100.0	100.0	100.0	NA	NA	NA
Non-MNCs	20682	10801	9881	76.0	70.3	73.9	NA	NA	NA
All MNCs	6539	4563	1976	24.0	29.7	26.1	100.0	100.0	100.0
USA MNCs	1123	1589	-466	4.1	10.3	6.4	17.2	34.8	24.4
ROW MNCs	5416	2974	2442	19.9	19.4	19.7	82.8	65.2	75.6
Petro MNCs	17	7	10	0.1	0.0	0.1	0.3	0.2	0.2
USA MNCs	0	0	0	0.0	0.0	0.0	0.0	0.0	0.0
ROW MNCs	17	7	10	0.1	0.0	0.1	0.3	0.2	0.2
Manu MNCs	774	1722	-948	2.8	11.2	5.9	11.8	37.7	22.5
USA MNCs	574	757	-183	2.1	4.9	3.1	8.8	16.6	12.0
ROW MNCs	200	965	-765	0.7	6.3	2.7	3.1	21.1	10.5
Whole MNCs	5419	2428	2991	19.9	15.8	18.4	82.9	53.2	70.7
USA MNCs	412	443	-31	1.5	2.9	2.0	6.3	9.7	7.7
ROW MNCs	5007	1985	3022	18.4	12.9	16.4	76.6	43.5	63.0
Other MNCs	329	406	-77	1.2	2.6	1.7	5.0	8.9	6.6
USA MNCs	137	389	-252	0.5	2.5	1.2	2.1	8.5	4.7
ROW MNCs	192	17	175	0.7	0.1	0.5	2.9	0.4	1.9

INDUSTRY TRADE ROLES

This section is based on the trade data shown in Tables 16.1, 16.2, and 16.3 for 1975, 1982, and 1989, respectively. The trade role of each affiliate industry group is discussed on the basis of affiliate related trade.

Petroleum Affiliates

Affiliate related trade was $812 million in 1975, adjusted for the affiliate trade overlap. This figure represented a 5.2% share of total trade and a 10.4% share of MNC-related trade. The industry category ranked third, tied with other affiliates, and was dominated by ROW-based firms. The industry trade balance was a surplus of $158 million, compared to a total merchandise surplus of $4,439 million.

By 1982, industry trade had decreased 88% to $99 million. This figure represented a 0.3% share of total trade (down 4.9 share points), and a 0.6% share of MNC-related trade (down 9.7 share points). The industry category now ranked last. The trade balance was a deficit of $32 million (a swing of $190 million), compared to a total merchandise surplus of $11,586 million (up $7,147 million).

Industry related trade was $98 million in 1989, a decrease of 1%. This figure represented a 0.2% share of total trade (down 0.1 share points), and a 0.5% share of MNC-related trade (down 0.1 share points). The industry category still ranked last (behind wholesale, manufacturing, and other industry categories) and continued to be dominated by ROW-based firms. The trade balance was a deficit of $33 million (up $1 million), compared to an overall merchandise trade balance which was in surplus by $11,857 million (up $271 million over 1982).

Manufacturing Affiliates

Affiliate related trade was $1,307 million in 1975, adjusted for the affiliate trade overlap. This figure represented a 8.4% share of total trade and a 16.7% share of MNC-related trade. The industry category ranked second and was dominated by U.S.-based firms. The industry trade balance was a surplus of $253 million, compared to a total merchandise balance which was in surplus by $4,439 million.

By 1982, industry trade had increased 169% to $3,515 million. This figure represented a 12.2% share of total trade (up 3.9 share points), and a 22.2% share of MNC-related trade (up 5.5 share points). The industry category ranked second, behind wholesale affiliates. The trade balance was a surplus of $794 million (up $541 million), compared to a total merchandise surplus of $11,586 million (up $7,147 million).

Industry related trade increased by 67% to $5,863 million in 1989. This figure represented a 13.8% share of total trade (up 1.5 share points), and a 30.2% share of MNC-related trade (up 8.1 share points). The industry category still ranked second, behind wholesale affiliates, but was now dominated by ROW-based firms. The trade balance was a deficit of $1,995 million (a swing of $2,789 million), compared to a total merchandise surplus of $11,857 million (up $271 million).

Wholesale Trade Affiliates

Affiliate related trade was $4,908 million in 1975, adjusted for the affiliate trade overlap. This figure represented a 31.4% share of total trade and a 62.7% share of MNC-related trade. The industry category ranked first and was dominated by ROW-based firms. The industry trade balance was a surplus of $1,570 million, compared to a total merchandise trade balance which was in surplus by $4,439 million.

By 1982, industry trade had increased 122% to $10,899 million. This figure represented a 37.9% share of total trade (up 6.5 share points), and a 68.8% share of MNC-related trade (up 6.1 share points). The industry category continued to rank first. The industry trade balance was a surplus of $5,353 million (up $3,783 million), compared to a total merchandise surplus position of $11,586 million (up $7,147 million).

Industry related trade increased by 8% to $11,812 million in 1989. This figure represented a 27.7% share of total trade (down 10.2 share points), and a 60.9% share of MNC-related trade (down 7.9 share points). The industry category continued to rank first, and continued to be dominated by ROW-based firms. The trade balance was a surplus of $4,239 million (down $1,114 million), compared to a total merchandise trade surplus of $11,857 million (up $271 million).

Other Industry Affiliates

Affiliate related trade was $805 million in 1975, adjusted for the affiliate trade overlap. This figure represented a 5.2% share of total trade and a 10.3% share of MNC-related trade. The industry category ranked third, tied with petroleum affiliates, and was dominated by U.S.-based firms. The industry trade balance was a deficit of $554 million, compared to a total merchandise surplus of $4,439 million.

By 1982, industry trade had increased 66% to $1,332 million. This figure represented a 4.6% share of total trade (down 0.5 share points), and a 8.4% share of MNC-related trade (down 1.9 share points). The industry category now ranked third. The trade balance was a deficit of $739 million (up $185 million), compared to a total merchandise balance which was in surplus by $11,586 million (up $7,147 million).

Industry related trade increased by 21% to $1,615 million in 1989. This figure represented a 3.8% share of total trade (down 0.8 share points), and a 8.3% share of MNC-related trade (down 0.1 share points). The industry category still ranked third (behind wholesale trade and manufacturing affiliate categories) and continued to be dominated by U.S.-based firms. The trade balance was a deficit of $597 million (down $142 million), compared to the total merchandise trade position which was in surplus of $11,857 million (up $271 million from 1985).

DERIVATION OF THE DATA

The derivation of the MNC-related product trade data is discussed at length in Chapter 12 on "Total Product Trade." Separate data on Crude Materials (SITC 2) trade have been collected in every FDI benchmark survey. No special modification of this data has been necessary.

CHAPTER 17

PETROLEUM AND PRODUCTS TRADE

Petroleum and Products is the leading product group in Non-Manufactures trade, accounting for over one-third of exports and imports. The product category includes 11.9% of total merchandise trade, ranking third. In affiliate related trade, multinational companies are involved in 50% of Petroleum and Products trade, compared to 52% for all Non-Manufactures. Petroleum affiliates are the dominant industry group, accounting for more than two-fifths of all Petroleum and Products trade.

DEFINITION OF PETROLEUM AND PRODUCTS

As defined by the Bureau of Economic Analysis, the "Petroleum and Products" foreign trade classification consists of products in "part" of the SITC 3 category. The items listed by BEA are actually SITC 33-34, which is the definition used in this book. Petroleum and Products trade includes the following products [BEA 1990 22]:

Petroleum and Products, Mineral Waxes, Natural and Manufactured Gas
(Part of SITC code 3)

Petroleum, petroleum products, and related materials (include crude and partly refined petroleum, and petroleum products such as gasoline, kerosene, distillate, and residual fuel oils, lubricating oils and greases, petroleum jelly and mineral waxes, petroleum coke, asphalt, and paving mixtures)

Gas, natural and manufactured

The petroleum product group described above is SITC 33 while the gas product group is SITC 34.

TRENDS IN PETROLEUM AND PRODUCTS TRADE

In 1975, Petroleum and Products trade totaled $27,259 million. The trade was dominated by imports; imports were $26,017 million while exports were $1,242 million yielding a large deficit of $24,775 million. Between 1975 and 1982, imports increased 151% or $39,314 million to reach $65,331 million. This import growth pushed total trade to a level of $72,398 million. The trade deficit more than doubled, rising 135% or $33,489 million to a staggering 1982 level of $58,264 million.

Between 1982 and 1989, all the components in Petroleum trade recorded declines in dollar value of roughly 20%. Imports dropped 22% or $14,449 million to a level of $50,882 million. Total trade fell to $56,518. The import decline improved the trade deficit by $13,018 million or 22%. However, the Petroleum and Products deficit still remained at $45,246 million in 1989.

The decline in Petroleum and Products trade between 1982 and 1989 had important effects on the Non-Manufactures and Manufactures trade aggregates. The trade share of Non-Manufactures was reduced while the associated deficit also decreased.

THE TRADE ROLE OF MULTINATIONAL COMPANIES

This section is based on the trade data shown in Tables 17.1, 17.2, and 17.3 for 1975, 1982, and 1989, respectively. The overall trade role of multinational companies ("All MNCs" in the tables) is discussed for both affiliate related trade and intrafirm related trade.

Affiliate Related Trade

Petroleum and Products trade totaled $27,259 million in 1975. Adjusted for the trade overlap, affiliate related trade was $15,083 million for a 55.3% share; Non-MNC trade was $12,177 million for a 44.7% share. The MNC-related trade position primarily reflected a 54.4% share of import trade, the dominant trade component; the export share was 75.5%. The dominant MNC group was U.S.-based firms with a 44.5% share of total trade; foreign-based firms held a 13.4% share. U.S. multinational companies had a larger share of both import and export trade.

The Petroleum and Products trade balance in 1975 was a deficit of $24,775 million. This reflected a $13,208 million deficit in MNC-related trade and a $11,568 million deficit in Non-MNC trade. The MNC-related deficit was linked to the deficit positions of both U.S. and ROW multinationals. Thus the overall deficit in Petroleum and Products was due to both components.

Between 1975 and 1982, Petroleum and Products trade grew 166% or $45,139 million to reach $72,398 million. In comparison, affiliate related trade

Table 17.1: Multinational Companies and
U.S. Petroleum and Products Trade (SITC 33-34) in 1975

	MERCHANDISE TRADE (Millions of Dollars)			TOTAL TRADE (Percent Share)			ALL MNCs TRADE (Percent Share)		
	EXPORTS	IMPORTS	BALANCE	EXP	IMP	AVG	EXP	IMP	AVG
Affiliate Related Trade									
Total	1242	26017	-24775	100.0	100.0	100.0	NA	NA	NA
Non-MNCs	305	11872	-11568	24.5	45.6	44.7	NA	NA	NA
All MNCs	938	14145	-13208	75.5	54.4	55.3	100.0	100.0	100.0
USA MNCs	548	11592	-11044	44.1	44.6	44.5	58.5	82.0	80.5
ROW MNCs	455	3194	-2739	36.6	12.3	13.4	48.5	22.6	24.2
Petro MNCs	569	14023	-13454	45.8	53.9	53.5	60.7	99.1	96.8
USA MNCs	437	11550	-11113	35.2	44.4	44.0	46.6	81.7	79.5
ROW MNCs	160	3104	-2944	12.9	11.9	12.0	17.1	21.9	21.6
Manu MNCs	67	35	32	5.4	0.1	0.4	7.2	0.2	0.7
USA MNCs	61	13	48	4.9	0.0	0.3	6.5	0.1	0.5
ROW MNCs	14	24	-10	1.1	0.1	0.1	1.5	0.2	0.3
Whole MNCs	275	67	208	22.2	0.3	1.3	29.4	0.5	2.3
USA MNCs	23	14	9	1.9	0.1	0.1	2.5	0.1	0.2
ROW MNCs	279	60	219	22.5	0.2	1.2	29.8	0.4	2.2
Other MNCs	26	20	6	2.1	0.1	0.2	2.8	0.1	0.3
USA MNCs	27	15	12	2.2	0.1	0.2	2.9	0.1	0.3
ROW MNCs	2	6	-4	0.2	0.0	0.0	0.2	0.0	0.1
Intrafirm Related Trade									
Total	1242	26017	-24775	100.0	100.0	100.0	NA	NA	NA
Non-MNCs	594	15123	-14529	47.8	58.1	57.7	NA	NA	NA
All MNCs	648	10894	-10246	52.2	41.9	42.3	100.0	100.0	100.0
USA MNCs	417	8982	-8565	33.6	34.5	34.5	64.4	82.4	81.4
ROW MNCs	231	1912	-1681	18.6	7.3	7.9	35.6	17.6	18.6
Petro MNCs	446	10824	-10378	35.9	41.6	41.3	68.8	99.4	97.6
USA MNCs	359	8953	-8594	28.9	34.4	34.2	55.4	82.2	80.7
ROW MNCs	87	1871	-1784	7.0	7.2	7.2	13.4	17.2	17.0
Manu MNCs	33	26	7	2.7	0.1	0.2	5.1	0.2	0.5
USA MNCs	33	5	28	2.7	0.0	0.1	5.1	0.0	0.3
ROW MNCs	0	21	-21	0.0	0.1	0.1	0.0	0.2	0.2
Whole MNCs	157	30	127	12.6	0.1	0.7	24.2	0.3	1.6
USA MNCs	15	10	5	1.2	0.0	0.1	2.3	0.1	0.2
ROW MNCs	142	20	122	11.4	0.1	0.6	21.9	0.2	1.4
Other MNCs	12	14	-2	1.0	0.1	0.1	1.9	0.1	0.2
USA MNCs	10	14	-4	0.8	0.1	0.1	1.5	0.1	0.2
ROW MNCs	2	0	2	0.2	0.0	0.0	0.3	0.0	0.0

increased $14,764 million or 98% to a level of $29,846 million (adjusted for the trade overlap). Accordingly, the overall affiliate position decreased from a 55.3% to a 41.2% share and Non-MNC trade rose to a 58.8% share. In addition, there was a change in the affiliate trade structure. The import share dropped to 35.8% and the export share increased to 91.0%. This structural change reflected a decline in the import share of U.S.-based MNCs, and an increase in the export share of foreign multinationals.

The Petroleum and Products trade balance in 1982 was a deficit of $58,264 million, up $33,489 million from 1975. The affiliate related trade deficit was $16,979 million in 1982, an increase of $3,772 million; the Non-MNC trade deficit increased $29,718 million to reach $41,285 million. Thus the deterioration in the Petroleum and Products trade balance was due to unfavorable trends in both components, especially Non-MNC trade. The MNC-related deficit continued to reflect deficit positions of both U.S. and ROW multinationals.

In the 1982 to 1989 period, Petroleum and Products trade declined 22% or $15,880 million to $56,518 million. In comparison, affiliate related trade rose $210 million or 1% to a level of $30,056 million (adjusted for the trade overlap). As a result, the overall affiliate position increased from a 41.2% to a 53.2% share and Non-MNC trade fell to a 46.8% share. The affiliate trade structure continued to change. The very significant import share increased to 48.9%, while the export share remained unchanged at 91.9%. The change in the import share reflected a 4.2% decline in U.S.-based share and a much larger 17.5% increase in ROW-based share. Compared to 1975, the U.S. MNC share of total trade had fallen from 44.5% to 20.6%; the ROW MNC share had risen from 13.4% to 35.2%. These changes primarily reflected import share changes.

The Petroleum and Products trade balance in 1989 was a deficit of $45,246 million, down $13,018 million from 1982. The affiliate related trade deficit was $19,698 million, an increase of $2,719 million; the Non-MNC trade deficit had improved $15,737 million to $25,548 million. Thus the reduction in the Petroleum and Products trade balance reflected trends in Non-MNC trade. The MNC-related deficit continued to reflect the deficit positions of both U.S. and ROW multinationals. The growth in this deficit was linked to a larger ROW MNC deficit which offset a decline in the U.S. MNC deficit.

Intrafirm Related Trade

Petroleum and Products trade totaled $27,259 million in 1975. Intrafirm related trade was $11,542 million for a 42.3% share (compared to a 55.3% share for affiliate related trade). Arms-length or Non-MNC trade was $15,717 million for a 57.7% share. The MNC-related trade position primarily reflected a 41.9% share of import trade, the dominant trade component; the export share was 52.2%. The dominant MNC group was U.S.-based firms with a 34.5% share of total trade; foreign-based firms held an 7.9% share. U.S. multinationals had a larger share of both import and export trade.

The Petroleum and Products trade balance in 1975 was a deficit of $24,775 million. This reflected a $10,246 million deficit in MNC-related trade and a $14,529 million deficit in Non-MNC trade. Thus the overall deficit was rooted in the trade balance position of both components. In turn, the MNC-related deficit was the result of the trade deficits of both U.S. and ROW multinationals,

Table 17.2: Multinational Companies and
U.S. Petroleum and Products Trade (SITC 33-34) in 1982

	MERCHANDISE TRADE (Millions of Dollars)			TOTAL TRADE (Percent Share)			ALL MNCs TRADE (Percent Share)		
	EXPORTS	IMPORTS	BALANCE	EXP	IMP	AVG	EXP	IMP	AVG
Affiliate Related Trade									
Total	7067	65331	-58264	100.0	100.0	100.0	NA	NA	NA
Non-MNCs	634	41919	-41285	9.0	64.2	58.8	NA	NA	NA
All MNCs	6434	23413	-16979	91.0	35.8	41.2	100.0	100.0	100.0
USA MNCs	1328	15671	-14343	18.8	24.0	23.5	20.6	66.9	57.0
ROW MNCs	5271	9290	-4019	74.6	14.2	20.1	81.9	39.7	48.8
Petro MNCs	1760	22096	-20336	24.9	33.8	33.0	27.4	94.4	79.9
USA MNCs	1063	15630	-14567	15.0	23.9	23.1	16.5	66.8	55.9
ROW MNCs	723	7821	-7098	10.2	12.0	11.8	11.2	33.4	28.6
Manu MNCs	314	43	271	4.4	0.1	0.5	4.9	0.2	1.2
USA MNCs	238	19	219	3.4	0.0	0.4	3.7	0.1	0.9
ROW MNCs	85	29	56	1.2	0.0	0.2	1.3	0.1	0.4
Whole MNCs	4347	1263	3084	61.5	1.9	7.7	67.6	5.4	18.8
USA MNCs	14	17	-3	0.2	0.0	0.0	0.2	0.1	0.1
ROW MNCs	4463	1434	3029	63.2	2.2	8.1	69.4	6.1	19.8
Other MNCs	13	10	2	0.2	0.0	0.0	0.2	0.0	0.1
USA MNCs	13	5	8	0.2	0.0	0.0	0.2	0.0	0.1
ROW MNCs	0	6	-6	0.0	0.0	0.0	0.0	0.0	0.0
Intrafirm Related Trade									
Total	7067	65331	-58264	100.0	100.0	100.0	NA	NA	NA
Non-MNCs	4300	50472	-46172	60.8	77.3	75.7	NA	NA	NA
All MNCs	2767	14859	-12092	39.2	22.7	24.3	100.0	100.0	100.0
USA MNCs	997	12574	-11577	14.1	19.2	18.7	36.0	84.6	77.0
ROW MNCs	1770	2285	-515	25.0	3.5	5.6	64.0	15.4	23.0
Petro MNCs	1176	14612	-13436	16.6	22.4	21.8	42.5	98.3	89.6
USA MNCs	870	12541	-11671	12.3	19.2	18.5	31.4	84.4	76.1
ROW MNCs	306	2071	-1765	4.3	3.2	3.3	11.1	13.9	13.5
Manu MNCs	119	14	105	1.7	0.0	0.2	4.3	0.1	0.8
USA MNCs	109	13	96	1.5	0.0	0.2	3.9	0.1	0.7
ROW MNCs	10	1	9	0.1	0.0	0.0	0.4	0.0	0.1
Whole MNCs	1466	227	1239	20.7	0.3	2.3	53.0	1.5	9.6
USA MNCs	12	15	-3	0.2	0.0	0.0	0.4	0.1	0.2
ROW MNCs	1454	212	1242	20.6	0.3	2.3	52.5	1.4	9.5
Other MNCs	6	6	0	0.1	0.0	0.0	0.2	0.0	0.1
USA MNCs	6	5	1	0.1	0.0	0.0	0.2	0.0	0.1
ROW MNCs	0	1	-1	0.0	0.0	0.0	0.0	0.0	0.0

especially U.S.-based MNCs.

Between 1975 and 1982, Petroleum and Products trade grew $45,139 million or 166% to reach $72,398 million. In comparison, intrafirm related trade increased $6,084 million or 53% to a level of $17,626 million. Accordingly, the overall intrafirm position decreased from a 42.3% to a 24.3% share (compared to a 55.3% to 41.2% share change for affiliate related trade).

Non-MNC trade rose to a 75.7% share. Within the intrafirm trade structure, the import share dropped to 22.7% and the export share to 39.2%. The import change primarily reflected declines in the shares of both U.S.-based and foreign-based MNCs.

The Petroleum and Products trade balance in 1982 was a deficit of $58,264 million, up $33,489 million from 1975. The intrafirm related trade deficit was $12,092 million, an increase of $1,846 million; the Non-MNC trade deficit had risen $31,643 million to $46,172 million. Thus the deterioration in the Petroleum and Products trade balance reflected unfavorable trends in both components. The MNC-related deficit continued to reflect deficit positions of both U.S. and ROW multinationals. The increase in the deficit was due entirely to a larger deficit in U.S. MNC trade; the ROW MNC deficit actually fell.

In the 1982 to 1989 period, Petroleum and Products trade declined $15,880 million or 22% to $56,518 million. In comparison, intrafirm related trade increased $607 million or three percent to a level of $18,233 million. As a result, the overall intrafirm position increased from a 24.3% to a 32.3% share (compared to a 41.2% to 53.2% share change for affiliate related trade). Non-MNC trade fell to a 67.7% share. Within the intrafirm trade structure, the import share rose to 30.7% and the export share to 46.3%. The import change reflected a 4.8% decrease in U.S. MNCs share and a 12.8% rise in ROW MNCs share. Compared to 1975, the U.S. MNC share of total trade had fallen from 34.5% to 15.3%; the ROW MNC share had risen from 7.9% to 17.0%. These changes in intrafirm trade structure primarily reflected shifts in import trade shares.

The Petroleum and Products trade balance in 1989 was a deficit of $45,246 million, down $13,018 million from 1982. The intrafirm related trade deficit was $13,009 million, an increase of $917 million; the Non-MNC trade deficit had fallen $13,935 million to $32,237 million. Thus the improvement in the Petroleum and Products trade balance reflected changes in arms-length transactions. The MNC-related deficit continued to reflect deficit positions of both U.S. and ROW multinationals. The increase in this deficit was linked to a larger ROW MNC deficit which offset a decline in the U.S. MNC deficit.

INDUSTRY TRADE ROLES

This section is based on the trade data shown in Tables 17.1, 17.2, and 17.3 for 1975, 1982, and 1989, respectively. The trade role of each affiliate industry group is discussed on the basis of affiliate related trade.

Petroleum Affiliates

Affiliate related trade was $14,592 million in 1975, adjusted for the affiliate trade overlap. This figure represented a 53.5% share of total trade and a 96.8%

Table 17.3: Multinational Companies and U.S. Petroleum and Products Trade (SITC 33-34) in 1989

	MERCHANDISE TRADE (Millions of Dollars)			TOTAL TRADE (Percent Share)			ALL MNCs TRADE (Percent Share)		
	EXPORTS	IMPORTS	BALANCE	EXP	IMP	AVG	EXP	IMP	AVG
Affiliate Related Trade									
Total	5636	50882	-45246	100.0	100.0	100.0	NA	NA	NA
Non-MNCs	457	26005	-25548	8.1	51.1	46.8	NA	NA	NA
All MNCs	5179	24877	-19698	91.9	48.9	53.2	100.0	100.0	100.0
USA MNCs	1559	10092	-8533	27.7	19.8	20.6	30.1	40.6	38.8
ROW MNCs	3748	16162	-12414	66.5	31.8	35.2	72.4	65.0	66.2
Petro MNCs	1721	22563	-20842	30.5	44.3	43.0	33.2	90.7	80.8
USA MNCs	1386	10061	-8675	24.6	19.8	20.3	26.8	40.4	38.1
ROW MNCs	355	13625	-13270	6.3	26.8	24.7	6.9	54.8	46.5
Manu MNCs	301	497	-196	5.3	1.0	1.4	5.8	2.0	2.7
USA MNCs	156	30	126	2.8	0.1	0.3	3.0	0.1	0.6
ROW MNCs	151	505	-354	2.7	1.0	1.2	2.9	2.0	2.2
Whole MNCs	3151	1038	2113	55.9	2.0	7.4	60.8	4.2	13.9
USA MNCs	11	1	10	0.2	0.0	0.0	0.2	0.0	0.0
ROW MNCs	3242	1176	2066	57.5	2.3	7.8	62.6	4.7	14.7
Other MNCs	6	779	-774	0.1	1.5	1.4	0.1	3.1	2.6
USA MNCs	6	0	6	0.1	0.0	0.0	0.1	0.0	0.0
ROW MNCs	0	856	-856	0.0	1.7	1.5	0.0	3.4	2.8
Intrafirm Related Trade									
Total	5636	50882	-45246	100.0	100.0	100.0	NA	NA	NA
Non-MNCs	3024	35261	-32237	53.7	69.3	67.7	NA	NA	NA
All MNCs	2612	15621	-13009	46.3	30.7	32.3	100.0	100.0	100.0
USA MNCs	1303	7338	-6035	23.1	14.4	15.3	49.9	47.0	47.4
ROW MNCs	1309	8283	-6974	23.2	16.3	17.0	50.1	53.0	52.6
Petro MNCs	1318	15011	-13693	23.4	29.5	28.9	50.5	96.1	89.6
USA MNCs	1168	7317	-6149	20.7	14.4	15.0	44.7	46.8	46.5
ROW MNCs	150	7694	-7544	2.7	15.1	13.9	5.7	49.3	43.0
Manu MNCs	190	242	-52	3.4	0.5	0.8	7.3	1.5	2.4
USA MNCs	119	21	98	2.1	0.0	0.2	4.6	0.1	0.8
ROW MNCs	71	221	-150	1.3	0.4	0.5	2.7	1.4	1.6
Whole MNCs	1099	103	996	19.5	0.2	2.1	42.1	0.7	6.6
USA MNCs	11	0	11	0.2	0.0	0.0	0.4	0.0	0.1
ROW MNCs	1088	103	985	19.3	0.2	2.1	41.7	0.7	6.5
Other MNCs	5	265	-260	0.1	0.5	0.5	0.2	1.7	1.5
USA MNCs	5	0	5	0.1	0.0	0.0	0.2	0.0	0.0
ROW MNCs	0	265	-265	0.0	0.5	0.5	0.0	1.7	1.5

share of MNC-related trade. The industry category ranked first, and was dominated by U.S.-based firms. The industry trade balance was a deficit of $13,454 million, compared to a total merchandise deficit of $24,775 million.

By 1982, industry trade had increased 64% to $23,856 million. This figure represented a 33.0% share of total trade (down 20.6 share points), and a 79.9% share of MNC-related trade (down 16.8 share points). The industry category continued to rank first. The trade balance was a deficit of $20,336 million (up $6,882 million), compared to a total merchandise deficit of $58,264 million (up $33,489 million).

Industry related trade increased only 2% to $24,283 million in 1989. This figure represented a 43.0% share of total trade (up 10.0 share points), and a 80.8% share of MNC-related trade (up 0.9 share points). The industry category still ranked first, but was now dominated by ROW-based firms. The trade balance was a deficit of $20,842 million (up $505 million), compared to a total merchandise deficit of $45,246 million (down $13,018 million).

Manufacturing Affiliates

Affiliate related trade was $102 million in 1975, adjusted for the affiliate trade overlap. This figure represented a 0.4% share of total trade and a 0.7% share of MNC-related trade. The industry category ranked third, behind petroleum and wholesale affiliates. The industry trade balance was a surplus of $32 million, compared to a total merchandise deficit of $24,775 million.

By 1982, industry trade had increased 249% to $357 million. This figure represented a 0.5% share of total trade (up 0.1 share points), and a 1.2% share of MNC-related trade (up 0.5 share points). The industry category continued to rank third. The trade balance was a surplus of $271 million (up $239 million), compared to a total merchandise deficit of $58,264 million (up $33,489 million).

Industry related trade increased by 124% to $798 million in 1989. This figure represented a 1.4% share of total trade (up 0.9 share points), and a 2.7% share of MNC-related trade (up 1.5 share points). The industry category still ranked third, just ahead of other affiliates. The trade balance was a deficit of $196 million (a swing of $467 million), compared to a total merchandise deficit of $45,246 million (down $13,018 million).

Wholesale Trade Affiliates

Affiliate related trade was $342 million in 1975, adjusted for the affiliate trade overlap. This figure represented a 1.3% share of total trade and a 2.3% share of MNC-related trade. The industry category ranked second and was dominated by ROW-based firms. The industry trade balance was a surplus of $208 million, compared to a total merchandise deficit of $24,775 million.

By 1982, industry trade had increased 1540% to $5,610 million. This figure represented a 7.7% share of total trade (up 6.5 share points), and a 18.8% share of MNC-related trade (up 16.5 share points). The industry category continued to rank second, behind petroleum affiliates. The trade balance was a surplus of $3,084 million (up $2,875 million), compared to a total merchandise deficit of $58,264 million (up $33,489 million).

Industry related trade decreased by 25% to $4,189 million in 1989. This figure represented a 7.4% share of total trade (down 0.3 share points), and a 13.9% share of MNC-related trade (down 4.9 share points). The industry category continued to rank second and to be dominated by ROW-based firms. The trade balance was a surplus of $2,113 million (down $971 million), compared to a total merchandise deficit of $45,246 million (down $13,018 million).

Other Industry Affiliates

Affiliate related trade was $46 million in 1975, adjusted for the affiliate trade overlap. This figure represented a 0.2% share of total trade and a 0.3% share of MNC-related trade. The industry category ranked last and was dominated by U.S.-based firms. The industry trade balance was a surplus of $6 million, compared to a total merchandise deficit of $24,775 million.

By 1982, industry trade had decreased 50% to $23 million. This figure represented a 0.0% share of total trade (down 0.1 share points), and a 0.1% share of MNC-related trade (down 0.2 share points). The industry category ranked last. The trade balance was a surplus of $2 million (down $4 million), compared to a total merchandise deficit of $58,264 million (up $33,489 million).

Industry related trade increased by 3325% to $785 million in 1989. This figure represented a 1.4% share of total trade (up 1.4 share points), and a 2.6% share of MNC-related trade (up 2.5 share points). The industry category still ranked last, but was now dominated by ROW-based firms. The trade balance was a deficit of $774 million (a swing of $776 million), compared to a total merchandise deficit of $45,246 million (down $13,018 million).

DERIVATION OF THE DATA

The derivation of the MNC-related product trade data is discussed at length in Chapter 12 on "Total Product Trade." As noted in that discussion, trade categories were combined in certain benchmark surveys. Coal and Coke (SITC 32) was combined with Petroleum and Products (SITC 33-34) in the outward benchmark for 1977. Separate data on Petroleum and Products trade have been collected in all other surveys.

The task was to allocate the combined Coal and Coke (SITC 32) trade and Petroleum and Products (SITC 33-34) trade in BM77 into the two component categories. As elsewhere, this was done with a set of allocation ratios.

The development of 1977 benchmark estimates for Coal and Coke and Petroleum and Products is described in the data derivation section of Chapter 18 on "Coal and Coke Trade." These data were used as the basis for the tables in this chapter.

COAL AND COKE TRADE

Coal and Coke, along with Beverages and Tobacco, are the smallest product groups in Non-Manufactures trade. The product category amounts to only 1.3% of total merchandise trade, and ranks last. In affiliate related trade, multinational companies are involved in 36% of Coal and Coke trade, compared to 52% for all Non-Manufactures. This level of MNC-related trade is among the lowest of all product categories. Wholesale affiliates are the dominant industry group, but account for less than one-fourth of all Coal and Coke trade.

DEFINITION OF COAL AND COKE PRODUCTS

As defined by the Bureau of Economic Analysis, the "Coal and Coke" trade classification consists of products in "part" of the SITC 3 category. The items listed by BEA are actually SITC 32, which is the definition used in this book. Coal and Coke trade includes the following products [BEA 1990 22]:

Coal, Coke, and Briquets
(Part of SITC code 3)

Coal, lignite, peat, coke and briquets thereof

TRENDS IN COAL AND COKE TRADE

In 1975, Coal and Coke trade totaled $3,925 million. The trade was dominated by exports; exports were $3,341 million and imports were $584 million yielding a surplus of $2,757 million. Between 1975 and 1982, exports increased 88% or $2,934 million to reach $6,275 million. This export growth pushed total trade to a level of $6,354 million. The trade surplus nearly tripled, rising 125% or $3,439 million to a level of $6,196 million.

Between 1982 and 1989, the structure of Coal and Coke trade changed significantly. The dollar value of exports fell 31% or $1,945 million to $4,330 million. Starting from practically nothing, imports increased by $1,667 million to $1,746 million. Total trade decreased four percent or $278 million to reach $6,076 million. Consequently, the trade balance deteriorated by 58% or $3,612 million, dropping the trade surplus to $2,584 million in 1989.

THE TRADE ROLE OF MULTINATIONAL COMPANIES

This section is based on the trade data shown in Tables 18.1, 18.2, and 18.3 for 1975, 1982, and 1989, respectively. The overall trade role of multinational companies ("All MNCs" in the tables) is discussed for both affiliate related trade and intrafirm related trade.

Affiliate Related Trade

Coal and Coke trade totaled $3,925 million in 1975. Adjusted for the trade overlap, affiliate related trade was $510 million for a 13.0% share; Non-MNC trade was $3,416 million for a 87.0% share. This trade category is dominated by export activity. The MNC-related trade position reflected a 14.1% share of export trade and a 6.4% share of import trade. The dominant MNC group was foreign-based firms with a 12.1% share; U.S.-based firms held a mere 1.1% share. ROW multinational companies held larger shares of both export and import trade.

The Coal and Coke trade balance in 1975 was a surplus of $2,757 million. This reflected a $435 million surplus in MNC-related trade and a $2,323 million surplus in Non-MNC trade. Thus the overall surplus in Coal and Coke trade was linked to both components. In turn, the MNC-related surplus reflected the surplus position of ROW and U.S. multinationals, especially the former.

Between 1975 and 1982, Coal and Coke trade grew 62% or $2,429 million to reach $6,354 million. In comparison, affiliate related trade increased $3,097 million or 608% to a level of $3,606 million (adjusted for the trade overlap). Accordingly, the overall affiliate position jumped from a 13.0% to a 56.8% share and Non-MNC trade fell to a 43.2% share. Within the affiliate trade structure, the export share rose to 56.5% and the import share to 74.7%. The change in the export share reflected a large increase in the export trade of ROW-based MNCs.

The Coal and Coke trade balance in 1982 was a surplus of $6,196 million, an increase of $3,439 million from 1975. The affiliate related trade surplus was $3,488 million, an increase of $3,054 million; the Non-MNC trade surplus had risen by $386 million to $2,708 million. Thus the improvement in the Coal and

Table 18.1: Multinational Companies and U.S. Coal and Coke Trade (SITC 32) in 1975

	MERCHANDISE TRADE (Millions of Dollars)			TOTAL TRADE (Percent Share)			ALL MNCs TRADE (Percent Share)		
	EXPORTS	IMPORTS	BALANCE	EXP	IMP	AVG	EXP	IMP	AVG
Affiliate Related Trade									
Total	3341	584	2757	100.0	100.0	100.0	NA	NA	NA
Non-MNCs	2869	547	2323	85.9	93.6	87.0	NA	NA	NA
All MNCs	472	38	435	14.1	6.4	13.0	100.0	100.0	100.0
USA MNCs	39	6	33	1.2	1.0	1.1	8.3	16.0	8.8
ROW MNCs	441	33	408	13.2	5.7	12.1	93.4	88.0	93.0
Petro MNCs	100	1	99	3.0	0.2	2.6	21.3	2.4	19.9
USA MNCs	0	0	0	0.0	0.0	0.0	0.0	0.0	0.0
ROW MNCs	101	1	100	3.0	0.2	2.6	21.4	2.7	20.0
Manu MNCs	42	36	7	1.3	6.1	2.0	9.0	94.9	15.3
USA MNCs	37	6	31	1.1	1.0	1.1	7.8	16.0	8.4
ROW MNCs	7	31	-24	0.2	5.3	1.0	1.5	82.7	7.5
Whole MNCs	255	1	254	7.6	0.2	6.5	54.0	2.7	50.3
USA MNCs	2	0	2	0.1	0.0	0.1	0.4	0.0	0.4
ROW MNCs	257	1	256	7.7	0.2	6.6	54.4	2.7	50.6
Other MNCs	74	0	74	2.2	0.0	1.9	15.7	0.0	14.5
USA MNCs	0	0	0	0.0	0.0	0.0	0.0	0.0	0.0
ROW MNCs	76	0	76	2.3	0.0	1.9	16.1	0.0	14.9
Intrafirm Related Trade									
Total	3341	584	2757	100.0	100.0	100.0	NA	NA	NA
Non-MNCs	2970	563	2407	88.9	96.4	90.0	NA	NA	NA
All MNCs	371	21	350	11.1	3.6	10.0	100.0	100.0	100.0
USA MNCs	23	3	20	0.7	0.5	0.7	6.2	14.3	6.6
ROW MNCs	348	18	330	10.4	3.1	9.3	93.8	85.7	93.4
Petro MNCs	93	0	93	2.8	0.0	2.4	25.1	0.0	23.7
USA MNCs	0	0	0	0.0	0.0	0.0	0.0	0.0	0.0
ROW MNCs	93	0	93	2.8	0.0	2.4	25.1	0.0	23.7
Manu MNCs	23	20	3	0.7	3.4	1.1	6.2	95.2	11.0
USA MNCs	23	3	20	0.7	0.5	0.7	6.2	14.3	6.6
ROW MNCs	0	17	-17	0.0	2.9	0.4	0.0	81.0	4.3
Whole MNCs	205	1	204	6.1	0.2	5.2	55.3	4.8	52.6
USA MNCs	0	0	0	0.0	0.0	0.0	0.0	0.0	0.0
ROW MNCs	205	1	204	6.1	0.2	5.2	55.3	4.8	52.6
Other MNCs	50	0	50	1.5	0.0	1.3	13.5	0.0	12.8
USA MNCs	0	0	0	0.0	0.0	0.0	0.0	0.0	0.0
ROW MNCs	50	0	50	1.5	0.0	1.3	13.5	0.0	12.8

Coke trade balance was due to favorable trends in both trade components. The size and growth of the MNC-related surplus was linked to the export activity of foreign-based MNCs.

In the 1982 to 1989 period, Coal and Coke trade fell 4% or $278 million to $6,076 million. In comparison, affiliate related trade declined $1,260 million or 35% percent to a level of $2,346 million (adjusted for the trade overlap). As a result, the overall affiliate position decreased from a 56.8% to a 38.6% share and Non-MNC trade rose to a 61.4% share. Within the affiliate trade structure, the export share decreased to 48.2% and the import share to 14.7%. The export change reflected a decrease in the share of ROW multinationals. Compared to 1975, the ROW MNC share of total trade had risen from 12.1% to 36.2%; the U.S. MNC share had increased from 1.1% to 3.0%.

The Coal and Coke trade balance in 1989 was a surplus of $2,584 million, a decrease of $3,612 million from the 1982 position. The affiliate related trade surplus was down to $1,832 million, a deterioration of $1,656 million; the Non-MNC trade surplus had fallen $1,956 million down to $752 million. Thus the decline in the Coal and Coke trade surplus reflected unfavorable trends in both components. The level and change in the MNC-related surplus continued to reflect ROW MNC export patterns.

Intrafirm Related Trade

Coal and Coke trade totaled $3,925 million in 1975. Intrafirm related trade was $392 million for a 10.0% share (compared to a 13.0% share for affiliate related trade). Arms-length or Non-MNC trade was $3,533 million for a 90.0% share. This trade category is dominated by export activity. The MNC-related trade position reflected a 11.1% share of export trade and a 3.6% share of import trade. The dominant MNC group was foreign-based firms with a 9.3% share of total trade; U.S.-based firms had only a 0.7% share. ROW multinational companies held larger shares of both export and import trade.

The Coal and Coke trade balance in 1975 was a surplus of $2,757 million. This reflected a $350 million surplus in MNC-related trade and a $2,407 million surplus in Non-MNC trade. The MNC-related surplus was linked to the surplus position of ROW and U.S. multinationals, especially the former.

Between 1975 and 1982, Coal and Coke trade grew $2,429 million or 62% to reach $6,354 million. In comparison, intrafirm related trade increased $2,266 million or 579% to a level of $2,660 million. Accordingly, the overall intrafirm position jumped from a 10.0% to a 41.9% share (compared to a 13.0% to 56.8% share change for affiliate related trade). Non-MNC trade fell to a 58.1% share. Within the intrafirm trade structure, the export share climbed to 42.0% and the import share to 27.8%. The export change reflected a large increase in the share of foreign-based MNCs.

The Coal and Coke trade balance in 1982 was a surplus of $6,196 million, an improvement of $3,439 million from 1975. The intrafirm related trade surplus was $2,616 million, an increase of $2,266 million; the Non-MNC trade surplus had grown by $1,173 million to a level of $3,580 million. Thus the improvement in the Coal and Coke trade balance reflected both components. The MNC-related surplus continued to be linked to growing export trade by ROW MNCs.

In the 1982 to 1989 period, Coal and Coke trade fell $278 million or 4%

Table 18.2: Multinational Companies and
U.S. Coal and Coke Trade (SITC 32) in 1982

	MERCHANDISE TRADE (Millions of Dollars)			TOTAL TRADE (Percent Share)			ALL MNCs TRADE (Percent Share)		
	EXPORTS	IMPORTS	BALANCE	EXP	IMP	AVG	EXP	IMP	AVG
Affiliate Related Trade									
Total	6275	79	6196	100.0	100.0	100.0	NA	NA	NA
Non-MNCs	2728	20	2708	43.5	25.3	43.2	NA	NA	NA
All MNCs	3547	59	3488	56.5	74.7	56.8	100.0	100.0	100.0
USA MNCs	96	7	89	1.5	8.9	1.6	2.7	11.9	2.9
ROW MNCs	3474	52	3422	55.4	65.8	55.5	97.9	88.1	97.8
Petro MNCs	259	2	257	4.1	2.5	4.1	7.3	3.4	7.3
USA MNCs	0	0	0	0.0	0.0	0.0	0.0	0.0	0.0
ROW MNCs	266	2	264	4.2	2.5	4.2	7.5	3.4	7.4
Manu MNCs	118	40	78	1.9	50.6	2.5	3.3	67.8	4.4
USA MNCs	95	7	88	1.5	8.9	1.6	2.7	11.9	2.8
ROW MNCs	24	33	-9	0.4	41.8	0.9	0.7	55.9	1.6
Whole MNCs	2379	17	2362	37.9	21.5	37.7	67.1	28.8	66.5
USA MNCs	1	0	1	0.0	0.0	0.0	0.0	0.0	0.0
ROW MNCs	2386	17	2369	38.0	21.5	37.8	67.3	28.8	66.6
Other MNCs	791	0	791	12.6	0.0	12.4	22.3	0.0	21.9
USA MNCs	0	0	0	0.0	0.0	0.0	0.0	0.0	0.0
ROW MNCs	798	0	798	12.7	0.0	12.6	22.5	0.0	22.1
Intrafirm Related Trade									
Total	6275	79	6196	100.0	100.0	100.0	NA	NA	NA
Non-MNCs	3637	57	3580	58.0	72.2	58.1	NA	NA	NA
All MNCs	2638	22	2616	42.0	27.8	41.9	100.0	100.0	100.0
USA MNCs	50	7	43	0.8	8.9	0.9	1.9	31.8	2.1
ROW MNCs	2588	15	2573	41.2	19.0	41.0	98.1	68.2	97.9
Petro MNCs	2	0	2	0.0	0.0	0.0	0.1	0.0	0.1
USA MNCs	0	0	0	0.0	0.0	0.0	0.0	0.0	0.0
ROW MNCs	2	0	2	0.0	0.0	0.0	0.1	0.0	0.1
Manu MNCs	63	8	55	1.0	10.1	1.1	2.4	36.4	2.7
USA MNCs	50	7	43	0.8	8.9	0.9	1.9	31.8	2.1
ROW MNCs	13	1	12	0.2	1.3	0.2	0.5	4.5	0.5
Whole MNCs	2071	14	2057	33.0	17.7	32.8	78.5	63.6	78.4
USA MNCs	0	0	0	0.0	0.0	0.0	0.0	0.0	0.0
ROW MNCs	2071	14	2057	33.0	17.7	32.8	78.5	63.6	78.4
Other MNCs	502	0	502	8.0	0.0	7.9	19.0	0.0	18.9
USA MNCs	0	0	0	0.0	0.0	0.0	0.0	0.0	0.0
ROW MNCs	502	0	502	8.0	0.0	7.9	19.0	0.0	18.9

to $6,076 million. In comparison, intrafirm related trade decreased $1,698 million or 64% to a level of $962 million. As a result, the overall intrafirm position decreased from a 41.9% to a 15.8% share (compared to a 56.8% to 38.6% share change for affiliate related trade). Non-MNC trade rose to a 84.2% share. Within the intrafirm trade structure, the export share dropped to 18.9% and the import share to 8.1%. The change in export share reflected a decline in ROW MNC exports. Compared to 1975, the ROW MNC share of total trade had risen from 9.3% to 14.0%; the U.S. MNC share had increased from 0.7% to 1.8% percent.

The Coal and Coke trade balance in 1989 was a surplus of $2,584 million, down $3,612 million from 1982. The intrafirm related trade surplus was $678 million, a decrease of $1,938 million; the Non-MNC trade surplus had fallen $1,674 million to $1,906 million. Thus the decline in the Coal and Coke trade balance was due to both components. The size and changes in the MNC-related surplus was again linked solely to ROW MNC export trade.

INDUSTRY TRADE ROLES

This section is based on the trade data shown in Tables 18.1, 18.2, and 18.3 for 1975, 1982, and 1989, respectively. The trade role of each affiliate industry group is discussed on the basis of affiliate related trade.

Petroleum Affiliates

Affiliate related trade was $101 million in 1975, adjusted for the affiliate trade overlap. This figure represented a 2.6% share of total trade and a 19.9% share of MNC-related trade. The industry category ranked second and was dominated by ROW-based firms. The industry trade balance was a surplus of $99 million, compared to a total merchandise surplus of $2,757 million.

By 1982, industry trade had increased 158% to $261 million. This figure represented a 4.1% share of total trade (up 1.5 share points), and a 7.3% share of MNC-related trade (down 12.6 share points). The industry category ranked third, behind wholesale and other affiliates. The trade balance was a surplus of $257 million (up $158 million), compared to a total merchandise surplus of $6,196 million (up $3,439 million).

Industry related trade was $82 million in 1989, a decrease of 69%. This figure represented a 1.3% share of total trade (down 2.8 share points), and a 3.5% share of MNC-related trade (down 3.8 share points). The industry category now ranked last, and continued to be dominated by ROW-based firms. The trade balance was a surplus of $82 million (down $176 million), compared to a total merchandise surplus of $2,584 million (down $3,612 million).

Manufacturing Affiliates

Affiliate related trade was $78 million in 1975, adjusted for the affiliate trade overlap, and represented a 2.0% share of total trade and a 15.3% share of MNC-related trade. The industry category ranked third and was dominated by U.S.-based firms by a slight margin. The industry balance was a surplus of $7 million, compared to a total merchandise trade surplus of $2,757 million.

Table 18.3: Multinational Companies and
U.S. Coal and Coke Trade (SITC 32) in 1989

	MERCHANDISE TRADE (Millions of Dollars)			TOTAL TRADE (Percent Share)			ALL MNCs TRADE (Percent Share)		
	EXPORTS	IMPORTS	BALANCE	EXP	IMP	AVG	EXP	IMP	AVG
Affiliate Related Trade									
Total	4330	1746	2584	100.0	100.0	100.0	NA	NA	NA
Non-MNCs	2241	1489	752	51.8	85.3	61.4	NA	NA	NA
All MNCs	2089	257	1832	48.2	14.7	38.6	100.0	100.0	100.0
USA MNCs	139	44	95	3.2	2.5	3.0	6.7	17.1	7.8
ROW MNCs	1969	231	1738	45.5	13.2	36.2	94.3	89.9	93.8
Petro MNCs	82	0	82	1.9	0.0	1.3	3.9	0.0	3.5
USA MNCs	12	0	12	0.3	0.0	0.2	0.6	0.0	0.5
ROW MNCs	71	0	71	1.6	0.0	1.2	3.4	0.0	3.0
Manu MNCs	749	84	666	17.3	4.8	13.7	35.9	32.5	35.5
USA MNCs	107	6	101	2.5	0.3	1.9	5.1	2.3	4.8
ROW MNCs	652	90	562	15.1	5.2	12.2	31.2	35.0	31.6
Whole MNCs	670	159	511	15.5	9.1	13.7	32.1	61.9	35.4
USA MNCs	19	31	-12	0.4	1.8	0.8	0.9	12.1	2.1
ROW MNCs	655	133	522	15.1	7.6	13.0	31.4	51.8	33.6
Other MNCs	588	14	573	13.6	0.8	9.9	28.1	5.6	25.7
USA MNCs	1	7	-6	0.0	0.4	0.1	0.0	2.7	0.3
ROW MNCs	591	8	583	13.6	0.5	9.9	28.3	3.1	25.5
Intrafirm Related Trade									
Total	4330	1746	2584	100.0	100.0	100.0	NA	NA	NA
Non-MNCs	3510	1604	1906	81.1	91.9	84.2	NA	NA	NA
All MNCs	820	142	678	18.9	8.1	15.8	100.0	100.0	100.0
USA MNCs	101	8	93	2.3	0.5	1.8	12.3	5.6	11.3
ROW MNCs	719	134	585	16.6	7.7	14.0	87.7	94.4	88.7
Petro MNCs	14	0	14	0.3	0.0	0.2	1.7	0.0	1.5
USA MNCs	12	0	12	0.3	0.0	0.2	1.5	0.0	1.2
ROW MNCs	2	0	2	0.0	0.0	0.0	0.2	0.0	0.2
Manu MNCs	87	4	83	2.0	0.2	1.5	10.6	2.8	9.5
USA MNCs	69	4	65	1.6	0.2	1.2	8.4	2.8	7.6
ROW MNCs	18	0	18	0.4	0.0	0.3	2.2	0.0	1.9
Whole MNCs	422	128	294	9.7	7.3	9.1	51.5	90.1	57.2
USA MNCs	19	0	19	0.4	0.0	0.3	2.3	0.0	2.0
ROW MNCs	403	128	275	9.3	7.3	8.7	49.1	90.1	55.2
Other MNCs	297	10	287	6.9	0.6	5.1	36.2	7.0	31.9
USA MNCs	1	4	-3	0.0	0.2	0.1	0.1	2.8	0.5
ROW MNCs	296	6	290	6.8	0.3	5.0	36.1	4.2	31.4

By 1982, industry trade had increased 102% to $158 million. This figure represented a 2.5% share of total trade (up 0.5 share points), and a 4.4% share of MNC-related trade (down 10.9 share points). The industry category now ranked last. The trade balance was a surplus of $78 million (up $71 million), compared to a total merchandise surplus of $6,196 million (up $3,439 million).

Industry related trade increased by 428% to $833 million in 1989. This figure represented a 13.7% share of total trade (up 11.2 share points), and a 35.5% share of MNC-related trade (up 31.1 share points). The industry category now ranked first, tied with wholesale affiliates, and was dominated by ROW-based firms. The trade balance was a surplus of $666 million (up $588 million), compared to a total merchandise surplus of $2,584 million (down $3,612 million).

Wholesale Trade Affiliates

Affiliate related trade was $256 million in 1975, adjusted for the affiliate trade overlap. This figure represented a 6.5% share of total trade and a 50.3% share of MNC-related trade. The industry category ranked first and was dominated by ROW-based firms. The industry trade balance was a surplus of $254 million, compared to a total merchandise surplus of $2,757 million.

By 1982, industry trade had increased 836% to $2,396 million. This figure represented a 37.7% share of total trade (up 31.2 share points), and a 66.5% share of MNC-related trade (up 16.2 share points). The industry category continued to rank first. The trade balance was a surplus of $2,362 million (up $2,108 million), compared to a total merchandise surplus of $6,196 million (up $3,439 million).

Industry related trade decreased by 65% to $829 million in 1989. This figure represented a 13.7% share of total trade (down 24.1 share points), and a 35.4% share of MNC-related trade (down 31.1 share points). The industry category was now tied for first with manufacturing, and continued to be dominated by ROW-based firms. The trade balance was a surplus of $511 million (down $1,851 million), compared to a total merchandise surplus of $2,584 million (down $3,612 million).

Other Industry Affiliates

Affiliate related trade was $74 million in 1975, adjusted for the affiliate trade overlap. This figure represented a 1.9% share of total trade and a 14.5% share of MNC-related trade. The industry category ranked last and was dominated by ROW-based firms. The industry trade balance was a surplus of $74 million, compared to a total merchandise surplus of $2,757 million.

By 1982, industry trade had increased 967% to $791 million. This figure represented a 12.4% share of total trade (up 10.6 share points), and a 21.9% share of MNC-related trade (up 7.4 share points). The industry category now ranked second, behind wholesale affiliates. The trade balance was a surplus of $791 million (up $717 million), compared to a total merchandise surplus of $6,196 million (an increase of $3,439 million).

Industry related trade decreased by 24% to $602 million in 1989. This figure represented a 9.9% share of total trade (down 2.5 share points), and a 25.7% share of MNC-related trade (up 3.7 share points). The industry category now ranked third, and continued to be dominated by ROW-based firms. The trade balance was a surplus of $573 million (down $217 million), compared to a total merchandise surplus of $2,584 million (down $3,612 million).

DERIVATION OF THE DATA

The derivation of the MNC-related product trade data is discussed at length in Chapter 12 on "Total Product Trade." As noted in that discussion, trade categories were combined in certain benchmark surveys. Coal and Coke (SITC 32) was combined with Other Products (SITC 4,9) in the reverse benchmark for 1974. Coal and Coke (SITC 32) was combined with Petroleum and Products (SITC 33-34) in the outward benchmark for 1977. Separate data on Coal and Coke trade have been collected in all later FDI surveys.

The task was to allocate the combined trade groupings into their component categories. As elsewhere, this was done with sets of allocation ratios. The coal category is special since it was combined with another product classification in both a reverse survey and an outward survey. Since cross-survey data were not usable for developing allocation ratios, each benchmark was treated separately.

In the 1974 benchmark, Coal and Coke (SITC 32) trade was combined with Other Products (SITC 4,9) trade into a expanded "other" category (SITC 32,4,9). In the two later reverse benchmarks, Other Products (SITC 4,9) was again combined with another trade category. Thus the 1980 and 1987 surveys could not be used to provide allocation ratios for the 1974 benchmark. The only approach possible was to estimate Coal and Coke for 1974, and derive Other Products as a residual.

The ratios of Coal and Coke (SITC 32) trade to Petroleum and Products (SITC 33-34) trade were calculated for BM80 and BM87. These ratios showed some variability, so the BM87 ratios were discarded. The BM80 ratios, being the closest reverse benchmark to BM74, were used to estimated Coal and Coke trade in 1974 as a function of Petroleum and Products trade. These Coal and Coke estimates were then used to calculate Other Products as a residual. Since Coal and Coke trade tends to be small, the expanded "other" category in the 1974 benchmark primarily represented Other Products trade.

In the 1977 benchmark, Coal and Coke (SITC 32) trade was combined with Petroleum and Products (SITC 33-34) into a Fuels (SITC 3) category. Coal and Coke trade and Petroleum and Products trade were separately reported in the 1982 and 1989 outward investment benchmarks. The ratios were calculated for each benchmark year, and the BM89 ratios were again discarded. The BM82 ratios, being the closest outward benchmark to 1977, were used to allocate the Fuels trade into the Coal and Coke category and the Petroleum and Products category.

These data for the 1974 reverse benchmark and the 1977 outward benchmark were used as the basis for the tables in this chapter.

CHAPTER 19

OTHER PRODUCTS TRADE

Other Products exports and imports include one-eighth of all Non-Manufactures trade, and is the fourth largest category. The product group accounts for only 4.4% of total merchandise trade, ranking ninth. In affiliate related trade, multinational companies are involved in 44% of Other Products trade, compared to 52% for all Non-Manufactures. Wholesale affiliates are the dominant industry group, accounting for one-third of Other Products trade.

DEFINITION OF OTHER PRODUCTS

As defined by the Bureau of Economic Analysis, the "Other Products" foreign trade classification consists of products in the SITC 4 and 9 categories. This is a residual and miscellaneous trade classification, and is usually placed at the end of the product groups [BEA 1990 21-24]. Under some trade definitions, SITC 9 is a part of manufactured goods trade [Bailey and Bowden 57-59]. However, since the two SITC categories are combined in the benchmark data, the Other Products trade must be placed with non-manufactured goods. Other Products trade includes the following products [BEA 1990 24]:

Animal and Vegetable Oils, Fats, and Waxes, and Commodities N.E.C. (SITC codes 4 and 9)

Crude and refined, edible and inedible animal and vegetable fats and oils (exclude margarine, shortening, and other prepared edible fats, which are in SITC 0)

Military apparel and footwear

Armored vehicles and ordnance, except for shotgun shells, other hunting and sporting ammunition, and nonmilitary arms

Pet and zoo animals

Gold, nonmonetary (exclude ores and concentrates)

TRENDS IN OTHER PRODUCTS TRADE

In 1975, Other Products trade totaled $7,767 million. Exports were $4,680 million and imports were $3,087 million yielding a surplus of $1,593 million. Between 1975 and 1982, total trade increased 119% or $9,220 million to reach $16,987 million. Both exports and imports enjoyed strong growth, but with imports growing twice as fast. Consequently, the trade surplus decreased $834 million or 52% to a 1982 level of only $759 million.

Between 1982 and 1989, the growth patterns in Other Products trade reversed with exports now growing three times faster than imports. Total trade increased 181% or $30,742 million to reach $47,729 million. Exports surged 267% while imports rose 87%. This resulted in a massive improvement in the trade balance of $16,612 million, driving the trade surplus to $17,371 million in 1989.

THE TRADE ROLE OF MULTINATIONAL COMPANIES

This section is based on the trade data shown in Tables 19.1, 19.2, and 19.3 for 1975, 1982, and 1989, respectively. The overall trade role of multinational companies ("All MNCs" in the tables) is discussed for both affiliate related trade and intrafirm related trade.

Affiliate Related Trade

Other Products trade totaled $7,767 million in 1975. Adjusted for the trade overlap, affiliate related trade was $4,575 million for a 58.9% share; Non-MNC trade was $3,193 million for a 41.1% share. The MNC-related trade position reflected a 50.0% share of export trade, and a 72.4% share of import trade. The dominant MNC group was foreign-based firms with a 57.5% share of total trade; U.S.-based firms held a mere 1.6% share. ROW multinational companies had a larger share of both export and import trade. Notably, these firms held a 71.3% share of Other Products import trade.

The Other Products trade balance in 1975 was a surplus of $1,593 million. This reflected a $108 million surplus in MNC-related trade and a $1,486 million surplus in Non-MNC trade. The MNC-related surplus reflected a small surplus position in both U.S. and ROW multinationals. While Other Products trade was dominated by MNCs, the trade surplus was due to non-MNC trade.

Between 1975 and 1982, Other Products trade grew 119% or $9,220 million

Table 19.1: Multinational Companies and
U.S. Other Products Trade (SITC 4,9) in 1975

	MERCHANDISE TRADE (Millions of Dollars)			TOTAL TRADE (Percent Share)			ALL MNCs TRADE (Percent Share)		
	EXPORTS	IMPORTS	BALANCE	EXP	IMP	AVG	EXP	IMP	AVG
Affiliate Related Trade									
Total	4680	3087	1593	100.0	100.0	100.0	NA	NA	NA
Non-MNCs	2339	854	1486	50.0	27.6	41.1	NA	NA	NA
All MNCs	2341	2234	108	50.0	72.4	58.9	100.0	100.0	100.0
USA MNCs	86	35	51	1.8	1.1	1.6	3.7	1.6	2.6
ROW MNCs	2267	2200	67	48.4	71.3	57.5	96.8	98.5	97.7
Petro MNCs	145	154	-9	3.1	5.0	3.8	6.2	6.9	6.5
USA MNCs	5	0	5	0.1	0.0	0.1	0.2	0.0	0.1
ROW MNCs	140	154	-14	3.0	5.0	3.8	6.0	6.9	6.4
Manu MNCs	255	172	83	5.4	5.6	5.5	10.9	7.7	9.3
USA MNCs	66	32	34	1.4	1.0	1.3	2.8	1.4	2.1
ROW MNCs	190	140	50	4.1	4.5	4.2	8.1	6.3	7.2
Whole MNCs	1719	1833	-114	36.7	59.4	45.7	73.4	82.1	77.6
USA MNCs	10	2	8	0.2	0.1	0.2	0.4	0.1	0.3
ROW MNCs	1719	1832	-113	36.7	59.3	45.7	73.4	82.0	77.6
Other MNCs	222	75	148	4.8	2.4	3.8	9.5	3.4	6.5
USA MNCs	5	1	4	0.1	0.0	0.1	0.2	0.0	0.1
ROW MNCs	218	74	144	4.7	2.4	3.8	9.3	3.3	6.4
Intrafirm Related Trade									
Total	4680	3087	1593	100.0	100.0	100.0	NA	NA	NA
Non-MNCs	3693	1670	2023	78.9	54.1	69.0	NA	NA	NA
All MNCs	987	1417	-430	21.1	45.9	31.0	100.0	100.0	100.0
USA MNCs	62	32	30	1.3	1.0	1.2	6.3	2.3	3.9
ROW MNCs	925	1385	-460	19.8	44.9	29.7	93.7	97.7	96.1
Petro MNCs	133	97	36	2.8	3.1	3.0	13.5	6.8	9.6
USA MNCs	5	0	5	0.1	0.0	0.1	0.5	0.0	0.2
ROW MNCs	128	97	31	2.7	3.1	2.9	13.0	6.8	9.4
Manu MNCs	140	84	56	3.0	2.7	2.9	14.2	5.9	9.3
USA MNCs	45	29	16	1.0	0.9	1.0	4.6	2.0	3.1
ROW MNCs	95	55	40	2.0	1.8	1.9	9.6	3.9	6.2
Whole MNCs	552	1199	-647	11.8	38.8	22.5	55.9	84.6	72.8
USA MNCs	8	2	6	0.2	0.1	0.1	0.8	0.1	0.4
ROW MNCs	544	1197	-653	11.6	38.8	22.4	55.1	84.5	72.4
Other MNCs	162	37	125	3.5	1.2	2.6	16.4	2.6	8.3
USA MNCs	4	1	3	0.1	0.0	0.1	0.4	0.1	0.2
ROW MNCs	158	36	122	3.4	1.2	2.5	16.0	2.5	8.1

to reach $16,987 million. In comparison, affiliate related trade increased $2,490 million or 54% to a level of $7,065 million (adjusted for the trade overlap). Accordingly, the overall affiliate position decreased from a 58.9% to a 41.6% share and Non-MNC trade rose to a 58.4% share. Within the affiliate trade structure, the shares for exports dropped to 24.4% and for imports to 60.4%. These changes reflected declines in the trade shares of ROW-based MNCs.

The Other Products trade balance in 1982 was a surplus of $759 million, down $834 million from 1975. The affiliate related trade balance had deteriorated by $2,842 million, converting the small 1975 surplus into a deficit of $2,735. In contrast, the Non-MNC surplus rose $2,008 million to $3,494 million. Thus the decline in the Other Products trade balance was due entirely to unfavorable trends in MNC-related trade. For its part, the MNC-related deficit was created by the growth of ROW MNC imports.

In the 1982 to 1989 period, Other Products trade grew 181% or $30,742 million to $47,729 million. In comparison, affiliate related trade rose $7,538 million or 107% to a level of $14,603 million (adjusted for the trade overlap). As a result, the overall affiliate position dropped from a 41.6% to a 30.6% share and Non-MNC trade rose to a 69.4% share. Within the affiliate trade structure, the export share dropped to 21.8% and the import share to 49.5%. These changes reflected declines in the export and import shares of foreign-based MNCs, the dominant MNC group. Compared to 1975, the ROW MNC share of total trade had fallen from 57.5% to 29.3%; the U.S. MNC share had remained small at 1.6% and 1.7%. Foreign-based MNCs still held 49.4% of import trade.

The Other Products trade balance in 1989 had jumped to a large surplus of $17,371 million, up $16,612 million from 1982. The affiliate related trade deficit was $431 million, a decrease of $2,304 million; the Non-MNC trade surplus had improved $14,308 million to $17,802 million. Thus the large increase in the Other Products trade surplus primarily reflected trends in Non-MNC trade. The MNC-related deficit continued to be rooted in ROW MNC trade.

Intrafirm Related Trade

Other Products trade totaled $7,767 million in 1975. Intrafirm related trade was $2,404 million for a 31.0% share (compared to a 58.9% share for affiliate related trade). Arms-length or Non-MNC trade was $5,363 million for a 69.0% share. The MNC-related trade position reflected a 21.1% share of export trade and a 45.9% share of import trade. The dominant MNC group was foreign-based firms with a 29.7% share of total trade; U.S.-based firms held only a 1.2% share. ROW multinationals had a larger part of both export and import trade.

The Other Products trade balance in 1975 was a surplus of $1,593 million. This reflected a $430 million deficit in MNC-related trade and a $2,023 million surplus in Non-MNC trade. Thus the overall surplus was due to Non-MNC trade. The MNC-related deficit reflected the deficit position of foreign-based MNCs.

Between 1975 and 1982, Other Products trade grew $9,220 million or 119% to reach $16,987 million. In comparison, intrafirm related trade increased $1,020 million or 42% to a level of $3,424 million. Accordingly, the overall

Table 19.2: Multinational Companies and
U.S. Other Products Trade (SITC 4,9) in 1982

	MERCHANDISE TRADE (Millions of Dollars)			TOTAL TRADE (Percent Share)			ALL MNCs TRADE (Percent Share)		
	EXPORTS	IMPORTS	BALANCE	EXP	IMP	AVG	EXP	IMP	AVG
Affiliate Related Trade									
Total	8873	8114	759	100.0	100.0	100.0	NA	NA	NA
Non-MNCs	6708	3215	3494	75.6	39.6	58.4	NA	NA	NA
All MNCs	2165	4900	-2735	24.4	60.4	41.6	100.0	100.0	100.0
USA MNCs	148	41	107	1.7	0.5	1.1	6.8	0.8	2.7
ROW MNCs	2036	4861	-2825	22.9	59.9	40.6	94.0	99.2	97.6
Petro MNCs	0	0	0	0.0	0.0	0.0	0.0	0.0	0.0
USA MNCs	0	0	0	0.0	0.0	0.0	0.0	0.0	0.0
ROW MNCs	0	0	0	0.0	0.0	0.0	0.0	0.0	0.0
Manu MNCs	463	356	107	5.2	4.4	4.8	21.4	7.3	11.6
USA MNCs	84	28	56	0.9	0.3	0.7	3.9	0.6	1.6
ROW MNCs	384	328	56	4.3	4.0	4.2	17.7	6.7	10.1
Whole MNCs	1324	4208	-2884	14.9	51.9	32.6	61.1	85.9	78.3
USA MNCs	59	11	48	0.7	0.1	0.4	2.7	0.2	1.0
ROW MNCs	1274	4199	-2925	14.4	51.8	32.2	58.8	85.7	77.5
Other MNCs	378	336	42	4.3	4.1	4.2	17.5	6.9	10.1
USA MNCs	5	2	3	0.1	0.0	0.0	0.2	0.0	0.1
ROW MNCs	378	334	44	4.3	4.1	4.2	17.5	6.8	10.1
Intrafirm Related Trade									
Total	8873	8114	759	100.0	100.0	100.0	NA	NA	NA
Non-MNCs	7946	5617	2329	89.6	69.2	79.8	NA	NA	NA
All MNCs	927	2497	-1570	10.4	30.8	20.2	100.0	100.0	100.0
USA MNCs	110	36	74	1.2	0.4	0.9	11.9	1.4	4.3
ROW MNCs	817	2461	-1644	9.2	30.3	19.3	88.1	98.6	95.7
Petro MNCs	0	0	0	0.0	0.0	0.0	0.0	0.0	0.0
USA MNCs	0	0	0	0.0	0.0	0.0	0.0	0.0	0.0
ROW MNCs	0	0	0	0.0	0.0	0.0	0.0	0.0	0.0
Manu MNCs	155	181	-26	1.7	2.2	2.0	16.7	7.2	9.8
USA MNCs	55	23	32	0.6	0.3	0.5	5.9	0.9	2.3
ROW MNCs	100	158	-58	1.1	1.9	1.5	10.8	6.3	7.5
Whole MNCs	723	2231	-1508	8.1	27.5	17.4	78.0	89.3	86.3
USA MNCs	53	11	42	0.6	0.1	0.4	5.7	0.4	1.9
ROW MNCs	670	2220	-1550	7.6	27.4	17.0	72.3	88.9	84.4
Other MNCs	49	85	-36	0.6	1.0	0.8	5.3	3.4	3.9
USA MNCs	2	2	0	0.0	0.0	0.0	0.2	0.1	0.1
ROW MNCs	47	83	-36	0.5	1.0	0.8	5.1	3.3	3.8

intrafirm position decreased from a 31.0% to a 20.2% share (compared to a 58.9% to 41.6% share change for affiliate related trade). Non-MNC trade rose to a 79.8% share. Within the intrafirm trade structure, the export share dropped to 10.4% and the import share to 30.8%. These changes reflected declines in the trade shares of foreign-based MNCs.

The Other Products trade balance in 1982 was a surplus of $759 million, down $834 million from 1975. The intrafirm trade deficit was $1,570 million, an increase of $1,140 million; the Non-MNC trade surplus had risen $306 million to $2,329 million. Thus the deterioration in the Other Products trade balance reflected unfavorable trends in MNC-related transactions. In turn, the MNC-related deficit continued linked to the position of ROW multinationals.

In the 1982 to 1989 period, Other Products trade grew $30,742 million or 181% to $47,729 million. In comparison, intrafirm related trade increased $4,007 million or 117% to a level of $7,431 million. As a result, the overall intrafirm position dropped from a 20.2% to a 15.6% share (compared to a 41.6% to 30.6% share change for affiliate related trade). Non-MNC trade rose to a 84.4% share. Within the intrafirm trade structure, the export share dropped to 7.8% and the import share increased to 32.2%. These changes reflected shifts in the trade shares of ROW MNCs. Compared to 1975, the ROW MNC share of total trade had fallen from 29.7% to 14.7%; the U.S. MNC share had fallen from 1.2% to 0.9%.

The Other Products trade balance in 1989 was a surplus of $17,371 million, up $16,612 million from 1982. The intrafirm related trade deficit was $2,353 million, an increase of $783 million; the Non-MNC trade surplus had risen $17,395 million to $19,724 million. Thus the dramatic increase in the Other Products trade balance reflected trends in Non-MNC trade. The MNC-related deficit continued to be linked to foreign-based MNC trade patterns.

INDUSTRY TRADE ROLES

This section is based on the trade data shown in Tables 19.1, 19.2, and 19.3 for 1975, 1982, and 1989, respectively. The trade role of each affiliate industry group is discussed on the basis of affiliate related trade.

Petroleum Affiliates

Affiliate related trade was $299 million in 1975, adjusted for the affiliate trade overlap. This figure represented a 3.8% share of total trade and a 6.5% share of MNC-related trade. The industry category ranked third, tied with other affiliates, and was dominated by ROW-based firms. The industry trade balance was a deficit of $9 million, compared to a total merchandise surplus of $1,593 million.

By 1982, industry trade had decreased 100% to $0 million. This figure represented a 0.0% share of total trade (down 3.8 share points), and a 0.0% share of MNC-related trade (down 6.5 share points). The industry category ranked last, behind wholesale, manufacturing, and other affiliates. The trade balance was $0 million (up $9 million), compared to a total merchandise surplus of $759 million (down $834 million).

Industry related trade increased to a level of $110 million in 1989. This figure

Table 19.3: Multinational Companies and U.S. Other Products Trade (SITC 4,9) in 1989

	MERCHANDISE TRADE (Millions of Dollars)			TOTAL TRADE (Percent Share)			ALL MNCs TRADE (Percent Share)		
	EXPORTS	IMPORTS	BALANCE	EXP	IMP	AVG	EXP	IMP	AVG
Affiliate Related Trade									
Total	32550	15179	17371	100.0	100.0	100.0	NA	NA	NA
Non-MNCs	25464	7663	17802	78.2	50.5	69.4	NA	NA	NA
All MNCs	7086	7517	-431	21.8	49.5	30.6	100.0	100.0	100.0
USA MNCs	788	41	747	2.4	0.3	1.7	11.1	0.5	5.7
ROW MNCs	6480	7491	-1011	19.9	49.4	29.3	91.4	99.7	95.7
Petro MNCs	31	80	-49	0.1	0.5	0.2	0.4	1.1	0.8
USA MNCs	0	0	0	0.0	0.0	0.0	0.0	0.0	0.0
ROW MNCs	32	80	-48	0.1	0.5	0.2	0.5	1.1	0.8
Manu MNCs	1824	1581	242	5.6	10.4	7.1	25.7	21.0	23.3
USA MNCs	360	19	341	1.1	0.1	0.8	5.1	0.3	2.6
ROW MNCs	1511	1568	-57	4.6	10.3	6.5	21.3	20.9	21.1
Whole MNCs	4015	5313	-1299	12.3	35.0	19.5	56.7	70.7	63.9
USA MNCs	201	22	179	0.6	0.1	0.5	2.8	0.3	1.5
ROW MNCs	3904	5299	-1395	12.0	34.9	19.3	55.1	70.5	63.0
Other MNCs	1217	542	674	3.7	3.6	3.7	17.2	7.2	12.0
USA MNCs	227	0	227	0.7	0.0	0.5	3.2	0.0	1.6
ROW MNCs	1033	544	489	3.2	3.6	3.3	14.6	7.2	10.8
Intrafirm Related Trade									
Total	32550	15179	17371	100.0	100.0	100.0	NA	NA	NA
Non-MNCs	30011	10287	19724	92.2	67.8	84.4	NA	NA	NA
All MNCs	2539	4892	-2353	7.8	32.2	15.6	100.0	100.0	100.0
USA MNCs	424	10	414	1.3	0.1	0.9	16.7	0.2	5.8
ROW MNCs	2115	4882	-2767	6.5	32.2	14.7	83.3	99.8	94.2
Petro MNCs	0	0	0	0.0	0.0	0.0	0.0	0.0	0.0
USA MNCs	0	0	0	0.0	0.0	0.0	0.0	0.0	0.0
ROW MNCs	0	0	0	0.0	0.0	0.0	0.0	0.0	0.0
Manu MNCs	641	629	12	2.0	4.1	2.7	25.2	12.9	17.1
USA MNCs	313	7	306	1.0	0.0	0.7	12.3	0.1	4.3
ROW MNCs	328	622	-294	1.0	4.1	2.0	12.9	12.7	12.8
Whole MNCs	1762	4015	-2253	5.4	26.5	12.1	69.4	82.1	77.7
USA MNCs	107	3	104	0.3	0.0	0.2	4.2	0.1	1.5
ROW MNCs	1655	4012	-2357	5.1	26.4	11.9	65.2	82.0	76.3
Other MNCs	136	248	-112	0.4	1.6	0.8	5.4	5.1	5.2
USA MNCs	4	0	4	0.0	0.0	0.0	0.2	0.0	0.1
ROW MNCs	132	248	-116	0.4	1.6	0.8	5.2	5.1	5.1

represented a 0.2% share of total trade (up 0.2 share points), and a 0.8% share of MNC-related trade (up 0.8 share points). The industry category still ranked last, and remained dominated by ROW-based firms. The trade balance for the industry group was a deficit of $49 million (down $49 million). In comparison, the total trade balance had moved to a surplus position of $17,371 million (up $16,612 million).

Manufacturing Affiliates

Affiliate related trade was $427 million in 1975, adjusted for the affiliate trade overlap. This figure represented a 5.5% share of total trade and a 9.3% share of MNC-related trade. The industry category ranked second and was dominated by ROW-based firms. The industry trade balance was a surplus of $83 million, compared to a total merchandise surplus of $1,593 million.

By 1982, industry trade had increased 92% to $819 million. This figure represented a 4.8% share of total trade (down 0.7 share points), and a 11.6% share of MNC-related trade (up 2.3 share points). The industry category continued to rank second, behind wholesale affiliates. The trade balance was a surplus of $107 million (up $24 million), compared to a total merchandise surplus of $759 million (down $834 million).

Industry related trade increased by 316% to $3,405 million in 1989. This figure represented a 7.1% share of total trade (up 2.3 share points), and a 23.3% share of MNC-related trade (up 11.7 share points). The industry category ranked second and was still dominated by ROW-based firms. The trade balance was a surplus of $242 million (up $135 million), compared to a total merchandise surplus of $17,371 million (up $16,612 million).

Wholesale Trade Affiliates

Affiliate related trade was $3,551 million in 1975, adjusted for the affiliate trade overlap. This figure represented a 45.7% share of total trade and a 77.6% share of MNC-related trade. The industry category ranked first and was dominated by ROW-based firms. The industry trade balance was a deficit of $114 million, compared to a total merchandise surplus of $1,593 million.

By 1982, industry trade had increased 56% to $5,532 million. This figure was a 32.6% share of total trade (down 13.2 share points), and a 78.3% share of MNC-related trade (up 0.7 share points). The industry category continued to rank first. The trade balance was a deficit of $2,884 million (up $2,770 million), compared to an overall surplus of $759 million (down $834 million).

Industry related trade increased by 69% to $9,328 million in 1989. This figure represented a 19.5% share of total trade (down 13.0 share points), and a 63.9% share of MNC-related trade (down 14.4 share points). The industry category still ranked first, and continued to be dominated by ROW-based firms. The trade balance was a deficit of $1,299 million (down $1,586 million), compared to a total surplus of $17,371 million (up $16,612 million).

Other Industry Affiliates

Affiliate related trade was $297 million in 1975, adjusted for the affiliate trade overlap. This figure represented a 3.8% share of total trade and a 6.5% share of MNC-related trade. The industry category was tied with petroleum affiliates for third place, and was dominated by ROW-based firms. The industry trade balance was a surplus of $148 million, compared to a total merchandise surplus of $1,593 million.

By 1982, industry trade had increased 140% to $714 million. This figure represented a 4.2% share of total trade (up 0.4 share points), and a 10.1% share of MNC-related trade (up 3.6 share points). The industry category now ranked third, ahead of petroleum. The trade balance was a surplus of $42 million (down $105 million), compared to a total merchandise surplus of $759 million (down $834 million).

Industry related trade increased by 147% to $1,759 million in 1989. This figure represented a 3.7% share of total trade (down 0.5 share points), and a 12.0% share of MNC-related trade (up 1.9 share points). The industry category still ranked third, and continued to be dominated by ROW-based firms. The trade balance was a surplus of $674 million (up $632 million), compared to a total merchandise surplus of $17,371 million (up $16,612 million).

DERIVATION OF THE DATA

The derivation of the MNC-related product trade data is discussed at length in Chapter 12 on "Total Product Trade." As noted in that discussion, trade categories were combined in certain benchmark surveys. Coal and Coke (SITC 32) was combined with Other Products (SITC 4,9) in the reverse benchmark for 1974. Other Manufactures (SITC 61-66,8) was combined with Other Products (SITC 4,9) in the reverse benchmarks for 1980 and 1987. Separate data on Other Products trade have been collected in all the three outward surveys.

The task was to allocate the combined "residual" groupings into their two component categories. As elsewhere, this was done with sets of allocation ratios. The only information available was from the reverse benchmark surveys. The data in the three outward benchmarks were not relevant.

The development of 1974 benchmark estimates for Coal and Coke and Other Products is described in the data derivation section of Chapter 18 on "Coal and Coke Trade." The development of 1980 and 1987 benchmark estimates for Other Manufactures and Other Products is described in the data derivation section of Chapter 26 on "Other Manufactures Trade." These data were used as the basis for the tables in this chapter.

CHAPTER 20

MANUFACTURED GOODS TRADE

Manufactured Goods trade includes 65.9 % of Total Product trade. Multinational companies are involved in 54 % of trade on an affiliate basis and 43 % on an intrafirm basis. Manufacturing affiliates are the dominant industry group, followed by wholesale affiliates.

DEFINITION OF MANUFACTURED GOODS PRODUCTS

Manufactured Goods and Non-Manufactured Goods are two trade aggregates within Total Product trade. Manufactured Goods trade is composed of six BEA product groups.

As defined by the Bureau of Economic Analysis, the "Manufactured Goods" foreign trade classification consists of products in the SITC 5-8 categories. This definition of manufactured goods trade is the narrow definition [Bailey and Bowden 57-59]. The broader definition includes the SITC 9 category, but this data is not available from the benchmark surveys. Manufactured Goods trade includes the following six product groups [BEA 1990 22-23]:

Chemicals and Related Products
(SITC code 5)

Machinery, Electrical and Nonelectrical, except Transportation Equipment
(SITC codes 71-77)

Road Vehicles (Including Air Cushion Vehicles) and Parts
(SITC code 78)

Other Transport Equipment
(SITC code 79)

Metal Manufactures
(SITC codes 67-69)

Other Manufactures
(SITC codes 61-66, and 8)

These BEA product groups serve as the basis for the following six product trade chapters. These chapters provide the core of the analysis of MNC-related trade in manufactured goods. Each chapter includes a detailed product listing of the items that constitute the trade category, and shows the affiliate and intrafirm related trade for the three comparison years of 1975, 1982, and 1989.

This chapter on "Manufactured Goods Trade" summarizes the MNC-related trade which is covered in the individual product chapters. The trade data shown in the following tables represents the aggregate dollar value of all manufactured goods trade combined.

TRENDS IN MANUFACTURED GOODS TRADE

In 1975, total Manufactures trade was $124,065 million. Exports were $72,744 million and imports were $51,321 million yielding a surplus of $21,423 million. In 1982, total trade reached a level of $289,799 million, an increase of 134% or $165,734 million. Both exports and imports enjoyed strong growth over the period, but with imports growing nearly twice as fast. This major imbalance reduced the trade surplus to only $1,755 by 1982. The total decline in the trade balance was 92% or $19,668 million.

Between 1982 and 1989, the growth rates in Manufactures trade slowed. Total trade grew 115% or $333,685 million to reach $632,685 million. Imports still continued increasing twice as fast as exports. This resulted in further deterioration in the trade balance of $108,273, creating a deficit of $106,518 million by 1989.

THE TRADE ROLE OF MULTINATIONAL COMPANIES

This section is based on the trade data shown in Tables 20.1, 20.2, and 20.3 for 1975, 1982, and 1989, respectively. The overall trade role of multinational companies ("All MNCs" in the tables) is discussed for both affiliate related trade and intrafirm related trade.

Affiliate Related Trade

Manufactured Goods trade totaled $124,065 million in 1975. Adjusted for the trade overlap, affiliate related trade was $67,257 million for a 54.2% share;

Table 20.1: Multinational Companies and
U.S. Manufactures Trade (SITC 5-8) in 1975

	MERCHANDISE TRADE (Millions of Dollars)			TOTAL TRADE (Percent Share)			ALL MNCs TRADE (Percent Share)		
	EXPORTS	IMPORTS	BALANCE	EXP	IMP	AVG	EXP	IMP '	AVG
Affiliate Related Trade									
Total	72744	51321	21423	100.0	100.0	100.0	NA	NA	NA
Non-MNCs	36668	20140	16528	50.4	39.2	45.8	NA	NA	NA
All MNCs	36076	31181	4895	49.6	60.8	54.2	100.0	100.0	100.0
USA MNCs	31558	13299	18259	43.4	25.9	36.2	87.5	42.7	66.7
ROW MNCs	5870	18911	-13041	8.1	36.8	20.0	16.3	60.6	36.8
Petro MNCs	2034	709	1325	2.8	1.4	2.2	5.6	2.3	4.1
USA MNCs	1345	96	1249	1.8	0.2	1.2	3.7	0.3	2.1
ROW MNCs	773	655	118	1.1	1.3	1.2	2.1	2.1	2.1
Manu MNCs	24216	13660	10556	33.3	26.6	30.5	67.1	43.8	56.3
USA MNCs	23093	11946	11147	31.7	23.3	28.2	64.0	38.3	52.1
ROW MNCs	1836	2219	-383	2.5	4.3	3.3	5.1	7.1	6.0
Whole MNCs	8263	15951	-7687	11.4	31.1	19.5	22.9	51.2	36.0
USA MNCs	5795	668	5127	8.0	1.3	5.2	16.1	2.1	9.6
ROW MNCs	2872	15732	-12860	3.9	30.7	15.0	8.0	50.5	27.7
Other MNCs	1563	861	702	2.1	1.7	2.0	4.3	2.8	3.6
USA MNCs	1325	589	736	1.8	1.1	1.5	3.7	1.9	2.8
ROW MNCs	389	305	84	0.5	0.6	0.6	1.1	1.0	1.0
Intrafirm Related Trade									
Total	72744	51321	21423	100.0	100.0	100.0	NA	NA	NA
Non-MNCs	44578	25247	19331	61.3	49.2	56.3	NA	NA	NA
All MNCs	28166	26074	2092	38.7	50.8	43.7	100.0	100.0	100.0
USA MNCs	25635	10875	14760	35.2	21.2	29.4	91.0	41.7	67.3
ROW MNCs	2531	15199	-12668	3.5	29.6	14.3	9.0	58.3	32.7
Petro MNCs	1650	516	1134	2.3	1.0	1.7	5.9	2.0	4.0
USA MNCs	1095	53	1042	1.5	0.1	0.9	3.9	0.2	2.1
ROW MNCs	555	463	92	0.8	0.9	0.8	2.0	1.8	1.9
Manu MNCs	19203	11426	7777	26.4	22.3	24.7	68.2	43.8	56.5
USA MNCs	18552	9667	8885	25.5	18.8	22.7	65.9	37.1	52.0
ROW MNCs	651	1759	-1108	0.9	3.4	1.9	2.3	6.7	4.4
Whole MNCs	6444	13420	-6976	8.9	26.1	16.0	22.9	51.5	36.6
USA MNCs	5200	609	4591	7.1	1.2	4.7	18.5	2.3	10.7
ROW MNCs	1244	12811	-11567	1.7	25.0	11.3	4.4	49.1	25.9
Other MNCs	869	712	157	1.2	1.4	1.3	3.1	2.7	2.9
USA MNCs	788	546	242	1.1	1.1	1.1	2.8	2.1	2.5
ROW MNCs	81	166	-85	0.1	0.3	0.2	0.3	0.6	0.5

Non-MNC trade was $56,808 million for a 45.8% share. The MNC-related trade position reflected a 49.6% share of export trade and a 60.8% share of import trade. The dominant MNC group was U.S.-based firms with a 36.2% share of total trade; ROW-based firms held a 20.0% share. U.S. multinational companies had a much larger share of exports; ROW MNCs held the larger share of imports.

The Manufactured Goods trade balance in 1975 was a surplus of $21,423 million. This reflected a $4,895 million surplus in MNC-related trade and a $16,528 million surplus in Non-MNC trade. Thus the overall trade surplus position in Manufactured Goods was due to both components. In turn, the MNC-related surplus was based on a surplus position of U.S.-based multinationals which offset a deficit position of ROW-based firms.

Between 1975 and 1982, Manufactured Goods trade grew 134% or $165,734 million to reach $289,799 million. In comparison, affiliate related trade increased $88,347 million or 131% to a level of $155,604 million (adjusted for the trade overlap). Accordingly, the overall affiliate position decreased slightly from a 54.2% to a 53.7% share and Non-MNC trade rose to a 46.3% share.

Within the affiliate trade structure, the export share fell to 46.1% and the import share increased to 61.4%. The export change reflected a decline in the U.S. MNC share which offset a rise in ROW MNC share. The import change was due to a share gain by ROW MNCs which offset a decline in the U.S. MNC share.

The Manufactured Goods trade balance in 1982 was a small surplus of $1,755 million, down $19,668 million from 1975. The affiliate related trade position had changed into a deficit of $21,295 million, a swing of $26,190 million; the Non-MNC trade surplus had risen $6,522 million to $23,050 million. Thus the deterioration in the Manufactured Goods trade balance was due to unfavorable trends in MNC-related trade. The conversion of MNC-related trade into a deficit was caused by the growing deficit position of ROW multinationals, linked to a decline in the size of the U.S. MNC surplus.

In the 1982 to 1989 period, Manufactured Goods trade grew 115% or $333,685 million to $623,484 million. In comparison, affiliate related trade rose $188,927 million or 121% to a level of $344,531 million (adjusted for the trade overlap). As a result, the overall affiliate position increased from a 53.7% to a 55.3% share and Non-MNC trade fell to a 44.7% share.

Within the affiliate trade structure the export share increased to 52.9% and the import share decreased to 57.0%. The export change reflected growth in the trade shares of U.S. and ROW MNCs; the import change was due to a decline in the trade share of ROW MNCs. Compared to 1975, the U.S. MNC share of total trade had fallen from 36.2% to 28.2%; the ROW MNC share had risen from 20.0% to 28.8%. By a scant 0.6% margin, ROW-based firms had supplanted U.S.-based firms as the dominant MNC group.

The Manufactured Goods trade balance in 1989 had become a deficit of $106,518 million, a decrease of $108,273 million over 1982. The affiliate related trade deficit was $71,284 million, an increase of $49,989 million; the Non-MNC trade had converted to a deficit of $35,235 million, a swing of $58,284 million. Thus the deterioration in the Manufactured Goods trade balance reflected trends in both components. The MNC-related deficit was based on the growing trade deficit of ROW MNCs.

Table 20.2: Multinational Companies and
U.S. Manufactures Trade (SITC 5-8) in 1982

	MERCHANDISE TRADE (Millions of Dollars)			TOTAL TRADE (Percent Share)			ALL MNCs TRADE (Percent Share)		
	EXPORTS	IMPORTS	BALANCE	EXP	IMP	AVG	EXP	IMP	AVG
Affiliate Related Trade									
Total	145777	144022	1755	100.0	100.0	100.0	NA	NA	NA
Non-MNCs	78623	55573	23050	53.9	38.6	46.3	NA	NA	NA
All MNCs	67155	88449	-21295	46.1	61.4	53.7	100.0	100.0	100.0
USA MNCs	49985	31661	18324	34.3	22.0	28.2	74.4	35.8	52.5
ROW MNCs	20668	59525	-38857	14.2	41.3	27.7	30.8	67.3	51.5
Petro MNCs	2498	714	1783	1.7	0.5	1.1	3.7	0.8	2.1
USA MNCs	2223	129	2094	1.5	0.1	0.8	3.3	0.1	1.5
ROW MNCs	519	604	-85	0.4	0.4	0.4	0.8	0.7	0.7
Manu MNCs	42781	38615	4166	29.3	26.8	28.1	63.7	43.7	52.3
USA MNCs	33800	29480	4320	23.2	20.5	21.8	50.3	33.3	40.7
ROW MNCs	11431	10415	1016	7.8	7.2	7.5	17.0	11.8	14.0
Whole MNCs	20142	47973	-27830	13.8	33.3	23.5	30.0	54.2	43.8
USA MNCs	12834	1852	10982	8.8	1.3	5.1	19.1	2.1	9.4
ROW MNCs	7948	47463	-39515	5.5	33.0	19.1	11.8	53.7	35.6
Other MNCs	1733	1147	587	1.2	0.8	1.0	2.6	1.3	1.9
USA MNCs	1128	200	928	0.8	0.1	0.5	1.7	0.2	0.9
ROW MNCs	770	1043	-273	0.5	0.7	0.6	1.1	1.2	1.2
Intrafirm Related Trade									
Total	145777	144022	1755	100.0	100.0	100.0	NA	NA	NA
Non-MNCs	95606	74095	21511	65.6	51.4	58.6	NA	NA	NA
All MNCs	50171	69927	-19756	34.4	48.6	41.4	100.0	100.0	100.0
USA MNCs	41913	25987	15926	28.8	18.0	23.4	83.5	37.2	56.5
ROW MNCs	8258	43940	-35682	5.7	30.5	18.0	16.5	62.8	43.5
Petro MNCs	1391	607	784	1.0	0.4	0.7	2.8	0.9	1.7
USA MNCs	1030	94	936	0.7	0.1	0.4	2.1	0.1	0.9
ROW MNCs	361	513	-152	0.2	0.4	0.3	0.7	0.7	0.7
Manu MNCs	31116	31008	108	21.3	21.5	21.4	62.0	44.3	51.7
USA MNCs	28456	24148	4308	19.5	16.8	18.2	56.7	34.5	43.8
ROW MNCs	2660	6860	-4200	1.8	4.8	3.3	5.3	9.8	7.9
Whole MNCs	16800	37758	-20958	11.5	26.2	18.8	33.5	54.0	45.4
USA MNCs	11760	1590	10170	8.1	1.1	4.6	23.4	2.3	11.1
ROW MNCs	5040	36168	-31128	3.5	25.1	14.2	10.0	51.7	34.3
Other MNCs	864	554	310	0.6	0.4	0.5	1.7	0.8	1.2
USA MNCs	667	155	512	0.5	0.1	0.3	1.3	0.2	0.7
ROW MNCs	197	399	-202	0.1	0.3	0.2	0.4	0.6	0.5

Intrafirm Related Trade

Manufactured Goods trade totaled $124,065 million in 1975. Intrafirm related trade was $54,240 million for a 43.7% share (compared to a 54.2% share for affiliate related trade). Arms-length or Non-MNC trade was $69,825 million for a 56.3% share. The MNC-related trade position reflected a 38.7%

share of export trade and a 50.8% share of import trade. The dominant MNC group was U.S.-based firms with a 29.4% share of total trade; ROW-based firms held a 14.3% share. U.S. multinationals had the much larger share of exports; ROW MNCs had the larger share of imports.

The Manufactured Goods trade balance in 1975 was a surplus of $21,423 million. This reflected a $2,092 million surplus in MNC-related trade and a $19,331 million surplus in Non-MNC trade. Both components contributed to the favorable balance in Manufactured Goods trade. The MNC-related surplus was linked to a surplus in U.S. MNC trade which offset a deficit in ROW MNC trade.

Between 1975 and 1982, Manufactured Goods trade grew $165,734 million or 134% to reach $289,799 million. In comparison, intrafirm related trade increased $65,858 million or 121% to a level of $120,098 million. Accordingly, the overall intrafirm position decreased slightly from a 43.7% to a 41.4% share (compared to a 54.2% to 53.7% share change for affiliate related trade). Non-MNC trade rose to a 58.6% share. Within the intrafirm trade structure, the export share dropped to 34.4% and the import share to 48.6%. These changes reflected a decline in the shares of U.S.-based MNCs offsetting increases in the shares of ROW-based MNCs.

The Manufactured Goods trade balance in 1982 was a surplus of only $1,755 million, down $19,668 million from 1975. Intrafirm related trade had changed into a deficit of $19,756 million, a deterioration of $21,848 million; the Non-MNC trade surplus had risen $2,180 million to $21,511 million. Thus the decline in the Manufactured Goods trade balance resulted from trends in MNC-related trade. The MNC-related deficit emerged due to a growing deficit in ROW MNC trade and a shrinking surplus in U.S. MNC trade.

In the 1982 to 1989 period, Manufactured Goods trade grew $333,685 million or 115% to $623,484 million. In comparison, intrafirm related trade increased $157,425 million or 131% to a level of $277,523 million. As a result, the overall intrafirm position increased from a 41.4% to a 44.5% share (compared to a 53.7% to 55.3% share change for affiliate related trade). Non-MNC trade fell to a 55.5% share. Within the intrafirm trade structure, the export share rose to 39.0% and the import share was unchanged at 48.4%. The export change reflected increases in the trade shares of both U.S. and ROW MNCs. Compared to 1975, the U.S. MNC share of total trade had fallen from 29.4% to 24.1%; the ROW MNC share had risen from 14.3% to 20.4%.

The Manufactured Goods trade balance in 1989 had converted to a deficit of $106,518 million, a deterioration of $108,273 million from 1982. The intrafirm related trade deficit was $75,937 million, an increase of $56,181 million; the Non-MNC trade balance had declined $52,092 million to a deficit position of $30,581 million. Thus the deterioration in the Manufactured Goods trade balance was due to unfavorable trends in both components. The MNC-related deficit was based on the ballooning ROW MNC deficit which offset the surplus in U.S. MNC trade.

Table 20.3: Multinational Companies and
U.S. Manufactures Trade (SITC 5-8) in 1989

	MERCHANDISE TRADE (Millions of Dollars)			TOTAL TRADE (Percent Share)			ALL MNCs TRADE (Percent Share)		
	EXPORTS	IMPORTS	BALANCE	EXP	IMP	AVG	EXP	IMP	AVG
Affiliate Related Trade									
Total	258483	365001	-106518	100.0	100.0	100.0	NA	NA	NA
Non-MNCs	121860	157094	-35235	47.1	43.0	44.7	NA	NA	NA
All MNCs	136624	207907	-71284	52.9	57.0	55.3	100.0	100.0	100.0
USA MNCs	95065	81058	14007	36.8	22.2	28.2	69.6	39.0	51.1
ROW MNCs	46072	133327	-87255	17.8	36.5	28.8	33.7	64.1	52.1
Petro MNCs	2508	351	2156	1.0	0.1	0.5	1.8	0.2	0.8
USA MNCs	1114	18	1096	0.4	0.0	0.2	0.8	0.0	0.3
ROW MNCs	1523	358	1165	0.6	0.1	0.3	1.1	0.2	0.5
Manu MNCs	89970	103849	-13879	34.8	28.5	31.1	65.9	49.9	56.3
USA MNCs	66875	74040	-7165	25.9	20.3	22.6	48.9	35.6	40.9
ROW MNCs	26513	33899	-7386	10.3	9.3	9.7	19.4	16.3	17.5
Whole MNCs	42121	102142	-60020	16.3	28.0	23.1	30.8	49.1	41.9
USA MNCs	25698	6461	19237	9.9	1.8	5.2	18.8	3.1	9.3
ROW MNCs	17236	97897	-80661	6.7	26.8	18.5	12.6	47.1	33.4
Other MNCs	2024	1565	459	0.8	0.4	0.6	1.5	0.8	1.0
USA MNCs	1378	539	839	0.5	0.1	0.3	1.0	0.3	0.6
ROW MNCs	800	1173	-373	0.3	0.3	0.3	0.6	0.6	0.6
Intrafirm Related Trade									
Total	258483	365001	-106518	100.0	100.0	100.0	NA	NA	NA
Non-MNCs	157690	188271	-30581	61.0	51.6	55.5	NA	NA	NA
All MNCs	100793	176730	-75937	39.0	48.4	44.5	100.0	100.0	100.0
USA MNCs	83878	66690	17188	32.5	18.3	24.1	83.2	37.7	54.3
ROW MNCs	16915	110040	-93125	6.5	30.1	20.4	16.8	62.3	45.7
Petro MNCs	1316	242	1074	0.5	0.1	0.2	1.3	0.1	0.6
USA MNCs	734	15	719	0.3	0.0	0.1	0.7	0.0	0.3
ROW MNCs	582	227	355	0.2	0.1	0.1	0.6	0.1	0.3
Manu MNCs	64490	85688	-21198	24.9	23.5	24.1	64.0	48.5	54.1
USA MNCs	57753	61084	-3331	22.3	16.7	19.1	57.3	34.6	42.8
ROW MNCs	6737	24604	-17867	2.6	6.7	5.0	6.7	13.9	11.3
Whole MNCs	33794	89880	-56086	13.1	24.6	19.8	33.5	50.9	44.6
USA MNCs	24387	5277	19110	9.4	1.4	4.8	24.2	3.0	10.7
ROW MNCs	9407	84603	-75196	3.6	23.2	15.1	9.3	47.9	33.9
Other MNCs	1193	920	273	0.5	0.3	0.3	1.2	0.5	0.8
USA MNCs	1004	314	690	0.4	0.1	0.2	1.0	0.2	0.5
ROW MNCs	189	606	-417	0.1	0.2	0.1	0.2	0.3	0.3

INDUSTRY TRADE ROLES

This section is based on the trade data shown in Tables 20.1, 20.2, and 20.3 for 1975, 1982, and 1989, respectively. The trade role of each affiliate industry group is discussed on the basis of affiliate related trade.

Petroleum Affiliates

Affiliate related trade was $2,742 million in 1975, adjusted for the affiliate trade overlap. This figure represented a 2.2% share of total trade and a 4.1% share of MNC-related trade. The industry category ranked third and was evenly split between U.S.-based and ROW-based firms. The industry trade balance was a surplus of $1,325 million, compared to a total merchandise surplus of $21,423 million.

By 1982, industry trade had increased 17% to $3,212 million. This figure represented a 1.1% share of total trade (down 1.1 share points), and a 2.1% share of MNC-related trade (down 2.0 share points). The industry category ranked third behind manufacturing and wholesale affiliates, and ahead of other industry affiliates. The trade balance was a surplus of $1,783 million (up $459 million), compared to a total merchandise surplus of $1,755 million (down $19,668 million).

Industry related trade decreased by 11% to $2,859 million in 1989, adjusted for the affiliate trade overlap. This figure represented a 0.5% share of total trade (down 0.6 share points), and a 0.8% share of MNC-related trade (down 1.2 share points). The industry category now ranked last, and was dominated by ROW-based firms. The trade balance was a surplus of $2,156 million (up $373 million), compared to a total merchandise deficit of $106,518 million (a swing of $108,273 million).

Manufacturing Affiliates

Affiliate related trade was $37,876 million in 1975, adjusted for the affiliate trade overlap. This figure represented a 30.5% share of total trade and a 56.3% share of MNC-related trade. The industry category ranked first and was dominated by U.S.-based firms. The industry trade balance was a surplus of $10,556 million, compared to a total merchandise surplus of $21,423 million.

By 1982, industry trade had increased 115% to $81,396 million. This figure represented a 28.1% share of total trade (down 2.4 share points), and a 52.3% share of MNC-related trade (down 4.0 share points). The industry category ranked first ahead of wholesale affiliates. The industry trade balance was a surplus of $4,166 million (down $6,390 million), compared to total merchandise trade which was in surplus by $1,755 million (down $19,668 million).

Industry related trade increased by 138% to $193,819 million in 1989, adjusted for the affiliate trade overlap. This figure represented a 31.1% share of total trade (up 3.0 share points), and a 56.3% share of MNC-related trade (up 3.9 share points). The industry category still ranked first, and remained dominated by U.S.-based firms. The trade balance was a deficit of $13,879 million (a swing of $18,044 million), compared to a total merchandise deficit of $106,518 million (a swing of $108,273 million).

Table 20.4: Product Structure of
"Total" Merchandise Trade in
U.S. Manufactures Trade (SITC 5-8)

	MERCHANDISE TRADE (Millions of Dollars)			TOTAL TRADE (Percent Share)			ALL MNCs TRADE (Percent Share)		
	EXPORTS	IMPORTS	BALANCE	EXP	IMP	AVG	EXP	IMP	AVG
1975									
Manufact	72744	51321	21423	100.0	100.0	100.0	NA	NA	NA
Chem	8911	3713	5198	12.2	7.2	10.2	NA	NA	NA
Machnry	29954	12027	17927	41.2	23.4	33.8	NA	NA	NA
Veh&Pts	9525	9968	-443	13.1	19.4	15.7	NA	NA	NA
OtherTrans	7343	1573	5770	10.1	3.1	7.2	NA	NA	NA
MetManu	5804	8986	-3182	8.0	17.5	11.9	NA	NA	NA
OtherManu	11207	15054	-3847	15.4	29.3	21.2	NA	NA	NA
1982									
Manufact	145777	144022	1755	100.0	100.0	100.0	NA	NA	NA
Chem	20848	9493	11355	14.3	6.6	10.5	NA	NA	NA
Machnry	62702	39457	23245	43.0	27.4	35.3	NA	NA	NA
Veh&Pts	13365	29218	-15853	9.2	20.3	14.7	NA	NA	NA
OtherTrans	14587	4645	9942	10.0	3.2	6.6	NA	NA	NA
MetManu	8640	19227	-10587	5.9	13.4	9.6	NA	NA	NA
OtherManu	25635	41982	-16347	17.6	29.1	23.3	NA	NA	NA
1989									
Manufact	258483	365001	-106518	100.0	100.0	100.0	NA	NA	NA
Chem	36856	20744	16112	14.3	5.7	9.2	NA	NA	NA
Machnry	110902	126708	-15806	42.9	34.7	38.1	NA	NA	NA
Veh&Pts	24334	70282	-45948	9.4	19.3	15.2	NA	NA	NA
OtherTrans	25902	8691	17211	10.0	2.4	5.5	NA	NA	NA
MetManu	12721	30449	-17728	4.9	8.3	6.9	NA	NA	NA
OtherManu	47768	108127	-60359	18.5	29.6	25.0	NA	NA	NA

Wholesale Trade Affiliates

Affiliate related trade was $24,214 million in 1975, adjusted for the affiliate trade overlap. This figure represented a 19.5% share of total trade and a 36.0% share of MNC-related trade. The industry category ranked second and was dominated by ROW-based firms. The industry trade balance was a deficit of $7,687 million, compared to a total merchandise surplus of $21,423 million.

By 1982, industry trade had increased 181% to $68,115 million. This figure represented a 23.5% share of total trade (up 4.0 share points), and a 43.8% share of MNC-related trade (up 7.8 share points). The industry category ranked second behind manufacturing affiliates. The trade balance was a deficit of $27,830 million (up $20,143 million), compared to a total merchandise surplus of $1,755 million (down $19,668 million).

Table 20.5: Product Structure of
Affiliate Related "All MNCs" Trade in
U.S. Manufactures Trade (SITC 5-8)

	MERCHANDISE TRADE (Millions of Dollars)			TOTAL TRADE (Percent Share)			ALL MNCs TRADE (Percent Share)		
	EXPORTS	IMPORTS	BALANCE	EXP	IMP	AVG	EXP	IMP	AVG
1975									
Manufact	36076	31181	4895	49.6	60.8	54.2	100.0	100.0	100.0
Chem	4627	1822	2805	6.4	3.6	5.2	12.8	5.8	9.6
Machnry	14107	7907	6200	19.4	15.4	17.7	39.1	25.4	32.7
Veh&Pts	8013	9389	-1377	11.0	18.3	14.0	22.2	30.1	25.9
OtherTrans	570	636	-66	0.8	1.2	1.0	1.6	2.0	1.8
MetManu	2786	6080	-3294	3.8	11.8	7.1	7.7	19.5	13.2
OtherManu	5974	5348	626	8.2	10.4	9.1	16.6	17.2	16.8
1982									
Manufact	67155	88449	-21295	46.1	61.4	53.7	100.0	100.0	100.0
Chem	11541	5318	6224	7.9	3.7	5.8	17.2	6.0	10.8
Machnry	30648	29299	1349	21.0	20.3	20.7	45.6	33.1	38.5
Veh&Pts	11381	24650	-13269	7.8	17.1	12.4	16.9	27.9	23.2
OtherTrans	1690	2082	-392	1.2	1.4	1.3	2.5	2.4	2.4
MetManu	4686	15088	-10402	3.2	10.5	6.8	7.0	17.1	12.7
OtherManu	7210	12014	-4805	4.9	8.3	6.6	10.7	13.6	12.4
1989									
Manufact	136624	207907	-71284	52.9	57.0	55.3	100.0	100.0	100.0
Chem	26931	15455	11477	10.4	4.2	6.8	19.7	7.4	12.3
Machnry	55753	86027	-30274	21.6	23.6	22.7	40.8	41.4	41.2
Veh&Pts	21541	56778	-35237	8.3	15.6	12.6	15.8	27.3	22.7
OtherTrans	2097	4513	-2416	0.8	1.2	1.1	1.5	2.2	1.9
MetManu	10420	17752	-7332	4.0	4.9	4.5	7.6	8.5	8.2
OtherManu	19882	27384	-7502	7.7	7.5	7.6	14.6	13.2	13.7

Industry related trade increased by 112% to $144,263 million in 1989. This figure represented a 23.1% share of total trade (down 0.4 share points), and a 41.9% share of MNC-related trade (down 1.9 share points). The industry category still ranked second, and remained dominated by ROW-based firms. The trade balance was a deficit of $60,020 million (up $32,190 million), compared to a total merchandise deficit of $106,518 million (a swing of $108,273 million).

Other Industry Affiliates

Affiliate related trade was $2,424 million in 1975, adjusted for the affiliate trade overlap. This figure represented a 2.0% share of total trade and a 3.6% share of MNC-related trade. Overall, the industry category ranked last and was

Table 20.6: Product Structure of
Intrafirm Related "All MNCs" Trade in
U.S. Manufactures Trade (SITC 5-8)

	MERCHANDISE TRADE (Millions of Dollars)			TOTAL TRADE (Percent Share)			ALL MNCs TRADE (Percent Share)		
	EXPORTS	IMPORTS	BALANCE	EXP	IMP	AVG	EXP	IMP	AVG
1975									
Manufact	28166	26074	2092	38.7	50.8	43.7	100.0	100.0	100.0
Chem	3626	1387	2239	5.0	2.7	4.0	12.9	5.3	9.2
Machnry	11552	7366	4186	15.9	14.4	15.2	41.0	28.3	34.9
Veh&Pts	6208	8457	-2249	8.5	16.5	11.8	22.0	32.4	27.0
OtherTrans	455	446	9	0.6	0.9	0.7	1.6	1.7	1.7
MetManu	1613	4410	-2797	2.2	8.6	4.9	5.7	16.9	11.1
OtherManu	4712	4008	704	6.5	7.8	7.0	16.7	15.4	16.1
1982									
Manufact	50171	69927	-19756	34.4	48.6	41.4	100.0	100.0	100.0
Chem	7636	3785	3851	5.2	2.6	3.9	15.2	5.4	9.5
Machnry	24600	25699	-1099	16.9	17.8	17.4	49.0	36.8	41.9
Veh&Pts	8689	20548	-11859	6.0	14.3	10.1	17.3	29.4	24.3
OtherTrans	968	1348	-380	0.7	0.9	0.8	1.9	1.9	1.9
MetManu	2769	10303	-7534	1.9	7.2	4.5	5.5	14.7	10.9
OtherManu	5509	8244	-2735	3.8	5.7	4.7	11.0	11.8	11.5
1989									
Manufact	100793	176730	-75937	39.0	48.4	44.5	100.0	100.0	100.0
Chem	16469	11436	5033	6.4	3.1	4.5	16.3	6.5	10.1
Machnry	45241	78321	-33080	17.5	21.5	19.8	44.9	44.3	44.5
Veh&Pts	18454	51465	-33011	7.1	14.1	11.2	18.3	29.1	25.2
OtherTrans	1361	3063	-1702	0.5	0.8	0.7	1.4	1.7	1.6
MetManu	4513	11309	-6796	1.7	3.1	2.5	4.5	6.4	5.7
OtherManu	14755	21136	-6381	5.7	5.8	5.8	14.6	12.0	12.9

dominated by U.S.-based firms. The industry trade balance was a surplus of $702 million, compared to a total merchandise surplus of $21,423 million.

By 1982, industry trade had increased 19% to $2,880 million. This figure represented a 1.0% share of total trade (down 1.0 share points), and a 1.9% share of MNC-related trade (down 1.8 share points). The industry category ranked last behind manufacturing, wholesale, and petroleum affiliates. The trade balance was a surplus of $587 million (down $116 million), compared to a total merchandise surplus of $1,755 million (down $19,668 million).

Industry related trade increased by 25% to $3,589 million in 1989. This figure represented a 0.6% share of total trade (down 0.4 share points), and a 1.0% share of MNC-related trade (down 0.8 share points). The industry category now ranked third, ahead of petroleum, and was evenly divided between U.S.-based and ROW-based firms. The trade balance was a surplus of $459

million (down $128 million), compared to a total merchandise deficit of
$106,518 million (a swing of $108,273 million).

THE STRUCTURE OF MANUFACTURED GOODS TRADE

The three tables on product structure are a bridge between the trade tables
in this chapter on "Manufactured Goods Trade" and the trade tables in the
subsequent six product trade chapters. Tables 20.4 to 20.6 provide direct
linkages between Tables 20.1 to 20.3 -- the trade tables for 1975, 1982, and
1989 -- and the related trade tables in the chapters which follow. There are
three product structure bridges or links: "Total" merchandise trade, affiliate
related "All MNCs" trade, and intrafirm related "All MNCs" trade.

"Total" Merchandise Trade

Table 20.4 covers the structure of "Total" Non-Manufactures merchandise
trade for 1975, 1982, and 1989. The term "Total" refers to the first data line
in the affiliate and intrafirm related trade sections of Tables 20.1 to 20.3. These
figures are total U.S. merchandise trade in Manufactured Goods.

The table covers "Total" Manufactures trade (the "Total" line in the table)
and the six product trade categories. Dollar values are shown for exports,
imports, and trade balances. Trade shares are shown on the "Total Trade"
basis; that is, the trade category is divided by total Manufactures trade. Trade
shares on the "All MNCs" basis are not applicable in this table.

The two leading product categories accounted for nearly 60% of total trade.
They were Machinery (35.9%) and Other Manufactures (23.3%). The two
intermediate product categories included 25% of Manufactures trade. They
were Vehicles and Parts (15.2%) and Chemicals (9.9%). The two smallest
product categories amounted to nearly 20% of total exports and imports. These
were Metal Manufactures (9.3%) and Other Transportation Equipment (6.4%).

Affiliate Related "All MNCs" Trade

Table 20.5 covers the structure of affiliate related "All MNCs" Non-
Manufactures trade for 1975, 1982, and 1989. The term "All MNCs" refers to
the third data line in the affiliate related trade section of Tables 20.1 to 20.3.
These figures are total MNC-related trade under the affiliate trade definition.

The table covers affiliate related "All MNCs" Manufactures trade (the
"Total" line in the table) and the six product trade categories. Dollar values are
shown for exports, imports, and trade balances. Trade shares are shown on two
bases.   The "Total Trade" basis is the trade category divided by total
Manufactures trade. The "All MNCs" basis is the trade category divided by
affiliate related All MNCs Manufactures trade.

The two leading product categories accounted for over 60% of total trade. They were Machinery (37.9%) and Vehicles and Parts (23.8%). The two intermediate product categories included 25% of Manufactures trade. They were Other Manufactures (14.2%) and Metal Manufactures (11.1%). The two smallest product categories amounted to less than 15% of total exports and imports. These categories were Chemicals (11.0%) and Other Transportation Equipment (2.0%).

Intrafirm Related "All MNCs" Trade

Table 20.6 covers the structure of intrafirm related "All MNCs" Non-Manufactures trade for 1975, 1982, and 1989. The term "All MNCs" refers to the third data line in the intrafirm related trade section of Tables 20.1 to 20.3. These figures are total MNC-related trade under the intrafirm trade definition.

The table covers intrafirm related "All MNCs" Manufactures trade (the "Total" line in the table) and the six product trade categories. Dollar values are shown for exports, imports, and trade balances. Trade shares are shown on two bases. The "Total Trade" basis is the trade category divided by total Manufactures trade. The "All MNCs" basis is the trade category divided by intrafirm related All MNCs Manufactures trade.

The two leading product categories accounted for 65% of total trade. They were Machinery (40.8%) and Vehicles and Parts (25.5%). Two intermediate product categories included less than 25% of Manufactures trade. They were Other Manufactures (13.4%) and Chemicals (9.6%). The two smallest product categories amounted to less than 15% of total exports and imports. These were Metal Manufactures (9.0%) and Other Transportation Equipment (1.7%).

DERIVATION OF THE DATA

The derivation of the MNC-related product trade data is covered at length in Chapter 12 on "Total Product Trade." As noted in that discussion, trade categories were combined in certain benchmark surveys. For example, in the 1980 and 1987 benchmarks, Other Manufactures (SITC 61-66,8) and Other Products (SITC 5,9) were combined into a single product grouping. These combined categories must be split into their component parts to derive consistent product trade data. These operations are discussed in the data derivation sections of the affected product chapters.

As mentioned earlier, the trade values shown in the tables in this chapter are aggregate values taken from the next six chapters. Thus the trade data shown in Table 20.1 for 1975 are the sum of the companion tables in Chapters 21 to 26. This includes the dollar value of the affiliate trade overlap.

CHAPTER 21

CHEMICALS TRADE

Chemicals exports and imports include one-tenth of all Manufactures trade, and are the fourth largest category. The product group accounts for 6.5% of total merchandise trade, ranking sixth. In affiliate related trade, multinational companies are involved in 60% of Chemicals trade, compared to 54% for all Manufactures. This level of MNC-related trade is among the highest of all product categories. Manufacturing affiliates are the dominant industry group, accounting for nearly two-fifths of all Chemicals trade.

DEFINITION OF CHEMICALS PRODUCTS

As defined by the Bureau of Economic Analysis, the "Chemicals" foreign trade classification consists of products in the SITC 5 category. Chemicals trade includes the following products [BEA 1990 22]:

Chemicals and Related Products
(SITC code 5)

Organic and inorganic chemical elements and compounds (include nuclear feed materials and fuels, and radioactive materials)

Dyeing, tanning, and coloring materials, natural and synthetic (include color lakes, tannins, printing inks, paints, enamels, and lacquers)

Medicinal and pharmaceutical products

Essential oils, perfume and flavor materials, including perfumes, cosmetics, and toilet preparations

Soap, cleansing and polishing preparations

Fertilizers, manufactured (mineral or chemical)

Explosives and pyrotechnic products (exclude ordnance and all other ammunition)

Artificial resins and plastic materials, cellulose esters and ethers

Other chemical products and materials, n.e.s. [not elsewhere specified] such as insecticides, herbicides, starches (include corn starch), disinfectants, glues and adhesives, wood and resin-based chemical products, artificial waxes, artificial graphite, etc.

NOTE. Exclude prepared photographic chemicals, synthetic rubber and cellulosic and noncellulosic manmade fibers

TRENDS IN CHEMICALS TRADE

In 1975, Chemicals trade totaled $12,624 million. Exports were $8,911 million and imports were $3,713 million yielding a surplus of $5,198 million. Between 1975 and 1982, total trade increased 140% or $17,717 million to reach $30,341 million. Both exports and imports enjoyed strong growth, with imports growing slightly faster. The trade surplus increased by 118% or $6,157 million to a 1982 level of $11,355 million.

Between 1982 and 1989, the growth rates slowed in Chemicals trade. Total trade increased 90% or $27,259 million to reach $57,600 million. Imports jumped 118% while exports rose 77%. This resulted in a 42% improvement in the trade balance of $4,757 million, creating a trade surplus of $16,112 million in 1989.

THE TRADE ROLE OF MULTINATIONAL COMPANIES

This section is based on the trade data shown in Tables 21.1, 21.2, and 21.3 for 1975, 1982, and 1989, respectively. The overall trade role of multinational companies ("All MNCs" in the tables) is discussed for both affiliate related trade and intrafirm related trade.

Affiliate Related Trade

Chemicals trade totaled $12,624 million in 1975. Adjusted for the trade overlap, affiliate related trade was $6,449 million for a 51.1% share; Non-MNC trade was $6,175 million for a 48.9% share. The MNC-related trade position reflected a 51.9% share of export trade and a 49.1% share of import trade. The

Table 21.1: Multinational Companies and
U.S. Chemicals Trade (SITC 5) in 1975

	MERCHANDISE TRADE (Millions of Dollars)			TOTAL TRADE (Percent Share)			ALL MNCs TRADE (Percent Share)		
	EXPORTS	IMPORTS	BALANCE	EXP	IMP	AVG	EXP	IMP	AVG
Affiliate Related Trade									
Total	8911	3713	5198	100.0	100.0	100.0	NA	NA	NA
Non-MNCs	4284	1891	2393	48.1	50.9	48.9	NA	NA	NA
All MNCs	4627	1822	2805	51.9	49.1	51.1	100.0	100.0	100.0
USA MNCs	3540	724	2816	39.7	19.5	33.8	76.5	39.7	66.1
ROW MNCs	1319	1175	144	14.8	31.6	19.8	28.5	64.5	38.7
Petro MNCs	433	166	267	4.9	4.5	4.7	9.4	9.1	9.3
USA MNCs	183	64	119	2.1	1.7	2.0	4.0	3.5	3.8
ROW MNCs	279	109	170	3.1	2.9	3.1	6.0	6.0	6.0
Manu MNCs	2833	851	1982	31.8	22.9	29.2	61.2	46.7	57.1
USA MNCs	2544	472	2072	28.5	12.7	23.9	55.0	25.9	46.8
ROW MNCs	385	408	-23	4.3	11.0	6.3	8.3	22.4	12.3
Whole MNCs	1225	601	624	13.7	16.2	14.5	26.5	33.0	28.3
USA MNCs	761	23	738	8.5	0.6	6.2	16.4	1.3	12.2
ROW MNCs	543	617	-74	6.1	16.6	9.2	11.7	33.9	18.0
Other MNCs	136	203	-67	1.5	5.5	2.7	2.9	11.1	5.3
USA MNCs	52	165	-113	0.6	4.4	1.7	1.1	9.1	3.4
ROW MNCs	112	41	71	1.3	1.1	1.2	2.4	2.3	2.4
Intrafirm Related Trade									
Total	8911	3713	5198	100.0	100.0	100.0	NA	NA	NA
Non-MNCs	5285	2326	2959	59.3	62.6	60.3	NA	NA	NA
All MNCs	3626	1387	2239	40.7	37.4	39.7	100.0	100.0	100.0
USA MNCs	3076	570	2506	34.5	15.4	28.9	84.8	41.1	72.7
ROW MNCs	550	817	-267	6.2	22.0	10.8	15.2	58.9	27.3
Petro MNCs	308	129	179	3.5	3.5	3.5	8.5	9.3	8.7
USA MNCs	137	48	89	1.5	1.3	1.5	3.8	3.5	3.7
ROW MNCs	171	81	90	1.9	2.2	2.0	4.7	5.8	5.0
Manu MNCs	2418	689	1729	27.1	18.6	24.6	66.7	49.7	62.0
USA MNCs	2222	342	1880	24.9	9.2	20.3	61.3	24.7	51.1
ROW MNCs	196	347	-151	2.2	9.3	4.3	5.4	25.0	10.8
Whole MNCs	885	382	503	9.9	10.3	10.0	24.4	27.5	25.3
USA MNCs	704	17	687	7.9	0.5	5.7	19.4	1.2	14.4
ROW MNCs	181	365	-184	2.0	9.8	4.3	5.0	26.3	10.9
Other MNCs	15	187	-172	0.2	5.0	1.6	0.4	13.5	4.0
USA MNCs	13	163	-150	0.1	4.4	1.4	0.4	11.8	3.5
ROW MNCs	2	24	-22	0.0	0.6	0.2	0.1	1.7	0.5

dominant MNC group was U.S.-based firms with a 33.8% share of total trade; ROW-based firms held a 19.8% share. U.S. multinational companies had a larger share of exports; ROW MNCs had a larger share of imports.

The Chemicals trade balance in 1975 was a surplus of $5,198 million. This reflected a $2,805 million surplus in MNC-related trade and a $2,393 million surplus in Non-MNC trade. The MNC-related surplus was based on surplus positions of both U.S. and ROW multinationals, primarily the U.S.-based MNCs. Thus the overall trade surplus position in Chemicals was due to both components.

Between 1975 and 1982, Chemicals trade grew 140% or $17,717 million to reach $30,341 million. In comparison, affiliate related trade increased $10,410 million or 161% to a level of $16,859 million (adjusted for the trade overlap). Accordingly, the overall affiliate position increased slightly from a 51.1% to a 55.6% share and Non-MNC trade fell to a 44.4% share. Within the affiliate trade structure, the export share increased to 55.4% and the import share to 56.0%. The export change reflected a jump in the ROW MNC share which offset a decline in U.S. MNC share. The import change was due to share gains by both MNC groups.

The Chemicals trade balance in 1982 was a surplus of $11,355 million, up $6,157 million from 1975. The affiliate related trade surplus was $6,224 million, an increase of $3,419 million; the Non-MNC trade surplus had risen $2,739 million to $5,132 million. Thus the improvement in the Chemicals trade balance was due to favorable trends in both components. The MNC-related surplus continued to reflect surplus positions of both U.S. and ROW multinationals.

In the 1982 to 1989 period, Chemicals trade grew 90% or $27,259 million to $57,600 million. In comparison, affiliate related trade rose $25,527 million or 151% to a level of $42,386 million (adjusted for the trade overlap). As a result, the overall affiliate position increased from a 55.6% to a 73.6% share and Non-MNC trade fell to a 26.4% share. Within the affiliate trade structure the export share increased to 73.1% and the import share to 74.5%. This change reflected growth in the trade shares of U.S. and ROW MNCs, especially the latter. Compared to 1975, the U.S. MNC share of total trade had fallen from 33.8% to 32.0%; the ROW MNC share had risen from 19.8% to 44.3%. ROW-based MNCs had supplanted U.S.-based firms as the dominant group.

The Chemicals trade balance in 1989 was a surplus of $16,112 million, up $4,757 million over 1982. The affiliate related trade surplus was $11,477 million, an increase of $5,253 million; the Non-MNC trade surplus had fallen $496 million to $4,636 million. Thus the improvement in the Chemicals trade balance reflected trends in MNC-related trade. The MNC-related surplus was based on the growing trade surplus in both MNC groups.

Intrafirm Related Trade

Chemicals trade totaled $12,624 million in 1975. Intrafirm related trade was $5,013 million for a 39.7% share (compared to a 51.1% share for affiliate related trade). Arms-length or Non-MNC trade was $7,611 million for a 60.3% share. The MNC-related trade position reflected a 40.7% share of export trade and a 37.4% share of import trade. The dominant MNC group was U.S.-based firms with a 28.9% share of total trade; ROW-based firms held a 10.8% share.

Table 21.2: Multinational Companies and U.S. Chemicals Trade (SITC 5) in 1982

	MERCHANDISE TRADE (Millions of Dollars)			TOTAL TRADE (Percent Share)			ALL MNCs TRADE (Percent Share)		
	EXPORTS	IMPORTS	BALANCE	EXP	IMP	AVG	EXP	IMP	AVG
Affiliate Related Trade									
Total	20848	9493	11355	100.0	100.0	100.0	NA	NA	NA
Non-MNCs	9307	4176	5132	44.6	44.0	44.4	NA	NA	NA
All MNCs	11541	5318	6224	55.4	56.0	55.6	100.0	100.0	100.0
USA MNCs	6487	2234	4253	31.1	23.5	28.7	56.2	42.0	51.7
ROW MNCs	5575	3466	2109	26.7	36.5	29.8	48.3	65.2	53.6
Petro MNCs	674	291	383	3.2	3.1	3.2	5.8	5.5	5.7
USA MNCs	388	122	266	1.9	1.3	1.7	3.4	2.3	3.0
ROW MNCs	316	184	132	1.5	1.9	1.6	2.7	3.5	3.0
Manu MNCs	6507	3510	2997	31.2	37.0	33.0	56.4	66.0	59.4
USA MNCs	4262	1910	2352	20.4	20.1	20.3	36.9	35.9	36.6
ROW MNCs	2519	1847	672	12.1	19.5	14.4	21.8	34.7	25.9
Whole MNCs	3893	1488	2406	18.7	15.7	17.7	33.7	28.0	31.9
USA MNCs	1730	192	1538	8.3	2.0	6.3	15.0	3.6	11.4
ROW MNCs	2327	1413	914	11.2	14.9	12.3	20.2	26.6	22.2
Other MNCs	467	29	437	2.2	0.3	1.6	4.0	0.5	2.9
USA MNCs	107	10	97	0.5	0.1	0.4	0.9	0.2	0.7
ROW MNCs	413	22	391	2.0	0.2	1.4	3.6	0.4	2.6
Intrafirm Related Trade									
Total	20848	9493	11355	100.0	100.0	100.0	NA	NA	NA
Non-MNCs	13212	5708	7504	63.4	60.1	62.4	NA	NA	NA
All MNCs	7636	3785	3851	36.6	39.9	37.6	100.0	100.0	100.0
USA MNCs	5445	1469	3976	26.1	15.5	22.8	71.3	38.8	60.5
ROW MNCs	2191	2316	-125	10.5	24.4	14.9	28.7	61.2	39.5
Petro MNCs	449	231	218	2.2	2.4	2.2	5.9	6.1	6.0
USA MNCs	211	90	121	1.0	0.9	1.0	2.8	2.4	2.6
ROW MNCs	238	141	97	1.1	1.5	1.2	3.1	3.7	3.3
Manu MNCs	4453	2519	1934	21.4	26.5	23.0	58.3	66.6	61.0
USA MNCs	3652	1268	2384	17.5	13.4	16.2	47.8	33.5	43.1
ROW MNCs	801	1251	-450	3.8	13.2	6.8	10.5	33.1	18.0
Whole MNCs	2667	1017	1650	12.8	10.7	12.1	34.9	26.9	32.3
USA MNCs	1517	102	1415	7.3	1.1	5.3	19.9	2.7	14.2
ROW MNCs	1150	915	235	5.5	9.6	6.8	15.1	24.2	18.1
Other MNCs	67	18	49	0.3	0.2	0.3	0.9	0.5	0.7
USA MNCs	65	9	56	0.3	0.1	0.2	0.9	0.2	0.6
ROW MNCs	2	9	-7	0.0	0.1	0.0	0.0	0.2	0.1

U.S. multinationals had the larger share of exports; ROW MNCs had the larger share of imports.

The Chemicals trade balance in 1975 was a surplus of $5,198 million. This reflected a $2,239 million surplus in MNC-related trade and a $2,959 million surplus in Non-MNC trade. Both components contributed to the favorable balance in Chemicals trade. The MNC-related surplus was linked to a surplus in U.S. MNC trade; foreign-based firms had a small deficit.

Between 1975 and 1982, Chemicals trade grew $17,717 million or 140%
to reach $30,341 million. In comparison, intrafirm related trade increased
$6,408 million or 128% to a level of $11,421 million. Accordingly, the overall
intrafirm position decreased slightly from a 39.7% to a 37.6% share (compared
to a 51.1% to 55.6% share change for affiliate related trade). Non-MNC trade
rose to a 62.4% share.

Within the intrafirm trade structure, the export share dropped to 36.6% and
the import share increased to 39.9%. This structural change reflected a decline
in the export share of U.S.-based MNCs, and an increase in the trade shares of
ROW-based MNCs.

The Chemicals trade balance in 1982 was a surplus of $11,355 million, up
$6,157 million from 1975. The intrafirm related trade surplus was $3,851
million, an increase of $1,612 million; the Non-MNC trade surplus had risen
$4,545 million to $7,504 million. Thus the improvement in the Chemicals trade
balance resulted from favorable trends in both components. The MNC-related
surplus continued to reflect the surplus in U.S. MNC trade while ROW MNC
trade again recorded a small deficit.

In the 1982 to 1989 period, Chemicals trade grew $27,259 million or 90%
to $57,600 million. In comparison, intrafirm related trade increased $16,484
million or 144% to a level of $27,905 million. As a result, the overall intrafirm
position increased from a 37.6% to a 48.4% share (compared to a 55.6% to
73.6% share change for affiliate related trade). Non-MNC trade rose to a
51.6% share.

Within the intrafirm trade structure, the export share rose to 44.7% and the
import share to 55.1%. This structural change reflected increases in the trade
shares of both U.S. and ROW MNCs. Compared to 1975, the U.S. MNC share
of total trade had fallen from 28.9% to 26.7%; the ROW MNC share had risen
from 10.7% to 21.7%.

The Chemicals trade balance in 1989 was a surplus of $16,112 million, up
$4,757 million from 1982. The intrafirm related trade surplus was $5,033
million, an increase of $1,182 million; the Non-MNC trade surplus had risen
$3,575 million to $11,079 million. Thus the improvement in the Chemicals
trade balance was due to favorable trends in both components, especially in
Non-MNC trade. The MNC-related surplus was rooted in the growing surplus
in U.S. MNC trade which offset a jump in the deficit associated with ROW
MNC trade.

INDUSTRY TRADE ROLES

This section is based on the trade data shown in Tables 21.1, 21.2, and 21.3
for 1975, 1982, and 1989, respectively. The trade role of each affiliate industry
group is discussed on the basis of affiliate related trade.

Table 21.3: Multinational Companies and U.S. Chemicals Trade (SITC 5) in 1989

	MERCHANDISE TRADE (Millions of Dollars)			TOTAL TRADE (Percent Share)			ALL MNCs TRADE (Percent Share)		
	EXPORTS	IMPORTS	BALANCE	EXP	IMP	AVG	EXP	IMP	AVG
Affiliate Related Trade									
Total	36856	20744	16112	100.0	100.0	100.0	NA	NA	NA
Non-MNCs	9925	5290	4636	26.9	25.5	26.4	NA	NA	NA
All MNCs	26931	15455	11477	73.1	74.5	73.6	100.0	100.0	100.0
USA MNCs	13218	5196	8022	35.9	25.0	32.0	49.1	33.6	43.4
ROW MNCs	14575	10913	3662	39.5	52.6	44.3	54.1	70.6	60.1
Petro MNCs	1687	276	1412	4.6	1.3	3.4	6.3	1.8	4.6
USA MNCs	314	17	297	0.9	0.1	0.6	1.2	0.1	0.8
ROW MNCs	1440	266	1174	3.9	1.3	3.0	5.3	1.7	4.0
Manu MNCs	17334	11588	5747	47.0	55.9	50.2	64.4	75.0	68.2
USA MNCs	7708	4813	2895	20.9	23.2	21.7	28.6	31.1	29.5
ROW MNCs	10293	7178	3115	27.9	34.6	30.3	38.2	46.4	41.2
Whole MNCs	7855	3542	4314	21.3	17.1	19.8	29.2	22.9	26.9
USA MNCs	5149	360	4789	14.0	1.7	9.6	19.1	2.3	13.0
ROW MNCs	2834	3420	-586	7.7	16.5	10.9	10.5	22.1	14.8
Other MNCs	54	50	5	0.1	0.2	0.2	0.2	0.3	0.2
USA MNCs	47	6	41	0.1	0.0	0.1	0.2	0.0	0.1
ROW MNCs	8	49	-41	0.0	0.2	0.1	0.0	0.3	0.1
Intrafirm Related Trade									
Total	36856	20744	16112	100.0	100.0	100.0	NA	NA	NA
Non-MNCs	20387	9308	11079	55.3	44.9	51.6	NA	NA	NA
All MNCs	16469	11436	5033	44.7	55.1	48.4	100.0	100.0	100.0
USA MNCs	11494	3887	7607	31.2	18.7	26.7	69.8	34.0	55.1
ROW MNCs	4975	7549	-2574	13.5	36.4	21.7	30.2	66.0	44.9
Petro MNCs	877	230	647	2.4	1.1	1.9	5.3	2.0	4.0
USA MNCs	304	14	290	0.8	0.1	0.6	1.8	0.1	1.1
ROW MNCs	573	216	357	1.6	1.0	1.4	3.5	1.9	2.8
Manu MNCs	9243	9112	131	25.1	43.9	31.9	56.1	79.7	65.8
USA MNCs	6673	3544	3129	18.1	17.1	17.7	40.5	31.0	36.6
ROW MNCs	2570	5568	-2998	7.0	26.8	14.1	15.6	48.7	29.2
Whole MNCs	6305	2078	4227	17.1	10.0	14.6	38.3	18.2	30.0
USA MNCs	4474	327	4147	12.1	1.6	8.3	27.2	2.9	17.2
ROW MNCs	1831	1751	80	5.0	8.4	6.2	11.1	15.3	12.8
Other MNCs	44	16	28	0.1	0.1	0.1	0.3	0.1	0.2
USA MNCs	43	2	41	0.1	0.0	0.1	0.3	0.0	0.2
ROW MNCs	1	14	-13	0.0	0.1	0.0	0.0	0.1	0.1

Petroleum Affiliates

Affiliate related trade was $599 million in 1975, adjusted for the affiliate trade overlap. This figure represented a 4.7% share of total trade and a 9.3% share of MNC-related trade. The industry category ranked third, behind manufacturing and wholesale affiliates, and was dominated by ROW-based firms. The industry trade balance was a surplus of $267 million, compared to a total merchandise surplus of $5,198 million.

By 1982, industry trade had increased 61% to $965 million. This figure represented a 3.2% share of total trade (down 1.6 share points), and a 5.7% share of MNC-related trade (down 3.6 share points). The industry category continued to rank third. The trade balance was a surplus of $383 million (up $116 million), compared to a total merchandise surplus of $11,355 million (up $6,157 million).

Industry related trade increased 103% to $1,963 million in 1989. This figure represented a 3.4% share of total trade (up 0.2 share points), and a 4.6% share of MNC-related trade (down 1.1 share points). The industry category still ranked third, and was dominated by ROW-based firms. The trade balance was a surplus of $1,412 million (up $1,029 million), compared to a total merchandise surplus of $16,112 million (up $4,757 million).

Manufacturing Affiliates

Affiliate related trade was $3,684 million in 1975, adjusted for the affiliate trade overlap. This figure represented a 29.2% share of total trade and a 57.1% share of MNC-related trade. The industry category ranked first, and was dominated by U.S.-based firms. The industry trade balance was a surplus of $1,982 million, compared to a total merchandise surplus of $5,198 million.

By 1982, industry trade had increased 172% to $10,017 million. This figure represented a 33.0% share of total trade (up 3.8 share points), and a 59.4% share of MNC-related trade (up 2.3 share points). The industry category continued to rank first. The trade balance was a surplus of $2,997 million (up $1,016 million), compared to a total merchandise surplus of $11,355 million (up $6,157 million).

Industry related trade increased by 189% to $28,922 million in 1989. This figure represented a 50.2% share of total trade (up 17.2 share points), and a 68.2% share of MNC-related trade (up 8.8 share points). The industry category continued to rank first, but was now dominated by ROW-based firms. The trade balance was a surplus of $5,747 million (up $2,749 million), compared to a total merchandise surplus of $16,112 million (up $4,757 million).

Wholesale Trade Affiliates

Affiliate related trade was $1,826 million in 1975, adjusted for the affiliate trade overlap. This figure represented a 14.5% share of total trade and a 28.3% share of MNC-related trade. The industry category ranked second, behind manufacturing affiliates, and was dominated by ROW-based firms. The industry trade balance was a surplus of $624 million, compared to a total merchandise surplus of $5,198 million.

By 1982, industry trade had increased 195% to $5,381 million. This figure represented a 17.7% share of total trade (up 3.3 share points), and a 31.9% share of MNC-related trade (up 3.6 share points). The industry category continued to rank second. The trade balance was a surplus of $2,406 million (up $1,782 million), compared to a total merchandise surplus of $11,355 million (up $6,157 million).

Industry related trade increased by 112% to $11,397 million in 1989. This figure represented a 19.8% share of total trade (up 2.1 share points), and a 26.9% share of MNC-related trade (down 5.0 share points). The industry category continued to rank second, and continued to be dominated by ROW-based firms. The trade balance was a surplus of $4,314 million (up $1,908 million), compared to a total merchandise surplus of $16,112 million (up $4,757 million).

Other Industry Affiliates

Affiliate related trade was $339 million in 1975, adjusted for the affiliate trade overlap. This figure represented a 2.7% share of total trade and a 5.3% share of MNC-related trade. The industry category ranked last and was dominated by U.S.-based firms. The industry trade balance was a deficit of $67 million, compared to a total merchandise surplus of $5,198 million.

By 1982, industry trade had increased 46% to $496 million. This figure represented a 1.6% share of total trade (down 1.1 share points), and a 2.9% share of MNC-related trade (down 2.3 share points). The industry category continued to rank last. The trade balance was a surplus of $437 million (a swing of $505 million), compared to a total merchandise surplus of $11,355 million (up $6,157 million).

Industry related trade decreased by 79% to $104 million in 1989. This figure represented a 0.2% share of total trade (down 1.5 share points), and a 0.2% share of MNC-related trade (down 2.7 share points). The industry category still ranked last. The trade balance was a surplus of $5 million (down $433 million), compared to a total merchandise surplus of $16,112 million (up $4,757 million).

DERIVATION OF THE DATA

The derivation of the MNC-related product trade data is discussed at length in Chapter 12 on "Total Product Trade." Separate data on Chemicals (SITC 5) trade have been collected in every FDI benchmark survey. No special modification of this data has been necessary.

CHAPTER 22

MACHINERY TRADE

Machinery is the leading product group in Manufactures trade, accounting for over one-third of exports and imports. The product category includes 23.7% of total merchandise trade, ranking first. In affiliate related trade, multinational companies are involved in 57% of Machinery trade, compared to 54% for all Manufactures. Manufacturing affiliates are the dominant industry group, accounting for nearly one-third of all Machinery trade.

DEFINITION OF MACHINERY PRODUCTS

As defined by the Bureau of Economic Analysis, the "Machinery" foreign trade classification consists of products in the SITC 71-77 categories. Machinery trade includes the following products [BEA 1990 22]:

Machinery, Electrical and Nonelectrical, Except Transportation Equipment (SITC codes 71-77)

Power-generating machinery, equipment and parts (include engines for transportation equipment and nuclear reactors)

Agricultural machinery (include tractors and parts)

Civil engineering and contractors' plant, equipment and parts

Textile and leather machinery and parts

Paper and pulp mill machinery, papercutting machines, etc., and parts

Printing and bookbinding machinery and parts

Food processing machines (except domestic) and parts

Metalworking and metalforming machinery, machine tools, and parts

Oil and gas field equipment and parts (exclude drill bits, core bits, and reamers)

Construction, maintenance, mining, and lifting and loading equipment and parts (exclude wheel or truck-mounted power cranes, draglines, shovels, and off-highway trucks and trailers)

Other industrial machinery and parts specialized to particular industries

Telecommunications and sound recording and reproducing apparatus and parts (include TV and radio receivers, telephone switchboards, phonographs, tape recorders, etc.)

Batteries

Electrical apparatus for medical purposes and radiological apparatus

Electrical equipment for internal combustion engines

Electrical hand tools

Electron tubes, semiconductors, etc.

Electrical machinery, apparatus and appliances, n.e.s, and parts (include electric household equipment, appliances and parts, and their nonelectric counterparts, but exclude nonelectric cooking stoves and ranges)

NOTE. See description of road vehicle parts, to determine which parts are included in machinery, and which in road vehicles (SITC 78) or in other transport equipment (SITC 79).

The note on road vehicle parts refers to the difficulty of assigning these products to the proper trade classification. It is apparent from the benchmark data that most respondents placed all automotive related trade into the Road Vehicles and Parts trade category, including trade that properly belongs in the Machinery category. Accordingly, the benchmark related data in this chapter have been adjusted upward. See the discussion at the end of Chapter 23.

TRENDS IN MACHINERY TRADE

In 1975, Machinery trade totaled $41,981 million. Exports were $29,954 million and imports were $12,027 million yielding a surplus of $17,927 million.

Table 22.1: Multinational Companies and
U.S. Machinery Trade (SITC 71-77) in 1975

	MERCHANDISE TRADE (Millions of Dollars)			TOTAL TRADE (Percent Share)			ALL MNCs TRADE (Percent Share)		
	EXPORTS	IMPORTS	BALANCE	EXP	IMP	AVG	EXP	IMP	AVG
Affiliate Related Trade									
Total	29954	12027	17927	100.0	100.0	100.0	NA	NA	NA
Non-MNCs	15848	4121	11727	52.9	34.3	47.6	NA	NA	NA
All MNCs	14107	7907	6200	47.1	65.7	52.4	100.0	100.0	100.0
USA MNCs	12571	4455	8116	42.0	37.0	40.6	89.1	56.3	77.3
ROW MNCs	2103	3621	-1518	7.0	30.1	13.6	14.9	45.8	26.0
Petro MNCs	869	67	802	2.9	0.6	2.2	6.2	0.8	4.3
USA MNCs	653	4	649	2.2	0.0	1.6	4.6	0.1	3.0
ROW MNCs	244	70	174	0.8	0.6	0.7	1.7	0.9	1.4
Manu MNCs	8158	4613	3545	27.2	38.4	30.4	57.8	58.3	58.0
USA MNCs	7905	4047	3858	26.4	33.6	28.5	56.0	51.2	54.3
ROW MNCs	550	655	-105	1.8	5.4	2.9	3.9	8.3	5.5
Whole MNCs	4562	3144	1417	15.2	26.1	18.4	32.3	39.8	35.0
USA MNCs	3518	342	3176	11.7	2.8	9.2	24.9	4.3	17.5
ROW MNCs	1243	2863	-1620	4.1	23.8	9.8	8.8	36.2	18.7
Other MNCs	517	82	435	1.7	0.7	1.4	3.7	1.0	2.7
USA MNCs	495	62	433	1.7	0.5	1.3	3.5	0.8	2.5
ROW MNCs	66	33	33	0.2	0.3	0.2	0.5	0.4	0.4
Intrafirm Related Trade									
Total	29954	12027	17927	100.0	100.0	100.0	NA	NA	NA
Non-MNCs	18402	4661	13741	61.4	38.8	54.9	NA	NA	NA
All MNCs	11552	7366	4186	38.6	61.2	45.1	100.0	100.0	100.0
USA MNCs	10584	4116	6468	35.3	34.2	35.0	91.6	55.9	77.7
ROW MNCs	968	3250	-2282	3.2	27.0	10.0	8.4	44.1	22.3
Petro MNCs	744	45	699	2.5	0.4	1.9	6.4	0.6	4.2
USA MNCs	540	1	539	1.8	0.0	1.3	4.7	0.0	2.9
ROW MNCs	204	44	160	0.7	0.4	0.6	1.8	0.6	1.3
Manu MNCs	6822	4329	2493	22.8	36.0	26.6	59.1	58.8	58.9
USA MNCs	6639	3772	2867	22.2	31.4	24.8	57.5	51.2	55.0
ROW MNCs	183	557	-374	0.6	4.6	1.8	1.6	7.6	3.9
Whole MNCs	3665	2951	714	12.2	24.5	15.8	31.7	40.1	35.0
USA MNCs	3123	318	2805	10.4	2.6	8.2	27.0	4.3	18.2
ROW MNCs	542	2633	-2091	1.8	21.9	7.6	4.7	35.7	16.8
Other MNCs	321	41	280	1.1	0.3	0.9	2.8	0.6	1.9
USA MNCs	282	25	257	0.9	0.2	0.7	2.4	0.3	1.6
ROW MNCs	39	16	23	0.1	0.1	0.1	0.3	0.2	0.3

Between 1975 and 1982, total trade increased 143% or $60,178 million to reach $102,159 million. Both exports and imports enjoyed strong growth, but with imports growing twice as fast. Consequently, the trade surplus increased only 30% or $5,318 million to a 1982 level of $23,245 million.

Between 1982 and 1989, the growth rate slowed in Machinery exports. Total trade increased 133% or $135,451 million to reach $237,610 million.

Import growth continued at 221% while export growth slumped to 77%. This resulted in a 168% deterioration in the trade balance of $39,051 million, turning the trade surplus into a $15,806 million deficit in 1989.

THE TRADE ROLE OF MULTINATIONAL COMPANIES

This section is based on the trade data shown in Tables 22.1, 22.2, and 22.3 for 1975, 1982, and 1989, respectively. The overall trade role of multinational companies ("All MNCs" in the tables) is discussed for both affiliate related trade and intrafirm related trade.

Affiliate Related Trade

Machinery trade totaled $41,981 million in 1975. Adjusted for the trade overlap, affiliate related trade was $22,013 million for a 52.4% share; Non-MNC trade was $19,968 million for a 47.6% share. The MNC-related trade position reflected a 47.1% share of export trade and a 65.7% share of import trade. The dominant MNC group was U.S.-based firms with a 40.6% share of total trade; ROW-based firms held a 13.6% share. U.S. multinational companies had a larger share of exports and imports, especially exports.

The Machinery trade balance in 1975 was a surplus of $17,927 million. This reflected a $6,200 million surplus in MNC-related trade and a $11,727 million surplus in Non-MNC trade. Thus, the overall trade surplus position in Machinery was due to both components. However, the MNC-related surplus was based on the surplus position of U.S. multinationals; ROW-based MNCs had a modest trade deficit.

Between 1975 and 1982, Machinery trade grew 143% or $60,178 million to reach $102,159 million. In comparison, affiliate related trade increased $37,933 million or 172% to a level of $59,946 million (adjusted for the trade overlap). Accordingly, the overall affiliate position increased from a 52.4% to a 58.7% share and Non-MNC trade fell to a 41.3% share. Within the affiliate trade structure, the export share increased to 48.9% and the import share to 74.3%. These changes reflected increases in ROW MNC trade shares which offset small declines in U.S. MNC shares.

The Machinery trade balance in 1982 was a surplus of $23,245 million, up $5,318 million from 1975. The affiliate related trade surplus was $1,349 million, a decrease of $4,851 million; the Non-MNC trade surplus had risen $10,169 million to $21,896 million. Thus the improvement in the Machinery trade balance was due to favorable trends in Non-MNC trade. The MNC-related surplus declined as the ROW MNC trade deficit increased more than the U.S. MNC trade surplus.

In the 1982 to 1989 period, Machinery trade grew 133% or $135,451 million to $237,610 million. In comparison, affiliate related trade rose $81,834

Table 22.2: Multinational Companies and
U.S. Machinery Trade (SITC 71-77) in 1982

	MERCHANDISE TRADE (Millions of Dollars)			TOTAL TRADE (Percent Share)			ALL MNCs TRADE (Percent Share)		
	EXPORTS	IMPORTS	BALANCE	EXP	IMP	AVG	EXP	IMP	AVG
Affiliate Related Trade									
Total	62702	39457	23245	100.0	100.0	100.0	NA	NA	NA
Non-MNCs	32055	10159	21896	51.1	25.7	41.3	NA	NA	NA
All MNCs	30648	29299	1349	48.9	74.3	58.7	100.0	100.0	100.0
USA MNCs	24327	13011	11316	38.8	33.0	36.5	79.4	44.4	62.3
ROW MNCs	7909	16950	-9041	12.6	43.0	24.3	25.8	57.9	41.5
Petro MNCs	1400	16	1385	2.2	0.0	1.4	4.6	0.1	2.4
USA MNCs	1383	5	1378	2.2	0.0	1.4	4.5	0.0	2.3
ROW MNCs	187	11	176	0.3	0.0	0.2	0.6	0.0	0.3
Manu MNCs	17313	15739	1574	27.6	39.9	32.4	56.5	53.7	55.1
USA MNCs	13667	12089	1578	21.8	30.6	25.2	44.6	41.3	43.0
ROW MNCs	4708	4054	654	7.5	10.3	8.6	15.4	13.8	14.6
Whole MNCs	11180	13270	-2089	17.8	33.6	23.9	36.5	45.3	40.8
USA MNCs	8717	893	7824	13.9	2.3	9.4	28.4	3.0	16.0
ROW MNCs	2756	12615	-9859	4.4	32.0	15.0	9.0	43.1	25.6
Other MNCs	754	274	479	1.2	0.7	1.0	2.5	0.9	1.7
USA MNCs	560	24	536	0.9	0.1	0.6	1.8	0.1	1.0
ROW MNCs	258	270	-12	0.4	0.7	0.5	0.8	0.9	0.9
Intrafirm Related Trade									
Total	62702	39457	23245	100.0	100.0	100.0	NA	NA	NA
Non-MNCs	38102	13758	24344	60.8	34.9	50.8	NA	NA	NA
All MNCs	24600	25699	-1099	39.2	65.1	49.2	100.0	100.0	100.0
USA MNCs	21150	11686	9464	33.7	29.6	32.1	86.0	45.5	65.3
ROW MNCs	3450	14013	-10563	5.5	35.5	17.1	14.0	54.5	34.7
Petro MNCs	755	14	741	1.2	0.0	0.8	3.1	0.1	1.5
USA MNCs	639	4	635	1.0	0.0	0.6	2.6	0.0	1.3
ROW MNCs	116	10	106	0.2	0.0	0.1	0.5	0.0	0.3
Manu MNCs	13271	13543	-272	21.2	34.3	26.2	53.9	52.7	53.3
USA MNCs	12018	10814	1204	19.2	27.4	22.3	48.9	42.1	45.4
ROW MNCs	1253	2729	-1476	2.0	6.9	3.9	5.1	10.6	7.9
Whole MNCs	10066	11974	-1908	16.1	30.3	21.6	40.9	46.6	43.8
USA MNCs	8147	846	7301	13.0	2.1	8.8	33.1	3.3	17.9
ROW MNCs	1919	11128	-9209	3.1	28.2	12.8	7.8	43.3	25.9
Other MNCs	508	168	340	0.8	0.4	0.7	2.1	0.7	1.3
USA MNCs	346	22	324	0.6	0.1	0.4	1.4	0.1	0.7
ROW MNCs	162	146	16	0.3	0.4	0.3	0.7	0.6	0.6

million or 137% to a level of $141,780 million (adjusted for the trade overlap). As noted above, most of this growth was imports which produced massive swings in the related trade balances. The overall affiliate position increased slightly from a 58.7% to a 59.7% share and Non-MNC trade fell to a 40.3% share. Within the affiliate trade structure the export share increased to 50.3% and the import share decreased to 67.9%. This change reflected growth in

ROW MNC shares and a decrease in U.S. MNC shares. Compared to 1975, the U.S. MNC share of total trade had fallen from 40.6% to 31.9%; the ROW MNC share had risen from 13.6% to 29.3%. ROW-based MNCs had achieved parity with U.S.-based firms, and were dominant in import trade.

The Machinery trade balance in 1989 was a deficit of $15,806 million, a deterioration of $39,051 million since 1982. The small affiliate related trade surplus was converted into a large deficit of $30,274 million, a swing of $31,623 million. The Non-MNC trade surplus remained, falling $7,429 million to a level of $14,468 million. Thus the deterioration in the Machinery trade balance was due to trends in MNC-related trade. Within MNC-related trade, the massive jump in imports had pushed the ROW MNC deficit to $39,893 million, completely offsetting the $9,356 million surplus created by U.S.-based firms.

Intrafirm Related Trade

Machinery trade totaled $41,981 million in 1975. Intrafirm related trade was $18,918 million for a 45.1% share (compared to a 52.4% share for affiliate related trade). Arms-length or Non-MNC trade was $23,063 million for a 54.9% share. The MNC-related trade position reflected a 38.6% share of export trade and a 61.2% share of import trade. The dominant MNC group was U.S.-based firms with a 35.0% share of total trade; ROW-based firms held a 10.0% share. U.S. multinationals had the larger share of exports and imports, especially exports.

The Machinery trade balance in 1975 was a surplus of $17,927 million. This reflected a $4,186 million surplus in MNC-related trade and a $13,741 million surplus in Non-MNC trade. Both components contributed to the favorable balance in Machinery trade. The MNC-related surplus was linked to a surplus in U.S. MNC trade which offset a deficit in ROW MNC trade.

Between 1975 and 1982, Machinery trade grew $60,178 million or 143% to reach $102,159 million. In comparison, intrafirm related trade increased $31,381 million or 166% to a level of $50,299 million. Accordingly, the overall intrafirm position increased slightly from a 45.1% to a 49.2% share (compared to a 52.4% to 58.7% share change for affiliate related trade). Non-MNC trade fell to a 50.8% share. Within the intrafirm trade structure, the export share increased to 39.2% and the import share to 65.1%. This structural change reflected a decline in the trade shares of U.S.-based MNCs which was offset by increases in the trade shares of ROW-based MNCs.

The Machinery trade balance in 1982 was a surplus of $23,245 million, up $5,318 million from 1975. The intrafirm related trade balance fell into a deficit of $1,099 million, a negative swing of $5,285 million. In contrast, the Non-MNC trade surplus had risen $10,603 million to $24,344 million. Thus the improvement in the Machinery trade balance resulted from favorable trends in Non-MNC trade only. The MNC-related deficit resulted from an increase in the

Table 22.3: Multinational Companies and
U.S. Machinery Trade (SITC 71-77) in 1989

	MERCHANDISE TRADE (Millions of Dollars)			TOTAL TRADE (Percent Share)			ALL MNCs TRADE (Percent Share)		
	EXPORTS	IMPORTS	BALANCE	EXP	IMP	AVG	EXP	IMP	AVG
Affiliate Related Trade									
Total	110902	126708	-15806	100.0	100.0	100.0	NA	NA	NA
Non-MNCs	55149	40682	14468	49.7	32.1	40.3	NA	NA	NA
All MNCs	55753	86027	-30274	50.3	67.9	59.7	100.0	100.0	100.0
USA MNCs	42615	33259	9356	38.4	26.2	31.9	76.4	38.7	53.5
ROW MNCs	14857	54750	-39893	13.4	43.2	29.3	26.6	63.6	49.1
Petro MNCs	695	16	679	0.6	0.0	0.3	1.2	0.0	0.5
USA MNCs	724	1	723	0.7	0.0	0.3	1.3	0.0	0.5
ROW MNCs	21	16	5	0.0	0.0	0.0	0.0	0.0	0.0
Manu MNCs	33482	42428	-8946	30.2	33.5	31.9	60.1	49.3	53.5
USA MNCs	26051	29911	-3860	23.5	23.6	23.6	46.7	34.8	39.5
ROW MNCs	8663	13968	-5305	7.8	11.0	9.5	15.5	16.2	16.0
Whole MNCs	20919	43174	-22255	18.9	34.1	27.0	37.5	50.2	45.2
USA MNCs	15377	3181	12196	13.9	2.5	7.8	27.6	3.7	13.1
ROW MNCs	5944	40498	-34554	5.4	32.0	19.5	10.7	47.1	32.8
Other MNCs	657	408	249	0.6	0.3	0.4	1.2	0.5	0.8
USA MNCs	463	166	297	0.4	0.1	0.3	0.8	0.2	0.4
ROW MNCs	229	268	-39	0.2	0.2	0.2	0.4	0.3	0.4
Intrafirm Related Trade									
Total	110902	126708	-15806	100.0	100.0	100.0	NA	NA	NA
Non-MNCs	65661	48387	17274	59.2	38.2	48.0	NA	NA	NA
All MNCs	45241	78321	-33080	40.8	61.8	52.0	100.0	100.0	100.0
USA MNCs	39177	29294	9883	35.3	23.1	28.8	86.6	37.4	55.4
ROW MNCs	6064	49027	-42963	5.5	38.7	23.2	13.4	62.6	44.6
Petro MNCs	387	12	375	0.3	0.0	0.2	0.9	0.0	0.3
USA MNCs	378	1	377	0.3	0.0	0.2	0.8	0.0	0.3
ROW MNCs	9	11	-2	0.0	0.0	0.0	0.0	0.0	0.0
Manu MNCs	25949	36788	-10839	23.4	29.0	26.4	57.4	47.0	50.8
USA MNCs	23295	26468	-3173	21.0	20.9	20.9	51.5	33.8	40.3
ROW MNCs	2654	10320	-7666	2.4	8.1	5.5	5.9	13.2	10.5
Whole MNCs	18459	41212	-22753	16.6	32.5	25.1	40.8	52.6	48.3
USA MNCs	15130	2697	12433	13.6	2.1	7.5	33.4	3.4	14.4
ROW MNCs	3329	38515	-35186	3.0	30.4	17.6	7.4	49.2	33.9
Other MNCs	446	309	137	0.4	0.2	0.3	1.0	0.4	0.6
USA MNCs	374	128	246	0.3	0.1	0.2	0.8	0.2	0.4
ROW MNCs	72	181	-109	0.1	0.1	0.1	0.2	0.2	0.2

ROW MNC deficit which swamped the surplus in U.S. MNC trade.

In the 1982 to 1989 period, Machinery trade grew $135,451 million or 133% to $237,610 million. In comparison, intrafirm related trade increased $73,263 million or 146% to a level of $123,562 million. Most of this growth was import trade, which caused large declines in trade balances. The overall intrafirm position saw a small increase from a 49.2% to a 52.0% share (compared to a 58.7% to 59.7% share change for affiliate related trade). Non-MNC trade fell to a 48.0% share. Within the intrafirm trade structure, the export share rose to 40.8% and the import share fell to 61.8%. The export change was due to an increase in the trade share of U.S. MNCs; the import change reflected a share loss by U.S. MNCs which was partially offset by a share gain by ROW MNCs. Compared to 1975, the U.S. MNC share of total trade had fallen from 35.0% to 28.8%; the ROW MNC share had risen from 10.0% to 23.2%. Foreign-based firms were now dominate in import trade.

The Machinery trade balance in 1989 was a deficit of $15,806 million, a deterioration of $39,051 million from 1982. The intrafirm related trade deficit was $33,080 million, an increase of $31,981 million; the Non-MNC trade surplus had fallen $7,070 million to $17,274 million. Thus the deterioration in the Machinery trade balance was due to unfavorable trends in both components, especially MNC-related trade. Within MNC-related trade, the massive jump in imports had pushed the ROW MNC deficit to $42,963 million, completely offsetting the $9,883 million surplus created by U.S.-based firms.

INDUSTRY TRADE ROLES

This section is based on the trade data shown in Tables 22.1, 22.2, and 22.3 for 1975, 1982, and 1989, respectively. The trade role of each affiliate industry group is discussed on the basis of affiliate related trade.

Petroleum Affiliates

Affiliate related trade was $936 million in 1975, adjusted for the affiliate trade overlap. This figure represented a 2.2% share of total trade and a 4.3% share of MNC-related trade. The industry category ranked third, behind manufacturing and wholesale affiliates, and was dominated by U.S.-based firms. The industry trade balance was a surplus of $802 million, compared to a total merchandise surplus of $17,927 million.

By 1982, industry trade had increased 51% to $1,416 million. This figure represented a 1.4% share of total trade (down 0.8 share points), and a 2.4% share of MNC-related trade (down 1.9 share points). The industry category continued to rank third. The trade balance was a surplus of $1,385 million (up $583 million), compared to a total merchandise surplus of $23,245 million (up $5,318 million).

Industry related trade decreased 50% to $711 million in 1989. This figure represented a 0.3% share of total trade (down 1.1 share points), and a 0.5% share of MNC-related trade (down 1.9 share points). The industry category now ranked last, but continued to be dominated by U.S.-based firms. The trade balance was a surplus of $679 million (down $706 million), compared to a total merchandise deficit of $15,806 million (a swing of $39,051 million).

Manufacturing Affiliates

Affiliate related trade was $12,771 million in 1975, adjusted for the affiliate trade overlap. This figure represented a 30.4% share of total trade and a 58.0% share of MNC-related trade. The industry category ranked first, and was dominated by U.S.-based firms. The industry trade balance was a surplus of $3,545 million, compared to total merchandise trade which was in a surplus position of $17,927 million.

By 1982, industry trade had increased 159% to $33,052 million. This figure represented a 32.4% share of total trade (up 1.9 share points), and a 55.1% share of MNC-related trade (down 2.9 share points). The industry category continued to rank first. The trade balance was a surplus of $1,574 million (down $1,971 million), compared to a total merchandise surplus of $23,245 million (up $5,318 million).

Industry related trade increased by 130% to $75,910 million in 1989. This figure represented a 31.9% share of total trade (down 0.4 share points), and a 53.5% share of MNC-related trade (down 1.6 share points). The industry category continued to rank first, and continued to be dominated by U.S.-based firms. The trade balance was a deficit of $8,946 million (a swing of $10,520 million), compared to a total merchandise deficit of $15,806 million (a swing of $39,051 million).

Wholesale Trade Affiliates

Affiliate related trade was $7,706 million in 1975, adjusted for the affiliate trade overlap. This figure represented a 18.4% share of total trade and a 35.0% share of MNC-related trade. The industry category ranked second, behind manufacturing affiliates, and was dominated by ROW-based firms by a slight margin. The industry trade balance was a surplus of $1,417 million, compared to the total merchandise trade in Machinery which was in surplus by $17,927 million.

By 1982, industry trade had increased 217% to $24,450 million. This figure represented a 23.9% share of total trade (up 5.6 share points), and a 40.8% share of MNC-related trade (up 5.8 share points). The industry category continued to rank second. The trade balance was a deficit of $2,089 million (a swing of $3,507 million), compared to a total merchandise surplus of $23,245 million (up $5,318 million).

Industry related trade increased by 162% to $64,093 million in 1989, adjusted for the affiliate trade overlap. This figure represented a 27.0% share of total trade (up 3.0 share points), and a 45.2% share of MNC-related trade (up 4.4 share points). The industry category still ranked second, and was now clearly dominated by ROW-based firms. The trade balance was a deficit of $22,255 million (up $20,166 million), compared to a total merchandise deficit of $15,806 million (a swing of $39,051 million).

Other Industry Affiliates

Affiliate related trade was $599 million in 1975, adjusted for the affiliate trade overlap. This figure represented a 1.4% share of total trade and a 2.7% share of MNC-related trade. The industry category ranked last and was dominated by U.S.-based firms. The industry trade balance was a surplus of $435 million, compared to a total merchandise surplus of $17,927 million.

By 1982, industry trade had increased 72% to $1,028 million. This figure represented a 1.0% share of total trade (down 0.4 share points), and a 1.7% share of MNC-related trade (down 1.0 share points). The industry category continued to rank last. The trade balance was a surplus of $479 million (up $44 million), compared to a total merchandise surplus of $23,245 million (up $5,318 million).

Industry related trade increased by 4% to $1,066 million in 1989. This figure represented a 0.4% share of total trade (down 0.6 share points), and a 0.8% share of MNC-related trade (down 1.0 share points). The industry category now ranked third, ahead of petroleum affiliates. The trade balance was a surplus of $249 million (down $230 million), compared to a total merchandise deficit of $15,806 million (a swing of $39,051 million).

DERIVATION OF THE DATA

The derivation of the MNC-related product trade data is discussed at length in Chapter 12 on "Total Product Trade." Separate data on Machinery (SITC 71-77) trade have been collected in every FDI benchmark survey. No special modification of this data seemed to be necessary at first.

The definition section above notes that certain automotive parts and components properly belong in the Machinery (SITC 71-77) trade classification and should not be included under Road Vehicles and Parts (SITC 78). As discussed in the data derivation section of Chapter 23 on "Road Vehicles and Parts Trade," such a reporting misclassification has occurred. Accordingly, the estimated values for MNC-related trade in Road Vehicles and Parts have been reduced, and part of the misclassified trade has been added to the Machinery category.

The data in the tables in this chapter include the reallocated trade from Chapter 23. The effect of the change is to increase the value of Machinery trade relative to other product categories. The adjustment does not affect the structural relationships and shifts within the Machinery trade category.

ROAD VEHICLES AND PARTS TRADE

Road Vehicles and Parts account for over one-sixth of all Manufactures trade, and are the third largest category. The product group includes 10.0% of total merchandise trade, ranking fourth. In affiliate related trade, multinational companies are involved in 86% of Road Vehicles and Parts trade, compared to 54% for Manufactures. This level of MNC-related trade is the highest of all product categories. Manufacturing affiliates are the dominant industry group, accounting for one-half of all Road Vehicles and Parts trade.

DEFINITION OF ROAD VEHICLES AND PARTS PRODUCTS

As defined by the Bureau of Economic Analysis, the "Road Vehicles and Parts" trade classification consists of products in the SITC code 78 group. Road Vehicles and Parts trade includes the following products [BEA 1990 22-23]:

Road Vehicles (Including Air Cushion Vehicles) and Parts (See Description of Parts Below)
(SITC code 78)

New and used passenger cars

Buses

Motorcycles, motorscooters, bicycles, and other cycles, motorized and nonmotorized

Trucks, except wheeled armored fighting vehicles

Truck trailers

Travel trailers and campers

Wheel- or truck-mounted power cranes, draglines, and shovels (except railway cranes)

Nonmilitary vehicles which operate in whole or in part on runners or skis

Motor vehicle stampings

Road vehicle parts -- Include all parts that are shipped with the vehicle. Product classification of parts that are shipped separately depends on the type of part. Some parts, such as bodies, chassis, shock absorbers, bumpers, mufflers, tailpipes, transmissions, motor vehicle floor coverings, and gaskets, always are classified in SITC 78 (or 79, if parts are for "other transport equipment"), whether or not shipped with the vehicles. Other types of parts are included with vehicles only when shipped with the vehicles; when shipped separately, such parts are classified in other product categories, according to the type of material or the general function of the part. As examples, if shipped separately from vehicles: tires and tubes, brake linings and pads, clutch facings and linings, and automotive glass and mirrors are in SITC 61-66; locks, hinges, and other automotive hardware, vehicle suspension springs and leaves are in SITC 69; and internal combustion piston engines and parts, turbines and parts, motor vehicle pumps and fans, blowers, radios, storage batteries, and electrical equipment for engines and vehicles are in SITC 71-77

The extended description of road vehicle parts shows the difficulty of assigning these products to the proper trade classification. It is apparent from the benchmark data that most respondents ignored these instructions and reported all their automotive related trade within the Road Vehicles and Parts trade category.

As a result, the reported MNC-related trade from the benchmark surveys actually exceeds the recorded merchandise trade. Accordingly, the benchmark derived data in this chapter have been adjusted downward, while the data in the related trade classifications have been adjusted upward. See the discussion at the end of this chapter.

TRENDS IN ROAD VEHICLES AND PARTS TRADE

In 1975, Road Vehicles and Parts trade totaled $19,493 million. Exports were $9,525 million and imports were $9,968 million yielding a small deficit of $443 million. Between 1975 and 1982, total trade in this very important category increased 119% or $23,090 million to reach $42,583 million. Imports showed the stronger growth, growing nearly five times faster than exports. As a result, the trade deficit ballooned by $15,410 million to a 1982 level of $15,853 million.

Table 23.1: Multinational Companies and U.S. Road Vehicles and Parts Trade (SITC 78) in 1975

	MERCHANDISE TRADE (Millions of Dollars)			TOTAL TRADE (Percent Share)			ALL MNCs TRADE (Percent Share)		
	EXPORTS	IMPORTS	BALANCE	EXP	IMP	AVG	EXP	IMP	AVG
Affiliate Related Trade									
Total	9525	9968	-443	100.0	100.0	100.0	NA	NA	NA
Non-MNCs	1513	579	934	15.9	5.8	10.7	NA	NA	NA
All MNCs	8013	9389	-1377	84.1	94.2	89.3	100.0	100.0	100.0
USA MNCs	7988	4400	3588	83.9	44.1	63.6	99.7	46.9	71.2
ROW MNCs	29	5267	-5238	0.3	52.8	27.2	0.4	56.1	30.4
Petro MNCs	21	20	1	0.2	0.2	0.2	0.3	0.2	0.2
USA MNCs	18	0	18	0.2	0.0	0.1	0.2	0.0	0.1
ROW MNCs	3	21	-18	0.0	0.2	0.1	0.0	0.2	0.1
Manu MNCs	7849	4269	3579	82.4	42.8	62.2	98.0	45.5	69.6
USA MNCs	7847	4382	3465	82.4	44.0	62.7	97.9	46.7	70.3
ROW MNCs	6	15	-9	0.1	0.2	0.1	0.1	0.2	0.1
Whole MNCs	106	5091	-4985	1.1	51.1	26.7	1.3	54.2	29.9
USA MNCs	89	18	71	0.9	0.2	0.5	1.1	0.2	0.6
ROW MNCs	17	5221	-5204	0.2	52.4	26.9	0.2	55.6	30.1
Other MNCs	37	9	28	0.4	0.1	0.2	0.5	0.1	0.3
USA MNCs	34	0	34	0.4	0.0	0.2	0.4	0.0	0.2
ROW MNCs	3	10	-7	0.0	0.1	0.1	0.0	0.1	0.1
Intrafirm Related Trade									
Total	9525	9968	-443	100.0	100.0	100.0	NA	NA	NA
Non-MNCs	3317	1511	1806	34.8	15.2	24.8	NA	NA	NA
All MNCs	6208	8457	-2249	65.2	84.8	75.2	100.0	100.0	100.0
USA MNCs	6188	3844	2344	65.0	38.6	51.5	99.7	45.5	68.4
ROW MNCs	20	4613	-4593	0.2	46.3	23.8	0.3	54.5	31.6
Petro MNCs	16	17	-1	0.2	0.2	0.2	0.3	0.2	0.2
USA MNCs	14	0	14	0.1	0.0	0.1	0.2	0.0	0.1
ROW MNCs	2	17	-15	0.0	0.2	0.1	0.0	0.2	0.1
Manu MNCs	6088	3841	2247	63.9	38.5	50.9	98.1	45.4	67.7
USA MNCs	6085	3827	2258	63.9	38.4	50.8	98.0	45.3	67.6
ROW MNCs	3	14	-11	0.0	0.1	0.1	0.0	0.2	0.1
Whole MNCs	91	4593	-4502	1.0	46.1	24.0	1.5	54.3	31.9
USA MNCs	79	17	62	0.8	0.2	0.5	1.3	0.2	0.7
ROW MNCs	12	4576	-4564	0.1	45.9	23.5	0.2	54.1	31.3
Other MNCs	13	6	7	0.1	0.1	0.1	0.2	0.1	0.1
USA MNCs	10	0	10	0.1	0.0	0.1	0.2	0.0	0.1
ROW MNCs	3	6	-3	0.0	0.1	0.0	0.0	0.1	0.1

Between 1982 and 1989, the disparity in import and export growth rates continued. Total trade in Road Vehicles and Parts increased 122% or $52,033 million to reach $94,616 million. Imports increased by 141% compared to an export growth of 82%. This disparity resulted in a 190% deterioration in the trade balance of $30,095 million, pushing the trade deficit to a level of $45,948 million in 1989.

THE TRADE ROLE OF MULTINATIONAL COMPANIES

This section is based on the trade data shown in Tables 23.1, 23.2, and 23.3 for 1975, 1982, and 1989, respectively. The overall trade role of multinational companies ("All MNCs" in the tables) is discussed for both affiliate related trade and intrafirm related trade.

Affiliate Related Trade

Road Vehicles and Parts trade totaled $19,493 million in 1975. Adjusted for the trade overlap, affiliate related trade was $17,402 million for a 89.3% share; Non-MNC trade was $2,092 million for a 10.7% share. The MNC-related trade position reflected a 84.1% share of export trade and a 94.2% share of import trade. The dominant MNC group was U.S.-based firms with a 63.6% share of total trade; ROW-based firms held a 27.2% share. U.S. multinational companies accounted for nearly all MNC-related exports; ROW MNCs had a slightly larger share of imports.

The Road Vehicles and Parts trade balance in 1975 was a small deficit of $443 million. This reflected a $1,377 million deficit in MNC-related trade and a $934 million surplus in Non-MNC trade. Thus the overall deficit position in Road Vehicles and Parts was due to MNC-related trade. In turn, the MNC-related deficit was caused by a ROW MNC deficit which offset the surplus in U.S. MNC trade.

Between 1975 and 1982, Road Vehicles and Parts trade grew 119% or $23,090 million to reach $42,583 million. In comparison, affiliate related trade increased $18,629 million or 107% to a level of $36,031 million (adjusted for the trade overlap). Accordingly, the overall affiliate position decreased slightly from a 89.3% to a 84.6% share and Non-MNC trade rose to a 15.4% share. Within the affiliate trade structure, the export share increased to 85.2% and the import share fell to 84.4%. The export change reflected a jump in the ROW MNC share which offset a decline in U.S. MNC share. The import change was due to share losses by both MNC groups, especially U.S.-based firms.

The Road Vehicles and Parts trade balance in 1982 was a deficit of $15,853 million, up $15,410 million from 1975. The affiliate related trade deficit was $13,269 million, an increase of $11,892 million; the Non-MNC trade surplus had changed into a $2,585 million deficit, a swing of $3,518 million. Thus the growth in the Road Vehicles and Parts trade deficit was due to unfavorable trends in both components. The increase in the MNC-related deficit was due to the higher ROW MNC deficit and a shrinking U.S. MNC surplus.

In the 1982 to 1989 period, Road Vehicles and Parts trade grew 122% or $52,033 million to $94,616 million. In comparison, affiliate related trade rose $42,289 million or 117% to a level of $78,319 million (adjusted for the trade overlap). As a result, the overall affiliate position fell slightly from a 84.6% to a 82.8% share and Non-MNC trade rose to a 17.2% share. Within the affiliate

Table 23.2: Multinational Companies and
U.S. Road Vehicles and Parts Trade (SITC 78) in 1982

	MERCHANDISE TRADE (Millions of Dollars)			TOTAL TRADE (Percent Share)			ALL MNCs TRADE (Percent Share)		
	EXPORTS	IMPORTS	BALANCE	EXP	IMP	AVG	EXP	IMP	AVG
Affiliate Related Trade									
Total	13365	29218	-15853	100.0	100.0	100.0	NA	NA	NA
Non-MNCs	1984	4569	-2585	14.8	15.6	15.4	NA	NA	NA
All MNCs	11381	24650	-13269	85.2	84.4	84.6	100.0	100.0	100.0
USA MNCs	10648	9776	872	79.7	33.5	48.0	93.6	39.7	56.7
ROW MNCs	1272	15355	-14083	9.5	52.6	39.0	11.2	62.3	46.1
Petro MNCs	119	8	111	0.9	0.0	0.3	1.0	0.0	0.4
USA MNCs	123	2	121	0.9	0.0	0.3	1.1	0.0	0.3
ROW MNCs	0	6	-6	0.0	0.0	0.0	0.0	0.0	0.0
Manu MNCs	10800	9995	804	80.8	34.2	48.8	94.9	40.6	57.7
USA MNCs	10274	9697	577	76.9	33.2	46.9	90.3	39.3	55.4
ROW MNCs	1039	437	602	7.8	1.5	3.5	9.1	1.8	4.1
Whole MNCs	413	14568	-14155	3.1	49.9	35.2	3.6	59.1	41.6
USA MNCs	194	77	117	1.5	0.3	0.6	1.7	0.3	0.8
ROW MNCs	231	14829	-14598	1.7	50.8	35.4	2.0	60.2	41.8
Other MNCs	49	78	-28	0.4	0.3	0.3	0.4	0.3	0.4
USA MNCs	57	0	57	0.4	0.0	0.1	0.5	0.0	0.2
ROW MNCs	2	83	-81	0.0	0.3	0.2	0.0	0.3	0.2
Intrafirm Related Trade									
Total	13365	29218	-15853	100.0	100.0	100.0	NA	NA	NA
Non-MNCs	4676	8670	-3994	35.0	29.7	31.3	NA	NA	NA
All MNCs	8689	20548	-11859	65.0	70.3	68.7	100.0	100.0	100.0
USA MNCs	8495	8813	-318	63.6	30.2	40.6	97.8	42.9	59.2
ROW MNCs	194	11735	-11541	1.5	40.2	28.0	2.2	57.1	40.8
Petro MNCs	98	6	92	0.7	0.0	0.2	1.1	0.0	0.4
USA MNCs	98	0	98	0.7	0.0	0.2	1.1	0.0	0.3
ROW MNCs	0	6	-6	0.0	0.0	0.0	0.0	0.0	0.0
Manu MNCs	8236	8815	-579	61.6	30.2	40.0	94.8	42.9	58.3
USA MNCs	8228	8741	-513	61.6	29.9	39.8	94.7	42.5	58.0
ROW MNCs	8	74	-66	0.1	0.3	0.2	0.1	0.4	0.3
Whole MNCs	353	11693	-11340	2.6	40.0	28.3	4.1	56.9	41.2
USA MNCs	167	72	95	1.2	0.2	0.6	1.9	0.4	0.8
ROW MNCs	186	11621	-11435	1.4	39.8	27.7	2.1	56.6	40.4
Other MNCs	2	34	-32	0.0	0.1	0.1	0.0	0.2	0.1
USA MNCs	2	0	2	0.0	0.0	0.0	0.0	0.0	0.0
ROW MNCs	0	34	-34	0.0	0.1	0.1	0.0	0.2	0.1

trade structure the export share rose to 88.5% and the import share declined to 80.8%. This change reflected gains in the trade shares of U.S. MNCs and declines in the shares of ROW MNCs. Compared to 1975, the U.S. MNC share of total trade had fallen from 63.6% to 47.6%; the ROW MNC share had risen from 27.2% to 36.8%.

The Road Vehicles and Parts trade balance in 1989 was a deficit of $45,948 million, up $30,095 million over 1982. The affiliate related trade deficit was $35,237 million, an increase of $21,969 million; the Non-MNC trade deficit had risen $8,127 million to $10,711 million. Thus the deterioration in the Road Vehicles and Parts trade balance reflected trends in both components. Within the MNC-related deficit, the ROW MNC deficit had doubled to $33,031 million while the balance on U.S. MNC trade had converted into a deficit of $3,099 million.

Intrafirm Related Trade

Road Vehicles and Parts trade totaled $19,493 million in 1975. Intrafirm related trade was $14,665 million for a 75.2% share (compared to a 89.3% share for affiliate related trade). Arms-length or Non-MNC trade was $4,828 million for a 24.8% share. The MNC-related trade position reflected a 65.2% share of export trade and a 84.8% share of import trade. The dominant MNC group was U.S.-based firms with a 51.5% share of total trade; ROW-based firms held a 23.8% share. U.S. multinationals held nearly all of the MNC-related exports; ROW MNCs had the larger share of imports.

The Road Vehicles and Parts trade balance in 1975 was a small deficit of $443 million. This reflected a $2,249 million deficit in MNC-related trade and a $1,806 million surplus in Non-MNC trade. The overall trade deficit was due to MNC-related trade. The MNC-related deficit was linked to a deficit in ROW MNC trade which offset a surplus in U.S. MNC trade.

Between 1975 and 1982, Road Vehicles and Parts trade grew $23,090 million or 119% to reach $42,583 million. In comparison, intrafirm related trade increased $14,572 million or 99% to a level of $29,237 million. Accordingly, the overall intrafirm position decreased from a 75.2% to a 68.7% share (compared to a 89.3% to 84.6% share change for affiliate related trade). Non-MNC trade rose to a 31.3% share. Within the intrafirm trade structure, the export share remained at 65.0% and the import share slumped to 70.3%. These changes reflected a decline in the import shares of U.S.-based and foreign-based MNCs.

The Road Vehicles and Parts trade balance in 1982 was a deficit of $15,853 million, up $15,410 million from 1975. The intrafirm related trade deficit was $11,859 million, an increase of $9,610 million; the Non-MNC trade surplus had switched to a deficit of $3,994 million, a swing of $5,800 million. Thus the deterioration in the Road Vehicles and Parts trade balance resulted from unfavorable trends in both components. The MNC-related deficit reflected a growing deficit in ROW MNC trade and a change of U.S. MNC trade into the deficit column.

In the 1982 to 1989 period, Road Vehicles and Parts trade grew $52,033 million or 122% to $94,616 million. In comparison, intrafirm related trade increased $40,682 million or 139% to a level of $69,919 million. As a result, the overall intrafirm position increased from a 68.7% share up to a 73.9% share

Table 23.3: Multinational Companies and
U.S. Road Vehicles and Parts Trade (SITC 78) in 1989

	MERCHANDISE TRADE (Millions of Dollars)			TOTAL TRADE (Percent Share)			ALL MNCs TRADE (Percent Share)		
	EXPORTS	IMPORTS	BALANCE	EXP	IMP	AVG	EXP	IMP	AVG
Affiliate Related Trade									
Total	24334	70282	-45948	100.0	100.0	100.0	NA	NA	NA
Non-MNCs	2793	13504	-10711	11.5	19.2	17.2	NA	NA	NA
All MNCs	21541	56778	-35237	88.5	80.8	82.8	100.0	100.0	100.0
USA MNCs	20954	24053	-3099	86.1	34.2	47.6	97.3	42.4	57.5
ROW MNCs	896	33927	-33031	3.7	48.3	36.8	4.2	59.8	44.5
Petro MNCs	5	0	5	0.0	0.0	0.0	0.0	0.0	0.0
USA MNCs	5	0	5	0.0	0.0	0.0	0.0	0.0	0.0
ROW MNCs	0	0	0	0.0	0.0	0.0	0.0	0.0	0.0
Manu MNCs	20821	24658	-3837	85.6	35.1	48.1	96.7	43.4	58.1
USA MNCs	20635	23717	-3082	84.8	33.7	46.9	95.8	41.8	56.6
ROW MNCs	480	1424	-944	2.0	2.0	2.0	2.2	2.5	2.4
Whole MNCs	709	32071	-31362	2.9	45.6	34.6	3.3	56.5	41.9
USA MNCs	310	287	23	1.3	0.4	0.6	1.4	0.5	0.8
ROW MNCs	414	32500	-32086	1.7	46.2	34.8	1.9	57.2	42.0
Other MNCs	6	48	-43	0.0	0.1	0.1	0.0	0.1	0.1
USA MNCs	4	49	-45	0.0	0.1	0.1	0.0	0.1	0.1
ROW MNCs	2	3	-1	0.0	0.0	0.0	0.0	0.0	0.0
Intrafirm Related Trade									
Total	24334	70282	-45948	100.0	100.0	100.0	NA	NA	NA
Non-MNCs	5880	18817	-12937	24.2	26.8	26.1	NA	NA	NA
All MNCs	18454	51465	-33011	75.8	73.2	73.9	100.0	100.0	100.0
USA MNCs	18176	21649	-3473	74.7	30.8	42.1	98.5	42.1	57.0
ROW MNCs	278	29816	-29538	1.1	42.4	31.8	1.5	57.9	43.0
Petro MNCs	1	0	1	0.0	0.0	0.0	0.0	0.0	0.0
USA MNCs	1	0	1	0.0	0.0	0.0	0.0	0.0	0.0
ROW MNCs	0	0	0	0.0	0.0	0.0	0.0	0.0	0.0
Manu MNCs	17886	22524	-4638	73.5	32.0	42.7	96.9	43.8	57.8
USA MNCs	17876	21334	-3458	73.5	30.4	41.4	96.9	41.5	56.1
ROW MNCs	10	1190	-1180	0.0	1.7	1.3	0.1	2.3	1.7
Whole MNCs	564	28908	-28344	2.3	41.1	31.1	3.1	56.2	42.2
USA MNCs	297	282	15	1.2	0.4	0.6	1.6	0.5	0.8
ROW MNCs	267	28626	-28359	1.1	40.7	30.5	1.4	55.6	41.3
Other MNCs	3	33	-30	0.0	0.0	0.0	0.0	0.1	0.1
USA MNCs	2	33	-31	0.0	0.0	0.0	0.0	0.1	0.1
ROW MNCs	1	0	1	0.0	0.0	0.0	0.0	0.0	0.0

(compared to a 84.6% to 82.8% share change for affiliate related trade). Non-MNC trade fell to a 26.1% share. Within the intrafirm trade structure, the export share rose to 75.8% and the import share to 73.2%. These changes reflected increases in the export share of U.S. MNCs and the import share of ROW MNCs. Compared to 1975, the U.S. MNC share of total trade had fallen from 51.5% to 42.1%; the ROW MNC share had risen from 23.8% to 31.8%.

The Road Vehicles and Parts trade balance in 1989 was a deficit of $45,948 million, up $30,095 million from 1982. The intrafirm related trade deficit was $33,011 million, an increase of $21,152 million; the Non-MNC trade deficit had risen $8,943 million to $12,937 million. Thus the deterioration in the Road Vehicles and Parts trade balance was due to unfavorable trends in both components. The MNC-related deficit was based on the growing deficits in both the MNC groups, but especially among foreign-based firms.

INDUSTRY TRADE ROLES

This section is based on the trade data shown in Tables 23.1, 23.2, and 23.3 for 1975, 1982, and 1989, respectively. The trade role of each affiliate industry group is discussed on the basis of affiliate related trade.

Petroleum Affiliates

Affiliate related trade was $41 million in 1975, adjusted for the affiliate trade overlap. This figure represented a 0.2% share of total trade and a 0.2% share of MNC-related trade. The industry category ranked third, tied with other affiliates. The industry trade balance was a surplus of $1 million, compared to a total merchandise deficit of $443 million.

By 1982, industry trade had increased 208% to $127 million. This figure represented a 0.3% share of total trade (up 0.1 share points), and a 0.4% share of MNC-related trade (up 0.1 share points). The industry category remained tied with other affiliates for third place. The trade balance was a surplus of $111 million (up $110 million), compared to a total merchandise deficit of $15,853 million (up $15,410 million).

Industry related trade decreased 96% to $5 million in 1989. This figure represented a 0.0% share of total trade (down 0.3 share points), and a 0.0% share of MNC-related trade (down 0.3 share points). The industry category now ranked last. The trade balance was a surplus of $5 million (down $106 million), compared to a total merchandise deficit of $45,948 million (up $30,095 million).

Manufacturing Affiliates

Affiliate related trade was $12,118 million in 1975, adjusted for the affiliate trade overlap. This figure represented a 62.2% share of total trade and a 69.6% share of MNC-related trade. The industry category ranked first, and was dominated by U.S.-based firms. The industry trade balance was a surplus of $3,579 million, compared to a total merchandise deficit of $443 million.

By 1982, industry trade had increased 72% to $20,795 million. This figure represented a 48.8% share of total trade (down 13.3 share points), and a 57.7%

share of MNC-related trade (down 11.9 share points). The industry category continued to rank first. The trade balance was a surplus of $804 million (down $2,775 million), compared to a total merchandise deficit of $15,853 million (up $15,410 million).

Industry related trade increased by 119% to $45,479 million in 1989. This figure represented a 48.1% share of total trade (down 0.8 share points), and a 58.1% share of MNC-related trade (up 0.4 share points). The industry category continued to rank first, and remained dominated by U.S.-based firms. The trade balance was a deficit of $3,837 million (a swing of $4,641 million), compared to a total merchandise deficit of $45,948 million (up $30,095 million).

Wholesale Trade Affiliates

Affiliate related trade was $5,197 million in 1975, adjusted for the affiliate trade overlap. This figure represented a 26.7% share of total trade and a 29.9% share of MNC-related trade. The industry category ranked second, behind manufacturing affiliates, and was dominated by ROW-based firms. The industry trade balance was a deficit of $4,985 million, compared to a total merchandise deficit of $443 million.

By 1982, industry trade had increased 188% to $14,981 million. This figure represented a 35.2% share of total trade (up 8.5 share points), and a 41.6% share of MNC-related trade (up 11.7 share points). The industry category continued to rank second. The trade balance was a deficit of $14,155 million (up $9,171 million), compared to a total merchandise deficit of $15,853 million (up $15,410 million).

Industry related trade increased by 119% to $32,781 million in 1989. This figure represented a 34.6% share of total trade (down 0.5 share points), and a 41.9% share of MNC-related trade (up 0.3 share points). The industry category continued to rank second, and continued to be dominated by ROW-based firms. The trade balance was a deficit of $31,362 million (up $17,206 million), compared to a total merchandise deficit of $45,948 million (up $30,095 million).

Other Industry Affiliates

Affiliate related trade was $46 million in 1975, adjusted for the affiliate trade overlap. This figure represented a 0.2% share of total trade and a 0.3% share of MNC-related trade. The industry category ranked third, tied with petroleum affiliates, and was dominated by U.S.-based firms. The industry trade balance was a surplus of $28 million, compared to a total merchandise deficit of $443 million.

By 1982, industry trade had increased 177% to $127 million. This figure represented a 0.3% share of total trade (up 0.1 share points), and a 0.4% share of MNC-related trade (up 0.1 share points). The industry category continued to be tied for third place. The trade balance was a deficit of $28 million (a swing of $56 million), compared to a total merchandise deficit of $15,853 million (up $15,410 million).

Industry related trade decreased by 57% to $54 million in 1989. This figure represented a 0.1% share of total trade (down 0.2 share points), and a 0.1% share of MNC-related trade (down 0.3 share points). The industry category now ranked third, and remained dominated by U.S.-based firms. The trade balance was a deficit of $43 million (up $14 million), compared to a total merchandise deficit of $45,948 million (up $30,095 million).

DERIVATION OF THE DATA

The derivation of the MNC-related product trade data is discussed at length in Chapter 12 on "Total Product Trade." Separate data on Road Vehicles and Parts (SITC 78) trade have been collected in every FDI benchmark survey. No special modification of this data seemed to be necessary at first.

When the MNC-related trade in Road Vehicles and Parts was compared to total U.S. trade in the category, the MNC-related share regularly exceeded a 100% share, even in intrafirm trade! This excessive level of reported MNC-related trade occurred in all three comparison years.

This excessive trade share was not an artifact of the product trade derivation procedure discussed in Chapter 12. It cannot be attributed to bias in the conversion from a majority-owned foreign affiliate (MOFA) to all-affiliate basis, or to time shifting. The intent was to use the 1982 and 1989 benchmark survey data without any alteration from the published figures. Yet even here, the claimed level of MNC-related trade, at the MOFA level, was greater than the recorded international trade of the United States. Examples of All MNCs trade shares are shown below.

Affiliate Related Trade

Year	Exports	Imports	Average
1975	112.2%	125.6%	119.0%
1982	113.5%	112.5%	112.8%
1989	118.0%	107.7%	110.4%

Intrafirm Related Trade

Year	Exports	Imports	Average
1975	86.9%	113.1%	100.3%
1982	86.7%	93.8%	91.5%
1989	101.1%	97.6%	98.5%

In considering the two data sets, it was very clear that the reported U.S. merchandise exports of SITC 78 were the higher quality data. The detailed instructions to benchmark respondents on trade categories belabor the point on the proper classification of automotive parts. These instructions are printed in full in the product definition section above [BEA 1990 22-23]. It was apparent that many respondents have nevertheless dumped all automotive related trade data into the SITC 78 category.

The two options were to use the data as is, or to modify the benchmark sourced data to be consistent with the reported merchandise trade data. Option one was not really an option. Option two required an arbitrary reduction in the level of MNC-related automotive trade and a reallocation of that reduction to other product categories. However, this latter option was really not as arbitrary as it may seem.

Automotive trade was dominated by multinational companies. The export trade was primarily shipments by the Big Three automakers to the Canadian market. Imports consisted of shipments by Japanese auto firms to the American market, and shipments by the Big Three from Canada to the United States. While these few multinational companies may not account for all of the automotive trade, they will account for close to 100%.

The initial dollar estimates of MNC-related Road Vehicles and Parts trade have been cut by 25% across the board. This reduced the highest claimed market share of 125.6% to a level of 94.2%, and placed the highest affiliate related share levels in the 80% to 90% range. The effect of this scalar reduction is shown below.

Affiliate Related Trade

Year	Exports	Imports	Average
1975	84.1%	94.2%	89.3%
1982	85.2%	84.4%	84.6%
1989	88.5%	80.8%	82.8%

Intrafirm Related Trade

Year	Exports	Imports	Average
1975	65.2%	84.8%	75.2%
1982	65.0%	70.3%	68.7%
1989	75.8%	73.2%	73.9%

It is important to note that such a scalar reduction has the advantage of preserving all structural relationships and shifts within the Road Vehicles and Parts trade category. It did reduce the value of this trade against other product categories, but after all, this was the intent of the adjustment.

The next question dealt with the disposition of the reductions in the dollar value of SITC 78 trade. Should it be discarded? It was reasonable to assume that these dollar figures represented actual MNC-related trade which had been reported in the wrong trade classification. The BEA instructions to benchmark respondents identified four other product categories as containing automotive related trade [BEA 1990 22-23].

The dollar reductions in the export and import value of Road Vehicles and Parts trade (SITC 78) were reallocated to these four product categories: Machinery (SITC 71-77), Other Transportation Equipment (SITC 79), Metal Manufactures (SITC 67-69), and Other Manufactures (SITC 61-66,8). These were related product groups which properly contained automotive parts and components. The dollar reductions were added to these categories using the initial MNC-related trade estimates as allocation weights.

This reallocation increased the value of the trade in these four categories against all other trade categories. Again, this was the intent of the adjustment. Structural relationships and shifts within the four trade categories were preserved.

It is important to note that this procedure reallocated reported MNC-related trade into appropriate trade classifications without affecting the integrity of larger product aggregates. The shift occurred within five of the six manufacturing product categories. Chemicals (SITC 5) was not affected by the changes. The aggregate figures for Manufactured Goods Trade (SITC 5-8) in Chapter 20, Non-Manufactured Goods Trade (SITC 0-4, 9) in Chapter 13, and Total Product Trade (SITC 0-9) in Chapter 12 were completely unaffected.

CHAPTER 24

OTHER TRANSPORT EQUIPMENT TRADE

Other Transport Equipment is the smallest product group in Manufactures trade. The product category amounts to only 4.2% of total merchandise trade, ranking tenth. In affiliate related trade, multinational companies are involved in 17% of Other Transport Equipment trade, compared to 54% for all Manufactures. This level of MNC-related trade is by far the lowest for all product categories. Manufacturing affiliates are the dominant industry group, but account for only one-tenth of all Other Transport Equipment trade.

DEFINITION OF OTHER TRANSPORT EQUIPMENT PRODUCTS

As defined by the Bureau of Economic Analysis, the "Other Transport Equipment" trade classification consists of products in the SITC 79 category. Other Transport Equipment includes the following products [BEA 1990 23]:

Other Transport Equipment
(SITC code 79)

Railway vehicles, new and rebuilt (include railway cranes, railway and tramway track fixtures and fittings, and hovertrains)

Aircraft and associated equipment and parts

Ships, boats (include hovercraft) and floating structures

Passenger car trailers (include housing-type coaches)

Parts for such transport equipment (the description of "road vehicle parts" applies also to parts for "other transport equipment")

The comment on road vehicle parts refers to the difficulty of assigning these products to the proper trade classification. It is apparent from the benchmark data that most respondents placed all automotive related trade into the Road Vehicles and Parts category, including trade that properly belongs in the Other Transport Equipment category. Accordingly, the benchmark related data in this chapter have been adjusted upward. See the discussion at the end of the "Road Vehicles and Parts Trade" chapter.

TRENDS IN OTHER TRANSPORT EQUIPMENT TRADE

In 1975, Other Transport Equipment trade totaled $8,916 million. Exports were $7,343 million and imports were $1,573 million yielding a surplus of $5,770 million. Between 1975 and 1982, total trade increased 116% or $10,316 million to reach $19,232 million. Both exports and imports enjoyed strong growth, with imports growing twice as fast. The trade surplus increased $4,172 million or 72% to a 1982 level of $9,942 million.

Between 1982 and 1989, the growth rates slowed in Other Transport Equipment trade, especially in imports. Total trade increased 80% or $15,361 million to reach $34,593 million. Imports grew 87% while exports rose 78%. This resulted in a 73% improvement in the trade balance of $7,269 million, pushing the trade surplus to $17,211 million in 1989.

THE TRADE ROLE OF MULTINATIONAL COMPANIES

This section is based on the trade data shown in Tables 24.1, 24.2, and 24.3 for 1975, 1982, and 1989, respectively. The overall trade role of multinational companies ("All MNCs" in the tables) is discussed for both affiliate related trade and intrafirm related trade.

Affiliate Related Trade

Other Transport Equipment trade totaled $8,916 million in 1975. Adjusted for the trade overlap, affiliate related trade was $1,206 million for a 13.5% share; Non-MNC trade was $7,710 million for a 86.5% share. The dominant trade category was exports. The MNC-related trade position reflected a 7.8% share of export trade and a 40.4% share of import trade. The dominant MNC group was U.S.-based firms with a 8.2% share of total trade; ROW-based firms held a 5.8% share. U.S. multinational companies had the larger shares of export and import trade. Note that MNC-related trade was concentrated in imports, the smaller trade category.

The Other Transport Equipment trade balance in 1975 was a surplus of $5,770 million. This reflected a small $66 million deficit in MNC-related trade

Table 24.1: Multinational Companies and U.S. Other Transport Equipment Trade (SITC 79) in 1975

	MERCHANDISE TRADE (Millions of Dollars)			TOTAL TRADE (Percent Share)			ALL MNCs TRADE (Percent Share)		
	EXPORTS	IMPORTS	BALANCE	EXP	IMP	AVG	EXP	IMP	AVG
Affiliate Related Trade									
Total	7343	1573	5770	100.0	100.0	100.0	NA	NA	NA
Non-MNCs	6773	937	5836	92.2	59.6	86.5	NA	NA	NA
All MNCs	570	636	-66	7.8	40.4	13.5	100.0	100.0	100.0
USA MNCs	380	347	33	5.2	22.1	8.2	66.7	54.6	60.3
ROW MNCs	214	301	-87	2.9	19.1	5.8	37.5	47.3	42.7
Petro MNCs	77	21	56	1.1	1.4	1.1	13.6	3.4	8.2
USA MNCs	7	0	7	0.1	0.0	0.1	1.2	0.0	0.6
ROW MNCs	71	22	49	1.0	1.4	1.0	12.5	3.5	7.7
Manu MNCs	252	348	-96	3.4	22.2	6.7	44.3	54.8	49.8
USA MNCs	239	343	-104	3.3	21.8	6.5	41.9	53.9	48.3
ROW MNCs	30	16	14	0.4	1.0	0.5	5.3	2.5	3.8
Whole MNCs	169	254	-85	2.3	16.2	4.8	29.7	40.0	35.1
USA MNCs	76	4	72	1.0	0.3	0.9	13.3	0.6	6.6
ROW MNCs	98	251	-153	1.3	16.0	3.9	17.2	39.5	28.9
Other MNCs	71	12	59	1.0	0.7	0.9	12.4	1.8	6.8
USA MNCs	58	0	58	0.8	0.0	0.7	10.2	0.0	4.8
ROW MNCs	15	12	3	0.2	0.8	0.3	2.6	1.9	2.2
Intrafirm Related Trade									
Total	7343	1573	5770	100.0	100.0	100.0	NA	NA	NA
Non-MNCs	6888	1127	5761	93.8	71.6	89.9	NA	NA	NA
All MNCs	455	446	9	6.2	28.4	10.1	100.0	100.0	100.0
USA MNCs	289	169	120	3.9	10.7	5.1	63.5	37.9	50.8
ROW MNCs	166	277	-111	2.3	17.6	5.0	36.5	62.1	49.2
Petro MNCs	74	13	61	1.0	0.8	1.0	16.3	2.9	9.7
USA MNCs	4	0	4	0.1	0.0	0.0	0.9	0.0	0.4
ROW MNCs	70	13	57	1.0	0.8	0.9	15.4	2.9	9.2
Manu MNCs	173	182	-9	2.4	11.6	4.0	38.0	40.8	39.4
USA MNCs	171	167	4	2.3	10.6	3.8	37.6	37.4	37.5
ROW MNCs	2	15	-13	0.0	1.0	0.2	0.4	3.4	1.9
Whole MNCs	147	245	-98	2.0	15.6	4.4	32.3	54.9	43.5
USA MNCs	67	2	65	0.9	0.1	0.8	14.7	0.4	7.7
ROW MNCs	80	243	-163	1.1	15.4	3.6	17.6	54.5	35.8
Other MNCs	61	6	55	0.8	0.4	0.8	13.4	1.3	7.4
USA MNCs	47	0	47	0.6	0.0	0.5	10.3	0.0	5.2
ROW MNCs	14	6	8	0.2	0.4	0.2	3.1	1.3	2.2

and a $5,836 million surplus in Non-MNC trade. Thus the overall trade surplus position in Other Transport Equipment was due to Non-MNC trade. The MNC-related deficit was the result of a small ROW MNC deficit offsetting a smaller U.S. MNC surplus.

Between 1975 and 1982, Other Transport Equipment trade grew 116% or $10,316 million to reach $19,232 million. In comparison, affiliate related trade increased $2,566 million or 213% to a level of $3,772 million (adjusted for the trade overlap). Accordingly, the overall affiliate position increased from a 13.5% to a 19.6% share and Non-MNC trade fell to a 80.4% share. Within the affiliate trade structure, the export share increased to 11.6% and the import share to 44.8%. These changes reflected higher ROW MNC shares which offset a decline in U.S. MNC shares.

The Other Transport Equipment trade balance in 1982 was a surplus of $9,942 million, up $4,172 million from 1975. The affiliate related trade deficit remained a small $392 million, an increase of $326 million; the Non-MNC trade surplus had risen $4,498 million to $10,334 million. Thus the improvement in the Other Transport Equipment trade balance was due to favorable trends in Non-MNC trade. Within the MNC-related deficit, both MNC groups now had small deficits.

In the 1982 to 1989 period, Other Transport Equipment trade grew 80% or $15,361 million to $34,593 million. In comparison, affiliate related trade rose $2,838 million or 75% to a level of $6,610 million (adjusted for the trade overlap). As a result, the overall affiliate position decreased slightly from a 19.6% to a 19.1% share and Non-MNC trade rose to a 80.9% share. Within the affiliate trade structure the export share decreased to 8.1% and the import share rose to 51.9%. This change reflected growth in the import share of U.S. MNCs. Compared to 1975, the U.S. MNC share of total trade had risen from 8.2% to 10.3%; the ROW MNC share had risen from 5.8% to 10.1%. These share increases were concentrated in imports (the smaller trade category) where MNC-related trade now accounted for more than half of the trade.

The Other Transport Equipment trade balance in 1989 was a surplus of $17,211 million, up $7,269 million over 1982. The affiliate related trade deficit was $2,416 million, an increase of $2,024 million; the Non-MNC trade surplus had risen $9,293 million to $19,627 million. Thus the improvement in the Other Transport Equipment trade balance again reflected trends in Non-MNC trade. The MNC-related deficit was based on deficits in both MNC groups.

Intrafirm Related Trade

Other Transport Equipment trade totaled $8,916 million in 1975. Intrafirm related trade was $901 million for a 10.1% share (compared to a 13.5% share for affiliate related trade). Arms-length or Non-MNC trade was $8,015 million for a 89.9% share. The MNC-related trade position reflected a 6.2% share of export trade and a 28.4% share of import trade. U.S.-based firms held a 5.1% share of total trade; ROW-based firms held a 5.0% share. U.S. multinationals had the larger share of exports; ROW MNCs had the larger share of imports.

The Other Transport Equipment trade balance in 1975 was a surplus of $5,770 million. This reflected a $9 million surplus in MNC-related trade and a $5,761 million surplus in Non-MNC trade. The favorable balance in Other Transport Equipment trade was based on Non-MNC trade. The MNC-related

Table 24.2: Multinational Companies and
U.S. Other Transport Equipment Trade (SITC 79) in 1982

	MERCHANDISE TRADE (Millions of Dollars)			TOTAL TRADE (Percent Share)			ALL MNCs TRADE (Percent Share)		
	EXPORTS	IMPORTS	BALANCE	EXP	IMP	AVG	EXP	IMP	AVG
Affiliate Related Trade									
Total	14587	4645	9942	100.0	100.0	100.0	NA	NA	NA
Non-MNCs	12897	2563	10334	88.4	55.2	80.4	NA	NA	NA
All MNCs	1690	2082	-392	11.6	44.8	19.6	100.0	100.0	100.0
USA MNCs	644	924	-280	4.4	19.9	8.2	38.1	44.4	41.6
ROW MNCs	1144	1336	-192	7.8	28.8	12.9	67.7	64.2	65.7
Petro MNCs	23	0	23	0.2	0.0	0.1	1.4	0.0	0.6
USA MNCs	22	0	22	0.2	0.0	0.1	1.3	0.0	0.6
ROW MNCs	4	0	4	0.0	0.0	0.0	0.2	0.0	0.1
Manu MNCs	896	1183	-287	6.1	25.5	10.8	53.0	56.8	55.1
USA MNCs	437	923	-486	3.0	19.9	7.1	25.9	44.3	36.1
ROW MNCs	537	394	143	3.7	8.5	4.8	31.8	18.9	24.7
Whole MNCs	675	830	-155	4.6	17.9	7.8	39.9	39.9	39.9
USA MNCs	108	0	108	0.7	0.0	0.6	6.4	0.0	2.9
ROW MNCs	579	869	-290	4.0	18.7	7.5	34.3	41.7	38.4
Other MNCs	96	69	27	0.7	1.5	0.9	5.7	3.3	4.4
USA MNCs	77	1	76	0.5	0.0	0.4	4.6	0.0	2.1
ROW MNCs	24	73	-49	0.2	1.6	0.5	1.4	3.5	2.6
Intrafirm Related Trade									
Total	14587	4645	9942	100.0	100.0	100.0	NA	NA	NA
Non-MNCs	13619	3297	10322	93.4	71.0	88.0	NA	NA	NA
All MNCs	968	1348	-380	6.6	29.0	12.0	100.0	100.0	100.0
USA MNCs	448	368	80	3.1	7.9	4.2	46.3	27.3	35.2
ROW MNCs	520	980	-460	3.6	21.1	7.8	53.7	72.7	64.8
Petro MNCs	4	0	4	0.0	0.0	0.0	0.4	0.0	0.2
USA MNCs	1	0	1	0.0	0.0	0.0	0.1	0.0	0.0
ROW MNCs	3	0	3	0.0	0.0	0.0	0.3	0.0	0.1
Manu MNCs	319	630	-311	2.2	13.6	4.9	33.0	46.7	41.0
USA MNCs	315	367	-52	2.2	7.9	3.5	32.5	27.2	29.4
ROW MNCs	4	263	-259	0.0	5.7	1.4	0.4	19.5	11.5
Whole MNCs	585	669	-84	4.0	14.4	6.5	60.4	49.6	54.1
USA MNCs	89	0	89	0.6	0.0	0.5	9.2	0.0	3.8
ROW MNCs	496	669	-173	3.4	14.4	6.1	51.2	49.6	50.3
Other MNCs	60	49	11	0.4	1.1	0.6	6.2	3.6	4.7
USA MNCs	43	1	42	0.3	0.0	0.2	4.4	0.1	1.9
ROW MNCs	17	48	-31	0.1	1.0	0.3	1.8	3.6	2.8

balance was created by a U.S. MNC surplus barely exceeding a ROW MNC deficit.

Between 1975 and 1982, Other Transport Equipment trade grew $10,316 million or 116% to reach $19,232 million. In comparison, intrafirm related trade increased $1,415 million or 157% to a level of $2,316 million. Accordingly, the overall intrafirm position increased slightly from a 10.1% to a 12.0% share (compared to a 13.5% to 19.6% share change for affiliate related trade). Non-MNC trade fell to a 88.0% share. Within the intrafirm trade structure, the trade shares increased a shade to 6.6% for exports and 29.0% for import. These changes reflected an increase in the trade shares of ROW-based firms exceeding a decrease in the trade shares of U.S.-based firms.

The Other Transport Equipment trade balance in 1982 was a surplus of $9,942 million, up $4,172 million from 1975. The intrafirm related trade balance was a small deficit of $380 million, a decline of $389 million; the Non-MNC trade surplus had risen $4,561 million to $10,322 million. Thus the improvement in the Other Transport Equipment trade balance resulted from favorable trends in Non-MNC trade. The MNC-related deficit reflected deficits in both MNC groups.

In the 1982 to 1989 period, Other Transport Equipment trade grew $15,361 million or 80% to $34,593 million. In comparison, intrafirm related trade increased $2,108 million or 91% to a level of $4,424 million. As a result, the overall intrafirm position edged up from a 12.0% to a 12.8% share (compared to a 19.6% to 19.1% share change for affiliate related trade). Non-MNC trade fell to a 87.2% share. Within the intrafirm trade structure, the export share fell to 5.3% and the import share rose to 35.2%. This structural change reflected an increase in the import share of U.S. MNCs. Compared to 1975, the U.S. MNC share of total trade had risen from 5.1% to 5.7%; the ROW MNC share had risen from 5.0% to 7.1%. The growth of MNC-related trade was concentrated in imports.

The Other Transport Equipment trade balance in 1989 was a surplus of $17,211 million, up $7,269 million from 1982. The intrafirm related trade deficit was $1,702 million, an increase of $1,322 million; the Non-MNC trade surplus had risen $8,591 million to $18,913 million. Thus the improvement in the Other Transport Equipment trade balance was again due to favorable trends in Non-MNC trade. The MNC-related deficit was based on growing deficits in both MNC groups.

INDUSTRY TRADE ROLES

This section is based on the trade data shown in Tables 24.1, 24.2, and 24.3 for 1975, 1982, and 1989, respectively. The trade role of each affiliate industry group is discussed on the basis of affiliate related trade.

Petroleum Affiliates

Affiliate related trade was $99 million in 1975, adjusted for the affiliate trade overlap. This figure represented a 1.1% share of total trade and a 8.2% share of MNC-related trade. The industry category ranked third, behind manufacturing and wholesale affiliates, and was dominated by the ROW-based

Table 24.3: Multinational Companies and
U.S. Other Transport Equipment Trade (SITC 79) in 1989

	MERCHANDISE TRADE (Millions of Dollars)			TOTAL TRADE (Percent Share)			ALL MNCs TRADE (Percent Share)		
	EXPORTS	IMPORTS	BALANCE	EXP	IMP	AVG	EXP	IMP	AVG
Affiliate Related Trade									
Total	25902	8691	17211	100.0	100.0	100.0	NA	NA	NA
Non-MNCs	23805	4179	19627	91.9	48.1	80.9	NA	NA	NA
All MNCs	2097	4513	-2416	8.1	51.9	19.1	100.0	100.0	100.0
USA MNCs	1025	2550	-1525	4.0	29.3	10.3	48.9	56.5	54.1
ROW MNCs	1273	2218	-945	4.9	25.5	10.1	60.7	49.2	52.8
Petro MNCs	5	0	5	0.0	0.0	0.0	0.2	0.0	0.1
USA MNCs	6	0	6	0.0	0.0	0.0	0.3	0.0	0.1
ROW MNCs	0	0	0	0.0	0.0	0.0	0.0	0.0	0.0
Manu MNCs	1002	3501	-2498	3.9	40.3	13.0	47.8	77.6	68.1
USA MNCs	783	2431	-1648	3.0	28.0	9.3	37.3	53.9	48.6
ROW MNCs	352	1261	-909	1.4	14.5	4.7	16.8	27.9	24.4
Whole MNCs	764	989	-224	3.0	11.4	5.1	36.4	21.9	26.5
USA MNCs	222	119	103	0.9	1.4	1.0	10.6	2.6	5.2
ROW MNCs	548	933	-385	2.1	10.7	4.3	26.1	20.7	22.4
Other MNCs	325	23	302	1.3	0.3	1.0	15.5	0.5	5.3
USA MNCs	14	0	14	0.1	0.0	0.0	0.7	0.0	0.2
ROW MNCs	373	24	349	1.4	0.3	1.1	17.8	0.5	6.0
Intrafirm Related Trade									
Total	25902	8691	17211	100.0	100.0	100.0	NA	NA	NA
Non-MNCs	24541	5628	18913	94.7	64.8	87.2	NA	NA	NA
All MNCs	1361	3063	-1702	5.3	35.2	12.8	100.0	100.0	100.0
USA MNCs	623	1356	-733	2.4	15.6	5.7	45.8	44.3	44.7
ROW MNCs	738	1707	-969	2.8	19.6	7.1	54.2	55.7	55.3
Petro MNCs	2	0	2	0.0	0.0	0.0	0.1	0.0	0.0
USA MNCs	2	0	2	0.0	0.0	0.0	0.1	0.0	0.0
ROW MNCs	0	0	0	0.0	0.0	0.0	0.0	0.0	0.0
Manu MNCs	516	2415	-1899	2.0	27.8	8.5	37.9	78.8	66.3
USA MNCs	402	1256	-854	1.6	14.5	4.8	29.5	41.0	37.5
ROW MNCs	114	1159	-1045	0.4	13.3	3.7	8.4	37.8	28.8
Whole MNCs	743	629	114	2.9	7.2	4.0	54.6	20.5	31.0
USA MNCs	208	100	108	0.8	1.2	0.9	15.3	3.3	7.0
ROW MNCs	535	529	6	2.1	6.1	3.1	39.3	17.3	24.1
Other MNCs	100	19	81	0.4	0.2	0.3	7.3	0.6	2.7
USA MNCs	11	0	11	0.0	0.0	0.0	0.8	0.0	0.2
ROW MNCs	89	19	70	0.3	0.2	0.3	6.5	0.6	2.4

firms. The industry trade balance was a surplus of $56 million, compared to a total merchandise surplus of $5,770 million.

By 1982, industry trade had decreased 76% to $23 million. This figure represented a 0.1% share of total trade (down 1.0 share points), and a 0.6% share of MNC-related trade (down 7.6 share points). The industry category now ranked last. The trade balance was a surplus of $23 million (down $32 million), compared to a total merchandise surplus in the trade category of $9,942 million (up $4,172 million).

Industry related trade decreased 78% to $5 million in 1989. This figure represented a 0.0% share of total trade (down 0.1 share points), and a 0.1% share of MNC-related trade (down 0.5 share points). The industry category ranked last. The trade balance was a surplus of $5 million (down $18 million), compared to a total merchandise surplus of $17,211 million (up $7,269 million).

Manufacturing Affiliates

Affiliate related trade was $601 million in 1975, adjusted for the affiliate trade overlap. This figure represented a 6.7% share of total trade and a 49.8% share of MNC-related trade. The industry category ranked first, and was dominated by U.S.-based firms. The industry trade balance was a deficit of $96 million, compared to a total merchandise surplus of $5,770 million.

By 1982, industry trade had increased 246% to $2,079 million. This figure represented a 10.8% share of total trade (up 4.1 share points), and a 55.1% share of MNC-related trade (up 5.3 share points). The industry category continued to rank first. The trade balance was a deficit of $287 million (up $191 million), compared to a total merchandise surplus of $9,942 million (up $4,172 million).

Industry related trade increased by 117% to $4,503 million in 1989. This figure represented a 13.0% share of total trade (up 2.2 share points), and a 68.1% share of MNC-related trade (up 13.0 share points). The industry category continued to rank first, and was still dominated by U.S.-based firms. The trade balance was a deficit of $2,498 million (up $2,211 million), compared to a total merchandise surplus of $17,211 million (up $7,269 million).

Wholesale Trade Affiliates

Affiliate related trade was $424 million in 1975, adjusted for the affiliate trade overlap. This figure represented a 4.8% share of total trade and a 35.1% share of MNC-related trade. The industry category ranked second, behind manufacturing affiliates, and was dominated by ROW-based firms. The industry trade balance was a deficit of $85 million, compared to a total merchandise surplus of $5,770 million.

By 1982, industry trade had increased 255% to $1,505 million. This figure represented a 7.8% share of total trade (up 3.1 share points), and a 39.9% share of MNC-related trade (up 4.8 share points). The industry category continued to rank second. The trade balance was a deficit of $155 million (up $70 million), compared to a total merchandise surplus of $9,942 million (up $4,172 million).

Industry related trade increased by 17% to $1,753 million in 1989, adjusted for the affiliate trade overlap. This figure represented a 5.1% share of total trade (down 2.8 share points), and a 26.5% share of MNC-related trade (down 13.4 share points). The industry category continued to rank second, and continued to be dominated by ROW-based firms. The trade balance was a deficit of $224 million (up $69 million), compared to a total merchandise surplus of $17,211 million (up $7,269 million).

Other Industry Affiliates

Affiliate related trade was $83 million in 1975, adjusted for the affiliate trade overlap. This figure represented a 0.9% share of total trade and a 6.8% share of MNC-related trade. The industry category ranked last and was dominated by U.S.-based firms. The industry trade balance was a surplus of $59 million, compared to a total merchandise surplus of $5,770 million.

By 1982, industry trade had increased 100% to $165 million. This figure represented a 0.9% share of total trade (down 0.1 share points), and a 4.4% share of MNC-related trade (down 2.5 share points). The industry category now ranked third, ahead of petroleum affiliates. The trade balance was a surplus of $27 million (down $32 million), compared to a total merchandise surplus of $9,942 million (up $4,172 million).

Industry related trade increased by 111% to $349 million in 1989, adjusted for the affiliate trade overlap. This figure represented a 1.0% share of total trade (up 0.1 share points), and a 5.3% share of MNC-related trade (up 0.9 share points). The industry category continued to rank third, but was now dominated by ROW-based firms. The industry trade balance was a surplus of $302 million (up $275 million), compared to a total surplus in the trade category of $17,211 million (up $7,269 million).

DERIVATION OF THE DATA

The derivation of the MNC-related product trade data is discussed at length in Chapter 12 on "Total Product Trade." Separate data on Other Transport Equipment (SITC 79) trade have been collected in every FDI benchmark survey. No special modification of this data seemed to be necessary at first.

The definition section above notes that certain automotive parts and components properly belong in the Other Transport Equipment (SITC 79) trade classification and should not be included under Road Vehicles and Parts (SITC 78). As discussed in the data derivation section of Chapter 23 on "Road Vehicles and Parts Trade," such a reporting misclassification has occurred. Accordingly, the estimated values for MNC-related trade in Road Vehicles and Parts have been reduced, and part of the misclassified trade has been added to the Other Transport Equipment category.

The data in the tables in this chapter include the reallocated trade from Chapter 23. The effect of the change is to increase the value of Other Transport

Equipment trade relative to other product categories. The adjustment does not affect the structural relationships and shifts within the Other Transport Equipment trade category.

CHAPTER 25

METAL MANUFACTURES TRADE

Metal Manufactures exports and imports include less than one-tenth of all Manufactures trade, and are the fifth largest category. The product group includes 6.1% of total merchandise trade, ranking eighth. In affiliate related trade, multinational companies are involved in 65% of Metal Manufactures trade, compared to 54% for all Manufactures. This level of MNC-related trade is among the highest of all product categories. Wholesale affiliates are the dominant industry group, accounting for nearly two-fifths of Metal Manufactures trade.

DEFINITION OF METAL MANUFACTURES PRODUCTS

As defined by the Bureau of Economic Analysis, the "Metal Manufactures" foreign trade classification consists of products in the SITC 67-69 categories. International trade in the Metal Manufactures category includes the following products [BEA 1990 23]:

Metal Manufactures
(SITC codes 67, 68, and 69)

Iron and steel products of blast furnaces, steel works, rolling mills and finishing mills

Cast iron articles, except ingot molds and railway car wheels

Nonferrous metals and metal products (except gold and insulated cable for communication, appliances, and building)

Nonferrous metal castings and forgings

Uranium depleted in U235 and thorium

Fabricated metal products (except ordnance, machinery, and transportation products and insulated electrical items), such as structures and parts of structures, metal containers, wire products, pipes and tubes, nails, screws, nuts and bolts, hand and edge tools, dies and cutting tools; drill bits, core bits and reamers for oil and gas field drilling machinery; metal venetian blinds, hardware, table flatware and cutlery, utensils and household equipment made of base metal, etc.

Metal stampings, except motor vehicle stampings and stamped vitreous enameled parts for washing machines and refrigerators

Nonelectric cooking stoves and ranges

NOTE. See description of road vehicle parts to determine which parts are classified in metal manufactures, and which in road vehicles (SITC 78) and in other transport equipment (SITC 79).

The note on road vehicle parts refers to the difficulty of assigning these products to the proper trade classification. It is apparent from the benchmark data that most respondents reported all automotive related trade under the Road Vehicles and Parts trade category, including trade that properly belongs in the Metal Manufactures category.

As a result, the reported MNC-related trade in Road Vehicles and Parts regularly exceeds the total recorded U.S. merchandise trade in the product category. Accordingly, the reported benchmark trade data in Road Vehicles and Parts was adjusted downward, and the related automotive trade categories -- including Metal Manufactures trade -- have been adjusted upward. See the discussion at the end of the "Road Vehicles and Parts Trade" chapter.

TRENDS IN METAL MANUFACTURES TRADE

In 1975, U.S. merchandise trade in Metal Manufactures totaled $14,790 million. Exports were $5,804 million and imports were $8,986 million yielding a deficit of $3,182 million. Between 1975 and 1982, total trade increased 88% or $13,077 million to reach $27,867 million. Both exports and imports increased, with imports growing over twice as fast. Accordingly, the trade deficit improved by $7,405 million or 233% to reach a 1982 level of $10,587 million.

Between 1982 and 1989, the growth rate slowed significantly in Metal Manufactures imports. Total trade increased 55% or $15,303 million to reach $43,170 million. Imports grew by 58% while exports rose 47%. This resulted in a 68% deterioration in the trade balance of $7,141 million, increasing the trade deficit to $17,728 million in 1989.

Table 25.1: Multinational Companies and
U.S. Metal Manufactures Trade (SITC 67-69) in 1975

	MERCHANDISE TRADE (Millions of Dollars)			TOTAL TRADE (Percent Share)			ALL MNCs TRADE (Percent Share)		
	EXPORTS	IMPORTS	BALANCE	EXP	IMP	AVG	EXP	IMP	AVG
Affiliate Related Trade									
Total	5804	8986	-3182	100.0	100.0	100.0	NA	NA	NA
Non-MNCs	3018	2907	112	52.0	32.3	40.1	NA	NA	NA
All MNCs	2786	6080	-3294	48.0	67.7	59.9	100.0	100.0	100.0
USA MNCs	1827	909	918	31.5	10.1	18.5	65.6	15.0	30.9
ROW MNCs	1240	5287	-4047	21.4	58.8	44.1	44.5	87.0	73.6
Petro MNCs	259	246	13	4.5	2.7	3.4	9.3	4.0	5.7
USA MNCs	195	12	183	3.4	0.1	1.4	7.0	0.2	2.3
ROW MNCs	78	236	-158	1.3	2.6	2.1	2.8	3.9	3.5
Manu MNCs	1427	1345	82	24.6	15.0	18.7	51.2	22.1	31.3
USA MNCs	1181	672	509	20.3	7.5	12.5	42.4	11.1	20.9
ROW MNCs	376	702	-326	6.5	7.8	7.3	13.5	11.5	12.2
Whole MNCs	769	4294	-3525	13.3	47.8	34.2	27.6	70.6	57.1
USA MNCs	238	143	95	4.1	1.6	2.6	8.5	2.4	4.3
ROW MNCs	613	4234	-3621	10.6	47.1	32.8	22.0	69.6	54.7
Other MNCs	331	195	137	5.7	2.2	3.6	11.9	3.2	5.9
USA MNCs	213	82	131	3.7	0.9	2.0	7.6	1.3	3.3
ROW MNCs	173	115	58	3.0	1.3	1.9	6.2	1.9	3.2
Intrafirm Related Trade									
Total	5804	8986	-3182	100.0	100.0	100.0	NA	NA	NA
Non-MNCs	4191	4576	-385	72.2	50.9	59.3	NA	NA	NA
All MNCs	1613	4410	-2797	27.8	49.1	40.7	100.0	100.0	100.0
USA MNCs	1265	676	589	21.8	7.5	13.1	78.4	15.3	32.2
ROW MNCs	348	3734	-3386	6.0	41.6	27.6	21.6	84.7	67.8
Petro MNCs	198	212	-14	3.4	2.4	2.8	12.3	4.8	6.8
USA MNCs	139	2	137	2.4	0.0	1.0	8.6	0.0	2.3
ROW MNCs	59	210	-151	1.0	2.3	1.8	3.7	4.8	4.5
Manu MNCs	885	937	-52	15.2	10.4	12.3	54.9	21.2	30.3
USA MNCs	816	453	363	14.1	5.0	8.6	50.6	10.3	21.1
ROW MNCs	69	484	-415	1.2	5.4	3.7	4.3	11.0	9.2
Whole MNCs	428	3102	-2674	7.4	34.5	23.9	26.5	70.3	58.6
USA MNCs	228	140	88	3.9	1.6	2.5	14.1	3.2	6.1
ROW MNCs	200	2962	-2762	3.4	33.0	21.4	12.4	67.2	52.5
Other MNCs	102	159	-57	1.8	1.8	1.8	6.3	3.6	4.3
USA MNCs	82	81	1	1.4	0.9	1.1	5.1	1.8	2.7
ROW MNCs	20	78	-58	0.3	0.9	0.7	1.2	1.8	1.6

THE TRADE ROLE OF MULTINATIONAL COMPANIES

This section is based on the trade data shown in Tables 25.1, 25.2, and 25.3 for 1975, 1982, and 1989, respectively. The role of multinational companies ("All MNCs" in the tables) is discussed for affiliate and intrafirm related trade.

Affiliate Related Trade

Metal Manufactures trade totaled $14,790 million in 1975. Adjusted for the trade overlap, affiliate related trade was $8,866 million for a 59.9% share; Non-MNC trade was $5,925 million for a 40.1% share. The MNC-related trade position reflected a 48.0% share of export trade and a 67.7% share of import trade. The dominant MNC group was ROW-based firms with a 44.1% share of total trade; U.S.-based firms held a 18.5% share. U.S. multinational companies had a larger share of exports; ROW MNCs had a much larger share of imports.

The Metal Manufactures trade balance in 1975 was a deficit of $3,182 million. This reflected a $3,294 million deficit in MNC-related trade and a small $112 million surplus in Non-MNC trade. Thus the overall trade deficit position in Metal Manufactures was due to MNC-related trade. In turn, the MNC-related deficit was created by a ROW MNC deficit which exceeded a U.S. MNC surplus.

Between 1975 and 1982, Metal Manufactures trade grew 88% or $13,077 million to reach $27,867 million. In comparison, affiliate related trade increased $10,908 million or 123% to a level of $19,773 million (adjusted for the trade overlap). Accordingly, the overall affiliate position increased from a 59.9% to a 71.0% share and Non-MNC trade fell to a 29.0% share. Within the affiliate trade structure, the export share increased to 54.2% and the import share to 78.5%. The export change reflected a jump in the ROW MNC share which offset a decline in U.S. MNC share. The import change was due to share gains by the ROW MNC group.

The Metal Manufactures trade balance in 1982 was a deficit of $10,587 million, up $7,405 million from 1975. The affiliate related trade deficit was $10,402 million, an increase of $7,109 million; the Non-MNC trade surplus shifted by $297 million to a small deficit of $185 million. Thus the increase in the Metal Manufactures trade deficit was due to MNC-related trade trends. The MNC-related deficit continued to reflect the deficit position of ROW MNCs; U.S.-based firms achieved a small surplus.

In the 1982 to 1989 period, Metal Manufactures trade grew 55% or $15,303 million to $43,170 million. In comparison, affiliate related trade rose $8,399 million or 43% to a level of $28,172 million (adjusted for the trade overlap). As a result, the overall affiliate position decreased from a 71.0% to a 65.3% share and Non-MNC trade rose to a 34.7% share. Within the affiliate trade structure the export share jumped to 81.9% and the import share slumped to 58.3%. These large changes reflected export and import share shifts in foreign-based MNCs. Compared to 1975, the U.S. MNC share of total trade had fallen from 18.5% to 13.0%; the ROW MNC share had risen from 44.1% to 54.2%. ROW-based MNCs now held majority shares of total trade in both exports and imports.

The Metal Manufactures trade balance in 1989 recorded a deficit of $17,728

Table 25.2: Multinational Companies and
U.S. Metal Manufactures Trade (SITC 67-69) in 1982

	MERCHANDISE TRADE (Millions of Dollars)			TOTAL TRADE (Percent Share)			ALL MNCs TRADE (Percent Share)		
	EXPORTS	IMPORTS	BALANCE	EXP	IMP	AVG	EXP	IMP	AVG
Affiliate Related Trade									
Total	8640	19227	-10587	100.0	100.0	100.0	NA	NA	NA
Non-MNCs	3955	4140	-185	45.8	21.5	29.0	NA	NA	NA
All MNCs	4686	15088	-10402	54.2	78.5	71.0	100.0	100.0	100.0
USA MNCs	2151	2009	142	24.9	10.4	14.9	45.9	13.3	21.0
ROW MNCs	2846	13419	-10573	32.9	69.8	58.4	60.7	88.9	82.3
Petro MNCs	199	399	-200	2.3	2.1	2.1	4.3	2.6	3.0
USA MNCs	210	0	210	2.4	0.0	0.8	4.5	0.0	1.1
ROW MNCs	11	402	-391	0.1	2.1	1.5	0.2	2.7	2.1
Manu MNCs	2407	3751	-1343	27.9	19.5	22.1	51.4	24.9	31.1
USA MNCs	1421	1531	-110	16.4	8.0	10.6	30.3	10.1	14.9
ROW MNCs	1166	2307	-1141	13.5	12.0	12.5	24.9	15.3	17.6
Whole MNCs	1976	10777	-8801	22.9	56.1	45.8	42.2	71.4	64.5
USA MNCs	446	441	5	5.2	2.3	3.2	9.5	2.9	4.5
ROW MNCs	1634	10579	-8945	18.9	55.0	43.8	34.9	70.1	61.8
Other MNCs	103	161	-58	1.2	0.8	0.9	2.2	1.1	1.3
USA MNCs	74	37	37	0.9	0.2	0.4	1.6	0.2	0.6
ROW MNCs	35	131	-96	0.4	0.7	0.6	0.7	0.9	0.8
Intrafirm Related Trade									
Total	8640	19227	-10587	100.0	100.0	100.0	NA	NA	NA
Non-MNCs	5871	8924	-3053	68.0	46.4	53.1	NA	NA	NA
All MNCs	2769	10303	-7534	32.0	53.6	46.9	100.0	100.0	100.0
USA MNCs	1528	1328	200	17.7	6.9	10.2	55.2	12.9	21.8
ROW MNCs	1241	8975	-7734	14.4	46.7	36.7	44.8	87.1	78.2
Petro MNCs	66	356	-290	0.8	1.9	1.5	2.4	3.5	3.2
USA MNCs	63	0	63	0.7	0.0	0.2	2.3	0.0	0.5
ROW MNCs	3	356	-353	0.0	1.9	1.3	0.1	3.5	2.7
Manu MNCs	1303	2525	-1222	15.1	13.1	13.7	47.1	24.5	29.3
USA MNCs	1013	955	58	11.7	5.0	7.1	36.6	9.3	15.1
ROW MNCs	290	1570	-1280	3.4	8.2	6.7	10.5	15.2	14.2
Whole MNCs	1337	7363	-6026	15.5	38.3	31.2	48.3	71.5	66.6
USA MNCs	403	373	30	4.7	1.9	2.8	14.6	3.6	5.9
ROW MNCs	934	6990	-6056	10.8	36.4	28.4	33.7	67.8	60.6
Other MNCs	63	59	4	0.7	0.3	0.4	2.3	0.6	0.9
USA MNCs	49	0	49	0.6	0.0	0.2	1.8	0.0	0.4
ROW MNCs	14	59	-45	0.2	0.3	0.3	0.5	0.6	0.6

million, up $7,141 million over 1982. The affiliate related trade deficit was $7,332 million, a decrease of $3,070 million; the small Non-MNC trade deficit had ballooned by $10,211 million to reach $10,396 million. Thus the deterioration in the Metal Manufactures trade balance reflected trends in Non-MNC trade, a reversal from the 1975 to 1982 period. The size and change in the MNC-related deficit was again based on the deficit in ROW MNC trade.

Intrafirm Related Trade

Metal Manufactures trade totaled $14,790 million in 1975. Intrafirm related trade was $6,023 million for a 40.7% share (compared to a 59.9% share for affiliate related trade). Arms-length or Non-MNC trade was $8,767 million for a 59.3% share. The MNC-related trade position reflected a 27.8% share of export trade and a 49.1% share of import trade. The dominant MNC group was ROW-based firms with a 27.6% share of total trade; U.S.-based firms held a 13.1% share. U.S. multinationals had the larger share of exports; ROW MNCs had a much larger share of imports.

The Metal Manufactures trade balance in 1975 was a deficit of $3,182 million. This reflected a $2,797 million deficit in MNC-related trade and a $385 million deficit in Non-MNC trade. Both components contributed to the negative balance in Metal Manufactures trade. The MNC-related deficit was linked to a deficit in ROW MNC trade; U.S.-based firms had a modest surplus.

Between 1975 and 1982, Metal Manufactures trade grew $13,077 million or 88% to reach $27,867 million. In comparison, intrafirm related trade increased $7,049 million or 117% to a level of $13,072 million. Accordingly, the overall intrafirm position increased from a 40.7% to a 46.9% share (compared to a 59.9% to 71.0% share change for affiliate related trade). Non-MNC trade fell to a 53.1% share.

Within the intrafirm trade structure, the export share rose to 32.0% and the import share to 53.6%. These changes reflected a decline in the trade shares of U.S.-based MNCs and an increase in the trade shares of ROW-based MNCs.

The Metal Manufactures trade balance in 1982 was a deficit of $10,587 million, up $7,405 million from 1975. The intrafirm related trade deficit was $7,534 million, an increase of $4,737 million; the Non-MNC trade deficit had risen $2,668 million to $3,053 million. Thus the deterioration in the Metal Manufactures trade balance resulted from unfavorable trends in both components. The MNC-related deficit continued to reflect the deficit in ROW MNC trade.

In the 1982 to 1989 period, Metal Manufactures trade grew $15,303 million or 55% to $43,170 million. In comparison, intrafirm related trade increased $2,750 million or 21% to a level of $15,822 million. As a result, the overall intrafirm position decreased from a 46.9% to a 36.7% share (compared to a 71.0% to 65.3% share change for affiliate related trade). Non-MNC trade rose to a 63.3% share.

Within the intrafirm trade structure, the export share rose to 35.5% while the import share plummeted to 37.1%. These changes reflected share changes in ROW MNCs trade. Compared to 1975, the U.S. MNC share of total trade had fallen from 13.0% to 9.0%; the ROW MNC share had remained the same at 27.6%.

The Metal Manufactures trade balance in 1989 was a deficit of $17,728 million, up $7,141 million from 1982. The intrafirm related trade deficit was

Table 25.3: Multinational Companies and
U.S. Metal Manufactures Trade (SITC 67-69) in 1989

	MERCHANDISE TRADE (Millions of Dollars)			TOTAL TRADE (Percent Share)			ALL MNCs TRADE (Percent Share)		
	EXPORTS	IMPORTS	BALANCE	EXP	IMP	AVG	EXP	IMP	AVG
Affiliate Related Trade									
Total	12721	30449	-17728	100.0	100.0	100.0	NA	NA	NA
Non-MNCs	2301	12697	-10396	18.1	41.7	34.7	NA	NA	NA
All MNCs	10420	17752	-7332	81.9	58.3	65.3	100.0	100.0	100.0
USA MNCs	2797	2812	-15	22.0	9.2	13.0	26.8	15.8	19.9
ROW MNCs	7931	15484	-7553	62.3	50.9	54.2	76.1	87.2	83.1
Petro MNCs	56	7	48	0.4	0.0	0.1	0.5	0.0	0.2
USA MNCs	42	0	42	0.3	0.0	0.1	0.4	0.0	0.1
ROW MNCs	15	8	7	0.1	0.0	0.1	0.1	0.0	0.1
Manu MNCs	3782	6424	-2642	29.7	21.1	23.6	36.3	36.2	36.2
USA MNCs	1932	2406	-474	15.2	7.9	10.0	18.5	13.6	15.4
ROW MNCs	1947	4198	-2251	15.3	13.8	14.2	18.7	23.6	21.8
Whole MNCs	6151	10961	-4810	48.4	36.0	39.6	59.0	61.7	60.7
USA MNCs	490	291	199	3.9	1.0	1.8	4.7	1.6	2.8
ROW MNCs	5863	11020	-5157	46.1	36.2	39.1	56.3	62.1	59.9
Other MNCs	431	360	71	3.4	1.2	1.8	4.1	2.0	2.8
USA MNCs	333	115	218	2.6	0.4	1.0	3.2	0.6	1.6
ROW MNCs	106	258	-152	0.8	0.8	0.8	1.0	1.5	1.3
Intrafirm Related Trade									
Total	12721	30449	-17728	100.0	100.0	100.0	NA	NA	NA
Non-MNCs	8208	19140	-10932	64.5	62.9	63.3	NA	NA	NA
All MNCs	4513	11309	-6796	35.5	37.1	36.7	100.0	100.0	100.0
USA MNCs	2181	1724	457	17.1	5.7	9.0	48.3	15.2	24.7
ROW MNCs	2332	9585	-7253	18.3	31.5	27.6	51.7	84.8	75.3
Petro MNCs	33	0	33	0.3	0.0	0.1	0.7	0.0	0.2
USA MNCs	33	0	33	0.3	0.0	0.1	0.7	0.0	0.2
ROW MNCs	0	0	0	0.0	0.0	0.0	0.0	0.0	0.0
Manu MNCs	1930	4291	-2361	15.2	14.1	14.4	42.8	37.9	39.3
USA MNCs	1448	1483	-35	11.4	4.9	6.8	32.1	13.1	18.5
ROW MNCs	482	2808	-2326	3.8	9.2	7.6	10.7	24.8	20.8
Whole MNCs	2279	6818	-4539	17.9	22.4	21.1	50.5	60.3	57.5
USA MNCs	453	212	241	3.6	0.7	1.5	10.0	1.9	4.2
ROW MNCs	1826	6606	-4780	14.4	21.7	19.5	40.5	58.4	53.3
Other MNCs	271	200	71	2.1	0.7	1.1	6.0	1.8	3.0
USA MNCs	247	29	218	1.9	0.1	0.6	5.5	0.3	1.7
ROW MNCs	24	171	-147	0.2	0.6	0.5	0.5	1.5	1.2

$6,796 million, a decrease of $738 million; in contrast the Non-MNC trade deficit had risen $7,879 million to $10,932 million. Thus the increase in the Metal Manufactures trade deficit was due to trends in Non-MNC trade, which was a significant reversal of earlier patterns. The size and change in the deficit resulting from MNC-related trade continued to be based in ROW MNC trade, while U.S. MNC trade continued to show a modest surplus.

INDUSTRY TRADE ROLES

This section is based on the trade data shown in Tables 25.1, 25.2, and 25.3 for 1975, 1982, and 1989, respectively. The trade role of each affiliate industry group is discussed on the basis of affiliate related trade.

Petroleum Affiliates

Affiliate related trade was $504 million in 1975, adjusted for the affiliate trade overlap. This figure represented a 3.4% share of total trade and a 5.7% share of MNC-related trade. The industry category ranked last, and was dominated by ROW-based firms. The industry trade balance was a surplus of $13 million, compared to a total merchandise deficit of $3,182 million.

By 1982, industry trade had increased 19% to $598 million. This figure represented a 2.1% share of total trade (down 1.3 share points), and a 3.0% share of MNC-related trade (down 2.7 share points). The industry category now ranked third, behind wholesale and manufacturing affiliates. The trade balance was a deficit of $200 million (a swing of $212 million), compared to a total merchandise deficit of $10,587 million (up $7,405 million).

Industry related trade decreased 89% to $63 million in 1989. This figure represented a 0.1% share of total trade (down 2.0 share points), and a 0.2% share of MNC-related trade (down 2.8 share points). The industry category again ranked last. The trade balance was a surplus of $48 million (a swing of $248 million), compared to a total merchandise deficit of $17,728 million (up $7,141 million).

Manufacturing Affiliates

Affiliate related trade was $2,773 million in 1975, adjusted for the affiliate trade overlap. This figure represented a 18.7% share of total trade and a 31.3% share of MNC-related trade. The industry category ranked second, behind wholesale affiliates, and was dominated by U.S.-based firms. The industry trade balance was a surplus of $82 million, compared to a total merchandise deficit of $3,182 million.

By 1982, industry trade had increased 122% to $6,158 million. This figure represented a 22.1% share of total trade (up 3.4 share points), and a 31.1% share of MNC-related trade (down 0.1 share points). The industry category continued to rank second, but was now dominated by ROW-based firms. The trade balance was a deficit of $1,343 million (a swing of $1,425 million), compared to a total merchandise deficit of $10,587 million (up $7,405 million).

Industry related trade increased by 66% to $10,206 million in 1989. This figure represented a 23.6% share of total trade (up 1.5 share points), and a 36.2% share of MNC-related trade (up 5.1 share points). The industry category continued to rank second and remained dominated by ROW-based firms. The trade balance was a deficit of $2,642 million (up $1,298 million), compared to a total merchandise deficit of $17,728 million (up $7,141 million).

Wholesale Trade Affiliates

Affiliate related trade was $5,063 million in 1975, adjusted for the affiliate trade overlap. This figure represented a 34.2% share of total trade and a 57.1% share of MNC-related trade. The industry category ranked first, and was dominated by ROW-based firms. The industry trade balance was a deficit of $3,525 million, compared to a total merchandise deficit of $3,182 million.

By 1982, industry trade had increased 152% to $12,753 million. This figure represented a 45.8% share of total trade (up 11.5 share points), and a 64.5% share of MNC-related trade (up 7.4 share points). The industry category continued to rank first. The trade balance was a deficit of $8,801 million (up $5,276 million), while total merchandise trade in Metal Manufactures was in deficit by $10,587 million (up $7,405 million).

Industry related trade increased by 34% to $17,112 million in 1989, adjusted for the affiliate trade overlap. This figure represented a 39.6% share of total trade (down 6.1 share points), and a 60.7% share of MNC-related trade (down 3.8 share points). The industry category continued to rank first, and continued to be dominated by ROW-based firms. The trade balance was a deficit of $4,810 million (down $3,991 million), compared to a total merchandise deficit of $17,728 million (up $7,141 million).

Other Industry Affiliates

Affiliate related trade was $526 million in 1975, adjusted for the affiliate trade overlap. This figure represented a 3.6% share of total trade and a 5.9% share of MNC-related trade. The industry category ranked third and was dominated by U.S.-based firms. The industry trade balance was a surplus of $137 million, compared to a total merchandise deficit of $3,182 million.

By 1982, industry trade had decreased 50% to $263 million. This figure represented a 0.9% share of total trade (down 2.6 share points), and a 1.3% share of MNC-related trade (down 4.6 share points). The industry category now ranked last. The trade balance was a deficit of $58 million (a swing of $195 million), compared to a total merchandise deficit of $10,587 million (up $7,405 million).

Industry related trade increased by 200% to $790 million in 1989, adjusted for the affiliate trade overlap. This figure represented a 1.8% share of total trade (up 0.9 share points), and a 2.8% share of MNC-related trade (up 1.5 share points). The industry category now ranked third, ahead of petroleum affiliates. The trade balance was a surplus of $71 million (a swing of $129 million), compared to a total Metal Manufactures deficit of $17,728 million (up $7,141 million).

DERIVATION OF THE DATA

The derivation of the MNC-related product trade data is discussed at length in Chapter 12 on "Total Product Trade." Separate data on Metal Manufactures (SITC 69-69) trade have been collected in every FDI benchmark survey. No special modification of this data seemed to be necessary at first.

The definition section above notes that certain automotive parts and components properly belong in the Metal Manufactures (SITC 67-69) trade classification and should not be included under Road Vehicles and Parts (SITC 78). As discussed in the data derivation section of Chapter 23 on "Road Vehicles and Parts Trade," such a reporting misclassification has occurred. Accordingly, the estimated values for MNC-related trade in Road Vehicles and Parts have been reduced, and part of the misclassified trade has been added to the Machinery category.

The data in the tables in this chapter include the reallocated trade from Chapter 23. The effect of the change is to increase the value of Metal Manufactures trade relative to other product categories. The adjustment does not affect the structural relationships and shifts within the Metal Manufactures trade category.

CHAPTER 26

OTHER MANUFACTURES TRADE

Other Manufactures exports and imports include nearly one-fourth of all Manufactures trade, ranking second only to Machinery. The product category accounts for 15.4% of total merchandise trade, ranking second. In affiliate related trade, multinational companies are involved in 34% of Other Manufactures trade, compared to 54% for all Manufactures. This level of MNC-related trade is among the lowest of all product categories. Manufacturing affiliates are the dominant industry group, accounting for nearly one-third of Other Manufactures trade.

DEFINITION OF OTHER MANUFACTURES PRODUCTS

As defined by the Bureau of Economic Analysis, the "Other Manufactures" foreign trade consists of products falling in the SITC 61-66 and 8 categories. This is a residual and miscellaneous trade classification for the narrow definition (SITC 5-8) of manufactured goods trade [Bailey and Bowden 57-59]. Other Manufactures trade includes the following products [BEA 1990 23]:

Other Manufactures
(SITC codes 61-66, and 8)

Leather, leather manufactures and dressed furskins (include composition leather with a basis of leather and manufactures of such composition leather)

Rubber manufactures, finished and semifinished (include sheet and plate materials, hardened rubber items, tires and tubes, hygienic and pharmaceutical articles, etc.)

Cork manufactures, agglomerated cork, and articles of same

Wood veneers, plywood, improved or reconstructed wood, and other worked wood (include cooperage, millwork, household utensils of wood, etc.)

Paper, paperboard, and articles of paper pulp, of paper, or of paperboard

Textile yarn, thread, and fabrics of manmade or natural fibers but exclude scouring and combing mill products

Made up articles of textile materials, apparel, clothing accessories, and related products

Footwear (exclude military apparel and footwear, which are in SITC 9)

Floor coverings (include linoleum, carpets, mats, etc.)

Nonmetallic mineral manufactures, such as glass and glass products, pottery, lime, cement, and fabricated construction materials, refractory materials, clay construction materials, etc. (exclude electrical porcelain goods and gaskets of laminated metals)

Sanitary, plumbing, heating and lighting fixtures and fittings

Furniture and parts (include chairs designed for medical, dental, surgical and veterinary use)

Travel goods, luggage, handbags and similar containers

Optical goods, instruments and apparatus

Medical and dental instruments and appliances

Meters, counters, and measuring, checking, analyzing, and controlling instruments

Photographic and motion picture apparatus, equipment, and supplies (include prepared photographic film and chemicals)

Watches, clocks and parts thereof

Phonograph records and record blanks

Magnetic tape, including computer recording, etc.

Printed matter, including books, magazines, newspapers, commercial printing, etc.

Baby carriages, toys, games, and sporting goods

Office and stationery supplies

Miscellaneous plastic products (except laminated sheets, rods, and tubes)

Works of art, collector's pieces, antiques

Jewelry and related articles

Musical instruments and parts and accessories

Nonmilitary arms, shotgun shells, other hunting and sporting ammunition

Other miscellaneous manufactured products

This trade category (specifically SITC 61-66) is also affected by the difficulty of assigning road vehicle parts to the proper trade classification. It is apparent from the benchmark data that most respondents placed all automotive related trade into the Road Vehicles and Parts category, including trade that properly belongs in the Other Manufactures category. Accordingly, the benchmark related trade data in this chapter have been adjusted upward. See the discussion at the end of the Road Vehicles and Parts chapter.

TRENDS IN OTHER MANUFACTURES TRADE

In 1975, Other Manufactures trade totaled $26,261 million. Exports were $11,207 million and imports were $15,054 million yielding a deficit of $3,847 million. Between 1975 and 1982, total trade increased 158% or $41,356 million to reach $67,617 million. Both exports and imports recorded strong growth, with imports growing faster. This imbalance increased the trade deficit by $12,500 million or 325% to a 1982 level of $16,347 million.

Between 1982 and 1989, the growth rates slowed in Other Manufactures trade, especially in exports. Total trade increased 131% or $88,278 million to reach $155,895 million. Imports increased by 158% compared to export growth of 86%. This resulted in a 269% deterioration in the trade balance of $44,012 million, pushing the trade deficit to $60,359 million in 1989.

THE TRADE ROLE OF MULTINATIONAL COMPANIES

This section is based on the trade data shown in Tables 26.1, 26.2, and 26.3 for 1975, 1982, and 1989, respectively. The role of multinational companies ("All MNCs" in the tables) is discussed for affiliate and intrafirm related trade.

Affiliate Related Trade

Other Manufactures trade totaled $26,261 million in 1975. Adjusted for the trade overlap, affiliate related trade was $11,322 million for a 43.1% share;

Non-MNC trade was $14,939 million for a 56.9% share. The MNC-related trade position reflected a 53.3% share of export trade and a 35.5% share of import trade. The dominant MNC group was U.S.-based firms with a 29.4% share of total trade; ROW-based firms held a 16.1% share. U.S. MNCs and ROW MNCs held the larger share of exports and imports, respectively.

The Other Manufactures trade balance in 1975 was a deficit of $3,847 million. This reflected a $626 million surplus in MNC-related trade and a $4,473 million deficit in Non-MNC trade. The MNC-related surplus was based on a surplus position of U.S.-based firms which exceeded a ROW MNC deficit. Thus the deficit in Other Manufactures trade was due to Non-MNC trade.

Between 1975 and 1982, Other Manufactures trade grew 158% or $41,356 million to reach $67,617 million. In comparison, affiliate related trade increased $7,902 million or 70% to a level of $19,224 million (adjusted for the trade overlap). Accordingly, the overall affiliate position decreased from a 43.1% to a 28.4% share and Non-MNC trade rose to a 71.6% share. Within the affiliate trade structure, the export share plummeted to 28.1% and the import share decreased to 28.6%. The export and import decreases reflected declines in U.S. MNC shares.

The Other Manufactures trade balance in 1982 was a deficit of $16,347 million, up $12,500 million from 1975. The affiliate related trade balance had changed to a deficit of $4,805 million, a deterioration of $5,431 million; the Non-MNC trade deficit had risen $7,070 million to $11,543 million. Thus the decline in the Other Manufactures trade balance was due to unfavorable trends in both components. The conversion of MNC-related trade into a deficit was caused by the growing deficit position of ROW multinationals, linked to a decline in the size of the U.S. MNC surplus.

In the 1982 to 1989 period, Other Manufactures trade grew 131% or $88,278 million to $155,895 million. In comparison, affiliate related trade rose $28,042 million or 146% to a level of $47,265 million (adjusted for the trade overlap). As a result, the overall affiliate position increased slightly from a 28.4% to a 30.3% share and Non-MNC trade fell to a 69.7% share.

Within the affiliate trade structure the export share jumped to 41.6% and the import share decreased to 30.3%. The export change reflected growth in the trade shares of U.S. and ROW MNCs; the import change was due to a decline in ROW MNC share which offset an increase in U.S. MNC share. Compared to 1975, the U.S. MNC share of total trade had fallen from 29.4% to 17.7% and the ROW MNC share from 16.1% to 14.5%.

The Other Manufactures trade balance in 1989 was a deficit of $60,359 million, up $44,012 million over 1982. The affiliate related trade deficit was $7,502 million, an increase of $2,698 million; the Non-MNC trade deficit had ballooned $41,315 million to $52,857 million. Thus the large increase in the Other Manufactures trade deficit primarily reflected trends in Non-MNC trade. The MNC-related deficit was again based on a growing trade deficit in ROW MNC trade and a declining surplus in U.S. MNC trade.

Table 26.1: Multinational Companies and
U.S. Other Manufactures Trade (SITC 61-66,8) in 1975

	MERCHANDISE TRADE (Millions of Dollars)			TOTAL TRADE (Percent Share)			ALL MNCs TRADE (Percent Share)		
	EXPORTS	IMPORTS	BALANCE	EXP	IMP	AVG	EXP	IMP	AVG
Affiliate Related Trade									
Total	11207	15054	-3847	100.0	100.0	100.0	NA	NA	NA
Non-MNCs	5233	9706	-4473	46.7	64.5	56.9	NA	NA	NA
All MNCs	5974	5348	626	53.3	35.5	43.1	100.0	100.0	100.0
USA MNCs	5252	2464	2788	46.9	16.4	29.4	87.9	46.1	68.2
ROW MNCs	965	3260	-2295	8.6	21.7	16.1	16.2	61.0	37.3
Petro MNCs	375	188	186	3.3	1.3	2.1	6.3	3.5	5.0
USA MNCs	289	16	273	2.6	0.1	1.2	4.8	0.3	2.7
ROW MNCs	98	197	-99	0.9	1.3	1.1	1.6	3.7	2.6
Manu MNCs	3697	2233	1464	33.0	14.8	22.6	61.9	41.8	52.4
USA MNCs	3377	2030	1347	30.1	13.5	20.6	56.5	38.0	47.8
ROW MNCs	489	423	66	4.4	2.8	3.5	8.2	7.9	8.1
Whole MNCs	1432	2566	-1135	12.8	17.0	15.2	24.0	48.0	35.3
USA MNCs	1113	138	975	9.9	0.9	4.8	18.6	2.6	11.0
ROW MNCs	358	2546	-2188	3.2	16.9	11.1	6.0	47.6	25.6
Other MNCs	471	361	110	4.2	2.4	3.2	7.9	6.7	7.3
USA MNCs	473	280	193	4.2	1.9	2.9	7.9	5.2	6.7
ROW MNCs	20	94	-74	0.2	0.6	0.4	0.3	1.8	1.0
Intrafirm Related Trade									
Total	11207	15054	-3847	100.0	100.0	100.0	NA	NA	NA
Non-MNCs	6495	11046	-4551	58.0	73.4	66.8	NA	NA	NA
All MNCs	4712	4008	704	42.0	26.6	33.2	100.0	100.0	100.0
USA MNCs	4233	1500	2733	37.8	10.0	21.8	89.8	37.4	65.7
ROW MNCs	479	2508	-2029	4.3	16.7	11.4	10.2	62.6	34.3
Petro MNCs	310	100	210	2.8	0.7	1.6	6.6	2.5	4.7
USA MNCs	261	2	259	2.3	0.0	1.0	5.5	0.0	3.0
ROW MNCs	49	98	-49	0.4	0.7	0.6	1.0	2.4	1.7
Manu MNCs	2817	1448	1369	25.1	9.6	16.2	59.8	36.1	48.9
USA MNCs	2619	1106	1513	23.4	7.3	14.2	55.6	27.6	42.7
ROW MNCs	198	342	-144	1.8	2.3	2.1	4.2	8.5	6.2
Whole MNCs	1228	2147	-919	11.0	14.3	12.9	26.1	53.6	38.7
USA MNCs	999	115	884	8.9	0.8	4.2	21.2	2.9	12.8
ROW MNCs	229	2032	-1803	2.0	13.5	8.6	4.9	50.7	25.9
Other MNCs	357	313	44	3.2	2.1	2.6	7.6	7.8	7.7
USA MNCs	354	277	77	3.2	1.8	2.4	7.5	6.9	7.2
ROW MNCs	3	36	-33	0.0	0.2	0.1	0.1	0.9	0.4

Intrafirm Related Trade

Other Manufactures trade totaled $26,261 million in 1975. Intrafirm related trade was $8,720 million for a 33.2% share (compared to a 43.1% share for affiliate related trade). Arms-length or Non-MNC trade was $17,541 million for a 66.8% share. The MNC-related trade position reflected a 42.0% share of export trade and a 26.6% share of import trade. The dominant MNC group was U.S.-based firms with a 21.8% share of total trade; ROW-based firms held a 11.4% share. U.S. multinationals had a much larger share of exports; ROW MNCs had the larger share of imports.

The Other Manufactures trade balance in 1975 was a deficit of $3,847 million. This reflected a $704 million surplus in MNC-related trade and a $4,551 million deficit in Non-MNC trade. Thus the unfavorable balance in Other Manufactures trade reflected a Non-MNC deficit. The MNC-related surplus was linked to a surplus in U.S. MNC trade which offset a deficit in ROW MNC trade.

Between 1975 and 1982, Other Manufactures trade grew $41,356 million or 158% to reach $67,617 million. In comparison, intrafirm related trade increased $5,033 million or 58% to a level of $13,753 million. Accordingly, the overall intrafirm position decreased from a 33.2% to a 20.3% share (compared to a 43.1% to 28.4% share change for affiliate related trade). Non-MNC trade rose to a 79.7% share. Within the intrafirm trade structure, the export share plummeted to 21.5% and the import share decreased to 19.6%. These changes reflected trade share declines in both MNC groups, especially an export share drop of U.S.-based firms.

The Other Manufactures trade balance in 1982 was a deficit of $16,347 million, up $12,500 million from 1975. The intrafirm related trade had converted to a deficit of $2,735 million, a swing of $3,439 million; the Non-MNC trade deficit had risen $9,061 million to $13,612 million. Thus the rise in the Other Manufactures trade deficit resulted from unfavorable trends in both components. The MNC-related deficit emerged due to the growing deficit position of ROW multinationals.

In the 1982 to 1989 period, Other Manufactures trade grew $88,278 million or 131% to $155,895 million. In comparison, intrafirm related trade increased $22,138 million or 161% to a level of $35,891 million. As a result, the overall intrafirm position increased from a 20.3% to a 23.0% share (compared to a 28.4% to 30.3% share change for affiliate related trade). Non-MNC trade fell to a 77.0% share. Within the intrafirm trade structure, the export share rose to 30.9% while the import share remained at 19.5%. The export change was due to increases in the trade shares of both U.S. and ROW MNCs. Compared to 1975, the U.S. MNC share of total trade had fallen from 21.8% to 13.5% and the ROW MNC share from 11.4% to 9.5%.

The Other Manufactures trade balance in 1989 was a deficit of $60,359 million, up $44,012 million from 1982. The intrafirm related trade deficit was $6,381 million, an increase of $3,646 million; the Non-MNC trade deficit had ballooned $40,366 million to $53,978 million. Thus the deterioration in the Other Manufactures trade balance was due to unfavorable trends in both components, especially Non-MNC trade. The MNC-related deficit was based on the growing ROW MNC deficit which offset a surplus in U.S. MNC trade.

Table 26.2: Multinational Companies and
U.S. Other Manufactures Trade (SITC 61-66,8) in 1982

	MERCHANDISE TRADE (Millions of Dollars)			TOTAL TRADE (Percent Share)			ALL MNCs TRADE (Percent Share)		
	EXPORTS	IMPORTS	BALANCE	EXP	IMP	AVG	EXP	IMP	AVG
Affiliate Related Trade									
Total	25635	41982	-16347	100.0	100.0	100.0	NA	NA	NA
Non-MNCs	18426	29968	-11543	71.9	71.4	71.6	NA	NA	NA
All MNCs	7210	12014	-4805	28.1	28.6	28.4	100.0	100.0	100.0
USA MNCs	5728	3707	2021	22.3	8.8	14.0	79.5	30.9	49.1
ROW MNCs	1922	8999	-7077	7.5	21.4	16.2	26.7	74.9	56.8
Petro MNCs	82	1	81	0.3	0.0	0.1	1.1	0.0	0.4
USA MNCs	97	0	97	0.4	0.0	0.1	1.3	0.0	0.5
ROW MNCs	1	1	0	0.0	0.0	0.0	0.0	0.0	0.0
Manu MNCs	4858	4438	420	19.0	10.6	13.7	67.4	36.9	48.4
USA MNCs	3739	3330	409	14.6	7.9	10.5	51.9	27.7	36.8
ROW MNCs	1462	1376	86	5.7	3.3	4.2	20.3	11.5	14.8
Whole MNCs	2005	7040	-5035	7.8	16.8	13.4	27.8	58.6	47.1
USA MNCs	1639	249	1390	6.4	0.6	2.8	22.7	2.1	9.8
ROW MNCs	421	7158	-6737	1.6	17.1	11.2	5.8	59.6	39.4
Other MNCs	265	535	-270	1.0	1.3	1.2	3.7	4.5	4.2
USA MNCs	253	128	125	1.0	0.3	0.6	3.5	1.1	2.0
ROW MNCs	38	464	-426	0.1	1.1	0.7	0.5	3.9	2.6
Intrafirm Related Trade									
Total	25635	41982	-16347	100.0	100.0	100.0	NA	NA	NA
Non-MNCs	20126	33738	-13612	78.5	80.4	79.7	NA	NA	NA
All MNCs	5509	8244	-2735	21.5	19.6	20.3	100.0	100.0	100.0
USA MNCs	4847	2323	2524	18.9	5.5	10.6	88.0	28.2	52.1
ROW MNCs	662	5921	-5259	2.6	14.1	9.7	12.0	71.8	47.9
Petro MNCs	19	0	19	0.1	0.0	0.0	0.3	0.0	0.1
USA MNCs	18	0	18	0.1	0.0	0.0	0.3	0.0	0.1
ROW MNCs	1	0	1	0.0	0.0	0.0	0.0	0.0	0.0
Manu MNCs	3534	2976	558	13.8	7.1	9.6	64.1	36.1	47.3
USA MNCs	3230	2003	1227	12.6	4.8	7.7	58.6	24.3	38.0
ROW MNCs	304	973	-669	1.2	2.3	1.9	5.5	11.8	9.3
Whole MNCs	1792	5042	-3250	7.0	12.0	10.1	32.5	61.2	49.7
USA MNCs	1437	197	1240	5.6	0.5	2.4	26.1	2.4	11.9
ROW MNCs	355	4845	-4490	1.4	11.5	7.7	6.4	58.8	37.8
Other MNCs	164	226	-62	0.6	0.5	0.6	3.0	2.7	2.8
USA MNCs	162	123	39	0.6	0.3	0.4	2.9	1.5	2.1
ROW MNCs	2	103	-101	0.0	0.2	0.2	0.0	1.2	0.8

INDUSTRY TRADE ROLES

This section is based on the trade data shown in Tables 26.1, 26.2, and 26.3 for 1975, 1982, and 1989, respectively. The trade role of each affiliate industry group is discussed on the basis of affiliate related trade.

Petroleum Affiliates

Affiliate related trade was $563 million in 1975, adjusted for the affiliate trade overlap. This figure represented a 2.1% share of total trade and a 5.0% share of MNC-related trade. The industry category ranked last, and was dominated by U.S.-based firms. The industry trade balance was a surplus of $186 million, compared to a total merchandise deficit of $3,847 million.

By 1982, industry trade had decreased 85% to $83 million. This figure represented a 0.1% share of total trade (down 2.0 share points), and a 0.4% share of MNC-related trade (down 4.5 share points). The industry category continued to rank last. The trade balance was a surplus of $81 million (down $105 million), compared to a total merchandise deficit of $16,347 million (up $12,500 million).

Industry related trade increased 37% to $113 million in 1989. This figure represented a 0.1% share of total trade (unchanged) and a 0.2% share of MNC-related trade (down 0.2 share points). The industry category continued to rank last, but was now dominated by ROW-based firms. The trade balance was a surplus of $8 million (down $73 million), compared to a total merchandise deficit of $60,359 million (up $44,012 million).

Manufacturing Affiliates

Affiliate related trade was $5,929 million in 1975, adjusted for the affiliate trade overlap. This figure represented a 22.6% share of total trade and a 52.4% share of MNC-related trade. The industry category ranked first, and was dominated by U.S.-based firms. The industry trade balance was a surplus of $1,464 million, compared to a total merchandise deficit of $3,847 million.

By 1982, industry trade had increased 57% to $9,296 million. This figure represented a 13.7% share of total trade (down 8.8 share points), and a 48.4% share of MNC-related trade (down 4.0 share points). The industry category continued to rank first by a slight margin over wholesale affiliates. The trade balance was a surplus of $420 million (down $1,044 million), compared to a total merchandise deficit of $16,347 million (up $12,500 million).

Industry related trade increased by 210% to $28,798 million in 1989. This figure represented a 18.5% share of total trade (up 4.7 share points), and a 60.9% share of MNC-related trade (up 12.6 share points). The industry category continued to rank first, and continued to be dominated by U.S.-based firms. The trade balance was a deficit of $1,702 million (a swing of $2,123 million), compared to an overall deficit of $60,359 million (up $44,012 million).

Wholesale Trade Affiliates

Affiliate related trade was $3,998 million in 1975, adjusted for the affiliate trade overlap. This figure represented a 15.2% share of total trade and a 35.3%

Table 26.3: Multinational Companies and
U.S. Other Manufactures Trade (SITC 61-66,8) in 1989

	MERCHANDISE TRADE (Millions of Dollars)			TOTAL TRADE (Percent Share)			ALL MNCs TRADE (Percent Share)		
	EXPORTS	IMPORTS	BALANCE	EXP	IMP	AVG	EXP	IMP	AVG
Affiliate Related Trade									
Total	47768	108127	-60359	100.0	100.0	100.0	NA	NA	NA
Non-MNCs	27887	80744	-52857	58.4	74.7	69.7	NA	NA	NA
All MNCs	19882	27384	-7502	41.6	25.3	30.3	100.0	100.0	100.0
USA MNCs	14456	13188	1268	30.3	12.2	17.7	72.7	48.2	58.5
ROW MNCs	6540	16035	-9495	13.7	14.8	14.5	32.9	58.6	47.8
Petro MNCs	60	53	8	0.1	0.0	0.1	0.3	0.2	0.2
USA MNCs	23	0	23	0.0	0.0	0.0	0.1	0.0	0.0
ROW MNCs	47	68	-21	0.1	0.1	0.1	0.2	0.2	0.2
Manu MNCs	13548	15250	-1702	28.4	14.1	18.5	68.1	55.7	60.9
USA MNCs	9766	10762	-996	20.4	10.0	13.2	49.1	39.3	43.4
ROW MNCs	4778	5870	-1092	10.0	5.4	6.8	24.0	21.4	22.5
Whole MNCs	5722	11405	-5682	12.0	10.5	11.0	28.8	41.6	36.2
USA MNCs	4150	2223	1927	8.7	2.1	4.1	20.9	8.1	13.5
ROW MNCs	1633	9526	-7893	3.4	8.8	7.2	8.2	34.8	23.6
Other MNCs	551	676	-125	1.2	0.6	0.8	2.8	2.5	2.6
USA MNCs	517	203	314	1.1	0.2	0.5	2.6	0.7	1.5
ROW MNCs	82	571	-489	0.2	0.5	0.4	0.4	2.1	1.4
Intrafirm Related Trade									
Total	47768	108127	-60359	100.0	100.0	100.0	NA	NA	NA
Non-MNCs	33013	86991	-53978	69.1	80.5	77.0	NA	NA	NA
All MNCs	14755	21136	-6381	30.9	19.5	23.0	100.0	100.0	100.0
USA MNCs	12227	8780	3447	25.6	8.1	13.5	82.9	41.5	58.5
ROW MNCs	2528	12356	-9828	5.3	11.4	9.5	17.1	58.5	41.5
Petro MNCs	16	0	16	0.0	0.0	0.0	0.1	0.0	0.0
USA MNCs	16	0	16	0.0	0.0	0.0	0.1	0.0	0.0
ROW MNCs	0	0	0	0.0	0.0	0.0	0.0	0.0	0.0
Manu MNCs	8966	10558	-1592	18.8	9.8	12.5	60.8	50.0	54.4
USA MNCs	8059	6999	1060	16.9	6.5	9.7	54.6	33.1	42.0
ROW MNCs	907	3559	-2652	1.9	3.3	2.9	6.1	16.8	12.4
Whole MNCs	5444	10235	-4791	11.4	9.5	10.1	36.9	48.4	43.7
USA MNCs	3825	1659	2166	8.0	1.5	3.5	25.9	7.8	15.3
ROW MNCs	1619	8576	-6957	3.4	7.9	6.5	11.0	40.6	28.4
Other MNCs	329	343	-14	0.7	0.3	0.4	2.2	1.6	1.9
USA MNCs	327	122	205	0.7	0.1	0.3	2.2	0.6	1.3
ROW MNCs	2	221	-219	0.0	0.2	0.1	0.0	1.0	0.6

share of MNC-related trade. The industry category ranked second, behind manufacturing affiliates, and was dominated by ROW-based firms. The industry trade balance was a deficit of $1,135 million, compared to a total merchandise deficit of $3,847 million.

By 1982, industry trade had increased 126% to $9,045 million. This figure represented a 13.4% share of total trade (down 1.8 share points), and a 47.1%

share of MNC-related trade (up 11.7 share points). By a small margin, the industry category continued to rank second behind manufacturing affiliates. The trade balance was a deficit of $5,035 million (up $3,901 million), compared to a total merchandise deficit of $16,347 million (up $12,500 million).

Industry related trade increased by 89% to $17,127 million in 1989. This figure represented a 11.0% share of total trade (down 2.4 share points), and a 36.2% share of MNC-related trade (down 10.8 share points). The industry category was now a distant second rank, and continued to be dominated by ROW-based firms. The trade balance was a deficit of $5,682 million (up $647 million), compared to a total merchandise deficit of $60,359 million (up $44,012 million).

Other Industry Affiliates

Affiliate related trade was $832 million in 1975, adjusted for the affiliate trade overlap. This figure represented a 3.2% share of total trade and a 7.3% share of MNC-related trade. The industry category ranked third and was dominated by U.S.-based firms. The industry trade balance was a surplus of $110 million, compared to a total merchandise deficit of $3,847 million.

By 1982, industry trade had decreased four percent to $800 million. This figure represented a 1.2% share of total trade (down 2.0 share points), and a 4.2% share of MNC-related trade (down 3.2 share points). The industry category continued to rank third, but was now dominated by ROW-based firms. The trade balance was a deficit of $270 million (a swing of $381 million), compared to a total merchandise deficit of $16,347 million (up $12,500 million).

Industry related trade increased by 53% to $1,227 million in 1989. This figure represented a 0.8% share of total trade (down 0.4 share points), and a 2.6% share of MNC-related trade (down 1.6 share points). The industry category continued to rank third, and was again dominated by U.S.-based firms. The trade balance was a deficit of $125 million (down $145 million), compared to a total merchandise deficit of $60,359 million (up $44,012 million).

DERIVATION OF THE DATA

The derivation of the MNC-related product trade data is discussed at length in Chapter 12 on "Total Product Trade." As noted in that discussion, trade categories were combined in certain benchmark surveys. Other Manufactures (SITC 61-66,8) was combined with Other Products (SITC 4,9) in the reverse benchmarks for 1980 and 1987. Separate data on Other Manufactures trade have been collected in the remaining reverse benchmark for 1974, and in all of the three outward surveys.

The task was to allocate the residual "other" grouping (SITC 4,61-66,8,9) into its two component categories. As elsewhere, this was done with a set of allocation ratios. The only information available was from the 1974 benchmark. The data in the three outward benchmarks were not relevant.

The first method was to generate the allocation ratios directly from Other Manufactures and Other Products categories in the 1974 benchmark. A minor problem was that this method generates identical ratios to be used on both the 1980 and 1987 benchmark data. The significant problem was that the Other Products (SITC 4,9) data in BM74 was partially an estimate. The benchmark source tables placed Coal and Coke (SITC 32) in the residual category. The development of 1974 benchmark estimates for Coal and Coke and Other Products is described in the data derivation section of Chapter 18 on "Coal and Coke Trade." The favorable factor was that the Coal and Coke trade was small, so the estimates developed for Other Products in the 1974 benchmark should possess the appropriate magnitudes.

Given these problems, a second method was employed to generate additional allocation ratios from the 1974 benchmark data. In this procedure, dollar estimates were developed for Other Manufactures and Other Products trade in 1980 and 1987. The ratio of these estimates served as allocation ratios. The dollar estimates were developed as follows.

In the 1974 benchmark, there was complete data on manufactures trade categories. The ratios between Other Manufactures (SITC 61-66,8) and "Known" Manufactures (SITC 5,71-77,78,79,67-69) were calculated. These ratios were then used with the "Known" Manufactures data from BM80 and BM87 to generate dollar values for Other Manufactures.

In the 1974 benchmark, there was good data on Other Products trade since the Coal and Coke component in the source tables was small. The ratios between Other Products (SITC 4,9) and Total Trade (SITC 0-9) were calculated. These ratios were then used with Total Trade data from BM80 and BM87 to generate dollar values for Other Products.

Each of the two methods generated a set of allocation ratios for the 1980 benchmark and the 1987 benchmark. Each set of ratios brought additional information to the process, so the two sets were averaged to find the final set of allocation ratios. This average set was used to generate the values for both Other Manufactures (SITC 61-66,8) and Other Products (SITC 4,9).

Note that at this point, special estimates of Other Manufactures trade had been developed for only the 1980 and 1987 benchmarks. The other four FDI surveys collected data for this trade category. It was thought that no further modification of the Other Manufactures trade data would be necessary.

The definition section above notes that certain automotive parts and components properly belong in the Other Manufactures (SITC 61-66,8) trade classification and should not be included under Road Vehicles and Parts (SITC 78). As discussed in the data derivation section of Chapter 23 on "Road Vehicles and Parts Trade," such a reporting misclassification occurred. Accordingly, the estimated values for MNC-related trade in Road Vehicles and Parts were reduced, and part of the misclassified trade was added to the Other

Manufactures category.

The data in the tables in this chapter include the reallocated trade from Chapter 23. The effect of the change was to increase the value of Other Manufactures trade relative to other product categories. The adjustment does not affect the structural relationships and shifts within the Other Manufactures trade category.

In summary, the initial estimates for Other Manufactures trade in the 1980 and 1987 benchmarks had to be developed out of a combined category that included Other Products. This affected only the data for BM80 and BM87. The subsequent adjustment for reallocated Road Vehicles and Parts trade affected all data in all benchmarks. These data were used as the basis for the tables in this chapter.

SELECTED BIBLIOGRAPHY

The principal sources of information for this book are the six benchmark surveys of foreign direct investment conducted by the U.S. Government over the past two decades. The convention is to refer to these sources by the benchmark year, rather than the year of publication. Thus a text reference could take the form of "the 1974 benchmark survey" or "BM74." A citation would refer to the benchmark year and a table number, such as [BM74 E-2].

The U.S. Bureau of Economic Analysis, together with the U.S. Bureau of the Census, are units of the U.S. Department of Commerce but are sufficiently well known to be cited directly without the Commerce designation. In contrast, a reference to the International Trade Administration would be confusing without the Commerce linkage.

Abbreviated source notations are shown in brackets [ ].

THE BENCHMARK SURVEYS OF FOREIGN DIRECT INVESTMENT

U.S. Department of Commerce, Office of the Secretary. *Foreign Direct Investment in the United States: Volume 2: Benchmark Survey, 1974.* Washington, DC: USGPO (April 1976). [BM74].

U.S. Bureau of Economic Analysis. *U.S. Direct Investment Abroad, 1977.* Washington, DC: USGPO (April 1981). [BM77].

___. *Foreign Direct Investment in the United States, 1980.* Washington, DC: USGPO (October 1983). [BM80].

___. *U.S. Direct Investment Abroad: 1982 Benchmark Survey Data.* Washington, DC: USGPO (December 1985). [BM82].

___. *Foreign Direct Investment in the United States: 1987 Benchmark Survey, Final Results.* Washington, DC: USGPO (August 1990). [BM87].

___. *U.S. Direct Investment Abroad: 1989 Benchmark Survey, Final Results.* Washington, DC: USGPO (October 1992). [BM89].

OTHER SOURCES

Bailey, Victor B. and Bowden, Sara R. *Understanding United States Foreign Trade Data.* U.S. Department of Commerce, International Trade Administration. Washington, DC: USGPO (August 1985).

Hipple, F. Steb. "The Changing Role of Multinational Corporations in U.S. International Trade," in Gray, H. Peter (ed). *The Modern International Environment.* Greenwich, CT: JAI Press (1989), 65-80.

___. "The Measurement of International Trade Related to Multinational Companies," *The American Economic Review* 80:1263-1270 (December 1990).

___. "Multinational Companies and the Growth of the U.S. Trade Deficit," *The International Trade Journal* 5:217-234 (Winter 1990).

___. "Multinational Companies and International Trade: The Impact of Intrafirm Shipments on U.S. Foreign Trade 1977-1982," *Journal of International Business Studies* 21:495-504 (Third Quarter 1990).

___. *The Role of Multinational Firms in U.S. International Trade.* Washington, DC: U.S. Department of Commerce, International Trade Administration (July 1982).

Mataloni, Raymond J., Jr. "U.S. Multinational Companies: Operations in 1992," *Survey of Current Business* 74:6:42-62 (June 1994).

Rutter, John W. "Recent Trends in International Direct Investment and the Implications for U.S. Business," *U.S. Industrial Outlook 1990.* Washington, DC: USGPO (January 1990), 6-11.

U.S. Bureau of the Census. *Statistical Abstract of the United States: 1979, 1985, 1991.* Washington, DC: USGPO (1980, 1986, 1992). [ABUS79], [ABUS85], [ABUS91].

U.S. Bureau of Economic Analysis. *Business Statistics: 1963-91.* 27th ed. Washington, DC: USGPO (June 1992). [BS6391].

___. *Foreign Direct Investment in the United States: Revised 1982 Estimates.* Washington, DC: USGPO (December 1985). [FDIUS82].

___. *Foreign Direct Investment in the United States: Revised 1989 Estimates.* Washington, DC: USGPO (August 1992). [FDIUS89].

___. *Guide to Industry and Foreign Trade Classifications for International Surveys BE-799.* Washington, DC: USGPO (1990).

Zeile, William J. "Foreign Direct Investment in the United States: 1992 Benchmark Survey Results," *Survey of Current Business* 74:7:154-186 (July 1994).

INDEX

About the Author

F. STEB HIPPLE holds a dual appointment as Professor of Economics and Director, Bureau of Business and Economic Research, at East Tennessee State University. Previously, he was an Economic Policy Fellow of the Brookings Institution, and a Senior International Economist with the U.S. Department of Commerce. He has published numerous papers on multinational companies over the past two decades.

ISBN 0-89930-820-1

90000>

EAN

9 780899 308203

HARDCOVER BAR CODE